DEBT AND DEVELOPMENT

DEBT AND DEVELOPMENT

EDITED BY
J. C. SÁNCHEZ ARNAU

With contributions by
Georges Corm, Abdelkader Sid-Ahmed,
Samuel Lichtensztejn, José Manuel Quijano,
and Gonzalo Daniel Martner

PRAEGER

PRAEGER SPECIAL STUDIES • PRAEGER SCIENTIFIC

Library of Congress Cataloging in Publication Data

Main entry under title:

Debt and development.

1. Underdeveloped areas—Debts, External—Addresses, essays, lectures. 2. Underdeveloped areas—Economic policy—Addresses, essays, lectures. I. Sánchez Arnau, J. C.
HJ8899.D4 336.3′435′091724 82-431
ISBN 0-03-061904-1 AACR2

Published in 1982 by Praeger Publishers
CBS Educational and Professional Publishing
a Division of CBS Inc.
521 Fifth Avenue, New York, New York 10175, U.S.A.

23456789 145 987654321

Printed in the United States of America

PREFACE

This book is the final result of a research project carried out by the International Center for Development (Paris, France), under the responsibility of its Executive Director, J.C. Sánchez Arnau, and with the participation of economists from different areas of the Third World. The project was financed by the International Foundations for Development Alternatives (Nyon, Switzerland).

This project was accomplished between mid-1978 and early 1980; during this period, the debt problem of the developing countries emerged as one of the main features of the international economic situation. The most recent evolution of international economy shows the significance of the debt problem and its increasing importance for any attempt to promote Third World development and a reasonable reorganization of the international economic structure.

The papers included in this book give particular attention to the historical origins and structural aspects of the debt problems of developing countries. Therefore, they intend to go beyond statistical evidence, and present a global interpretation of such a phenomenon.

CONTENTS

Chapter I

DEBT AND DEVELOPMENT

J. C. Sánchez Arnau

DEBT AND DEVELOPMENT

Much has been said and written about Third World indebtedness problems and much more will be in the future. Industrialised countries indicate clear symptoms of a long generalized recession. As in the past, they will probably transfer a great part of the effects of their recession or of its implicit costs of adjustment, to the developing countries. Greater protectionism, lower imports, export subsidies, a drop of official financial flows, more or less disguised expulsion of immigrant workers, will be amongst the measures bringing about this transfer. To these will be added the drop in the prices of some raw materials due to the fall in demand.

The impact on the Third World will depend on the scale of the recession, and the time it takes industrialized countries, in particular the United States, to react. Under the assumption that this is a more or less traditional cyclical crisis albeit aggravated by new elements, it can be avoided by adopting traditional neoclassical economic remedies. If, however, as many suspect, the present recession is more an expression of structural problems affecting the very basis of the functioning of present growth models of industrialized countries, then the impact of recession on developing countries will be greater and more prolonged. In such circumstances, the "debt" problem will become particularly relevant, since it will be the most obvious expression of the incapacity of many LDCs to resist an aggravation of their balance of payments problems.

Furthermore, if the vulnerability of the external and payment situation of many LDCs has not yet emerged, it has been due to a sub-product of the recession and of the international monetary disorder: the high level of international liquidity. Without such a recession, the multinational and large companies of the industrialized world would have already absorbed most of the liquid resources available in world financial markets, which are at present being used to finance the Third World's indebtedness. Hence one of the paradoxes of the present situation: the same recession which deprives many LDCs of their external resources derived form their exports or the remittances of their migrant workers,generates the liquidity which enables them to contract debts, thus escaping the risk of economic collapse.

This paradox can become a trap with few exits. If the industrialized countries took measures to limit this liquidity, which for orthodox economists is one of the main causes of the monetary disorder at the root of the present crisis, many LDCs resorting massively to indebtedness would be deprived of these resources, but would continue to be faced with the other aspects of recession which have compelled them to contract new debts. With the continuous increase in interest rates in Industrialised countries, backed by daily demands for a greater control on the flow of dollars and activities of the Euro-market, is such a moment far away?

However, it would not be intellectually fair to present just this grim scenario. In more cases than one, indebtedness may well have been a well-calculated risk, and even a considerable drop in international liquidity within the framework of generalized recession would permit more then one considerably indebted developing country to escape the risk of default.

However, reservations concerning this possibility must also be expressed because there is not just "an indebtedness problem" but various other problems. Besides which, the pressent situation and the future prospects differ greatly from one country to another.

A. Size and characteristics of Third World Indebtedness

This study does not aim at presenting another survey of Third World indebtedness, but at investigating its causes. If indebtedness occasionally occurs voluntarily as the result of a calculated risk it is most often the inevitable outcome of an economic policy -or of a policy "tout court". However, a few figures are necessary to situate the extent and characteristics of the problem.

They may also help to de-dramatize certain aspects, and give a real dimension to others which have not always been treated with the seriousness they deserve.

OECD statistics[1/] show that from 1970 to 1978, the external indebtedness of developing countries increased from $74.7 to $321.5 billion, growing at an annual rate varying from 13% in 1972 to 23% in 1975. In real terms, the increase was equally significant: at 1970 prices, it augmented from $72.9 billion to $103.9 billion at the end of 1976, while the annual growth rate in real terms varied between 5% in 1972 to 29% in 1975. Though this rate was only 9% and 10% in 1973 and 1974, which were the most difficult years of the start of the present recession (implying that in real terms Third World countries had less resources and had to reimburse a part of their debt at the depths of the recession).

This global development involves major changes in the composition of the debt. First, the share of debts arising out of non-official loans increased from 28.1% in 1969 to 41.1% in 1976 -and have certainly increased further since. According to UNCTAD, 72% of the total of non-official debt in 1976 comprised of bank loans, as compared to 51% in 1967. On the other hand, the share of suppliers' credits dropped from 40% to 25% between 1967 and 1976. This can be explained both by increasing preference of developing countries to borrow from the capital market and by the growing restrictions imposed by the OECD countries on such credits.

As far as terms indebtedness is concerned, the average maturity of loans has been declining in recent years. It decreased from 19.3 years in

(1) i.e. public and private disbursed debt.

1970 to 14.1 in 1977. In the same period, the average grace time dropped from 5.2 to 3.9 years while the average interest rate increased from 5.3 to 6.9%, and the grant element of loans declined from 31% to 18%.

However, the individual situation of developing countries varies. The bulk of indebtedness of developing countries is accounted for by a small number of countries. Figures for the end of 1976 show that 12 developing countries accounted for 58% of the total public and private debt of the Third World, i.e. $152 billion out of a total of $264.4 billion. In order of importance of their indebtedness these countries were Brazil, Mexico, India, Indonesia, Algeria, South Korea, Yugoslavia, Iran Egypt, and Argentina. But there are of course many other developing countries whose debts, though not sizeable, are nevertheless considerable in terms of their capacity to pay.

The indebtedness of most of these countries, but also of Venezuela and Peru has been growing even faster in recent years. With the exception of Iran, India and Indonesia, their total debt increases between 1973 and 1976 in real terms, deflated by export prices, from 25% for Yugoslavia to 204% for Venezuela. In cases such as Mexico, the total amount of indebtedness exceeds three years' exports of goods and services, and more than two years for Brazil, Chile, Peru and India. Also, according to World Financial Markets, the debt service coefficient, (i.e. amortization and interest payments as a percentage of the exports of goods and services) was nearly 45% for Brazil and Chile in 1976, 41% for Argentina, 32% for Mexico and 38% for Peru -all Latin American countries. The remaining major debtors had debt service coefficient of less than 15%, with the exception of Yugoslavia which went slightly over this average. The most interesting feature is debt service as a percentage of gross external indebtedness, the so-called "roll over ratio" -which expresses the share of new debts used to amortize overall indebtedness and pay interest; this was especially high for Argentina (110.3%0), India (69.1%) Yugoslavia (66.5%) and Chile (64.6%).

If from the global and quantitative point of view the debt problem of developing countries was basically concentrated on these countries, any analysis of the future development of the problem must survey the situation of many other developing countries whose debts, though modest, are significant in terms of their capacity to pay.

There are basically four types of situations. First, that of the two largest debtors, Brazil and Mexico. Together they account for 25% of the total debt of developing countries ($32.1 and $25.5 billion respectively, at the end of 1977). Their debt is growing, thus compromising significant amounts of their future external resources, as well as weighing on present resorces. However, these countries do not seem to present the greatest problems in the short term. Mexico's extensive oil resources will enable it to meet its debt service; whereas Brazil's creditors will be anxious to avoid a financial collapse which could have repercussions on the entire world banking system if its balance of payments gets worse, which is probable, due to its relative lack of oil resourses and the growing obstacles to its exports inherent in the increasing protectionism of industrialised countries. This subject will be further analysed from another angle latter on.

The second type of debtor country includes South Korea, Philippines, Chile, Argentina, Peru, and Yugoslavia. Most of them have adopted economic policies aimed at increasing integration with the international market and are strongly oriented towards promoting exports of manufactured and semi-manufactured products. As long as the present level of international liquidity is maintained, the debt situation of most of these countries will get worse, especially if they persist in their policies of assimilation with the international economy when it is in full recession. There will of course be exceptions: the oil and gas of Indonesia,or the Korean economy's capacity for adaptation. In any case, this group of countries displays many signs of external vulnerability and increasing indebtedness.

The third type of country comprises a varied group of countries with fairly low per capita income levels, with external debts arising essentially out of public loans, their debt service coefficients increasing from 18 to 40% and whose external vulnerability is due either to the lack of diversification or the need for the development of its economy. This category comprises India, Pakistan, Egypt, Bolivia, Jamaica, Angola, Congo, Guinea, Mauritania, Sudan, Togo, Bangladesh, Burma and Sri Lanka. However, several of these countries have commercial debts,either bank loans or suppliers' credits- accounting for a significant share of their total debt. This is the case of Egypt, Bolivia, Jamaica, Congo, Guinea, Mauritania, Sudan, Togo and to a lesser extent, Bangladesh.

According to the World Bank, countries with per capita income between $161 and $300 a year -comprising the majority of the countries mentioned- showed the highest increase in indebtedness between 1970 and 1976 with an annual growth rate of 25%. Private bank loans multiplied by 30, increasing 75% each year. Debt service increased 26%, while interest rate payments grew faster than amortization. Various countries within the group could well encounter serious difficulties in their balance of payments in the short term. Those with debts arising mainly from official loans could obtain some measure of debt relief. But the recent experience of Pakistan clearly demonstrates that this possibility is essentially conditioned by political considerations.

Finally, a fourth group of countries consists of those without debts, but highly dependent on grants from industrialized countries to finance their essential imports. A number of African countries belong to this group: Upper Volta, Benin, Chad, Ethiopia, Central Africa, Mali, Rwanda, Madagascar and Somalia amongst others.

Some of these countries, such as Ethiopia for example, often finance up to 100% of their current account deficit with donations. The vulnerability of this group is very great, and even if industrialised and OPEC countries hopefully continue to support them financially, their economic future is nevertheless a cause for grave concern especially if present recessionary trends intensify.

B. The causes of the indebtedness process

The question now arises as to how such a large number of developing countries could have arrived at such a high level of indebtedness, especially when most of their leaders realize that historically, indebtedness has been one of the most usual ways of losing important areas of economic autonomy, or even political independence.

However when one analyzes the indebtedness of the Third World it becomes evident that it is a central circular mechanism within the numerous vicious circles of underdevelopment. It is astonishing that this problem has so far been given only limited attention and that it has been viewed more as a consequence of underdevelopment than as one of its causes or at least as one of the principal means by which underdevelopment perpetuates itself.

In trying to answer this question, two basis types of situations should be distinguished. First, that corresponding to countries which are totally lacking in resources, with limited capacity or autonomy for self-financing. These countries which are extremely dependent on foreign aid, have been unable -although in some cases one may wonder whether they had no other alternative- to escape from strong external indebtedness to maintain essential imports to ensure basic consumer levels.

The second, more common case, relates to those countries whose indebtedness is strongly linked to the type or model of development which they have chosen, or to the economic and social policy followed as a consequence of the adoption by the dominating groups, of a certain ideology of development. This is the case that we shall analyze in depth.

C. Development as an ideology and its consequences on indebtedness

In the last thirty years, a great deal of literature on development has emerged, together with new theories on growth. At the same time "the myth of development", to use the expression of C. Furtado, has become an integral part of the national ideology of Third World countries, regardless of whether they have Socialistic or Liberal overtones. The prospects opened up in the 19th century by "Europeanisation" -a prolongation of the myth of progress which emerged from the 18th century and the dawn of the industrial revolution.

The notion of development has been used to influence popular masses with a view to modifying socio-professional structures which the ruling or merging social groups see as an obstacle to the perpetuation of their situation in society. These notions have given rise to the illusion that a few periodic plans, implying the massive use of capital goods and Western technology can close the gap between the centre and the periphery of the world economic system and ensure the satisfaction of popular aspirations in the near future.

But development as the official ideology of the Third World, representing the promotion of vast "modernisation" programmes has fully coincided with the interests of the industrialised countries, insofar as their own model of society, and therefore model of consumption and technology thus fallaciously acquires a universal character. Development as an ideology only reflects the situation and the needs of the economy of countries which are already developed. The majority of development theories ignore the historic processes of the economic evolution, and thus the possibility of using the enriching lessons taught by historical experience which should underlie any development theory.

Almost no country has been able to industrialise by resorting solely to imported technology, and even less, by only importing the means of production. The 19th century is full of exaggerated examples of the Europeanising "modernisations" (the Ottoman Empire, Egypt, Tunisia, Iran, as well as some Latin American countries) which led to financial bankruptcies, grave losses of autonomy and even in certain extreme cases, to the loss of national independence.

Thus the fallacy of the pseudo-scientific, mathematically formulated theories of income growth presently in fashion, based on a mechanical relationship between investment and production, constructing production functions whose theoretical shortcomings have been demonstrated, contributed to granting additional legitimacy to the developmentalist economic policies of Third World countries. Such theories were usually conceived to justify encouragement of massive investments in the "modern" industrial sector, seen as capable of generating multiplying effects to disseminate technical progress in national economies. Such investments involved massive importation of production goods from the out-side and encouraged the Third World to enter into technological commercial channels controlled by the transnational firms which finally resulted in, the greatest indebtedness known in modern history.

Various mechanisms resulted in a significant process of acculturation (colonisation being the most obvious) and the aspiration to achieve the Western consumer model was generalised through the impact of the demostration effect, as pointed out by Duesenberry in the 1950's.

Within the framework of this model, demand cannot be satisfied except by the acquisition of technology from industrial centers, in the form of indiscriminate imports instead of a global and systematic effort to acquire mastery of technology. As in the 19th century, the nature of the internal economic policies in the last instance reflects both the interests of the ruling classes in the Third World and the excessive power of the industrialised countries: this has permitted developing countries disparate integration into channels of international trade. The lack of interest in an autonomous effort to master technological processes likely to increase the welfare of the population is thus perpetuated into this century. Modernisation strategies are reduced to instruments of subordination to industrialised countries. There has been a dangerous acceleration of the technological and financial dependence since the end of the last war. Beyond its various forms, the result has been the passive consumption of technology, a fragmented economy, loss of control of the economic system and growing indebtedness.

As indicated in the study of George Corm included in this volume, the accumulation of capital, enriching society, depends on the capacity to generate productive capability and not on the increased ability to import productive capacity from abroad. Economic relations between the centre and the periphery as they have developed since the previous century, help industrialised countries to develop their technological capacity further, whereas the Third World remains dependent, lacking dynamism, and incapable of satisfying the basic needs of the majority of its population. The multiplier effects tend to occur in the country of the origin of the production means rather than in the importing country.

To sum up, the development model described above has resulted in an industrialisation model built on foreign investments and massive indebtedness to import capital goods and inputs which ensure its functioning. With the option of substituting imports and/or generating new exports, this approach has coincided with the interest of transnational capital in favour of an international division of labour adjusted to its global interests.

D. Mechanisms of indebtedness

Following the description of the basic causes of indebtedness, the mechanisms through which it is brought about will be explained.

The development model generally adopted in Third World countries with more or less chronic indebtedness problems is centred on the satisfaction of the demands of those groups in society which have the highest purchasing power, and are interested in copying the consumption models of the industrialized societies. This is effectuated through a process of modernization of the infrastructure and an accelerated industrialization process generally based on import substitution.

Both processes are linked and usually mutually reinforced. This can be illustrated by the introduction of motorcar manufacture or assembly, requiring the contruction of roads, which in turn requires the development of a road equipment industry. This kind of process leads many development theorists to maintain that it is self-sustaining. But the reality is slightly different.

The establishment of the motorcar industry is within the reach of very few developing countries. Capital needs are enormous and though technology is fairly dispersed, it is always in the hands of the transnational companies dominating the world car markets. Consequently, there is a need for foreign investment by TNCs to establish terminal plants.

Local sub-contracting factories then develop around these plants, many of these factories being owned by small or medium-sized national companies resorting to public credit to begin and develop operations and needing State guarantees to obtain foreign credits needed to import capital goods. Many in turn are associated to other foreign firms providing them with the technology necessary to manufacture automobile parts. Generally, the percentage of national integration of the final product is not very high, since often the TNCs controlling the motor car plant prefer to import parts from other countries as a function of their overall costs or inter-firm financial movements. On the other hand, the State embarks on ambitious road construction programmes, even though they have a low coefficient of use, except around large cities, although other public services such as railways are outdated and overloaded with passengers -most of whom, moreover, will never be able to own a car.

In order to build these roads, the State will resort to credits extended by international organisations and will use the services of foreign consulting engineering firms to satisfy the technical requirements of these organisations. Also, the State will import road equipment or if the programme is very ambitious, will promote the establishment of a road equipment industry, resorting to their specialised TNCs, which in turn will resort to local companies for the manufacture of some of the necessary parts.

The result of this series of operations will imply: a degree of indebtedness with respect to credits accompanying the entry of foreign capital; futher indebtedness for capital goods imports of local companies manufacturing some parts; the increase in imports corresponding to parts not manufactured locally and further sums for inputs to be used in the manufacture of parts. If the country has no oil, then there will also be an increase in oil imports, and refined products, and perhaps the country will undertake to set up a plant to refine the imported oil. Most of these imports except for oil, will be on credit, backed by a government guarantee. The State will have in turn contracted debts for the roadbuilding programme.

The volume of debt generated in this way can be considerable but it is assumed that the development of the motorcar industry will result in an increase in economic activity permitting increased exports of other products. This increase will cover the payments of debt service and the regular increase in imports of inputs, renewal of equipment and fuels.

The problems begin when it becomes evident that the massive introduction of the motor car, while satisfying the expectations of most of the middle and upper income groups, has not solved the transport problem, nor has it generated either directly or indirectly greater exports, which can look after the indebtedness. Something similar happens with the television industry, with refrigerators, radios and many other consumer durables, which contribute to increasing the welfare of population groups with purchasing power and increasing GNP... but also indebtedness.

In relation to the economy as a whole, when based on the economic model being described here, various factors which underlie indebtedness are reflected in the balance of payments in the following manner. First, the increase in imports of capital goods not financed by foreign investments. To these should be added increased imports in inputs. Significantly, the further industrialisation advances according to the model described, the more difficult it becomes to limit or diminish such imports of inputs. The reason is that industrial sectors which have emerged through this process, become the most dynamic centre of the economy and it thus becomes almost impossible to restrict imports of inputs without endangering the rhythm of economic activity and the level of employment. Thus when balance of payments problems start becoming serious, it is usual for governments to run away from their problems by promoting new investments to increase import substitution, but since investments are usually made on the same basis as the preceding ones,the balance of payment effects of this substitution are cancelled out over time.

Second, there is an increase in payments and remittances made by the foreign companies. These can become so important that the balance of inflows from investments plus the eventual exports they generate are less than the outflows for dividends capital repatriation of part of the principal, royalties for pattents and trade marks and additional imports.

Factors such as the overbilling which takes place in interfirm transactions and the burden on developing countries arising from R and D expenditures already amortised in the industrialised countries, also play a role in this process. Statistical analysis carried out in Latin American countries clearly demonstrates the above. In addition, a good part of the profits made by the TNCs are at the expense either of local credit, or external credits with the official guarantee of the host country, when not based on tax breaks offered to attract investments. Taken together, all these factors give a clearer view of the negative impact of this type of investment on the balance of payments.

But balance of payments problems also have other origins. One of them, little analysed until the present, is the financial cost of their external debts incurred to promote public works. Due to the basket of currencies in which the loans of some international financial organizations are expressed, their real cost is much higher -due to the constant appreciation of some of these currencies- than the nominal rate of loans.

Thus, for example, the IBRD, which is financed largely on the Japanese, German and Swiss national markets, passes on exchange rate risks entirely to its debtors, who thus find the actual rate of interest charges on their borrowings from the IBRD market several points higher than the nominal rate.[1/]

Also, expenditures on armaments should be mentioned as one of the usual causes of excessive indebtedness.

Data on this type of expenditure is scarce and is never reflected in official indebtedness figures but each time a developing country has come forward to renegotiate its external debt, it has been possible to infer that most of the differences between figures by creditors and debtors was due to unregistered purchases of military material, due to its confidentiality, in the books of the central monetary authority. Of course this does not give even a vague idea of the burden of financing such purchases on the indebtedness of many LDCs, but permits the assumption that in many Third World countries indebtedness is considerably higher than the official figures.

The theoretical models of planners of this type of development assume that all these pressures on the balance of payments will be compensated by increased exports arising out of stepped up economic activity. However, this is not normally the case, due first to the weakness of the exporting sector of most developing countries (with the predominance of products characterized by unstable prices, some declining over the long term) and difficulties in moving from export of primary products to exports of manufactures. Either by the influence of the frowth in internal demand, and the inefficiency of industries which have been developed on the basis of high tariff protection and thus cannot compete with costs on the international market, or finally due to the increasing protectionism of industrialized countries against products in which developing countries manage to become competitive.

The result of this lack of symmetry between growth of imports and outflows on current account and the slow growth of exports, is a more or less chronic deficit in the balance of payments, leading to increasing indebtedness described earlier.

In recent years, the governments of some Third World countries, in particular Latin America, have chosen to apply a model whose final objectives are the same -to satisfy demand of the sectors with the highest purchasing power but which are achieved under different policies. These have consisted in eliminating external protection benefitting their industries, while proceeding to major income redistribution resulting in the notable drop in real wages, while promoting the entry of foreign capital and meeting balance of payments problems by increasing indebtedness in the form of bank loans.

These policies have been aimed at making their industries "competitive" and facilitating the increase of exports of manufac-

1/ An article published in 1978 in a Colombian review edited by a former Minister of Economy, stated that Colombia was: "... paying to the World Bank an approximate rate of interest in dollars of 18% for the portion of our debt expressed in Swiss francs, and a dollar interest of 15% for the portion expressed in DM. and it compared these rates with that of 7.6% payable on month to month Eurodollar loans in December 1977. In "Estrategia económica y financiera", Bogotá, March 1980.

tures and semi-manufactures, based on low labour costs and in some cases on the availability of comparative advantages derived from the low production costs of certain inputs.

Until now, the result has been almost the same in all cases. First, a considerable social cost, in terms of high unemployment and repressive measures to oblige wage earners to accept the reduction of their real earnings as well as the weight of income redistribution in favour of higher income groups, assumed to have a higher propensity to save and invest.

Second, a major recession which in many cases resulted in significant drops in GNP. Third, the liquidation of a considerable part of national industry, due to the interplay of the reduction in sales due to the recession, competition from imports whose entry is favoured by the dismantling of effective protection and by the exchange policies, and the high cost of many, due to the freeing of interest rates. Fourth, the emergence of a new financial class, monopolizing most of the benefits of this type of policy, a class which replaced the previous industrial bourgeoisie -which turned to speculative activities or the import of products that it used to manufacture. The entry of foreign capital in the form of direct investments has not been very great in any case -except perhaps when it has been for the sale of public companies or the handing over to private interests of natural resources previously nationalised. Inflation reached impressive levels and indebtedness which it was thought could be rapidly eliminated either remained at the same level, or augmented, due to the increase in imports arising from the liquidation of industry and tariff dismantling; as well as to the disappointing performance of exports -due either to internal production problems, to difficulties of access to markets of industrialised countries, or to decreasing demand due to the general recession.

E. Conclusion

On a general level, the immediate alternatives facing leaders of Third World countries once they have reached the critical level of external indebtedness -which can be measured by indicators showing that debt service tends to become an objective obstacle to development- are analysed in three of the studies presented in this volume. They endeavour to identify the principal aspects of the present international financial structure concerning developing countries, i.e. the role of the IMF, of international private banking, and of debt rescheduling mechanisms.

First, the overwhelming role of the IMF must be emphasised as an institution set up at the end of the Second World War to regulate international monetary and financial movements in the Capitalist world. The IMF emerges as a body which can correct the balance of payments disequilibria of developing countries, by granting short-term finance, subject to conditions (proportional to the volume of liquidity requested) based upon national economic policies. In the view of the IMF, the latter are generally held responsible for the generation of these desequilibrea, while reference to the structural factors is avoided.

Consequently, developing countries have access to drawings on their reserve position at the IMF (reserve tranches and drawing rights) on their credit tranches (first tranche and upper tranches, up to in general no more then 200$ of the country's quota), on the Extended Facility, the Compensatory Finance system, the Buffer Stock Financing Facility, the Supplementary Finance Facility, representing these various entitlements amounting to about five times a member country's quota.

But the approach of the IMF towards "stabilisation plans" in exchange for which it extends these financial resources, has resulted in the imposition of markedly recessionary policies with negative consequences for the growth of the affected countries. Most often, this has not resolved the continuously remaining structural disequilibria.

A study by IMF staff members analysing 75 stabilization plans shows that the net foreign exchange reserve position only improved in 18 cases, thus there was no improvement in 76% of the cases. Out of 29 anti-inflation programmes on which relevant information was available, the rate of inflation had dropped only in 7 cases, thus goals were not achieved in 76% of the cases. According to IMF thinking, these are two key variables.

In addition, the GNP growth rate weakened or was negative in 53% of the cases analysed[1/]. To this should be added the drop in investment and employment levels, the deterioration in income distribution, the denationalisation of the economy, the decrease in import capacities caused by repatriation of earnings and amortization of foreign capital due to the lifting of exchange control and the increased pressure on wages.

Affected economies thus remain in debt, while debt service capacity shrinks with the mortgaging of medium and long term growth potential.

It is therefore hardly surprising, that Third World countries tend to avoid resorting to the IMF. In 1976 these countries as a group used Fund credit facilities up to 72.4% of their total quotas, of which only 10% were drawings on the ordinary tranches.

Consequently, as has been pointed out in the first part of this introduction, developing countries increasingly resort to private capitals markets, seeking to maintain their import capacity and reserves at a level which can sustain an adequate growth rate.

1/ Figures are from the article by T. Reichmann and R.T. Stillson "Experience with Programmes of Balance of Payments Adjustments: Stand-by arrangements in the Higher Tranches 1963-1971" IMF Staff Papers Vol. 25 N°2 June 1978, IMF Washington.

This is particularly the case of countries with per capita incomes in excess of $800 dollars, since they absorb nearly 70% of private international bank credits. It is mainly these countries which play a leading role in the geographical shift and re-articulation on a world scale of productive structures going on at present -that are a pre-eminent area of activity for the transnational companies. International private banks thus manage to finance a good part of such activities accompanying pari passu their cycle of internationalisation, with the inevitable sequels of oligopolistic concentration, denationalisation and destructuring of the recipient economies.

Private bank credits have much more disadvantageous maturities and interest rates than those granted by official bodies. Their repayment becomes a growing burden, representing 15% of total interest payments of developing countries in 1970, and 39% in 1976. This deterioration in indebtedness conditions increases both the vulnerability of debt service capacity and medium and long-term pressures on import capacity, tending to dislocate these countries' balance of payments. Moreover, after a period of relative informality based on the prospect of substantial short-term earnings for private banks, the scope of conditionality now extends to financial operations with private bodies, not only via the "country risk" process of evaluation, and the direct intervention by big banks, but above all by the tight links between their operations and the control over national economic policies imposed by the IMF.

Debt rescheduling operations can be similarly evaluated. They take place in exceptional and extreme circumstances and are merely temporary palliatives. The concentration of these operations in a limited number of countries, and their recurrent character indicate that the present methods are far from satisfactory. All the more so, since they are most often conditional, and are subject to the application of stabilisation plans supervised by the IMF, and sometimes under the iron control and intervention of creditors. Thus, the logic with which the IMF operates in the various areas of external financing and the results of its policies harm the interests of the developing countries, without solving the problem of indebtedness.

We can infer from the above that the present international financial structure and the position of Third World countries therein, reproduce if not augment, the trend towards excessive indebtedness, whose substrata consists of development models prevailing in the last few decades, and reproducing the experiences of the last century. Excessive indebtedness is one of the most significant symptoms of the incapacity of such development models to offer solutions for the grave problems of the Third World.

The studies presented here endeavour to establish a balance of evidence in this direction, and formulate outlines both for alternative proposals for further reflexion, and for practical initiatives in the relevant field of the economic problems of developing countries.

Chapter II

THE INDEBTEDNESS OF THE DEVELOPING COUNTRIES: ORIGINS AND MECHANISMS

Georges Corm

"Capital is made at home." (Ragnar Nurske)

"Capital is the product of collective labor and can be set in motion only by the common activity of a large number of members of society, and even, in the last resort, by all of its members."

(Karl Marx)

INTRODUCTION

In recent years the problems of indebtedness of the countries of the Third World have taken on a new dimension, both in terms of the amounts involved and the increasing number of countries caught in the web of indebtedness.(1) The recent moratoriums and rescheduling of external debts of certain Third World countries (Turkey, Peru, Zaire, Zambia) have heightened the anxiety and led the International Monetary Fund to play an even greater role in the direction of the economic policies of the developing countries. As early as the late sixties, the World Bank had considerably increased its influence in the economic management of the countries of the Third World, through a dynamic policy of boosting its lending operations to levels which, only a few years earlier, would have been scarcely conceivable. At the same time, the major commercial banks of the Western countries opened their windows to a wide range of countries, thus making available a source of credit which, until the end of the sixties, had been accessible only to a small number of Latin American countries (Brazil, Argentian, Chile, Mexico).

It is true that, according to the classical theory of underdevelopment which was formed during the fifties, lack of capital was always regarded as one of the main causes of the backwardness of the Third World. For that reason, recourse to foreign credit and investments was viewed as a normal element of economic policy in the countries of the Third World. However, bilateral credits with the former metropolitan power or aid from international bodies, as well as loans from the World Bank or the International Development Association, were considered to be the prime ways of injecting capital into the Third World. Until the end of the sixties, it would have been unthinkable for the countries of the Third World to become the leading borrowers on the international capital markets, or for the amounts borrowed to reach today's levels; this was so for several reasons:

- the weakness of the economic structures of the majority of the countries of the Third World and their consequent lack of creditworthiness.
- the erratic fluctuations of their external earnings and of their foreign exchange reserves, which made it even harder for them to repay what they had borrowed.
- their limited capacity for the absorption of capital, due to the classical features of underdevelopment:

(1) For a description of the recent evolution of Third World debt, see G. Corm: "Endettement du Tiers-Monde et Commerce de Technologie", _Le Monde Diplomatique_, October, 1977.

lack of qualified personnel, lack of infrastructure, lack of skilled labor, etc...

- past experience on the national capital markets, where most of the non-industrialized countries had proved unable to keep up their regular debt-service payments (Ottoman debt and debts of the Latin American countries, for example), while some of them (such as Russia in 1917) had simply repudiated their external financial commitments altogether.

The evolution of Third World debt over the past ten years raises certain valid questions about the significance of the fundamental changes which have occured and about their possible consequences. The sheer magnitude of the amounts involved requires some profound thinking, on the part of lending and borrowing countries alike. The resulting inter-dependence could well give rise to a general crisis of international payments, should one of the major debtor countries, for whatever reason, become unable to keep up with the servicing of its external debt (Brazil, with debts totalling 40 billion is a relevant case). Such a crisis would have extremely grave consequences for the economies of the industrialized countries, with inevitable repercussions for the developing countries, many of which cannot keep their balance of payments in order without recourse to external credit. If the foreign debt of the countries of the Third World continues to grow at its present rate they are gradually going to find themselves increasingly cornered in their dealings with the international capital markets and, therefore, with the industrialized countries, and also with the two principal bodies for international financial intervention, the IBRD and the IMF, and the series of regional bodies whose intervention procedures are closely patterned after the ones used by those two bodies (Inter-American Development Bank, Asian Development Bank, Arab Development Fund, Arab Monetary Fund, African Development Bank, etc...).

The sudden massive entry of the People's Republic of China into the network of trade with the industrialized countries, after an absence lasting more than a quarter of a century, will cause a considerable additional expansion of the already overloaded international lending machinery. All the more reason, therefore, to enquire as to the consequences of this accumulation of debts, both for relations between the developing countries and the industrialized countries, and the capacity of the structures of the world economy to cope with the imbalances implied by the continuation of the existing debt machinery.

Moreover, in order to realize exactly what is at stake, one should view the current phenomena of Third World indebtedness in the context of the structural crisis which has afflicted the industrialized countries since 1973, the three main manifestations of which are inflation, unemployment and the excessive power and prosperity of the multinational corporations (MNC), which have been playing an elaborate game of dislocation and relocation of productive activities on a worldwide level.

The massive increase in the debts of the CMEA countries on the international capital markets also deserves a mention here: it also began towards the end of the sixties; it is estimated that, by the end of the century, it will reach a total of 200 billion.(1) This increase is also due to the expansion of trade between Soviet Russia and the Western industrialized countries, and, in particular, the large-scale import of ready-made technology in the form of the delivery of factories under the turn-key system.

In the light of all these facts, one cannot help thinking that the expansion of international credit mechanisms, in terms of the amounts involved and also the number and kind of borrowers, on such an unexpectedly massive scale, is not conducive to fundamental changes in the structures of the world economy. This expansion is all the more significant when one considers that, during the half-century between 1914 and the decade of the sixties, starting with the monetary disorder which followed the first World War and the protectionism of the twenties and thirties, the international economy had lacked international credit mechanisms even remotely comparable to those which, before 1914, had made Europe, and particularly the London and Paris markets, the "world's banker".(2) The large international financing operations which took place during that period, especially those involving reconstruction after the two world wars, relied on bilateral mechanisms or transfers (Marshall Plan) or multilateral aid bodies such as the IBRD. Until the end of the sixties, this was the framework in which the financing of development operations in the Third World was conducted.

Morecver, one cannot fail to be struck by the coincidence between, on the one hand, the sudden renewal of the international credit mechanisms and their expansion to the Third World and, on the other hand, the dislocation of the international monetary system, the fall of the gold standard and, in fact, of any set of rules governing the mechanisms for the issuance

(1) See Chapter III.
(2) H. Feis: Europe, the world's banker, 1870-1914, (New Haven Connecticut, 1930).

and distribution of international liquidity.

Considerable changes are therefore taking place in the international economy; the sudden re-emergence, on a gigantic scale, of the international credit mechanisms provides unmistakable evidence of those changes. Their meaning and consequences for the different participants of international economic affairs are of course difficult to assess at this stage. It is naturally tempting to revert to certain classics of Marxism, particularly to Hobson, Hilferding, Lenin and Rosa Luxembourg, to show that the current expansion of the international credit mechanisms signals the beginning of a new phase of imperialism which has been generated by the capitalism of the industrialized countries. It is actually quite surprising that comtemporary Marxist authors have not devoted greater attention to recent developments in the international capital markets which, as we shall see, are curiously reminiscent of financial trends at the end of the 19th century.(1)

We shall not, however, take that approach. It is evident to us that the industrialized countries and their MNCs are doing their best to promote a new international division of labor (IDL) in keeping with the technological evolution of their production apparatus and its profitability. Nonetheless, we feel it is risky to attempt to formulate a global theory for the functioning of the IDL as a mechanism from which the developing countries cannot escape, because the very essence of the IDL is the fact that it is constantly moving in response to the obstacles or the opportunities with which the MNCs - the main actors of today's economic scene - are faced. That it why we intend to determine the internal mechanisms in the Third World countries which make them agree to enter this new IDL, rather than to add further refinements to a Marxist analysis of imperialism or neo-imperialism and to devise sophisticated theories about the behavior of the MNCs. When all is said and done, any possibility of gradually escaping from exploitation and of devising ways of achieving economic liberation must be based on a correct analysis of the inner workings of under-development and its relationship with the external mechanisms of exploitation.

From this point of view, we shall devote the first chapter to the phenomenon of the historical recurrence of Third World indebtedness. In the 19th century, Latin America, the Middle East and North Africa, as well as India, China and Japan piled up impressive amounts of debt on the financial markets of

---

(1) With the exception of H. Magdoff: <u>The Age of Imperialism: the economics of US foreign policy</u>, (New York: Modern Reader Paperbacks, 1969), which has a chapter on the expansion of the American financial network, pp. 67 - 115.

the industrialized countries, in different developmental contexts. It is therefore necessary to restore the historical perspective in order to appreciate the significance of present-day mechanisms of Third World debt and find ways of circumventing them.

This presentation of the historical background will lead us, in a third chapter, to focus more accurately on the immediate causes of the mechanisms of indebtedness in the 20th century, which reflect the paradigm "modernization - technology - pattern of consumption - national construction" which underlay the unfortunate experiences of indebtedness in the 19th century. In this context we shall present some more advanced epistemological thinking of a fundamental variant of this paradigm which lies at the basis of all theories of development. This variant can be summarized in the dual notion "capital - modernization", which is central to the whole range of problems posed by alternative development models. It will, moreover, be necessary to determine to what extent those models can be expressed in concrete terms. The fundamental policy change made by China in the middle of 1978 towards a return to the classic "modernization" model eliminates the basic assumptions about alternative development models which had hitherto existed in contemporary development literature.

Having thus completed the historical and geographical exploration of the mechanisms of indebtedness in the Third World, we shall then outline, by way of conclusion, not so much global - and for that reason unrealistic - alternatives to a situation which is at many points irreversible, but gradual corrective measures which, with time, will restore an authentic freedom of economic choice. The application of such corrective measures will, of course, depend wholly on the inter-play of political forces within Third World societies. This does not mean that a knowledge of the functioning of practical reality and of the way that reality is perceived by the social forces involved in both local and international economic life cannot provide that political inter-play with the right conditions for more democratic decision-making on economic affairs. Finance is the one area in which the mechanisms for decision-making in the Third World are most autocratic and the choice of society which they imply is most blurred. This is the spirit in which this study has been prepared; this is why it has steered well clear of the dogmatic and deterministic patterns of thought which underly so many theories of development and actually obscure the perception of reality and, consequently, the exercise of freedom.

I. HISTORICAL RECURRENCE OF THE PHENOMENON OF INDEBTEDNESS: THIRD WORLD DEBTS IN THE 19th CENTURY

"In scanning over the riches of civilization, spread out before him for acceptance, he contemptuously rejects those calculated to benefit his people, and chooses the modern scientific governing machine, result of ages of experiments, with its patent screws for extracting blood and treasure, conscription and taxations". (From an account of travels in the Ottoman Empire in the 19th century).[1]

(1) Quoted by B. Lewis: The emergence of modern Turkey, (Oxford University Press, 1966), p. 73.

There is abundant literature dealing with capital flow in the 19th century. It naturally focusses on the phenomenon from the point of view of the capital-exporting countries and on the significance of international investment within neo-classical economic theories. This same literature, however, was used as a basis for the Marxist analyses of imperialism at the beginning of the century (Hilferding, Lenin, Bukharin and Rosa Luxembourg, in particular); on the other hand, the literature on capital flow was used much less by modern neo-Marxist authors or even by the Latin American economists who developed the theory of dependence and who made a point of criticizing the neo-classical theories of international trade or of demonstrating the lack of autonomy in the processes of growth in the Third World, i.e., the periphery in relation to the center. Such a non-deterministic use of the economic facts available to us has helped conceal a very important similarity between the financial experience of the Third World countries in the 19th century and their current experiences - a similarity from which important lessons can be learnt and which makes it possible to reconstitute a repetitive historical process which poses many questions.

Here we shall deal with the period between the end of the Napoleonic Wars (1814) and the first World War (1914), and which corresponds to the Golden Age of imperialism. It will be seen, however, that the bulk of the debts of the non-industrialized countries (thus including Russia) during that period was contracted by independent governments, without direct military pressure. Military interventions were often the result of the inability of the borrowing States to manage an external debt which had become very large and which thus affected major interests in the capital-exporting countries, which had overwhelming military and industrial superiority. While gun-boat diplomacy certainly played a decisive role in opening up some countries, particularly in Asia, to trade with the industrialized countries, recourse to borrowings from those same countries was not a direct outcome of "free trade imperialism".[1] Moreover, certain colonies, such as Austrailia and Canada, were to achieve balanced development despite recourse to indebtedness; Japan, which had also contracted debts, was nonetheless to become the first great industrial power in Asia, whereas Portugal, which had accumulated an empire and heavy debts on the British and French financial markets, could do no better than maintain a profound economic stagnation.

(1) Expression taken from an article by J. Gallagher and R. Robinson: "The imperialism of free trade", The Economic History Review, 2nd series, Vo. VI, No. 1, 1953, pp. 1-15.

Since the situations involved are complex and it is extremely difficult to make generalizations, any conclusions one may arrive at about the laws of growth and development must be necessarily modest. It does seem, however, that in financial matters indebtedness in most cases helped develop and consolidate an essentially extroverted economy, the general mechanisms of which have been described in Chapter I.

The following summary of the debts of the countries of the Third World is intended principally to illustrate the internal mechanisms of the cycle of indebtedness. The European aspects of those mechanisms, which have been abundantly described in the literature on international capital flows or on capitalism, will therefore be mentioned only incidentally.

A. The debts of the Ottoman Empire and Egypt.[1]

The history of the indebtedness of these two entities is different in one essential sense: the Empire had to finance an army which was finding it increasingly difficult to maintain the imperial boundaries, whereas the period of Egyptian military expansion came to an end in 1848, with the end of the reign of Mehemet Ali, and before the beginning of the cycle of indebtedness. The intrigues involved in the Ottoman debt were thus far more widespread than in the case of the Egyptian debt. Even so, the link between the histories of those two debts lies in the desire for "Europeanization" which the regimes then in power in Constantinople and Cairo shared. While Mehemet Ali proved capable of withstanding the temptation of indebtedness, his successors-particularly the Khedive Ismail, whose policy of modernization clearly indicated that he regarded his country as a part of Europe[2] - plunged into a series of loans, starting in 1854 and especially in 1864, which far exceeded the capacity of repayment of the Egyptian economy of the day. As for the Ottoman debt, its beginning coincided with the enactment of the second decree or reorganization of the Empire, based on "modern" and European notions, in 1856. One of the paragraphs of that decree stipulates that:

---

(1) The most recent and best documented basic work is J. Ducruet: Les capitaux Européens au Proche-Orient,(Paris: Puf, 1964) which contains an exhaustive bibliography.

(2) The Khedive was fond of saying: "My country is no longer in Africa, we are now a part of Europe", (in:Documents diplomatiques francais, Affaires d'Egypte, 1880, p. 115). For his part, Khalil Pasha, grand admiral of the Ottoman fleet in 1830, used to say: "I am more and more convinced that if we do not quickly imitate Europe, we will have to resign ourselves to slipping back into Asia" (in: E. Engelhardt, La Turquie et le Tanzimat, Paris: 1882, Vol.I, p. 2.)

> "Steps shall be taken for the formation of banks and other similar institutions so as to effect a reform in the monetary and financial system as well as to create funds to be employed in augmenting the sources of the material wealth of my empire. Steps shall also be taken for the formation of roads and canals to increase the facilities of communication and increase the sources of the wealth of the country".[1]

For both Egypt and the ruling circles of the Ottoman Empire, the first half of the 19th century was a time of intense contacts with the Europe of the Code Civil and the Industrial Revolution. Missions were sent to Europe and a number of colleges and academies were founded locally. The most remarkable accomplishments clearly took place in Egypt, where Mehemet Ali established State manufacturing concerns, thus laying the foundations of a State capitalism reminiscent of the Japanese experience of the Meiji era. However, in the Ottoman Empire, which, from a legal point of view, still had sovereign rights over Egypt, the Tanzimat ("Organization") movement set in motion a juridical revolution, as classical Islamic law was to be replaced in all sectors except family law by the Napoleonic law. The trade code, penal code, municipal and prefectoral mode of organization, the council of State, the law on nationality and, lastly, the constitution were all innovations which amounted to a real break with the past.[2] It will be noted that during the first half of the 19th century, when the cultural impact of Europe was the strongest, no debts were contracted. The industrialization carried out by Mehemet Ali relied entirely on Egypt's own resources.

In both cases, however, the state of the national finances was deplorable, particularly for the Ottoman Empire, and military ventures weighed heavily on the budget. There was no rational tax system to provide a regular flow of income, and both the State and the peasants who made up the bulk of the population were exploited by local cliques of bankers and usurers. Moreover, in Egypt as in the rest of the Empire, the first phases of Westernization did not produce the hoped-for results. The first Ottoman decree of the Tanzimat, 1839, remained a dead letter: Mehemet Ali suffered military defeats and the fragile social foundations of the renaissance which he had sought to

(1) From J.C. Hurewitz: Diplomacy in the Near and Middle East, Vol. I., p. 153.

(2) On this period of the Empire, see: B. Lewis: The Emergence of Modern Turkey, (Oxford University Press 1965); and R. H. Davidson: Reform in the Ottoman Empire 1856-1876, (Princeton 1963).

create were no match for the collusion between Britain and the Ottoman Empire and for the consequent opening up of the whole Empire, including Egypt, to free trade and the dismantling of the State monopolies set up by the Pasha of Egypt. The age of foreign debt had begun: in a headlong rush, the complex causes of which we shall consider later, the modernization of the Empire and of Egypt was left to the Western powers, the European bankers and to businessman with few scruples.

From 1854 onwards the pace of Egyptian and Ottoman indebtedness increased to such an extent that 25 years later Egyptian sovereignty had been alienated, and in 1882 Egypt was occupied by Britain, while the Council of Administration of the Ottoman Public Debt which was set up in 1880 was to become an organ of economic tutelage in the hands of the European powers.

In 1876, a year in which Egypt was obliged to cease payments altogether, the Egyptian debt reached 68.5 billion pounds at nominal values (compared to 3 million in 1863), but for a real product of only 46.6 million (see Table I). The real rate of interest on these debts varied from 9 to 11%, whereas the rates on the European capital markets were about 5 or 6%. In addition to this amount there were floating unfinanced debts of 26 million pounds on which annual interest of as high as 25% was payable. During that same period the State's income had risen from 2 million pounds to 10 million: in other words, external debts had increased 23 times and income only five times, which meant that the rate of increase of the debts was more than four times higher than that of income. In these circumstances external debt servicing absorbed 2/3 of State revenues and 50% of the value of exports (13.8 million pounds in 1880) which only doubled between 1863 and 1880.(1)

Debt consolidation operations which took place in 1876 after the default greatly restricted the already limited freedom of action of the Egyptian government. A commission on the public debt was founded; it was to be used by the European powers as an organ for control over the economy and finances of Egypt, until the country was completely taken over by Britain in 1882.

The Ottoman Empire, for its part, had suspended payments in 1875. In the meanwhile its external debt had risen from 5.5 million Turkish pounds in 1858 to 218 million nominal value,

(1) Details in J. Ducruet, *op.cit.*, pp. 19-76, and D. K. Fieldhouse: *Economics and Empire, 1830-1914*, (London: Weindenfeld and Nicholson, 1973), pp. 383-397. For Egypt see D. Landes: *Bankers and Pashas: international finance and economic imperialism in Egypt*, (London 1958).

but for a real product of 177.6 million, in other words with an actual rate of interest of over 10%. (Exchange rate: 4.4 Turkish pounds to the dollar: see Table II). From 1882 onwards, German loans played an important part in the development of the Ottoman external debt, which had hitherto been financed by the British and French markets; the German loans were more directly linked than other loans to infrastructure operations, particularly the Anatolia and Baghdad railroads. This was very much a part of the German power politics, which here coincided with the desire of the Ottoman Empire for a rail infrastructure giving it better control over the Asian provinces of the Empire.

A parallel may be drawn here with the Suez Canal, although the direct usefulness of the Canal for Egypt is less evident than that of the Baghdad railroad for the Empire. It is well known that Egypt, failing to meet the financial obligations it had assumed towards the Compagnie Universelle du Canal de Suez was forced to yield the greater part of its shares to Britain and to sell its 15% participation in the Company's profits for a lump sum to the Crédit Foncier.

For Egypt in particular, and also for the Empire, part of the debts made it possible to finance large-scale modernization projects: dams, roads, railroads, water supplies, telegraph. These projects were carried out, however, entirely by foreign companies, with considerable over-charging due to the greed of the entrepreneurs and the corruption and incompetence of the local administration. In the words of J. Ducruet, "many of these projects were carried out at very high prices: those in the port of Alexandria, listed here as costing 2.3 million, were estimated some years later by a commission of enquiry to be worth 1.4 million; the sugar mills were not worth one third of their cost, etc... Despite this leakage, the economic development of Egypt is a fact which can be demonstrated by a few figures"(1) (See Table III). In a similar vein, a British financier, the author of a fact-finding report, wrote as follows in 1876; "Vast amounts of money have been spent either on unproductive projects, or on projects which were carried out deficiently or too soon...The Khedive has clearly tried to do in a few years and with limited income jobs which need to be spread out over a long time; they would have strained the finances of many much richer countries..."(2)

In modern economic parlance this means that modernization largely remained a process in which the imported technology was not grafted onto an internal process of indigenous technological development, but continued to be a foreign body beyond the control of the country itself - hence the excess costs of the technological transfer, which are a major cause of the vicious circle of indebtedness.

---

(1) J. Ducruet, _op.cit._, p. 29.
(2) Quoted by J. Ducruet, _op.cit._, p. 30.

It would be tedious to examine in detail the history of the Ottoman and Egyptian debts, but in both cases there was a clear desire on the part of the governing élites for modernization; this desire was first motivated by the need to cope with the threat of European expansionism, or, in the case of Mehemet Ali, to acquire the status of an autonomous industrial power. This desire for modernization takes the form of rapid economic changes, as well as changes in the political and legal superstructures (Tanzimat), but also of an absence of dissemination of technological progress among the peasant and urban masses. The first élites which emerged from the initial wave of modernization (1800-1850) may have increased their number but did not help disseminate technological progress in forms accessible to other social strata. This did, however, give rise to popular opposition movements led by élites unaffected by modernization. Then followed a pendulum motion in the modernization policy, in which periods of receptivity to modern things alternated with phases of withdrawal and reaction. This unsettling pendulum motion greatly emphasized the need for foreign management of the inevitable process of modernization. Legal reforms remained incomplete and the administration heavily influenced by traditional attitudes, with mounting administrative contradictions and spreading corruption.

The entire history of the Europeanization of Egypt under the Khedive or of the Tanzimat in the Ottoman Empire is evidence of this pendulum motion, which was all the more pronounced in that the local agents of modernization were for the most part members of religious and ethnic minorities which, in the words of Bernard Lewis describing the Ottoman Empire,"were to act as a cushion - absorbing the impact of regular Western commercial and diplomatic activities in Turkey and thus protecting the Turks from direct contact and contamination".[1] Finding modernization thus blocked, the rulers found no other solution besides an even faster pace of modernization, on the assumption that cultural adaptation would eventually take place; for this reason direct colonization had its advocates everywhere.

(1) G. Lewis, *op.cit.*, p. 62. In Egypt the political élite is Turkish or Circassian, the economic élite Levantine or Syro-Lebanese. On this point see also M.A.R. Gibb and M.B. Owen: *Islamic Society and the West*, (Oxford University Press 1967), 2 vols., particularly Vol. I, chapter VI, pp. 289-313.

Blockages, however, led to excess costs; excess costs led to an increase in debt; and this increase led to a worsening of the terms under which credit was granted and the consequent need for new sources of financing to pay for the charges on past borrowings which had to be refinanced. At the same time the repatriation of profits on foreign investments, which were expected to produce a compelling modernizing effect, represent an additional burden, besides the need for external financing. These investments were for the most part linked to the obtaining of concessions for the operation of public services (transport, water, telegraph) or of mines or basic consumer goods (salt, tobacco).

The mechanism is very clear: one merely has to read the literature about the Ottoman public debt or the Egyptian debt in order to see it at work and to see the astonishing similarity between that mechanism and that of the current debts of the Third World. In the case of Egypt in particular the pattern of events is strikingly similar: in the 19th century Mehemet Ali and the abortive experiment of State capitalism, followed by the headlong rush into Europeanization by the Khedive Ismail, with a massive appeal for foreign aid; in the 20th century, Abdel Nasser and a new fruitless experiment with State capitalism, followed by the headlong rush to open the country to foreign investments with massive reliance on foreign aid. The similarity exists also in the case of Turkey, though less strikingly so, because Ataturk's experiment in the early part of the 20th century relied as little as possible on foreign aid, while his successors opened up the country and fell into the external indebtedness which led Turkey to a partial default in 1978. On the other hand, the evolution of modernization in Iran fits the pattern perfectly.

B. The Tunisian and Persian experience of indebtedness in the 19th century.

The cases of Tunisia and Persia complete and confirm the Ottoman and Egyptian experiences. The two main sources of indebtedness were, on the one hand, the need for capital equipment and military modernization and, on the other hand, the general desire for economic development. Like Egypt and Ottoman Turkey, both these countries were to be influenced by a strong Europeanization movement among certain élites. In Tunisia, for example, Khaireddine called simultaneously for a resurgence of Islam and for modernization; in this sense he was part of a pattern of Islamic, Indian, Egyptian, Iranian and Turkish reformers who tried to reconcile tradition and modernity, and thus to find ideological compromise formulas which would conceal the clash of social interests generated by the modalities of a modernization entirely imported from abroad; in this way, an emphasis on tradition and the spiritual heritage satisfied those social groups which were not affected by the social and economic benefits of Europeanization, as well as their élites, while at the same time lending legitimacy to the "modernity" of the élites which did benefit from Westernization.

Tunisian indebtedness began in 1830, mainly on the French capital market. In 1859, however, the external debt was still moderate, amounting to 12 million francs for annual State revenues of 11 million; it was thus possible for debt servicing not to exceed 10% of those revenues. In 1867, after excessive recourse to the capital market had led to an increase in the cost of credit and higher debt charges, Túnisia suspended its external payments; its debt had then risen to 160 million francs. After the opposition of the other European powers had led to the failure of an attempt, in 1869, to set up a Franco-Tunisian commission to control the country's finances, an expanded commission consisting of the representatives of France, Italy and Britain was set up for that purpose. The commission eventually restored the finances of the State of Tunisia, which had, through its bankruptcy, lost its economic autonomy; but bitter rivalry developed among the European powers over the concessions which should be extracted from the Dey of Tunis. European rivalries culminated in the French military occupation of 1881.

We shall not examine in detail the Moroccan experience of indebtedness, which is clearly similar to that of Tunisia though the Moroccan régime remained more arbitrary and more hostile to Europeanization until Sultan Abdel Azis came to power in 1894. Indebtedness began shortly thereafter; as early as 1902 the first problems of repayment occurred.(1)

As in the case of Egypt, the debts of Tunisia and Morocco preceded direct colonialism and were motivated by the desire of the national authorities to carry out a rapid Westernization of the country.(2) Fieldhouse, referring to Tunisia, sums up the situation accurately when he writes:

> "Here was a relatively wealthy society, with an increasing taste for European products - capital, consumer goods, military equipment - which wanted to modernize itself and was prepared to cooperate with European finance and technology. It was therefore an attractive target for the expanding European economy, resembling Latin American countries in that economic penetration was physically easy and the indigenous government was prepared to collaborate with foreign enterprise" (3)

---

(1) Details in H. Feiss, op.cit., pp. 397-421, and Fieldhouse, op.cit., pp. 269-311.

(2) Details in Fieldhouse, op.cit., pp. 110-118.

(3) Ibid., p. 112.

As we shall see in none of these cases was there anything like the fierce resistance to foreign control in Japan, which was accompanied by constant efforts to maintain internal control of technology.

The case of Persia is strongly reminiscent of that of Ottoman Turkey, but the inadequacy of the reigning dynasty, which, despite the adoption of a constitution and the inauguration of a Parliament in 1906, had been driven out by a general uprising in 1909, culminated in the Russo-British takeover of the country. Persian debts, however, remained very low in comparison to those of the Ottoman Empire or Egypt; this was particularly due to the inability of Persian structures to accomodate even a mere facade of modernization.(1)

C. <u>The debts of Latin America</u>.

Here again, as in the case of the Near East and North Africa, one is surprised to find that the process of indebtedness of the countries of Latin America was set in motion by the ruling élites at a time when their freedom of manoeuvre was all the greater in that economic extraversion, though admittedly quite pronounced even then, was nowhere near the threshold at which a headlong rush to modernize was the only way of coping with the imperialism of free trade. Moreover, it was after independence that the extraverted plantation and mining economies were to achieve their greatest expansion, the ruling élites being quite well disposed to free trade because of their need for modernization as a means of consolidating their power. We may refer in this respect, as one example among many others, to the policy of Porfirio Diaz which left the doors of Mexico wide open to foreign capital - an experiment which was to end in civil war and xenophobia.

It is do to this reason that we also find once again the same two principal causes of indebtedness:

- military equipment and the costs of military operations;
- setting up the basic infrastructure and the development of mining and agricultural activities.

A difference of general historical background separates the two cases, while at the same time confirming the similarity of events occurring so many years apart. Latin America emerged from Spanish Colonialism at the beginning of the 19th century and the economic policy of its élites steered it into the vicious circle of neo-colonial dependence which continues today through the phases of truncated but nonetheless progressive industrialization.

(1) Details in H. Feiss, <u>op.cit.</u>, pp. 361-381.

The Near East and North Africa were societies which remained closed to Europe until the beginning of the 19th century; they began to open up at a faster pace towards the middle of the century and, here again, it was the policies of the ruling êlites which set in motion a neo-colonial dependence which, by the end of the century or the beginning of the 20th century, had been transformed into direct or semi-direct colonization. In both cases, the channels of modernization passed through certain social, religious or ethnic groups, to the exclusion of others. Development was then distorted and impeded by the contradictory reactións of the various social groups to the modalities for the import of "modernism". This in turn was reflected in a ideological kaleidoscope which is hardly conducive to a clear understanding of the economic issues involved; this kaleidoscope continues in the 20th century, taking the concrete form of doctrines such as Peronism, the Middle East equivalent of which is the "specific" types of socialism, and in which right-wing conservatism and left-wing liberalism coexist uneasily.

Cardoso and Faletto, who reacted against the deterministic aspects of Marxist analyses of development and dependence in Latin America, deserve credit for showing the complex links which unite the "modern" groups, consisting of export-oriented sectors and more traditional groups, as well as the advantages obtained by the dominant groups as a result of the opening towards the outside world.(1) These two authors also make it clear that alternatives could have existed, but that the options chosen were more fully in keeping with the interests of the various dominant socio-economic groups. For example, speaking of the principal products of Latin America in the first half of the 19th century, they point out that:

> "It is interesting to note that these products could still be exploited with capital and that local resources were insufficient to finance diversified production on a large scale";

---

(1) F.H. Cardoso and E. Faletto, Dêpendence et dêveloppment en Amêrique Latine, (Paris: PUF, 1978). They say the following:

> "The exporter, planter, mine-owner, businessmen and banker groups played a vital intermediary role between(Cont'd)

> the European and American institutions on the one hand and the "traditional" agricultural sectors on the other. The national political institutions served not only the interests of the "modernizing" groups which were generated by the export system, but also those of the regional oligarchies which were generally opposed to the prospect of dominant paternalism becoming a more effective bureaucracy. The political contradictions between the contending dominant sectors went on into the 20th century when, with the success of the export model integrated into the world economy, new groups emerged to complete the economy of certain countries: the urban industrial sectors, the commercial sectors and the tertiary sector. From then on, the middle classes began to work for political reforms, thus making the reconciliation of the dominant groups possible." pp. 86-87.

The same analysis is found in C. Furtado: L'Amérique Latine, (Sirey 1970) who writes:

> " The setting up of the new States was influenced by two factors: the lack of real interdependence between the lords of the land who united or submitted to one individual as a result of the struggle for power, and the action taken by the urban bourgeoisie which had contacts with foreign countries and used every possibility of stepping up foreign trade, with the support of certain sectors of the rural sector. In this way, as possibilities opened up for this or that export sector, the urban group tended to strengthen its position and become integrated into a rural group, laying the foundations for an effective system of power". p.22

while further on they add that:

> "The problem was not that national capital should be available for investments made by foreigners; the owners of such capital, when they existed, were not interested in those sectors".(1)

The most interesting aspect of the mechanism of debts in Latin America is the fact that it would permit the development of a capitalist class even though that class had never had to take the responsibility for a genuine internal accumulation, that is, for an autonomous process of formation of capital in the sense of setting in motion a locally controlled technological accumulation of capital. The independence of the countries of Latin America does not, in fact, represent a break with the régime of colonization: the mechanisms for enrichment remain essentially mercantile and the dominant social groups are the ones which have continued that trend by seeking integration in British and then American free trade. The controversy about the political or economic causes of imperialism also provides us with a number of examples in which military constraints were not applied when a Latin American government practised a policy harmful to the economic interests of Britain.(2) We may even say that Latin America, by comparison with the other regions of the world, was treated quite favorably, as the policy of gunboat diplomacy was used only infrequently, particularly by Britain, which carried out an armed intervention only once, in Venezuela in 1903, to defend the interests of the bearer of State funds.(3)

In fact it was Rosa Luxembourg who, though deterministic in her long-term view of the collapse of world capitalism, best described the double role of international borrowing. In her book on the accumulation of capital she described as follows:

- continuation of capitalist accumulation in the center, while placing in the hands of the young countries the

(1) Cardoso and Faletto, op.cit., pp. 78 and 79.
(2) See W.M. Mathew: "The imperialism of free trade, Peru, 1820-1870", in The Economic History Review, 2nd series, 21, 1968, pp. 562-579; see also Fieldhouse, op.cit.
(3) D.C.M. Platt, "British bondholders in nineteenth-century Latin America: Injury and remedy", Inter-American Economic Affairs, XIV, 1960, p.41, quoted in D. Joslin: A Century of banking in Latin America, (Oxford University Press 1963), p. 103.

means of payments (through borrowings) which will make it possible for them to pay for purchases of goods produced in the center, on the one hand(1)

- emancipation of the new States which thus enter the arena of capitalism, sometimes by force, but often of their own free will.

---

(1) Rosa Luxembourg: L'accumulation du capital, (Paris: Maspero 1969), has the following to say:

"What Sismondi regarded as sheer madness actually occurred in this example: the British built railroads in the United States with their own iron and their own materials, paying for them with their own capital and refraining from "enjoying" those railroads. Despite all the periodical crises, European capital derived such profits from this madness that, around 1875, the London Stock Exchange was seized by a fever for foreign loans. Between 1870 and 1875 borrowings were contracted in London to a total value of 260 million pounds sterling - which immediately led to a rapid growth of British exports to the overseas countries. Although those countries occasionally went bankrupt, the capital kept pouring in. Towards the end of the 1870s, certain countries had partially or wholly suspended payment of interest: Turkey, Egypt, Greece, Bolivia, Costa Rica, Ecuador, Honduras, Mexico, Paraguay, Santo Domingo, Peru, Uruguay and Venezuela. However, by the end of the 1880s the fever for making loans to overseas States was back again: the States of South America, the colonies of South Africa absorbed enormous quantities of European capital. For example, the borrowings of the Argentine Republic amounted in 1874 to 10 million pounds sterling, and in 1890 to 59.1 million. Here again, Britain was building railroads with its own iron and its own coal and paying for them with its own capital". Vol. II, pp. 92-93.

> "These borrowings - the words of R. Luxembourg - are indispensable for the emancipation of the rising young capitalist States, and at the same time they are the most reliable way for the old capitalist countries to keep the young countries under their tutelage, to control their finances and to put pressure on their foreign customs and trade policies. They are the most effective way of opening up new spheres of investment for the accumulated capital of the old countries, and at the same time of creating new sources of competition for them, and of suddenly broadening the field of action of capitalist accumulation while at the same time causing it to shrink"(1)

In this way the surplus accumulated capital of the industrialized countries is invested abroad, expanding its range and its capacities for development, whereas in the young countries capitalism develops without accumulation in the real sense of the term because savings and technology are both provided from outside. To use Marxist terminology, the accumulation of the industrial capital of the countries which are already industrialized enables the Third World to enter the cycle of industrialization while preserving the pre-capitalist modalities for the mercantile accumulation of money capital. The wealth and savings of the dominant segments of the Third World, particularly in the 19th century, were considerable; they did not need to be invested, as foreign capital was available and was ready to take the losses. Proof of this is to be found in the fact that, despite the frequent defaults, the States of the Third World eventually managed to return to the capital markets. The truth of the matter is that, since the 19th century, international borrowing has blocked the process of autonomous industrialization by distorting the role of savings in its international distribution. We shall come back later to this important aspect of the indebtedness of the Third World.

We do not feel there is much point in going into the details of Latin American debts in the 19th century.(2) The movement followed, on the one hand, the vicissitudes of local politics and, on the other, the crises of the European stock markets.

(1) R. Luxembourg, op.cit., Vol. II, p.89.

(2) See in particular: J.F. Rippy: British investment in Latin America, 1822 - 1949, (Minneapolis 1959); L.H.Jenks: The migration of British capital to 1875, (New York: Alfred A. Knopf 1938); R.C. Conde: The first stages of modernization in Spanish America, (New York: Harper and Row, 1974); R. Sosa-Rodriquez: Les problemes structurels des relations économiques internationales de l'Amérique Latine, (Geneva: Droz, 1963); F. Mauro: Histoire de l'économie mondiale, (Paris: Sirey, 1971).

Indebtedness started with the wars of independence, which had the sympathy of British public opinion. From 1820 onwards Colombia, Chile, Peru, Buenos Aires, Mexico and Guatemala borrowed on the London market. A fictitious kingdom known as "Poyais" even succeeded in raising a loan of 200,000 pounds. -(see Table IV). By 1825 the total nominal amount of Latin American debts had already reached 21 million pounds, for an actual yield of 16.9 million, i.e., with a real rate of interest varying, depending on the loans from 5.9% to 10%. In 1880 the investment of Britain alone reached 179.5 million pounds, 123 million of which were in State bond issues; by 1913 these figures were, respectively 99.3 million and 314.3 million (see Table V). In 1913, French investments stood at 8.4 million francs, 2.6 million of which were invested in State bonds; German capital amounted to 3.8 billion marks. As for American investments,they rose between 1897 and 1914 from 308 million dollars to 1.6 billion; of this last figure only 368 million represented portfolio investments.(1) It should be noted that, at this time, the United States was still heavily in debt on the European capital markets.

These figures, when compared to those for investments in other regions of the Third World, show that Latin America was the largest consumer of the capital of the industrialized countries in the 19th century. Moreover, this situation was to continue in the 20th century. As the new Latin American States gradually became consolidated in the 19th century, investment in State bond issues were replaced by direct investments which, as in the Near East and North Africa, were carried out by a scramble for concessions for basic public services, particularly transport, and mines.

The numerous defaults which occurred in Latin America were no more of a deterrent there than they were in the other regions: both lenders and debtors alike returned to the vicious cycle of indebtedness, thus proving that it was of benefit to both of them.

Detailed debt figures make it clear, moreover, that the countries most heavily in debt in the 19th century were those where persons of European extraction were most strongly in control and where integration with the capitalism of the developed countries was fastest (Argentina, Brazil, Mexico, Uruguay, Venezuela, Chile, Peru). This situation was to recur in the 20th century, as was the preponderance of private investment.

---

(1) Figures taken from R. Sosa-Rodriguez, op.cit., pp. 32-51

D. The debts of the countries of Asia and the case of Japan.

When one considers the debts of the Asian countries, the case of Japan clearly poses a special problem, since we are dealing here with a country which, while having recourse to indebtedness for purposes of modernization, managed to prevent external financial flow from becoming the destructive mechansim which we have seen at work in the preceding cases. Japan thereby carried out an inward-focussing modernization which did not allow itself to be blocked by the classical mechanisms of extraversion.

It could be argued that the success of Japanese capitalism was due to its foreign expansion and its colonial conquests. In our opinion it is more reasonable to view the imperialist successes of Japan as the result of a successful process of technological autonomy which then drew Japan into an "expanded reproduction" cycle of capital, relying on the internal market, supported during phases of stagnation and depression by the external market. Against a background of keen imperialist rivalries in Asia, it is clear that Japan, competing against the European powers, could not even have ensured respect for its independence, much less carved out an empire for itself, had it not been for the fact that the vigor of its industrialization process and its technological autonomy had equipped it with a suitable military apparatus.

It should be remembered, moreover, that Japan during the years 1840-1870 was, like other countries, subject to the policy of gunboat diplomacy in the service of the imperialism of free trade, and that it was to be forced to accept commercial treaties opening its ports to Western merchandise without customs protection.

There is vast literature on the causes of Japanese industrialization.[(1)] Here we shall simply refer to those points which continue our analysis of the various experiences of indebtedness, particularly from the point of view of the attitudes of the intellectual and ruling élites to the choice of the modernization policy.[(2)]

---

(1) See, inter alia, J. Halliday: A political history of Japanese capitalism,(New York: Pantheon 1975); E.M. Norman: Selected writings. Origin of the modern Japanese state, (New York: Pantheon 1975); Japanese industrialization and its social consequences, H. Patrick (ed) (London: University of California Press, 1976).

(2) See in particular the important work by P. Akamatsu: Meiji - 1968. Révolution et contre-révolution au Japon, (Paris: Calmann-Lévy 1968)

a. Japanese xenophobia, like that of the Chinese, was widespread: Europeans were regarded as "barbarians". However, the crisis of the Japanese institution known as the "shogun", which ended in 1868 with the restoration of the powers of the Emperor, was a particularly fertile crisis in that it focussed attention on the problem of the choice of policy with which to resist European economic pressures. The dispute between the advisors to the Emperor and the last shogun was about the extent to which Japan, in response to foreign threats, should allow itself to be exposed to Western influences. The victory of the xenophobic party, which was predominant at the imperial court, did not, however, mean an absolute rejection of such exposure, but only that its extent should be limited to the minimum necessary to master European technology; at the same time the process of modernization was to be essentially inward looking, involving the gradual transformation of the highly decentralized feudal structures of traditional Japan into centralized capitalist structures. The process of technological control had already begun in 1840, though it had been greatly impeded by the obscurantist sectors of the xenophobic party who did not hesitate to murder Japanese scientists who "imported" European sciences.[1]

b. The military sphere was the one in which Western science was immediately applied, particularly for the casting of cannons; the Japanese élite proved capable of enough flexibility and judgment not to provoke the European powers until their technological backwardness had been overcome.

c. In the circumstances, therefore, it is not surprising that the financing of the industrial take-off relied mainly on internal sources (land tax, inflation and internal debt). Between 1868 and 1897, despite the numerous overtures made by European bankers, the Japanese government concluded only two modest loans: one in 1870 of 1 million pounds sterling, to help with the financing of the railroads, contracted at an interest rate of 9%, and the other of 2.3 million pounds, in 1873, to help buy out feudal rights, at an interest rate of 7%. The next foreign borrowings did not occur until 1897, and were used to finance

(1) See P. Akamatsu, <u>op.cit.</u>, p. 73. It was through the Dutch trading station of Nagasaki, the only European trading station allowed until the Japanese-American treaty of 1859, that Western science reached small groups of educated Japanese anxious to find out about the progress of Western technology. However, everything that came out of this Dutch enclave was severely censored.

the wars of Japanese expansion; however, the amount owed in 1913 - 1.6 billion yen - was commensurate with the size and power of the Japanese economy.(1)

In China, on the other hand, besides the fact that the ruling dynasty was foreign, the Chinese élite of the early part of the 19th century showed little interest in technological progress in Europe. It was not until European interests had given rise to the development of a bourgeoisie integrated into the trade network of Western capitalism that modernizing ideologies made their appearance. As in India, these ideologies fluctuated with a pendulum motion such as we have described in the case of other countries - phases of precipitous modernization based on the import of both technology and models of consumption, followed by phases of nationalist and traditionalist rejection. This pendulum motion reflects the complex evolution of the relations of endogenous interests between socio-professional groups in reaction to the impact of exogenous factors; this is a somewhat neglected field of study, though its main outlines at least have been described by J. Chesnaux.(2) At any rate it is

(1) Details in F. Mattard: Finances et développement, une approche historique, (Cuja 1974), pp. 79-102; and H. Feis: op.cit., pp. 422-429; F. Mauro, op.cit.,pp. 165-166; note the improvement in the interest rates at which the borrowings were concluded - as low as 5% in 1897.

(2) J. Chesnaux: L'Asie Orientale au XIXe et XXe siècles, (Paris: PUF 1973) in particular pp. 247-336. Referring to the various political tendencies among the Chinese élites at the beginning of the 20th century, Chesnaux writes: "The attitude of these parties and these groups to tradition is also highly complex. The initial modernism of the founders of the Congress or the Tong-meng-hui was gradually replaced by a desire to respect the national traditions and to exalt "spiritual values". This tendency may reflect the desire to better assert the national personality through religion and to be in touch with the popular masses, among whom these traditions are very strong. The emphasis laid by Tilak on Brahmanism, by the Indonesian nationalists on Islam and by the movements in Burma, Cambodia and Ceylon, has this dual meaning. This exaltation of traditional values could also be based on the desire to offset the revolutionary ideologies. Jiang Jie-Shi exalted Confucianism at the time of the struggle against Communism; the same sponsorship was invoked by the conservative nationalists of Vietnam, like Tran Trongkim, head of the pro-Japanese government of Jue Hue in 1945, and by the pro-Japanese politicians of the Nankin government in 1940-1945, (p.306); see also A.D. Gordon: "Businessmen and politics in a developing colonial economy; Bombay City, 1918-1933", in The imperial impact: studies in the economic history of Africa and India, C. Dewey and A.G. Hopkins (eds) (London: The Athlone Press 1978), pp. 194-213.

hardly conducive to the formulation and application of a coherent policy of modernization, beginning with the mobilization of internal savings, since such a mobilization implies profound reforms which the dominant groups are not always prepared to make.

The Chinese borrowings were to be devoted essentially to the payment of compensation for lost wars (Sino-Japanese war of 1894-1895, and, above all, the Boxer Rebellion) and the financing of railroads. Part of the money was borrowed from the Russian government - itself a heavy borrower of European capital, mainly on the French market - in return for the concession of the Trans-Manchurian railroad. As in the case of other countries, the scramble for concessions started in China, thus adding a sizeable external financial burden. As elsewhere, moreover, China had been obliged to pledge its customs and tax revenues as collateral for its external debts. In 1902 the external governmental public debt stood at 279.7 million dollars; in 1914 it was close to 500 million (496.2 million). During the same period, investment in business capital rose from 503.2 million dollars to 1,084.5 million.(1)

The case of India is obviously highly specific because since the beginning of the 19th century the East India Company had consolidated the direct or indirect control of the British colonial power over most of the Indian peninsula. The main source of Indian indebtedness was the building of the railroad network in the middle of the 19th century; this was warmly encouraged by the colonial power in order to facilitate its military control, but was also necessary for the speedy movement of grains to famine-stricken areas. Funds invested in railroads therefore carried a guaranteed rate of interest of 5%. In 12 years, between 1858 and 1869, 70 million pounds sterling was spent entirely on the railroads. It is interesting to note the remarks of a keen observer of Indian finances to the effect that the cost of construction was far higher than originally planned: 18,000 pounds sterling per mile, instead of 8,000.(2) He goes on to add:

> "For the case of the railway in India is that of the machine in all lands where it is imported from without. It destroys occupations in economizing labor. And the compensating demand for workmen to mine coal and to make machines which characterized the coming industrialism in Great Britain, Germany and the United States, was not manifested. India had coal and she had iron. But enterprise and empire could not wait

(1) Details in C.F. Remer: Foreign investments in China, (New York: 1933); and in Fieldhouse, Chesnaux and Mauro, op.cit.
(2) L.H. Jenks, op.cit., p. 222.

> upon their development. These things had to be provided from England. More than one third of the capital invested in Indian railways down to the early eighties was spent in England for railway iron and the cost of its transport to the East".(1)

The same observer admits, however, that neither the railroads of France nor those of Britain had been laid as fast as the railroads of India, and that, if they had been built by the local authorities they would probably have been cheaper but would have taken infinitely longer to complete. The same observer points out that the *Economist* of 12 June 1858 (p. 664) felt, with reference to the Indian railroads, that fewer and cheaper railroads as well as a greater number of roads and canals would have been better investments.(2)

It is not certain that, if the Indian government had had freedom of action it would have pursued a different policy, because we have seen governments which were still fairly free do exactly the same thing; and, in the 20th century, many Third World governments adopt similar policies.

---

(1) L.H. Jenks, *op.cit.*, p. 227.
(2) L.H. Jenks, *op.cit.*, p. 216.

TABLE I

Consolidated Debt of Egypt From 1862 to 1876.

(in thousands of pounds Sterling)

Year of borrow-	Nominal capital	Flota- tion	Real product	Real rate	Nominal inter- est	Real in- ter- est	End of amor- tiza- tion	Annuity
1862	3,293	83%	2,500	76%	7%	9 %	1892	265
1864	5,704	93%	4,864	85%	7%	8.2	1879	620
1865	3,387	90%	2,750	81%	7%	8.6	1881	368
1866	3,000	92%	2,640	88%	7%	8.0	1874	710
1867	2,080	90%	1,700	82%	9%	11.0	1881	258
1868	11,890	75%	7,193	61%	7%	11.5	1898	953
1870	7,143	75%	5,000	70%	7%	10.0	1890	669
1873	32,000	70%	19,974	63%	7%	11.0	1903	2,566
	68,497		46,621					6,409

SOURCE: J. Ducruet: Les capitaux européens au Proche-Orient, op.cit., p. 26.

TABLE II

Evolution of the Ottoman Public Debt 1858-1874

(in thousands of Turkish pounds)

	Nominal capital	Flotation rate	Actual product	End of amorti- zation	Interest and an- nuity		Principal contracting agent
1858	5,500	76.0%	4,180	1893	6%	385	Dent,Palmer
1860	2,241	62.5%	1,401	1896	6%	152	Mires
1862	8,800	68.0%	5,984	1886	6%	704	Ott.Bank
1863	8,800	71.0%	6,248	1887	6%	704	B.Imp.Ott.
1865a	6,600	66.0%	4,350	1887	6%	557	B.Imp.Ott.
1865b	40,000	50.0%	20,000	1898	5%	1,960	Engl.Syndic.
1869	24,444	61.0%	14,911	1902	6%	1,711	Comp.d'Esc.
1870	34,848	32.125%	11,915	1969	3%	1,232	Hirsch
1872	12,239	98.5%	12,055	1878	9%	1,101	B.Aust.Ott.
1873	30,555	59.5%	18,180	1903	6%	2,139	Crédit Gnl.
1874	44,000	43.5%	19,140	--	5%	2,200	B.Imp.Ott.
	218,027		117,650			12,845	

SOURCE: J. Ducruet: <u>Les capitaux européens au Proche-Orient</u>, op.cit., p.94.

TABLE III

Development of Egypt from 1863 to 1880

	Unit of measurement	1863	1880
Population	Thousands of inhabitants	4,833	5,818
Cultivated land	Thousands of acres	4,103	5,493
Public schools	Units	185	4,817
Value of imports	Thousands of pounds	1,991	5,410
Value of exports	Thousands of pounds	4,454	13,810
State revenues (1864)	Thousands of pounds	4,937	8,468
Railroads	Miles	275	1,196
Telegraph lines	Miles	634	5,858
Irrigation canals	Miles	44,625	52,400

SOURCE: J. Ducruet: Les capitaux européens au Proche-Orient, op.cit., p. 29.

TABLE IV

Latin American borrowings on the London market, 1822-1825

Date and debtor	Nominal value	Flotation price	Interest Nominal %	Interest Real %	Amounts received
1822					
Colombia	2,000,000	84	6	7.5	1,680,000
Chile	1,000,000	70	6	8.6	700,000
Poyais	200,000	80	6	7.5	160,000
Peru	450,000	88	6	6.8	396,000
1824					
Peru	750,000	82	6	7.3	615,000
Buenos Aires	1,000,000	85	6	7.0	850,000
Colombia	4,750,000	88.5	6	6.8	4,203,750
Brazil	1,200,000	75	5	6.7	900,000
Mexico	3,200,000	58	5	8.6	1,856,000
1825					
Brazil	2,000,000	85	5	5.9	1,700,000
Mexico	3,200,000	89.75	6	6.7	2,872,000
Peru	616,000	78	6	7.7	480,000
Guadalajara	600,000	60	6	10.0	360,000
Central America	163,000	73	6	8.2	118,990
TOTAL	21,129,000				16,891,740

SOURCE: R. Sosa-Rodriquez: Les problemes structurels des relations économiques internationales de l'Amérique Latine, op.cit., pp. 33-34.

TABLE V

British Investments in Latin America, 1880-1913.

(thousands of pounds sterling)

Country	1880 Total investments, nominal value	1880 State funds	1913 Total investments, nominal value	1913 State funds.
Argentina	20,339	11,234	357,740	81,582
Bolivia	1,654	1,654	--	--
Brazil	38,869	23,060	223,895	117,363
Mexico	32,741	23,541	159,024	28,596
Chile	8,466	7,765	63,938	34,676
Uruguay	7,644	3,519	46,145	25,552
Colombia	3,073	2,100	6,654	3,388
Costa Rica	3,304	3,304	6,660	2,005
Cuba	1,231	--	44,444	9,687
Dominican Republic	714	714	--	--
Ecuador	1,959	1,724	2,780	183
Guatemala	544	544	10,445	1,445
Honduras	3,222	3,222	3,143	3,143
Nicaragua	206	--	--	--
Paraguay	1,505	1,505	2,995	752
Peru	36,177	32,688	25,658	1,742
Venezuela	7,564	6,403	7,950	4,228
Companies operating in various countries	10,274	--	--	--
Banks	--	--	18,514	--
Shipping Companies	--	--	15,362	--
TOTAL	179,486	122,977	995,347	314,342

SOURCE: R. Sosa-Rodriguez: Les problemes structurels des relations économiques internationales d l'Amérique Latine, op.cit., pp. 36-37.

E. Savings, indebtedness and international monetary system.

The economic history of the Third World in the 19th century, including the general pattern of disruption of self-sufficient rural economics in favour of individual agricultural ownership, as well as the separation of agricultural and craft activities, led to the development of two financial circuits for the accumulation of money capital:

- the internal usury circuit which feeds on the lack of funds of the small cultivators, farmers or share-croppers, all of whom are overwhelmed by taxes, forced labor or rent payable to the landowners,

- the external mercantile circuit based on profits from exports.

In an economy which imports both capital and technology, there will be no incentive for either of these two circuits to become transformed into productive local savings, in other words, into a source of internal accumulation linked to technological progress. On the contrary, the external availability of technology and capital, and the fact that the foreign holders of capital and technology are in charge of the functioning of the technology which is introduced, leads the local classes which possess loan capital and mercantile capital to broaden the basis of their unproductive accumulation of money capital. In actual fact, as Knapp has shown, the internal rate of savings in the borrower country comes to be dependent on the maintenance of a certain level of external indebtedness. (1) Knapp gives several examples in which indebtedness exceeds the level warranted by balance - of - payments considerations. (2) Brown, enlarging on Knapp's arguments, points out that the exports of capital from

---

(1) J.A. Knapp: "Capital, exports and growth", in Economic Journal, Vol, 67, no. 267, September 1957.

(2) J.A. Knapp: "Capital, exports and growth for Argentina", in Economic Journal, September 1959.

the industrialized countries to the Third World have more often financed the constant rise in the debts of the borrowing countries than a real transfer of goods and services; interest and profits, during the period 1815-1914, partly covered the increase in those debts and occasionally even exceeded it. Summarizing Knapp's conclusion he goes on to say:

> "...there was "excess borrowing" during this period, due to a failure not of domestic saving but of domestic lending in the borrowing countries, either because of the undeveloped state of the banking system and capital market in these countries or because of a "tradition that capital should come in from abroad".

Knapp's argument is designed to show that there is little evidence for a real transfer of resources needed for growth in developing countries. The example that he gives of the capital movements between Britain and Argentina shows the huge size of the "excess borrowing". Only a third of the sum provided by British loans to Argentina in the 1880s was needed to cover Argentina's foreign payments deficits in those years. The rest financed the local costs of railway and port building, thus greatly increasing Argentina's indebtedness. According to another calculation, "Argentina's exports expanded six times between 1881-1885 and 1910-1914, whilst imports expanded five times and foreign debt service eight times."[(1)]

In the circumstances local capital was clearly not interested in setting up banking capital which could serve as an effective intermediary for savings to the benefit of those in the society who sought to obtain capital.

The accumulation of capital then becomes so large that it is naturally attracted to the financial centers of the industrialized countries, where it will be managed under conditions of greater financial and political security. For this reason the vacuum in the banking institutions is very quickly filled by the banks of the industrialized countries, which make it perform a dual function:

- helping the local government to mobilize its loans abroad.

- helping local savings to leave the country in order to be invested on foreign financial markets.

---

(1) M.B. Brown: Economics of imperialism, (London: Penguin Books, 1976), pp. 174-175.

It is not surprising, in this case, that throughout the 19th century foreign banks wove a formidable banking network in the Third World;(1) this delaying of local savings was later responsible for the weakness of the banking set-up which emerged in the Third World in the 20th century. Many attempts at local industrialization in the 19th century (e.g., Mexico, India) made by certain entrepreneurs from the traditional merchant or big landowner classes were blocked by a lack of capital, particularly in the light of the abundance of capital available to the other sectors of the economy, which were connected to trade with the industrialized countries.

In a remarkable study, De Cecco has shown that monetary manipulations were not merely due to British or French conspiracies, but were profitable to certain interests among the local élites. For example, the Latin American devaluations admittedly increased the amount of external debt, for both the State and the taxpayers in general; but at the same time they greatly enriched the dominant segments of the export sectors. Similarly, the fact that many countries kept a system of monetary bimetallism enabled those holding mercantile or loan capital to rid themselves advantageously of their silver holdings in order to buy gold when the price of silver was declining against that of gold. De Cecco concludes with reference to the spread of the gold standard:

> "In none of the cases reviewed did those who implemented monetary reform have the slightest intention of linking their countries to an international monetary system which would then automatically produce a kind of intentional economic meritocracy, based on differences in prices and interest rates among the various nations. In reality, we have seen how silver was used until its inflation became intolerable; how by going on to gold, countries tried to defend themselves against the immense slump in the price of primary commodities and silver. Where the ruling class could benefit from a depreciating standard, they kept silver in the saddle; and they never tried to change to gold except, of course, for the wrong reasons. When they did decide in favour of such a change, it was sometimes in order to obtain political credit in their countries or hard-currency abroad; but more often their arm was simply twisted by

(1) Details will be found in works already referred to, in particular Ducruet, Feis, Jenks and Joslin.

> other forces that, temporarily at least, challenged their supremacy. And, just as they had easily adopted gold, the ruling classes as carelessly repudiated it when, during and after the Great War, it did not suit their interests to retain it. However, nineteenth century public opinion did not create the Gold Standard myth; nor did it believe in an "ubi consistam" of eternal duration as was claimed by Keynes... After the Great War, it was the utopia jeremiads of a few day-dreamers which were responsible for the distorted image of the pre-1914 gold standard that has been so commonly accepted ever since. But the present study clearly shows that international economic events followed a pattern which could not possibly be called automatic. The various governments adopted such economic policies and as they deemed it would best serve the interest of the ruling classes. They favoured fixed exchange rates when they were expedient and progressive devaluation when it appeared possible. Nor were they afraid to change course whenever they felt it was necessary. Moreover, uncertain and even downright self-contradictory economic policies were adopted - as they often are nowadays. It would therefore be misleading to postulate any important qualitative differences between the monetary policies of the period under review and those of our own time."(1)

De Cecco also shows how, in the 19th century, many Third World governments anxious to have plenty of financial manoeuvrability, deposited vast sums of cash on the London and Paris markets. This leads him to the conclusion that the short-term balances of those countries, invested on the markets of the industrialized countries, make it easier for the latter to expand their external lending operations. Like Knapp, De Cecco concludes with an analysis of this phenomenon:

> "The greater liquidity preference that monetary authorities in smaller countries showed in this period was, from the point of view of the countries where they held their deposits, an advantage. Great Britain, and to a lesser extent France and Germany, could afford to spend more abroad, both

(1) M. De Cecco: Money and Empire, the international gold standard, 1890-1914, (Oxford: Basil Blackwell, 1974), pp. 60-61.

> on current and on capital account, than would have been possible had peripheral countries not preferred international credit to real resources."(1)

The imperialism of the international monetary system, like that of capital, is therefore the result of the policy of the Third World countries in the 19th century. The banking trusts and industrial trusts were as much a result of the economic policies of the peripheral countries as of gunboat diplomacy. The conditions for underdevelopment in the 20th century were in fact set up in the 19th century and without doubt in earlier centuries; they were to operate quite as effectively, despite the numerous political events which were supposed to have accelerated the liberation of the Third World - the difference being that this time the mechanisms of indebtedness were to help widen the technological gap even more spectacularly.

---

(1) De Cecco, op.cit. p. 119. Brown, referring to Rippy, op. cit., mentions that certain Latin American governments could have liquidity equivalent to about 60% of the debt contracted (op.cit., p.192). Here we are probably dealing with another problem which later recurred in the 20th century: that of the capacity of execution of those projects for which debts have been contracted.

CONCLUSION

It is not necessary to give further examples, because in all cases we see at work the same processes and mechanisms whereby the burden of debt servicing always rises faster than the volume of exports.(1) However, we should refer to those cases of indebtedness which did not lead to the reproduction of underdevelopment. Besides that of Japan, to which we have already referred, the United States, Canada, Australia and New Zealand were all heavy borrowers on the British capital market in the 19th century. These examples are all the more interesting in that all of these countries were at one time or another colonies which for many years were specialized in the production of raw materials, within the context of the international division of labor imposed by Britain from the beginning of the 19th century onwards.(2) Of course, one must not underestimate the fact that these countries, having been colonies of European settlement, enjoyed a favorable prejudice which facilitated the mobilization of loans on the European markets under good conditions. Yet for the United States, particularly at the time of the Civil War, the conditions of external borrowing were very severe. In another sense one should not underestimate the internal factors which made recourse to external indebtedness an additional source of economic stagnation and dependence. The experience of Japan and the countries quoted above shows beyond a doubt the need for a minimum level of local technological expertise as a means of preventing external indebtedness from becoming the central pivot of external dependence. That is why the notion, espoused by some authors, that absolute technological dependence is a variable depending exclusively on imperialism is clearly not a serious working hypothesis; in any case for the 19th century, when differences in technological levels between Europe and the rest of the world, were not the huge gap that exists today.

As we have seen, numerous internal socio-political causes are involved; in the light of our own 20th century experience these causes are now more clearly discernible and we are thus better able to understand the past. The mounting debts of Portugal and Tsarist Russia in the 19th century provide, in a different sense, additional proof that it is not enough to be situated in Europe and to have a colonial empire in order to become an industrialized capitalist power.

(1) For Argentina, for example, see A.G. Ford; "Capital exports and growth for Argentina", in Economic Journal, Vol. 68, no. 271, Sept. 1958.

(2) For Canada and Australia, see F. Mattard, op.cit. For the United States many details will be found in H. Feis and L.H. Jenks, op.cit.

It is the knowledge of the Third World's experience of foreign aid, indebtedness and investment which has led us to certain of the internal causes which, in the 19th century, made recourse to external debt, a source of dependence which could go as far as total subjugation. We shall see that socio-economic trends in the countries of the Third World in the 20th century are merely the continuation of those perceived in the 19th century, since the past cannot fail, in turn, to shed light on the present. It therefore is not surprising that recourse to external indebtedness continues to be the pivot of the mechanisms of dependence, together with policies pertaining to the transfer of technology.

When reading specialized works on European capital movements, one is struck by the similarity between the situations in the 20th century: take for example the feverish investment in railroads in Europe, the resulting prosperity and the consequent belief that such investments in the Third World would open the door to modernization and boost international trade. This fever was originally derived from the interest of the British builders and industrialists, who had a technological edge over their European competitors; consortiums of engineering contracting, management and suppliers companies were set up in conjunction with banking consortiums in order to beat their competitors in the race for concessions, financing and building contracts. In the 20th century we are witnessing the same processes involving the construction, for example, of airports, but also of highways, dams, telephone networks, etc...

In the next chapter we shall try to set forth in detail, to the extent possible, the complex relations linking the phenomena of technology, indebtedness and "modernization" to the economic system and to the models of consumption. In the light of the historical experience of the Third World, however, it appears immediately evident that indebtedness and technology are closely linked; the relationship between those two phenomena and the problems of savings and the economic system, and thence with the problems of "capital" will be examined in the light of the contemporary experiences of the countries of the Third World.

It is therefore truly regrettable that the economic literature does not, on the whole, pay much attention to an analysis of the internal mechanisms of decision-taking on the question of economic recourse to external sources. The literature on the movement of capital is almost exclusively based on an analysis from the point of view of the countries which are already industrialized or on mechanistic models of the functioning of balances of payments, from a neo-classical standpoint. As for the literature on dependence and imperialism, with a few exceptions which we have already examined, its models are quite as mechanistic, and its analyses give very scant treatment to the Third World, concentrating instead on the functioning of capitalism in the industrialized countries.

II. THE DEBTS OF THE THIRD WORLD IN THE 20th CENTURY: MODELS OF CONSUMPTION, TECHNOLOGY AND MODERNIZATION

"Technology is the magic mill which produces wealth and power: and human beings have always been prepared to pay almost any price for wealth and power". (Arnold Toynbee)

"For any country, if it wants to develop itself, it must mainly rely on itself and its own potentialities. But it is also necessary to obtain capital from the developed countries..."

Teng Hsiao-P'ing (Interview in Time 5/7/79)

It was not until the beginning of the seventies that the countries of the Third World reappeared as major borrowers on the international financial markets. This was because the international monetary upheavals which followed the first World War prevented the international financial markets, particularly those of London and Paris, from functioning as in the past. Moreover, there was a tendency for financial and trade flows to become bilateral operations between the metropolitan powers and the colonies, within the framework of the general rise of protectionism and the great depression of 1929. In fact it was not until the early sixties that operations began once more to become multilateral, on the one hand through the progressive dismantling of exchange controls, and on the other hand with the accession to independence of increasing numbers of Third World countries. This trend towards multilateralism encountered many obstacles, as the bulk of aid still came from the former metropolitan powers and the international institutions for aid and financing pursued relatively strict policies. Lastly, a period of great dynamism in the industrialized countries left little capital available for the countries of the Third World on the national financial markets and on the Euro-currency market, which was beginning its great period of expansion. In actual fact it was the oil crisis, with the burgeoning of oil-based capital and the recession in the industrialized countries which gave the countries of the Third World wider access to the international financial markets. At the same time the International Bank for Reconstruction and Development, as well as the International Monetary Fund, became much more extensively involved in the developing countries.

This does not mean that financial flows between the Third World and the industrialized countries dried up between 1919 and 1960. Those flows never stopped; they even increased because of the extraordinary expansion of American capital, particularly in Latin America and the Middle East - an expansion which offset the drop in European investments. But the importing of capital by the developing countries during this period mainly took the form of direct investments, whereas in the 19th century States' borrowings had usually occupied a very important place in the mechanisms of external finance of the non-industrialized countries. In the same way, from 1945 onwards aid was to become an increasingly important element in the various forms of capital import and its share in the flow of external capital did not decline until the Western financial markets were once more opened to borrowers from the developing countries.

Under the influence of American financial expansion, Latin America was to be a prominent capital-importing region; the Great Crash on the New York stock exchange in 1929 obviously dampened this trend, while at the same time leading to moratoriums on payments in most of the Latin American countries which effectively "rang the death knell of the external credit of the region".(1) This was to strengthen the trend towards direct investment which we have already noted. But it is interesting to note that it was precisely the external payments crisis of 1929 and the collapse of external demand which enabled Latin America to carry out a process of industrialization based on import substitution. In the case of Brazil, for example, C. Furtado has the following to say:

> "The origin of this principal thrust lay in the economic forces of the country, as a result of the tensions created by the foreign trade crisis. The action taken by the State was in fact largely a response to those tensions, the final result being the resumption of the process of industrialization. Indirectly the foreign trade crisis brought about a privileged situation, with regard to activities linked to the domestic market. The reduction of import capacity compelled those industries which depended on imports to make savings or find subsitutes for imported products. The high cost or the lack of imported parts turned out to be a sort of challenge to the engineers and the local mechanical industries."(2)

---

(1) R. Sosa-Rodriguez, _op.cit_., p. 99.

(2) C. Furtado, _Analyse du "modèle" brésilien_, (Paris: Anthropos, 1974), pp. 32-33. With reference to our period, the author writes: "Because he favored the hegemony of no particular region or group of interests - a fact made possible by the vacuum resulting from the decline of the coffee interests - Vargas enjoyed great independence in the exercise of power as no other previous government of the country ever had before. Thanks to developments during that period, the national State became an important factor in the Brazilian economic system. Trade policy, which had traditionally been subordinate to the interests of external debt, was transformed into a powerful instrument for the encouragement of capital formation", pp.31-32.

One should not forget, however, that it was during this period that European agriculture became modernized, while that of the Third World remained completely stagnant in terms of productivity - a fact which did not fail to influence subsequent trade between industrialized and developing countries.

It will moreover be noted that in Turkey, under Mustapha Kemal, and also in Egypt, there was a considerable improvement in the external financial situation, as the Turkish and Egyptian governments incurred no foreign debts at all during the period 1919-1945; at the same time, definite progress was made in the development of local industries, particularly in Egypt with the emergence of the Misr group, under the leadership of Talaat Harb.

The movement towards industrialization continued throughout the war, at a time when international trade was seriously impeded. Unfortunately, from 1945 onwards, the development of American aid programs brought about renewed recourse to external capital, and the need for raw materials caused by the Korean War boosted the activity of those Third World sectors which were geared for foreign trade. The purchasing power thus generated was to lead most countries into development programs which, by their very nature and conception, would eventually require a complement of increasing external financing and massive imports of technology.

The mechanisms of the dual technological/financial dependence were set in motion once again and led, 20 years later, to a situation in which the MNCs and the international capital markets had become the pivot of the mechanisms for development and modernization in the Third World, and the international financial organs had acquired the position of arbiters of the politico-social problems of the Third World. All other things being equal, in fact, the Third World thus found itself back in the 19th-century situations which we have described earlier.

Therefore in this section, we shall concentrate on the evolution of external indebtedness since 1945, since the "positive interlude" of the years 1919-1945 had failed fairly completely to generate self-sustaining industrialization based on a certain minimum level of technological autonomy. On the contrary, it is surprising that the need for supplementary external resources - either directly through increased aid and broader access to the international capital market, or indirectly through the stabilization of commodity prices - was one of the main demands made by the great movement of opposition to the international economic order, as expressed in particular by the United Nations Special Session on Commodities and

Development and the opening of the North-South dialogue (1974-1975).

At the same time, as we shall see, the increase in the external debt of the countries of the SMEA and the reversal of Chinese policy on external debt have once more raised the acute problem of recourse to external capital.

In the first part we shall thus try to quantify the increase in the external public debt of the Third World and the centrally planned economies (CMEA) and determine its significance for the general functioning of international trade in the era of the great technological modernizations controlled by the MNCs. Then, in the second part, we shall try to pinpoint those institutional and ideological causes within the Third World which accentuate the phenomena of financial and technological dependence; this will enable us to examine more systematically the relationship between financial dependence and technological dependence.

A. The quantitative factors and their meaning.

These factors are difficult to express in homogeneous terms, mainly for two reasons:

a) On the one hand, the survey made by the World Bank, which is the main available statistical source, takes account only of external public debt, to the exclusion of the external debts of the private sector; in countries where the market economy plays an important role, these debts can run into huge amounts of money, and their omission from a survey clearly detracts from the value of World Bank data. To take just the example of Brazil, while the external public debt at the end of 1979 amounted, according to World Bank Statistics, to 35.9 billion dollars, estimates of the total debt (including the private sector) were around 50 billion dollars. Moreover, the debts recorded here are only those lasting more than a year; yet, in the case of many countries, floating short-term debt is almost as large as the medium-term debt. Lastly, military debts are usually excluded from data provided by countries to the World Bank.

b) On the other hand, the World Bank's presentation of global statistical tables is never homogenous from one year to the next, because of increasingly sophisticated "refinements" in the sub-categories, by groups of countries or statistical magnitude, which are analyzed. Moreover, the statistical series are given sometimes on the basis of debts including amounts not disbursed, and sometimes without those amounts. For example, the statistical series included in the 1973 annual report of the World Bank only gives figures on the basis of amounts paid for the period 1965-1971, whereas the 1978 report gives figures solely on the basis of the total amounts, including the part of the debt which had not been disbursed, for the period 1970-1976. In addition, the statistical series are contantly reviewed by the World Bank, as the debts of newly surveyed countries are introduced into the series, and as improvements are gradually made in the reporting system for countries already surveyed.

Moreover, the other complementary statisical sources which are available - such as studies by OECD, the Development Assistance Committee, the Bank for International Settlements, or, more recently, UNCTAD - are rarely compatible with each other.

Lastly, a precise study of the statistical data should take account, on the one hand of domestic and international inflation rates, and, on the other hand, of variations in the exchange rates. In both cases, the necessary adjustments would be extremely delicate and could not fail to pose tough problems.

This is why, by merely taking the figures of the World Bank for external public debt in current dollars, and comparing them, still in current dollars, with the amount which seems to us to have the most significant bearing on the evolution of debt (exports), and even before dealing with estimates of the debts of private enterprises in the Third World, one can draw certain conclusions without being obliged to separate oil-exporting countries from the other developing countries.

1 Annual rates of growth of public debt rose sharply from 1970 onwards. Whereas for the period 1967-71 the average annual rate was 13.3%,(1) the rate rose to 20.3% for the period 1970-1976.

2 This increase was due essentially to the growth of borrowings on the international financial market, particularly the Euro-currency market; these borrowings, which accounted for only 4% of total external public indebtedness in 1967, reached 26% in 1976. Information available on the years 1977-1978 illustrates the very fast rise in such borrowings.

---

(1) Same rate as for the period 1961-69, on which statistics will be found in: Debt problems of the developing countries, Report of the UNCTAD Secretariat, New York, 1972, TD/118/Supp.6/Rev.1.

TABLE VI

Borrowing by Developing Countries

on the Euromarket

(in billions of dollars)

	Annual Average 1975/1978	1975	1976	1977	1978
I. Non-oil Exporting Countries:					
Argentina	170.24%	72	957	849	1.421
Brazil	35.50%	2.152	3.232	2.814	5.354
Chile	116.51%	--	208	591	975
Korea	95.81%	347	738	1.265	2.605
Malasia	26.39%	425	207	212	858
Mexico	45.55%	2.311	1.993	2.727	7.126
Morocco	44.62%	200	641	797	605
Peru	-24.78%	334	395	189	--
Philippines	76.38%	363	970	698	1.992
Taiwan	23.61%	135	219	524	255
Other Countries	28.72%	1.860	1.458	2.828	3.967
TOTAL		8.199	11.019	13.494	25.158
II. Oil Exporting Countries:					
Algeria	71.34%	500	643	723	2.515
Indonesia	-6.02%	1.347	469	817	1.118
Iran	61.05%	265	1.411	1.220	1.107
United Arab Emirates	65.41%	156	55	1.086	706
Venezuela	266.19%	38	1.185	1.666	1.866
Other Countries	66.31%	593	235	1.969	2.728
TOTAL		2.899	3.999	7.481	10.040
Total I and II	46.94%	11.098	15.016	20.975	35.198

SOURCE: Morgan Guarantee Trust Co. of New York: World Financial Markets, Dec. 1978

3 This change in the courses of indebtedness undoubtedly aggravated the debt servicing burden, particularly interest payments, the average annual growth rate of which for the period 1969-1975, was higher than the rate of increase of the debt itself. This was due to the fact that borrowings on the international capital market were concluded for relatively short periods and at market rates, plus a risk premium of between 1 and 2.5%. When one remembers that Euro-dollar rates between 1969 and 1976 fluctuated between 6 and 12%, that gives an interest rate rarely below 7% and going as high as 14.5%.

4 The average annual rate of increase of the debt of the developing countries for the period 1967-1971 was about 1.4% higher per annum than the rate of their exports. It was only because of the steep rise in oil prices in 1973 and 1974 that the rate of growth of exports for the period 1970-76 was higher than that of indebtedness, but in 1975 the trend was reversed; on the other hand the rate of increase of the import of services which, as we shall see, may be regarded as a reliable indicator of the level of technological dependence in the case of the developing countries was far higher than the rate of increase of debt (27.2% against 20.3%) for the period 1970-76.

5 Certain oil producing countries (Algeria, Iran, Venezuela, Indonesia, Nigeria), despite the increase in oil revenues in 1973-74 became net borrowers on the capital markets from 1975 onwards because of the deficit of their balance of goods and services. This proves, moreover, that despite the inflow of capital from oil revenues, their external debt situation had not changed basically; worse still, those countries, because of the absolute and relative decline of their other types of production (in particular agriculture) became more dependent than ever before on their energy exports.

6 It was actually the middle-income countries - a category which includes the oil exporting countries and many countries of Latin America - which increased their external debt most markedly during the period 1969-75. On the whole these were countries for which the great multinational corporations were privileged partners. The mounting size of the indebtedness of the low-income countries is also striking, although their share in the total debt of the developing countries declined.

At the end of 1978 the external debt of the developing countries was in the region of $300 billion on the basis of debt contracted, and $215 billion on the basis of debt disbursed. These figures presuppose a rate increase of 15% per annum for 1977 and 1978 - a conservative rate when one remembers that bank credits to the developing countries rose by 40% in 1977 and 67% in 1978. About 75% of the Euro-currency credits extended to the developing countries are borrowings for the State or the public sectors, or borrowings guaranteed by the State.

To this figure one should add the debts of the private sectors of the developing countries, which the World Bank estimated at $45 billion at the end of 1976;(1) this figure seems well below the real amount, if one takes into account the large floating debts which exist in the form of promissory notes drawn by suppliers on the importers of the developing countries and which are discounted without recourse with certain specialized institutions, particularly in Switzerland and Germany, and which are difficult to express in statistical terms.

The new statistical elements provided by the Bank for International Settlements (August 1978) concerning the structure of loan maturities at the banks of the Group of Ten, Switzerland, Austria, Denmark and Ireland as of 31/12/1977, show in all cases the predominance of one-year maturities. The statistics obviously include all bank loans and, accordingly, medium-term loans falling due during the year.(2)

The total public and private debt of the developing countries at the end of 1978 may be estimated to be somewhere between $350 billion and $400 billion - a vast amount, which shows the increasing extent to which investment in the Third World is being taken over by foreign capital.

Foreign loans are in themselves only one element in a series of external factors which affect the growth of the Third World. For example one must take into account:

i. The investments of the MNCs in the Third World, increasing from an annual average of $2 billion for the period 1964/1966 to $6.7 billion in 1973, $10.6 billion in 1975, and $8.8 billion in 1977.

---

(1) See World Bank report, 1978, p. 25.
(2) See *IMF Survey*, 11 September 1978, pp. 261-263, and *Financial Times*, 1/8/1978.

ii. The traditional forms of bilateral and multilateral aid, now greatly expanded by aid from the OPEC countries, in particular the Arab members, either individually or collectively (Assistance Fund of OPEC, Arab Bank for the Development of Africa, etc...).

iii. The rate of growth of the deficit of the balance of services, despite the large tourist revenues; this deficit is due to payments for patents, licenses, royalties, technical assistance and foreign consultants, besides the more traditional headings of insurance and transport, in which the Third World is generally in deficit.

iv. The rate of growth of the burden of debt servicing; for many countries the statistics of the World Bank do not faithfully reflect this burden, as the debts of the private sector are not taken into account. For example, in the case of Brazil the burden of debt servicing as a proportion of export earnings is between 50 and 60%, while the figure for Mexico is 55%.(1)

v. As in the 19th century, there are surprisingly large foreign exchange balances held by the developing countries in the banks of the Group of Ten, and surprisingly large foreign exchange reserves in the developing countries themselves.

vi. An important point to note is that an increasing share of the profits of the major international banks comes from their international lending operations. For First National City Bank, for example, the percentage of profits derived from international loans rose from 54% to 82% between 1972 and 1977; for the Bankers Trust during the same period, from 31% to 79%, and for the Chase Manhattan Bank from 42% to 65%.(2) This trend has been matched by an extraordinary expansion of the foreign networks of those banks, mostly in the Middle East and Asia, where French, German and American banks are engaged in keen competition. According to certain sources, American banks hold 52% of all claims on the developing countries and the CMEA countries, but 64% in the case of the debts of Latin

---

(1) According to the _Financial Times_ of 13/1/1978, quoting an article by E. Bacha, published in Brazil and printed in _World Development Magazine_, February 1978; see also supplement of _Financial Times_, "Brazilian Banking and Insurance", 28/6/78, p. 21; see also supplement of _International Herald Tribune_, "The Euromarket", Part One, December 1977, p. 55.

(2) See _Financial Times_, 6/6/78: "US authorities tighten up on overseas bank lending".

America.[1]

vii. One should also note the increasing importance of borrowings concluded by the countries of East Europe and the Soviet Union, and which are now thought to be in the region of $50 billion.[2] This indebtedness came into being and developed with the opening up of trade between the CMEA countries and Western Europe, and the very large turnkey plant contracts concluded between those countries and the MNCs since the end of the sixties.[3] According to certain sources, this indebtedness will reach $200 billion by the year 1980.[4]

viii. Lastly, China's program of modernization makes it likely that the indebtedness of those countries over the next four or five years will rise to 20 billion dollars, and then to 40 billion by 1985. For the past six months the international financial press has echoed the rivalries of the major Western banks as they vie with each other to offer the best terms of credit so as to enable the multinational corporations to capture the new Chinese markets.

In actual fact, it seems to us that since 1970 the international financial structures have entered a phase which, with all due reservations, is strikingly similar to that which preceded the first World War. The expansion, since the "reforms" of the international monetary system, of the dollar area to the whole of the world, the greater predominance of the major international banks in international financing, the capacity of the international monetary system to manage unlimited amounts of international financing, and, lastly, the de facto monopoly - both technological and financial - of the MNCs in the conduct of all significant investments in both the industrialized countries and the Third World, and partly

(1) See supplement of International Herald Tribune, "The Euromarket", Part One, p. 9.
(2) Supplement International Herald Tribune, quoted above, p. 3; see also Financial Times: "Comecon's debts to the West: a cause for concern", and Le Monde, 20-21 March 1977, "L'endettement des pays de l'Est devrait au moins doubler d'ici 1980".
(3) For a description of the big business between MNCs and socialist countries see C. Levinson: Vodka Cola, (Paris: Stock, 1977).
(4) See Financial Times, 19/12/78, "Comecon's debt of $200 billion by 1990 predicted".

also in the CMEA countries: (1) all these factors are evidence of the new world-wide status of the economy which the countries of the Third World seem ill-equipped to resist, assuming that their ruling élites actually do want to resist it(2).

The essential difference with the 19th century is that in those days the capitalism which sustained international trade was still largely national in nature. Britain's predominance was declining in the industrial sphere but still intact on the international financial circuits. In the present situation national capitalisms have been directly internationalized by the transnational operations of the major corporations of the leading industrialized countries. There are, nevertheless, some areas in which the similarity with the 19th century is discernible: there is a marked preponderance of American banking institutions in the international financial machinery, moreover, there is a definite preponderance of transnational corporations of American nationality in international trade and investment. This dual preponderance is, however, meeting increasingly stiff resistance as a result of the dynamism and the technological progress of the transnational corporations and the banks of the other capitalist industrialized countries, particularly Japan and Germany, but also France, with the growing part played by French banks in international financing, and, in particular the Crédit Agricole, which is the third largest bank in the world in terms of its turnover.(3)

The transnational capitalism of the close of the 20th century continues to bear the imprint of the national origins of the financial bodies and industrial corporations; the result is world-wide competition based on modern technology, especially in the fields of engineering, electronics, communications and the exploitation of the sources of energy. This competition takes place in an advertising climate from which the competing messages are conveyed to all levels of society, and, through modern media, reach even the remotest villages on earth. The advertising campaigns of the MNCs often link the

---

(1) See G. Corm: "Les firmes multinationales et l'acces du Tiers Monde a la technologie moderne", Le Monde Diplomatique, November 1978, and also "Endettement du Tiers-Monde et commerce de technologie", quoted above.

(2) This spread to a worldwide scale has been particularly well described by C.A. Michalet: Le Capitalisme Mondial (Paris: PUF 1976).

(3) On all these points, see G. Corm: "Systemes financiers et relations économiques internationales", in Problemes économiques du Tiers-Monde, studies by the Center for Research in Applied Economics, Algiers, prepared for the 1st Congress of Economists of the Third World, held at Algiers in February, 1976.

symbols of technological progress to images of the pleasure to be derived from the consumption of everyday objects (cigarettes, watches, radio, canned food, etc...), thus closely welding together a model of consumption and its supposed technological basis in the social ideologies. The symbols and images of Europeanization in the 19th century and the beginning of the 20th century (parliamentary democracy, free enterprises, national spirit, dress, Latin alphabet, etc...) have now been succeeded by new symbols and new images, which are well described by Baudrillard and Guillaume.[1] For individuals as members of society, this means the consumption and ownership of objects, and for States the ownership of the technological equipment capable of producing those objects and those models of consumption. The ideology of modernization is largely sustained by these symbols and images, and the profusion of financial means made available to buyers in the countries of the Third World makes it possible to feed the enormous machine of trade in technology which keeps the industrialized countries prosperous.[2]

It is not surprising that China, with its radical change in favour of the four modernizations and its overtures to the capitalist industrialized countries, has re-introduced Coca Cola into China, allowed Intercontinental, the famous American Hotel chain, to build several hotels on Chinese territory, and at the same time made massive purchases of Western technology. China is now also actively seeking the aid of the international institutions. Thus we find ourselves confronted with the paradigm "modernization-modern technology-model of consumption-national construction" which we mentioned in the introduction to this chapter and which is central to the problems of indebtedness of the Third World. This paradigm is based essentially on the dual notion "capital - modernization", on which, at the end of this chapter, we shall try to present certain ideas which might clarify the nature of the economic choices made by the governments of the Third World.

---

(1) See J. Baudrillard: Le système des objets, (Paris: Gallimard, 1968), and Pour une critique de l'économie politique du signe, (Paris: Gallimard, 1972); also M. Guillaume: Le capital et son double, (Paris: PUF, 1975).

(2) See G. Corm: Les firmes multinationales..., op.cit., and also Saper l'idéologie du développement, op.cit.

B. General Disadvantages of Indebtedness

Permanent recourse to external indebtedness by Third World countries seeking to lay the foundation for their autonomous development involves two kinds of disadvantages. The first kind occurs upstream from the process of indebtedness in its relation with the model for development, and produces a certain number of harmful effects which result from the very fact of recourse to indebtedness. The second kind occurs downstream from this process and produces consequences which have the effect of distorting the economic structures which result from a development process based on external indebtedness. Moreover, external indebtedness adds one more element to the various mechanisms for the reverse transfer of resources from the Third World countries to the industrialized countries, and one which, in today's economic situation, is fast acquiring crucial importance. Lastly, such indebtedness adds to the numerous causes of instability in the functioning of the international monetary system; in particular, it cannot fail to lead to increasingly greater dependence for the Third World.

1. Upstream harmful effects caused by recourse to external indebtedness.

a. Discouragement of the mobilization of potential savings.

In any country where the local capacity for capital formation is not fully mobilized - which is the case in most of the countries of the Third World - recourse to external indebtedness will have the effect of discouraging attempts to mobilize local savings, whether actual or potential. This can, in extreme cases, take the form of persistent unemployment and the marginalization of certain social groups or the maintenance of ostentatious consumption by other groups.

As we shall see, however, capital can be imported "wholesale" from abroad without major difficulties, the establishment of a dynamic network for the collection and redistribution of savings is greatly slowed down. What is said about indebtedness is valid also for aid, as numerous authors have emphasized.[1]

(1) In particular T.Mende: De l'aide a la recolonisation,(Paris: Seuil, 1972); R. Dumont: L'Afrique noire est mal partie, (Paris: Seuil, 1962); C.R. Hensman: Rich against poor - the reality of aid, (London: Penguin, 1971); C. Payer: The debt trap, (London: Penguin, 1975); and above all R.I. McKinnon: Money and capital in economic development, (Washington: The Brookins Institution, 1973); and also R. Nurske: Problems of capital formation in underdeveloped countries, (Oxford: Basil Blackwell, 1953); G. Ardant: Le monde en friche,(Payot 1954).

The economic history of the developing countries since the 19th century shows that disruption of the traditional economy leads to the development of usury, which paralyzes the self-financing capacity of small producers trying to achieve better productivity. This usurious capital, on the contrary, is used for sumptuous consumption, hoarding or investment abroad; it is rarely re-injected into the economy in the form of productive investments. In the best of circumstances, this capital will be invested in sectors which promote the extraversion of the economy and its specialization in the production of agricultural or mining raw materials for export.

In Chapter III we shall see how the functioning of local financial organs rarely corrects the distortions in savings brought about by modernization as it is understood in most developing countries. The distribution of savings is actually a fundamental part of productivity. If the savings of the "traditional" groups are confiscated, by the imposition of price-controls for agricultural products, by taxation or by price increases for industrial and semi-manufactured products used in farming or the cottage-industry sector, there will be very little chance of improvement in productivity occurring in the farming and cottage-industry sectors. Instead, such improvements will remain confined to the export-oriented sectors. The dissemination of technical progress thus becomes very difficult.

b. Discouragement of the growth of local productivity.

The availability of external means of payments, in addition to those earned by a country through its balance-of-payments surplus increases the tendency to import capital goods - a tendency which is also promoted by a number of other measures adopted locally by governments, such as exemption from customs duty, preferential rates of interest, etc...(1)

---

(1) A process well described by R.I. McKinnon: Money and Capital, op.cit.; by Paul Bairoch: Révolution industrielle et sous-développement, (Paris: Mouton, 1974) who has this to say: "a country imports machines because it does not have sufficient technological potential, and it is unable to bring that potential to a sufficiently high level because there is no local incentive for the industrial sectors where technicians could be trained and used to do anything about it". (p. 180); also N. Rosenberg: "reliance on borrowed technology perpetuates a posture of dependency and passivity. It deprives a country of the development of precisely those skills which are needed if she is to design and construct capital goods that are properly adapted to her own needs", in Perspectives on Technology, (Cambridge University Press, 1976) p. 166.

In this way the mechanisms for the acquisition of technological know-how are greatly hampered by the combined economic and financial policies of individual governments. A dual slowdown thus occurs, affecting the mobilization of local savings, on the one hand, and their transformation into productive capacity generated by local capacities, on the other. One immediate consequence of this situation is the complete discouragement of the emergence of local engineering capacities, in particular the capital goods sector and the installation of new plants.[1] It is precisely the availability of external financial resources which almost irresistibly impels those responsible for such matters to draw on the industrialized countries' stock of capacities for the production of capital goods; in other words, engineering is imported ready-made. Any real possibility of acquiring technology through "learning by doing" is thus short-circuited. Furthermore, the large-scale introduction of foreign standards and specifications into the productive sectors sets in motion an irreversible mechanism of technological dependence, whereby local engineering finds itself confined to the least complex tasks (in particular the construction of simple dwellings) or to subcontracting of the simple components of complex industrial operations, the processes and designs for which remain under the control of foreign design offices.

Here we are faced with a very distinct preference for visible success over the short term, to the detriment of real success over a longer term in the establishment of even a relatively autonomous process of growth and modernization. We shall later see that this harmful preference derives largely from the popular ideologies of development, and their influence on those who make economic policy decisions in the Third World.

By popular ideologies of development we mean the various doctrines, either Marxist or liberal in inspiration, which remain within a framework of pure economism, viewing development as a mechanical relationship between certain economic aggregates ("investment income", for example) or between certain abstractly and arbitrarily defined and qualified social classes. A feature common to virtually all these theories is their reliance on a quasi-metaphysical belief in the effect of these mechanical

---

(1) On the question of foreign investment, McKinnon writes: "relying on direct investment from abroad may break the external financial constraint at the cost of relinquishing investments opportunities to foreigners at bargain basement prices. Domestic entrepreneurial development may thereby be retarded. Learning by doing becomes learning by watching. (Our emphasis) In Money and capital, op.cit., p. 29. As we shall see this reasoning also applies to direct recourse to external indebtedness.

relationships and their confident disregard for the historical dimension of the economic phenomena pertaining to industrialization and the contemporary model for urban development. Even when the historical dimension is taken into account in the "popular" doctrines of development, it is treated selectively, with great emphasis being placed on the metaphysical and often the messianic aspect.[1]

We shall later return to the impact of developmental doctrines on the mechanisms of indebtedness, particularly in Chapter III. Our point is well illustrated by the fact that, in most Third World countries, the best industrial performances were achieved during the second World War, at a time, in other words, when the financial markets were closed, and when the disruption of international communications made the large-scale import of capital goods extremely difficult.

2. Downstream distorting effects caused by recourse to external indebtedness.

a. Distortions in the structure of prices and incomes.

By discouraging savings the cycle of indebtedness also discourages self-financing. As a result, financial charges weigh heavily on cost price, and, therefore, on the development of self-financing capacity. These additional costs, together with the extra charges imposed by current arrangements for the transfer of packaged technology (overcharging, patent fees, preferential dividends, etc...) to which we shall return later, impose a price structure which has two things wrong with it:

- Exports are made uncompetitive with the same goods produced in the industrialized countries, except in sectors making intensive use of cheap labor (textile) or in sectors producing semi-manufactured or intermediate products and under the absolute control of the transnational corporations. This inability to compete makes it difficult to boost exports in order to raise money with which to pay back the loans.

- The prices of industrial products on the domestic market are too high when compared with the average level of earnings, the result of which is:

(1) This mythological and messianic aspect of developmental doctrines is well described by P.L. Berger: Pyramids of sacrifice - political ethics and social change, (New York: Basic Books, Inc.) Chapter I; see also G. Corm: "Saper l'idéologie du développement", Le Monde Diplomatique, April 1978.

- Saving is discouraged among huge segments of the population which do, however, buy the goods produced, for reasons either of necessity (e.g., building materials) or of prestige (refrigerators, washing machines, etc...) and, increasingly, for both reasons at the same time, as urban development proceeds apace, imposing the way of life and the pattern of consumption of the already industrialized countries.

- Attempts to distribute income more evenly and thereby to improve the global savings capacity of the country are blocked. The capacity of saving in the rural sector is hardest hit, although the farming sector is precisely the one which most needs a general boost in productivity through the development of self-financing capacities.

These distortions are further aggravated by the current conditions in which the increase in Third World debt is taking place, that is through increasingly frequent recourse to commercial credits on the Euro-currency markets at high rates of interest and for average periods of 5 to 7 years.

b. <u>Distortions in the distribution of investments and reduction of the overall capacity for the absorption of new investments</u>.

In actual fact, however, it frequently happens that the modern industrial or even the agricultural sector either:

-does not pay the real price of foreign capital, when the State subsidizes interest rates, [(1)]

-or does not even have to endure the external constraints when the State, in one way or another, pays for the financing or refinancing of the external debts of those sectors; in this case, these charges are passed on to other sectors of the economy, which cope with them by boosting exports, particularly in the energy and mining sector, and in the sector of non-foodstuff agricultural produce such as coffee, tea, cotton, etc. Such an increase in exports often requires additional external investments, particularly in the mining sector.

(1) Particularly through development banks which contract external debts and then re-lend the funds thus borrowed at subsidized interest rates.

These mechanisms do the greatest harm in the case of the oil-exporting countries which in this way part with precious non-renewable resources which are indispensable for genuine industrialization. In the case of agricultural produce for export, the increase in production obviously takes place at the expense of foodstuff crops.

It remains true, however, that, in the overall economy of the importing State, the financial costs, whether they result from borrowings made directly in hard currencies or from external borrowings converted into local currency, often eventually become an abnormally large permanent component of the cost price, as local companies are rarely able to repay their loans. These companies then find themselves in a negative cash-flow situation, which leads to a constant aggravation of their financial burdens. These deficit sectors thus seize a growing share of the available savings, both internal and external.

Distortions thus spread throughout the investment structure; it often happens that the diversified distribution of investments required by a global plan is made impossible because a small number of industrial or agricultural sectors have seized the available financial resources. Nor is it a mere coincidence that those sectors are precisely the ones which call for large-scale imports of ready-made technology which is not under the control of the local engineering industry, or the mining sectors with an agricultural specialization - the so-called "enclave" sectors.

Both downstream and upstream from external indebtedness, we see a series of harmful effects on the mobilization of internal savings, the potential of the local engineering industry and thus of technological control, the structures and prices and consequently of incomes, and, lastly, the control of the distribution of investments. In many countries, and particularly in those which are semi-industrialized and where external debt is highest, the burden of debt servicing may thus cause a considerable reduction of a country's capacity to absorb capital. When debt servicing charges exceed 20-25% of total foreign exchange earnings from the export of goods and services, the country's capacity for manoeuvre in the investment sphere has been seriously reduced. This is all the more true in that the technological dependence of the modern agricultural and industrial sectors creates a permanent need for external resources in order to keep production going (spare parts, technical assistance, sudden replacement of equipment due to defective maintenance). A situation thus frequently comes about in which, under the pretext of a short-term increase in capacity to invest, a country might find itself over a longer period with a volume of financial flows which may admittedly be larger, but with a smaller capacity to invest and, in particular, to control the distribution of such investments. When this kind of blockage occurs the natural solution is to continue with even more investment in the export-oriented sectors of the economy, in the hope that they will expand its capacity to generate external resources.

This interlocking of external indebtedness and dependence is clearly of benefit to the industrialized countries.

3. External indebtedness as a source of reverse transfer of resources.

External indebtedness is closely linked to the different sources of the reverse transfer of resources from the exploited countries towards the industrialized countries. The repatriation of interest payments and the constant need to refinance the debts which most Third World countries cannot repay make external indebtedness an increasingly costly burden. These costs amount to a considerable reverse flow of resources for the developing countries. In the historical section we shall see how advantageous for the financiers of the creditor counties were the terms on which Third World debts were refinanced, particularly when compared to the terms which existed then and exist now in the industrialized countries themselves.

At the present time total annual interest payments made by the Third World States to the industrialized countries amount to some 15 billion dollars (not counting interest payments made in the private sector). One must add to this reverse flow of resources:[1]

(1) We have not quoted UNCTAD figures because they are too fragmentary and out of date. As an overall indication of costs associated with the transfer of technology we have used, in Chapter III, the evolution of the deficit in the balance of services (see Annex, Table 7). The main UNCTAD documents on these various points are:

- Financing and invisibles, Vol.III of the records of UNCTAD III, held in Santiago de Chile (F.73.II.D.6).
- Major issues arising for the transfer of technology to developing countries.(TD/B/AC. 11/10/Rev.2).
- The reverse transfer of technology: its dimensions, economic effects and policiy implications. (TD/B/C/6/7).

- repatriation of profits by transnational corporations with investments in the Third World,

- payments for patents and licenses,

- payments for services (technical assistance, consultants and engineering, insurance, transport),

- charges due to over-billing for imported capital goods or manufactured goods,

- losses resulting from the restrictive business practices imposed by the MNCs,

- losses resulting from the reverse transfer of technology in the form of the brain drain.[(1)]

In actual fact, one of the main causes of external indebtedness stems from the need to find foreign exchange resources in order to pay all these charges.

The other cause lies in the large-scale purchase of ready-made technology from the industrialized countries which far exeeds the external financial capacities of the Third World countries. This form of indebtedness became much more widespread between 1950 and 1970.[(2)]

At this stage it is already evident that indebtedness and transfer of technology are closely linked.

The new purchasing power of the oil exporting developing countries, which is for the most part recycled through the international financial circuits and partly through other developing countries by means of various types of aid and loans, as well as the considerable expansion of lending operations by the IBRD and the Euro-currency market to the Third World, are two factors which eventually are certain to strengthen the trend towards the reverse transfer of technology. Moreover, the most

---

(1) On all these points see G. Corm: "Finance and technology transfer", in Technology transfer and change in the Arab world, edited by A.B. Zahlan, (Oxford: Pergamon Press 1980)

(2) These problems are well summarized by D.C. Lambert: Les Economies du Tiers-Monde, (Paris: Armand Colin, 1974), pp. 183-190. See also T. Mende: De l'aide a la recolonisation, op. cit., p.107 ff.

dynamic industrial sectors in the industrialized countries are increasingly those which are directly oriented towards the markets of the Third World; it is the transnational corporations of those sectors which are pressing the financial markets and the international financial bodies to expand their lending operations in the Third World.

This expansion has, moreover, been possible only because all the orthodox rules governing the functioning of the international monetary system were scrapped and because, as a result, there has been an uncontrolled creation of international means of payment since 1971. The rules were abandoned as a consequence of the United States policy, in response to its own needs and its desire to maintain its position in the world economy. The Euro-currency markets and the satellite markets gravitating around it (Asia-dollars, Arabo-dollars) may also be viewed as nothing more than an extension of the American financial power. The integration of the Third World into this field obviously cannot fail to enhance the possibilities for action of the transnational corporations, particularly in the Third World, where their presence , until the end of the sixties, was slight. compared to the position they enjoyed in the industrialized countries.

4. Terms of trade, inflation and devaluation in the total debt service load.

One argument which is frequently advanced to justify indebtedness is that inflation reduces the burden of the debt. Those who make this claim forget, however, that this proposition is correct only when the income of the debtor rises at a higher rate than the rate of inflation. At the level of a country, this means that the terms of trade must improve before the burden of external debt is lightened. On the other hand, if the terms of trade deteriorate, the burden of debt servicing becomes heavier.

Yet, despite the increase in the price of energy and of certain agricultural export items in 1973/74, it is not at all certain that, over the long or even the medium term, the terms of trade are improving for Third World countries as a whole. Moreover, it is necessary to include the increase in the cost of imported services in order to form a more accurate idea of the terms of trade.

Another factor aggravating the external debt burden is the internal rate of inflation and the consecutive devaluation of the national currency against the currencies in which foreign borrowings are expressed. The situation is made even worse by the revaluations of the currencies of the borrowings: for example, borrowings contracted in strong currencies (Yens, DMs, Swiss Francs) mean extra charges for the debtors amounting to an annual average of 4 to 5% over the past five years.

On this last point it is important to note that the IBRD, which is financed largely on the Japanese, German and Swiss national markets, passes on exchange rate risks wholly to its debtors, who thus find the actual rate of interest charged on their borrowings from the IBRD marked up several points above the nominal rate.

Indebtedness, modalities for the transfer of technology and international monetary destabilization are thus the three facets of the reverse transfer of resources which is keeping the societies of the Third World in a state of dependence and exploitation.

4. <u>The indebtedness of the Third World as an additional source of instability for the international monetary system</u>.

Even though it has been made possible by the destabilization of the international monetary system, the current magnitude of the debt of the Third World countries has nonetheless now become a factor, among many others, capable of threatening the international system of payments. There can be no doubt that, if the countries most heavily in debt were to default, the entire system of international payments would be in danger of collapse, particularly because the bulk of the loans extended to the most heavily indebted countries is concentrated in the major international banks. Those are the banks which play a dominant role in the international financial circuits.

It is beyond doubt that the sheer size of the debts of certain countries is such that it is not in the interest of the creditors to allow those countries to drift towards default; for that reason the refinancing needs of the most heavily indebted countries are regularly provided for. Moreover, this mechanism can now function without any limitation as there is no institutional brake in the international monetary system:

- either on the United States balance of payments deficit which is thus enabled to create international currency when it feels so inclined;(1)

- or on the proliferation of deposits and borrowings on the Euro-currency market, which is not subject to direct control by any monetary or financial authority.

In fact the debts of the Third World have become an important component of the complex and gigantic pyramid of international and local credits managed by the networks of the major international banks which, like the transnational corporations, evolve in a world environment which gives them every opportunity

(1) This mechanism is well analyzed in M. Lelart: <u>Le dollar monnaie internationale: Le role des Etats-Unis dans la création monétaire internationale</u>,(Paris: Editions Albatros, 1975).

of evading both national and, all the more easily, regional or international controls. In the present situation of international inflation, unemployment and balance of payments deficits, there is a great risk of a break at one point or another in the pyramidal chain of credits; the Third World, moreover, is most definitely a weak link in the chain.

Being a weak link, the Third World is obviously on the receiving end of the most efficient efforts at control - a fact which raises yet again the problems of dependence.

5. Indebtedness as an additional source of dependence for the Third World.

In paragraphs 1, 2 and 3 we have seen that in actual fact indebtedness, because of the impediments and distortions it generates in the structures of savings, prices and investments, and also the mechanisms for the reverse tranfer of resources which it nourishes, becomes a self-sustaining and continually growing phenomenon completely beyond the control of the economic policy of the local authorities. Yet the creditor countries, through their national credit organs and also through the international bodies in which they usually wield a preponderant influence, do their best to control the economic management of the debtor countries. These controls have recently been strengthened by the establishment of a system of improved mutual information and coordination between the international banks on the one hand and the International Monetary Fund and the IBRD on the other. For example, since 1976 the negotiations on the refinancing of the debts of countries in default (Zaire, Turkey, Peru) have shown that the international banks are prepared to arrange new loans only after the defaulting countries have agreed to follow the recovery program imposed by the International Monetary Fund.

Even without a default, loan contracts often contain clauses imposing special constraints, in particular cross default clauses and also covenants and warranties clauses; in this latter case countries undertake to remain eligible for the facilities of the International Monetary Fund or not to violate the rules and recommendations of that Fund. These clauses frequently have the effect of leaving a government wishing to change its internal economic policy with very little room for manoeuvre. An increase in indebtedness means a greater number of restrictive clauses in the loan contracts and, consequently, even less possibility for the debtor country to attempt a change of policy in order to reduce its external dependence. The only alternative which exists is that which we have referred to previously: concentration on the export sectors in the hope that additional revenues will make it possible to reduce external indebtedness, thereby recovering some freedom of manoeuvre to steer local economic policy towards greater diversification.

Industrial sectors such as engineering and automobiles, which were originally promoted with the domestic market in mind, now often find their products being exported. In order to guarantee the success of this reconversion (marketing and competitive pricing) it is not unusual for transnational corporations to step up their role in the management and control of those sectors. In this case, the other sources of financial draining referred to in paragraph 3 are brought into play: in particular the repatriation of dividends and payment of royalties, for which external financing will eventually have to be found, particularly if the export effort runs out of steam for reasons such as the loss of markets due to a crisis in the importing countries or the emergence of better placed competitors.

C. CONCLUSION

However when one analyzes the indebtedness of the Third World it becomes clear that it is a central circular mechanism within the numerous vicious circles of underdevelopment. It is astonishing that this problem has so far been given only limited attention and that it has been viewed more as a consquence of underdevelopment than as one of its causes or at least as one of the principal means by which it perpetuates itself.

In these circumstances it is not surprising to see governments which cherish their independence in relation to the industrialized countries recklessly embarking on development programs which involve more or less intensive recourse to external indebtedness. The latest example, and the one which will have the greatest impact on the future of North-South relations, is that of China, which, since July 1978, has been scrambling to import ready-made technology with recourse to external financing. Further study will be needed to determine the underlying causes of this reversal of economic policy on the part of a country which had previously rejected any form of large-scale foreign debt, precisely so as not to compromise its political independence. There can be no doubt that geo-political reasons were involved in bringing about this abrupt change of economic policy. One is inclined to wonder as to the exact nature of the process which could account for the preference of the new Chinese rulers for short-term results to the detriment of the balance of society over the longer term. We have already referred to this preference in paragraph 1-b, in connection with the relationship between external indebtedness and technological control.

A consideration of the historical processes of indebtedness in the Third World will enable us to form a better overall picture of the way these phenomena are related to the problems of development and modernization.

III. IDEOLOGICAL AND INSTITUTIONAL FACTORS LEADING TO INDEBTEDNESS

There are four series of mutually interacting, and mutually intensifying factors which underly the renewal of indebtedness of the countries of the Third World in this quarter of the 20th century.

A. Vulgar theories of development: the persistence of the Ricardian universe.

There has been a great outpouring of "developmental" literature over the past thirty years. In all Third World countries it has become an integral part of the national ideology, whether it takes a socialist or liberal form. Everywhere this ideology has led to an expansion of the public sector: the State has thus been placed in charge of "development" at all levels, the notion of development now being practically synonymous with integration and national contruction. What was expected of "Europeanization" in the 19th century is now required of "development", while development ideology now performs the role played by the doctrine of free trade in the last century.

There is little point in attempting a description and a critique of the countless doctrines on development. However, it is necessary to note that these doctrines have for the most part been elaborated by the economists of the industrialized countries, and that they have been enlarged by the organs of the United Nations, which have become a major source of development literature. Marxist economics is also directly involved in the elaboration of "developmental" ideologies, and is even a fundamental source in the emergence of the very concept of development.(1) Marx's analyses of the liberating force of capital, and its role as a lever for material and technical progress have prolonged the European humanist philosophy of the Age of Enlightenment and its humanistic belief in the linearity of progress.

As in the last century with the ideology of free trade, the continued technical, material and military superiority of the Western countries and Russia have done much to give the doctrines of development and their various prescriptions a powerful hold on the élites of the Third World. However, like

(1) The famous ethnologist, Claude Levi-Strauss, recently made an interesting statement: "I think that the Communist and totalitarian Marxist ideology is merely a trick of history to promote the accelerated Westernization of the peoples which had been left outside until recently", Le Monde, 21-22 January 1979, p. 14.

free trade, development as an ideology does no more than reflect the situation and needs of the economy of the countries which are already developed; most development theories take no account whatsoever of the historical aspect of the processes of economic evolution. This is a paradoxical phenomenon, because the notion of development is barely conceivable except over a long period.

The paradox actually stems from the ideological degradation which the notion of development has undergone by being used as a State ideology to mobilize the popular masses and break the socio-professional structures which the dominant or rising élites regard as obstacles to development. In this respect, development as a State ideology in the independent Third World, with its vast modernization programs, has coincided perfectly with the interests of the industrialized countries, since it is their model of society, and their models of consumption and technology, which are thereby made universal.

The simple-minded idea that one or two five-year plans making massive use of equipment supplied by the developed countries can give a country a chance of quickly "catching up" with the industrialized countries has often been the corollary of State ideology on development. Bogus pseudo-scientific mathematical equations of the growth of revenue, based on investment/production ratios through capital coefficients, have lent additional legitimacy to the plans of Third World countries. These mechanistic calculations have been enriched by various more or less brilliant and superficial theories, which are almost always designed to justify a special drive for massive investments in the "modern" industrial sector, which is supposed to generate spin-off effects which will greatly accelerate a country's progress.

Generally speaking the development theories based on State ideologies in the developing countries have all helped set in motion a scramble for investments intended to bring about modernization; these investments have thus led to massive and abrupt imports of production equipment from abroad and have driven the Third World deep into the technological trade circuits run by the MNCs.

It is true that the popular theories of development, including the doctrine of industrialization through import substitution, are now in a state of crisis.[1] So far, however, this crisis has had only a marginal effect on the ruling élites of the Third World and has hardly made a dent in the State ideologies of development. The interesting thing about such criticism, which concentrates either on internal blockages due to the inadequate distribution of income, or on the global functioning of dependence, is that it has never been aimed directly at these ideologies from the point of view of their demands on the industrialized countries - an aspect which has become crystallized in the new formulation concerning the new international economic order. This new formulation was promptly taken over and broadened by the international institutions and by the Club of Rome, because it is actually far from being a challenge to the present economic order.[2] What the Third World countries are calling for is an expansion of the capacity of the system of international trade in order that they may be able to become more easily integrated into it. This expansion is viewed as taking place essentially through two mechanisms:

1. Increase of the external financial resources available to the countries of the Third World, by means of:

- higher prices for commodities
- the stabilization of commodity prices (UNCTAD Common Fund project)
- an increase in aid,
- expanded access to the international capital markets.

2. The lifting of the restrictions on the transfer of technology (proposed code of conduct for the multinational corporations).

(1) For a bibliography of the main works on the development crisis, see G. Corm: Saper l'idéologie du développement, op.cit.. On the crisis of developmentalist ideologies in Latin America, see T. Dos Santos: "The crisis of development theory and the problems of dependence in Latin America", in Underdevelopment and Development, H. Bernstein (ed), (Penguin Books 1973), pp. 57-80; also M. Wolfe: "Approaches to development: who is approaching what", in ECLA Review, 1st half 1976, pp. 131-172. Lastly, note in particular the works of Illich, especially: Une société sans école, (Paris: Seuil, 1971), and Libérer l'Avenir, (Paris: Seuil, 1971).

(2) Rio: reshaping the international order - a report to the Club of Rome, J. Tingergen, coordinator,(New York: E.P. Dutton, 1976).

We therefore find ourselves back in a wholly Ricardian universe in which the Third World sees its salvation mainly in expanded trade in which more expensive commodities will be exchanged for demonopolized technology, to the benefit of all concerned. In actual fact, beneath the appearances of State control introduced by the "modern" doctrines of development, belief in the virtues of Ricardian free trade still lies at the core of development policies. It is not the essence of the trade in technology which is being questioned, but rather its mode of functioning: and it is in this area that the MNCs and their monopolistic practices are being criticized. In the circumstances it is not surprising that the public sectors of the Third World countries have become the best customers of the MNCs, particularly when their relationship excludes the risks and disadvantages of joint ventures for the MNC by confining it to the role of supplier of industrial plants delivered on a turnkey basis. Nor is it particularly surprising that the Third World has become increasingly the prisoner of the international division of labor to which, in other contexts, it seems so vehemently opposed.

One cannot fail to note the similarity of the vocabularies used in the financial and technological spheres, both of which talk of transfers - transfers of resources, on the one hand, thus making possible transfers of technology on the other - both of them being thought to be capable, over the long term, of bringing equality and prosperity to the disadvantaged partner. And this is no mere coincidence, as technology has become the major source of profits in the industrialized countries and its present cost calls for large financial resources both to produce it and to buy the equipment which it produces and which leads to the way of life characteristic of the industrialized urban societies.

At least in the writings of Illich and Furtado one finds significant and broad criticism of the model of consumption of the industrialized countries as a factor causing blockages at different levels of the development process in the developing countries.[1] However, apart from Vaitsos[2] critics of the popular theories of development have tended to neglect the analysis of the devastating mechanisms of the transfer of technology and the damage done by the very fact of the transfer of resources, as well as the absurdity of the policies of the

(1) For Illich, note in particular: Une société sans école, op.cit., and Libérer l'Avenir, op.cit.; C. Furtado: Le mythe du développement économique, (Paris: Antropos, 1976).

(2) C.V. Vaitsos: "Bargaining and the distribution of returns in the purchase of technology and development", in Underdevelopment and Development, op.cit., pp. 315-323.

developing countries in this respect. Authors writing from the Marxist point of view usually do not even take up the question of technology, viewing it as an abstract variable entirely dependent on capital; in this way the autonomy of the process of technological mastery is only a variable, the fate of which follows that of the autonomy of the process of accumulation. This accounts for the belief, widely held in the Third World, that the mere fact of State control or the appropriation by the State of natural resources and the key sectors of the economy will suffice to set in motion the process of technological mastery.

Only liberal specialists in economic history have analyzed in detail the processes of the emergence of technological innovation and its relationship with economic growth, but their work has always been completely ignored by specialists on theories of development, who are obsessed by the direct ratio between investment and income which corresponds to the current problem of the maintenance of growth in the industrialized countries. In the past, however, it is evident that increases in income and the consequent progressive development of investments by self-financing or by loans arranged in a family or a professional context were made possible by advances in individual productivity, or of productivity in small production units, without recourse to massive investments.(1) It should be noted here that, since the Middle Ages, the development of major credit operations has been based on colonial trade. The emergence of modern banking in Europe owes as much to overseas as to local operations, if not more. It also owes a great deal to the construction of the national State, in which monarchs, in their attempts at centralization, needed to borrow in order to develop their armed forces and finance war efforts. In comparison with the amounts devoted to overseas expansion, the technological accumulation and domestic economic growth of the European countries actually required little indebtedness until the end of the 19th century. If it had been otherwise, it is to be doubted whether Britain, France and Germany would have been able to devote such a large share of their savings to foreign loans; on the other hand, Spain, whose colonial expansion, unlike that of the other European powers, led to an extraordinary accumulation of monetary capital, had no industrial revolution and no surplus savings invested abroad: such a phenomenon suggests the need

(1) For example, N. Rosenberg: Perspectives on Technology, op.cit., who has this to say about technical change:

> "The problem takes on additional importance when we adopt a more realistic conception of the nature of technical change than we have inherited from Schumpeter. Schumpeter accustomed economists to thinking

of technical change as involving major breaks, giant discontinuities or disruptions with the past. This rather melodramatic conception fitted in well with his charismatic approach to entrepreneurship. But technological change is also (and perhaps even more importantly) a continuous stream of innumerable minor adjustments, modifications,and adaptations by skilled personnel, and the technical vitality of an economy employing a machine technology is critically affected by its capacity to make these adaptations. The necessary skills, in the past, were developed and diffused in large measure by the capital goods sector. The skills are, inevitably, embodied in the human agent and not in the machine, and unless these skills are somehow made available, the prospects for the viability of machine technology may not be very good." p.166.

See also S. Kuznets: Croissance et structures économiques, (Paris: Calman-Lévy, 1972) who shows that a growth in the crude formation of capital has not always accompanied the growth of income in the industrialized countries during their process of industrialization. Some interesting studies have been prepared on the comparative economic evolution of the USA and Britain, showing the technological causes of the American advance and the British decline. See, inter alia, Technological change: the United States and Britain in the 19th century, S.B. Saul (ed), (London: Methuen and Co., Ltd., 1972), and particularly the contribution of D.L. Burn: "The genesis of American engineering competition, 1850-1870".

for further thought about the existence of the capital/modernization relationship.

It was not until the appearance of "mass capitalism" that credit, through the introduction of consumer credit, became the pivot of growth; in fact one wonders whether the shadow of Keynes might not be hovering behind all the development doctrines which call on the rich countries to devote a part of their national income to the injection of purchasing power into the developing countries.

All of this leads us to question the role of technology in the Third World as a variable almost exclusively dependent on capital, because of this point Marxists and liberals, behind their doctrinal confrontations, espouse positions which lead, as far as the developing countries are concerned, to the same conclusions: it is the formation of capital, or its accumulation, - depending on one's choice of vocabulary - which determines the degree of a country's command of technology; if capital is lacking it will be imported or transferred from where it is available. The notion of backwardness, of underdevelopment, of time-lag, together with the anguish which it arouses among the élites of the non-industrialized countries, means that this transfer has to take place at any price, in order to skip the intervening stages of development and catch up with the industrialized countries. Technology, techniques, automation, sciences, urban development, capital, modernization of the State: these are so many conceptual notions which are used abundantly in all the "developmental" literature, without any prior epistemological clarification whatever.(1) Moreover, the general institutional framework set up to "promote" development and modernization does nothing to facilitate such a clarification, and helps make the import of technical and financial capital the cornerstone of the economic policies of the countries of the Third World.

B. Institutional and administrative framework.

There is no need for us to review the institutions of development as a whole, as they have already been dealt with by numerous authors.(2) It should be borne in mind that generalizations are difficult because of the wide variety in levels of development: for example, the countries of Latin America, particularly those which have achieved a significant level of

(1) On this point see G. Corm: Possibilités économiques et distribution des revenus dans les pays arabes:effets sur l'éducation et les opportunités d'emploi, (Réflexion sur les rapports entre la culture, la technologie et l'économie), Expert seminar of UNESCO: Population - Education - Development in the Arab countries, held in Egypt from 21 to 29 February 1976, UNEDBAS/44/75/BS2.

(2) Here we shall merely mention the Gunnar Myrdal's classic, Asian drama - an inquiry into the poverty of nations, 3 vols., (New York: Pantheon, 1968).

diversification of their industrial structures (Argentina, Mexico, Brazil) find their autonomy reduced more by the functioning of the mechanisms for the distribution of income, and the major and irreversible role which the MNCs have played in their economies since the 19th century, than by the effects of the institutions of development. However, in recently independent countries the institutions in charge of development are much more directly responsible for their external dependence. For this reason we shall merely dwell at this point on the various institutional aspects which are conducive to a development dependent on the external sector. These aspects make it clear that there is a close link between the mechanisms of technological dependence and those of financial dependence.

1.)Qualitative dualism within the administrative machine.

The dualism which affects the economies of the developing countries occurs in their administrative institutions. Those sectors of the administration which are geared to the external sector usually enjoy better working conditions and higher salaries than those which are not in contact with the outside world. They are the first to attract the administrative "élites", which are in turn better placed to obtain privileged treatment from the governmental authorities; they are helped in this respect by the international institutions with which they deal as spokesmen for their countries and which press the governmental authorities to make increased resources available to those administrative structures. This administrative élite, which constitutes the modern sector of the administration, eventually becomes a powerful lobby working on behalf of the international institutions and the MNCs, which, as we shall see, often operate in the wake of the international bodies. The fact of belonging to the modern administrative sector, even in the poorest countries, makes it possible for one to move in several circuits which may offer a variety of benefits but which invariably provide access to the way of life and the pattern of consumption of the industrialized countries. These benefits range from travel and periods of residence abroad at the expense of the international institutions, the administrations of the industrialized countries or the MNCs, to the kind of widespread corruption which US Senate investigations of American transnational corporations have brought to light.

The governmental institutions which are most fully geared to the external sector are often those which bear the heaviest responsibilities for development: planning organs, central banks and development banks, ministries of industry and State industrial enterprises. It is hardly surprising that these bureaucracies have rarely developed an autonomous capacity for intervention, as in many cases the bulk of the technical work is done by foreign consultants: experts from the United Nations or the international financial institutions (IBRD, IMF, IFS, etc.), foreign engineering and management concerns, American investment banks, etc., which gradually impose their working methods. Since these local organs, geared to the external sector, are the real centers at which governmental decisions are prepared on economic policy and particularly on the choice of projects, it is clear that they are one of the main channels for a policy of reliance on the external sector in economic and social matters.

2.)Planning bodies and their working methods.

We do not propose to embark on another critical discussion of the effectiveness of planning as it is now practised in the developing countries.(1) It should be emphasized, however, that planning bodies have rarely developed a capacity for a command of technology which would enable them to help the organs in charge of industrial or agricultural policy to gradually become technologically independent. Without such a minimum capacity, contracts concluded with foreign corporations are more often than not unfavorable to the local party and do much to lay the foundations for future dependence. In any case, the plans of the developing countries are for the most part a mere shopping list of large-scale projects involving infrastructure or industrial complexes, for which profitability studies are prepared by foreign engineering offices or consultants, and which always involve massive recourse to foreign equipment and foreign corporations.

The rare efforts made by the international or national financial institutions to promote technology drawing more extensively on local capacities have been thwarted by the inertia of existing bureaucracies, by excessively low levels of productivity among the insufficiently motivated local labor force, and lastly by the structure of local prices and salaries.(2) Given the kind of methods which are used in the choice of investments, which are themselves based on manuals for project evaluation of the United Nations and the World Bank, the decisions taken have always favored investment requiring entirely imported technology, which means in most cases, the help of the MNCs.

(1) See the excellent critique by T. Killick, "The possibilities of development planning", Oxford Economic Papers, February 1977.

(2) See the valuable study by the Economic and Social Department of the United Nations: Appropriate technologies in civil engineering in works in developing countries: an exploratory appraisal of the state of the art, (New York: 1976), (E.76.II A.2).

In fact this trend has been greatly favored by the international financial institutions, which, besides their inadequate methods for project evaluation, have always made their participation conditional on the existence of preliminary studies made by international consultants and on the awarding of contracts through international bidding, the criteria for the submission of bids being such that the MNCs are placed in a virtual monopoly position with regard to the developing countries. The financial facilities granted for the preparation of the studies themselves have meant, in actual fact, that most planning organs, whether at a general level or within the technical ministries and State corporations, have now become totally dependent on external sources.

Increasingly widespread use of turnkey contract formulas, or more recently of similar contracts for the delivery of merchandise, has been so severely criticized that it deserves some attention here. Although these formulas do accelerate the completion of work, they condemn the local structures to technological dependence and discourage the emergence of local engineering capacities. They then lead to permanent dependence on the external supplier for maintenance and the acquisition of spare parts, thus aggravating tension on the balance of payments. There are countless examples of factories delivered through turnkey arrangements which have soon become paralyzed or have to work at a very low level of capacity because of the lack of spare parts which the supplier does not have in stock or which the country cannot afford to buy, or because there is no foreign technician available to spot the precise nature of the breakdowns which periodically occur in equipment which is not properly maintained.

In many countries the dependence, inertia and inefficiency of the administrative bureaucracies leads the planning organs and the governmental authorities to bring in the external financial institutions in order to guarantee a minimum level of thoroughness and continuity in the implementation of projects. In this way, local administrations geared to the external sector gradually turn into organs for the mere rubber-stamping of the bills of foreign corporations, instead of becoming the principal centers for the acquisition of technological know-how. In particular, the planning organs and study services fail to play any positive role in the decision-making machinery on investments. This machinery is thus left entirely under the influence of pressure groups and the attitude of the governmental authorities to those groups. The short-term interests of the groups then prevail; the preference for the short-term, as we have seen, means using foreign corporations which, unlike local industry, have the means to complete projects quickly.

The use of foreign corporations always involves an additional drain on foreign resources, which is why the criterion which predominates in the methods of project-evaluation is always the capacity of a project to generate foreign exchange, whether directly or indirectly. This leads straight into the vicious cycle of technological dependence causing financial dependence, and financial dependence increasing technological dependence, because, in order to resolve the problem of the foreign exchange gap, projects are designed with the foreign sector in mind, and therefore inevitably involve the use of either wholly or largely imported technology.

The planning organs are often a central link in sustaining this vicious cycle; and they will cease to be so only when they become centers for the planning of the development of local capacities in engineering, and the storage and distribution of economic and technical information, instead of being merely chambers for the recording of projects which satisfy the appetites of local pressure groups and for which in many cases even the initial idea was produced by foreign design offices which are themselves linked to the MNCs.

3.)<u>Local financing bodies and their modes of operation</u>.

The functioning of the local financing bodies is another very important link in the chain of technological/financial dependence. These organs do nothing more than reproduce the working methods and the methods for project evaluation of the international institutions. General administrative dualism is very advanced here: organs geared externally to the international financial institutions, and which are often internally geared to the "modern sectors", are those with the most dynamic capacity for intervention. On the other hand, the organs in charge of the financing of the "traditional" sectors (small-scale agriculture, cottage-industries, mass housing) are those which work at the slowest pace and which are most lacking in an effective capacity for intervention; in addition, they are paralyzed by a stifling administrative routine.

As a general rule the developing countries have only slight control over their own financial affairs which tend, on the whole, to be very dependent on the external sector at all levels, from factors affecting the control of the money supply, in which levels of foreign exchange holdings are often of prime importance, to those which affect the internal distribution of credit, in which external credits, because of the high proportion of foreign exchange involved in most investments, are of crucial importance. Besides the artificial manipulation of exchange rates, which, as Furtado and DeCecco have shown, are of benefit to certain social groups, the fact that the prices of exported commodities are set in foreign currencies also greatly weakens government control over the country's finances and, as the example of Latin America shows, can lead to wildly abnormal rates of inflation.

The practice of making rebates on interest rates or exchange rates is often another means of encouraging investments involving large foreign exchange expenditures, particularly when the repayment periods of internal borrowings based on external credits are much longer than the periods for local credits not related to the external sector which are usually short-term credits secured by real collateral, without regard to the merit of the project being financed. In the so-called "social" sectors (rural loans and loans to cottage-industries) the granting of rebates on interest as well as the inefficient administration of loans have the effect of transforming the granting of credit into a disguised form of subsidy, since the loans are rarely actually reimbursed. This serves as a deterrent to the transformation of these sectors and to an increase in their productivity; the dualism of the economy between the modern and the social or traditional sectors is intensified. It will be noted that the doctrine of the international financial institutions has always required that the developing countries make a rigid distinction between credit for agriculture and the "social" sectors on the one hand, and credits for the modern sectors on the other, each category being handled by different financing institutions.

The fragmentation of interest rates in most Third World countries - a fragmentation which is fostered by the impact of foreign aid and loans - does much to keep the productivity of the economy fragmented and to discourage savings and self-financing.[(1)] The fact that the structure of prices and earnings between the modern and traditional sectors is also fragmented further aggravates the general looseness of the economy. From this point of view, social credit in the form of subsidies is only a modest and ineffective counterweight to the drain inflicted on the traditional sectors by the system of prices and earnings. In any case social credit has never succeeded in eliminating the practice of attrition of the traditional sectors, which also prevents improvements in productivity and, accordingly, the formation of savings ca-

---

(1) The subject is given through treatment in R.I. McKinnon: Money and Capital, op.cit.

pacity or self-financing capacities. Indeed it often happens that subsidized credit facilities in the rural or cottage-industry sectors are beneficial mainly to those categories which are already privileged, at the expense of those less well endowed with land and the means of production. In such cases, the fragmentation is greatly intensified.

The financial institutions in the developing countries thus rarely play a positive role in the sphere of financial/technological dependence, since they are an important source of such dependence. For example, it is not rare to see substantial amounts of credit made available for projects involving intensive use of foreign heavy equipment, while peasants or small craftsmen are unable to find money with which to finance an artesian well, a pump or simple tools which are usually not available on the local market anyway, and continue to be a prey for moneylenders in order to provide for their mere subsistence. The more dynamic the "modern" financial sector, the greater the increase in dependence it will cause. It often happens that the dynamism of the modern financial sector paralyzes efforts made to boost the productivity of the rural and cottage-industry sectors, since whatever foreign capital is available is devoted, as a matter of priority, to the execution of projects which tend to integrate the local economy into the circuits of international trade. This is all the more likely to happen in that external financial institutions, besides financial facilities for preliminary studies and engineering studies by foreign firms, sometimes even provide financing for certain expenses in local currencies if the component of foreign imported material is large enough. In this way projects not included in the development plans are thus often carried out, to the detriment of other projects of a "social" nature, because the necessary external resources have been found by the foreign suppliers of the material. And even in "social" projects, the intervention of the international financial institutions greatly boosts the foreign exchange component in the cost of the projects.(1)

---

(1) See, for example, for school construction projects, H. Reiff: "Pour un réexamen de l'aide aux pays les moins développés", Perspectives, Vol. VI, No. 4, 1976. In the case of contruction and buildings it is the local administrations which are mainly responsible for the massive recourse to external technologies to the detriment of local capacities. See also H. Fathi: Construire avec le peuple, La Bibliotheque Arabe, (Paris: J.Marineau, 1970) and the UN study: Appropriate technologies in civil engineering, op.cit.

In many developing countries the availability of external financing greatly influences decisions on investments, and the financial sector is far from playing its proper role in limiting the use of external finance and in fully mobilizing domestic savings. The traditonal method for the evaluation of projects on which most instances of recourse to external financing are based, does not encourage the local financial organs to develop autonomous capacities for analysis which might have the effect of better mobilizing local resources; local financial organs are even more dependent on international consultancy firms than the planning organs when it comes to making choices as to financing.

Lastly, the general financial policy of the authorities usually has the effect of discouraging the mobilization of savings, either by causing high rates of inflation which lead to the confiscation of the savings of certain social segments to the advantage of others, or by keeping the return on savings deposited in the financial and banking institutions blocked at artificially low levels.

As in the case of the planning organs, the financial institutions will not play a positive role until they cease to be a link in the chain of technological/financial dependence and become an instrument really capable of bringing about a general improvement in local productivity. To do that they are going to have to completely change their working methods and equip themselves with extensive study and research services designed to promote the development of local technological know-how, in the framework of an overall governmental policy; such a policy would ensure that recourse to external technical and financial capital is carefully planned and kept down to the strict minimum necessary in the context of local attempts to promote productivity and a command of technology.

4.) Educational structures.

The educational structures of the Third World have been criticized so abundantly and from so many quarters that little remains to be said. Numerous authors, from widely different backgrounds, have denounced the aberrations of systems copied from those of the former colonial powers. Radicals (Freire, Reimer, Illich) and liberals (Myrdal, Balogh, Mende) alike have amply demonstrated the ineptitude of systems which devour previous resources in return for economically and socially negative results. (1)

(1) P. Freire: Pedagogy of the oppressed, (Middlesex: Penguin Education, 1972) and L'éducation pratique de la liberté, (Paris: Cerf, 1971); E. Reimer: School is dead: an essay on alternative education, (Middlesex: Penguin Education, 1971); for Illich, Myrdal and Mende, works quoted above; T. Balogh: The economics of poverty, (London: Weidenfeld and Nicholson, 1974).

On the whole, all observers agree that Third World educational systems suffer from three major flaws:

1. They are a major source of social inequality, and are "far and away the most powerful instrument for the perpetuation of the concepts, outlook and values on which the priviledged classes are based". (1)

2. They discourage innovation, and they perpetuate, and often aggravate, employment problems and help spread mala-adjustment among the "traditional" sector of the population.

3. In the light of the cost of modern educational infrastructure, the persistence of those systems leads to monumental social waste.

The failure of all educational reforms in the Third World is certainly due to the formidable resistance of the structure of social inequality set up by existing educational systems - a structure which keeps alive among the disadvantaged classes the hope that education will help them rise to higher levels of society.

Moreover, the educational systems now in use all favor purely academic studies, at the expense of technical education of a quality which might help mobilize local capacities for technological know-how. The democratization of academic education which has occurred in most Third World countries has been detrimental to technological autonomy, while the functioning of the economic and administrative institutions, far from correcting the state of dependence induced by the educational structures, has aggravated it. In actual fact, the educational systems themselves are a kind of ante-chamber leading to the reverse transfer of technology; since they are geared to the academic and research equipment of the industrialized countries and guided by them, it is only natural that the most dynamic and creative students in the systems should tend to emigrate particularly from countries where the socio-economic environment is hardly conducive to the development of a local command of technology. Apart from that, the modern sectors of administration and of the economic and financial institutions amplify the effects of the educational system in the sphere of the reverse transfer of technology: the most dynamic products of the system are eventually recruited either by the MNCs or by the international institutions.

Lastly, as investments, the educational systems of the countries of the Third World rank with the mass media as an extraordinarily efficient way of anchoring the model of consumption of the industrialized countries among the younger segments of the population.

(1) T. Mende, <u>op.cit.</u>, pp. 131-132.

C. <u>Income distribution, model of consumption and ideology of underdevelopment</u>.

Latin American authors, in particular Celso Furtado, have well illustrated the mechanisms by which import substitution can impede industrialization. All these mechanisms are derived from the unequal distribution of income which, in turn, is sustained by imitation of the models of consumption of the industrialized countries. For example, Furtado, describing the origins of the phenomenon of dependence, writes:

> "The phenomenon of dependence first takes the form of the adoption of models of consumption imposed from outside, using for this purpose the surplus produced by foreign trade. But it is the dynamism of this sector of consumption which transforms dependence into a process which it is difficult to reverse. When industrialization substitutes manufactured products for the same products imported from abroad, the production apparatus tends to split in two: one segment being engaged in traditional activities intended for export and for the domestic market (both rural and urban), and another segment involving capital-intensive industries whose output is intended for the "modernized" minority. Economists who view the economies of the underdeveloped countries as closed systems have seen in this cleavage of the production apparatus "an imbalance at the level of factors" due to the existence of fixed co-efficients in the functions of production or to the adoption of inadequate techniques. This approach conveniently ignores the fact that those consumer goods could be produced only with those techniques, and that for the ruling classes at the center the problem of choosing between this or that constellation of goods simply does not arise. To the extent that the models of consumption of those classes which appropriate the surplus for themselves must keep pace with the rapid evolution of lifestyles at the center of the system, no attempt to "adapt" a technology could possibly succeed.(1)

(1) C. Furtado: <u>Le mythe du développement économique</u>,op.cit., pp. 110-111. Note that we disagree with Furtado when he says that the models of consumption are "imposed from outside"; in actual fact, the models are ardently desired by the dominant élites to begin with, and then, by contagion and under the impact of the modern media, by the whole of the population.

The more intensive the attempt to industrialize, the greater the dependence on the industrialized countries will be, to the extent that the process of industrialization is viewed by the local élites as a pure process of imitation, excluding even the possibility of adaptation. The official vocabulary of the Third World nicely reflects this desire to merely imitate, when demands are addressed solely to the obstacles of the "transfer" of technology and to quantities of the products of technology which can be bought with any given amount of commodities. At the same time this attempt to industrialize can only lead to a concentration of earnings and of sources of profits in the sectors which are in one way or another, geared to the "transfer" of technology, i.e., to relations with the external sector. From this point of view, and quite apart from the juridical appearances, the results are the same whether industrialization is carried out by the public or the private sector, because involvement of certain segments of the population at the expense of the others in the external circuits linked to the external sector always carries with it certain privileges, which may be either directly material or on the other hand social, that is, pertaining to choice of lifestyle.

It is actually quite common for the very élites which at the local ideological level, emphasize the need for the mode of development to be authentic, specific and in keeping with the cultural and religious heritage of the country, to be themselves responsible for the adoption of economic policies which draw the country irremediably into a state of technological dependence. Here we have one of the numerous examples of the cultural alienation of the Third World in relation to the industrialized countries - a factor which contributes greatly to the deepening economic dependence of the Third World.

From this point of view we may say that the economy of underdevelopment itself, particularly as it has evolved over the past forty years, is a basic factor in the cultural alienation of the Third World. The economy of development constitutes a global ideology which serves as a political philosophy in most developing countries. In the words of a famous Nicaraguan author:

> "The false concept of underdevelopment exists solely and necessarily with reference to developed capitalist society. The so-called "underdeveloped" societies do not exist as entities in their own right, but only as potential entities; their reality is that process of becoming a future which they have already chosen.

> The ideology of underdevelopment is the admiring contemplation of that heavily mortgaged future and a limited affirmation of their choice."(1)

In actual fact - and this a point we shall consider once more in our conclusion - it is not so much the models of consumption of the industrialized countries which need to be challenged; the fact is that they now represent a virtually universal aspiration which permeates all social segments of the developing countries. It is rather the measures taken through local development policies which deserve to be denounced, because they unfailingly lead to dependent development, blocked industrialization and the decline of agriculture. As in the last century, the governing élites of the Third World want modernization but refuse to pay the price; they block the mechanisms of social evolution, yet they do not make a sufficient effort, as the dominant social classes, to devise a coherent and autonomous type of society. The various Third World ideologies - third ways, specific forms of socialism, etc. - which try to reconcile what are really non-existent contradictions between tradition and modernity, are nothing more than an expression of the "modernizations" imposed from above, in circumstances of dependence on the industrialized world. They are the ideologies of dependent modernization, which accelerates the blockages of development since they are addressed only to the external aspects of development, that is the model of consumption rather than the mastery of the domestic processes which lead to development.

C. Furtado has perfectly defined modernization as:

> "...a process of adaptation of more sophisticated models of consumption (public and private) and which occurs in the absence of the corresponding process of the accumulation of capital and of progress in the methods of production."(2)

This is why the development plans of the developing countries are so concerned with assembling a window-display of development by means of various spectacular infrastructure projects or the construction of industrial complexes based on the latest technology, while neglecting the internal building of

(1) R. Pallais: Incitation a la réfutation du Tiers-Monde, (Paris: Editions Champ Libre, 1978), p. 36; see also the introduction of our study Le développement introuvable, to be published in 1979 by Anthropos. For a stimulating analysis of the ideological significance of the economy of development for the economists of the industrialized countries, see M. Simoeon Simeon: L'économie et le sauvage, (Paris: Hallier, 1978).

(2) C. Furtado: Le mythe du développement, op.cit., p. 102.

development. There is thus complete confusion between the causes and the effects of development, accompanied by a preference for visible short-term success, to the detriment of the kind of truly integrated national construction which can only take place over a longer period.

D. Agricultural decline and uncontrolled urban growth.

The various factors analyzed above have the effect of speeding up the decline of agriculture and causing uncontrolled urban growth in the Third World. These two phenomena have been vigorously denounced for many years, and the World Bank, since MacNamara became its president, has not ceased to express its most acute concern. These aspects of external dependence have now assumed such proportions that there is a very real danger of famine and the breakdown of the social order of the countries of the Third World which underpins the current international economic order.

Our purpose here is to show that the decline of traditional food crop agriculture and the increase in urban concentrations now occurring in the Third World countries are factors which further intensify the irreversible process of external dependence. In agriculture, the decline in the production of foodstuffs causes local officials to turn increasingly to imports of foreign agricultural technology, in the form of equipment and methods of production. This fact, together with the very rapid development of the urban way of life and the general adoption of the patterns of food consumption of the industrialized countries soon obliges those same officials to consider entering the process of agribusiness with an appeal for a massive intervention of the MNCs which are specialized in this area.(1)

The rate of population growth in the towns of the Third World is such that local means are practically incapable of providirg the urban infrastructure which is needed for those towns to function properly. The solution which then inevitably suggests itself is recourse to the MNCs, since they alone have the technological capacity to rapidly modernize urban infrastructures, so that at least the business districts and the middle-class residental districts will be able to have the facilities expected in an urban setting.

In this way, these two contradictory phenomena of urban and rural evolution have a cumulative and amplifying effect on each other, leading to greater external dependence. The

(1) The evils of agribusiness have been amply described: see in particular S. George: Comment meurt l'autre moitié du monde, (Paris: Laffont, 1978); and G. Gareau: L'Agro-Business, (Paris: Calman-Lévy, 1977).

amounts involved in the development of urban infrastructures are usually far in excess of local financial capacities, particularly as the municipal authorities make no serious attempt to tax the more privileged inhabitants of the urban areas. Whether through inflation or indirect taxation, attempts to provide local financing, where they are made at all, are borne by the rural population or by that part of the urban population which is not truly integrated into the urban way of life as it is practised by the privileged segments. The result is a further blocking of the mechanisms of local savings which sustains the mechanisms for the uneven distribution of income, while increased recourse to the MNCs adds to the tension on the balance of payments. The gradual devaluation of the national currency which then occurs means an increase in the prices of imported products and in the inputs of local industry, which usually have a very large external component.

E. CONCLUSION

The gradual take-over of the economies of the developing countries by the MNCs is not merely a result of the excessive power of the industrialized countries. As in the 19th century, the integration of the Third World on unequal terms in the trade circuits dominated by the industrialized countries is due quite as much to the nature of the local economic policies, which reflect, above all, the interests of the dominant groups in the developing countries. It seems to us that the 20th century is repeating the unfortunate experience of the 19th century, when the lack of interest in an autonomous effort to achieve a mastery of the technological processes at the national level meant that the policies of modernization were doomed to be nothing more than an instrument for the promotion of the supremacy of the industrialized countries. The current phase, which, for the countries of the Third World, has lasted since 1950, indicates that there has been a dangerous acceleration of their technological/financial dependence, in the form of a faster rise in rates of indebtedness as well as the undisputed supremacy of the MNCS in the execution of all major investments in the Third World. Whether the technology-consuming countries have liberal régimes favoring joint ventures with the MNCs or whether they have régimes of State capitalism and use turnkey arrangements, the result is the same: a passive consumption of technology, an increasingly fragmented economy and the loss of control over the economic system implied by the decline of agriculture and by uncontrolled urban growth. One is thus entitled to be sceptical as to the possibility of the present process of modernization leading to a fundamental qualitative change in North-South relations which would reduce the exploitation inflicted on the societies of the Third World and enable them to recover control of their development, and, accordingly, of their potential.

The basic problem remains that of the attitude of the dominant groups in the societies of the Third World and the nature of their economic and cultural relations with the industrialized countries. Breaking out of the vicious cycle of unequal trade between the countries of the Third World and the industrialized countries, particularly that of trade in commodities for technology - which is not only unequal, but also destructuring and destructive - presupposes a general political attitude in which awareness of the dangers of uncontrolled acculturation causes a positive and active reaction to technology, that is, a desire to produce technology through the autonomous efforts of society. This is what Russia and Japan managed to do - and, before them, Germany which was industrially very far behind Britain. On the other hand, the countries which are now in the worst state of dependence are often those whose fear of acculturation leads to a fatal waste of intellectual energies, crystallizing in the emergence of the ideologies of specificity and authenticity, while their reaction to the challenge of technical progress is a passive reaction, which takes the form of demands for the "transfer of resources" and the "transfer of technology". This passive reaction leads the countries of the Third World to gradually lose control of their domestic economic and social evolution; indeed underdevelopment appears more and more as an ecological phenomenon, as society loses its capacity for natural adaptation to the fundamental changes in the environment.

The tendency to consider technical progress and a command of technology as a mere variable of the economic régime - a tendency for which Marxism and neo-liberalism are largely responsible - continues to steer the policies of the Third World countries towards the appearances of development but not its profound causes. From this point of view, most of the demands for a new international economic order seem quite irrelevant. Even the adoption of a code of conduct for the multinational corporations will remain ineffective so long as a minimum level of technological know-how is not achieved in the developing countries. On the other hand, it is to be feared that if the industrialized countries were to grant the demands being made by the Third World, the consequences might be an increase in external means of payment, leading to greater dependence on the ready-made technology of the MNCs, and, over the longer term, to a far worse state of financial dependence.

It is obviously difficult to reach general conclusions about such a diverse group of countries as the Third World. The range is enormous: it includes the technological sophistication of certain industrial sectors sustained by the MNCs in a number of Latin American countries; the Korean and Taiwanese models of modernization in which integration into the international division of labor of the MNCs is accompanied by successful technological grafts which seem to be spreading gradually to the whole of the economy; India, where a considerable technological autonomy has been developed in several sectors, while technological progress has not generalized; and also the numerous countries where there have been no technological autonomy and no external technological grafts. From this point of view one cannot rule out the possibility that a limited number of countries may gradually succeed in becoming integrated in a positive manner into the international trade circuits, thus breaking out of the vicious cycle of technological/financial dependence. But these limited cases should not make us lose sight of the general historical functioning of the obstacles to modernization. The obstacles of the 20th century, just as those of the 19th century were the basis of those occurring in the 20th century. This historical process of blockage obviously does not exclude the occasional short-lived period of success, of which there were many in the 19th century and the first half of the 20th century, any more than it excludes the possibility of individual societies breaking the chain of obstacles.

Development is by definition a historical process, and, therefore, primarily a global response of society to change and disruption of the traditional balances: rates of population growth, the onslaught of foreign cultures and new modes of production, changes in transport, trade flows and patterns of economic domination, etc... It is impossible to prescribe a remedy which is not tainted with the kind of intellectual posturing or inaccurate concepts conveyed by the ideology of development. At the very most, an analysis of experiments that have failed, in relation to the popular theories of development which inspired them, will enable us to see which social groups derived benefits from these experiments and thus to understand why they were undertaken. In this respect there can be no doubt that most developmental experiments in the 19th century, as in the 20th, have actually weakened the ability of the societies of the Third World to adapt to the ecological disruptions caused by the triumphant industrialization of Europe. The analysis which we have made of the mechanisms of indebtedness is one approach among many others to this recurrent phenomenon. It forms part of a rather vast paradigm which we have tried to circumscribe throughout this study and which is based on the notions of "modernization - technology - model of consumption - national construction.

An exhaustive study of this paradigm clearly goes well beyond the limits of this study. We hope, however, that our efforts to situate the phenomenon of indebtedness in a broader framework will help dispel the illusions of the purely economic approach which prevails in the literature on development and underdevelopment as well as in the solutions advocated, both locally and internationally, to combat exploitation and poverty. It is for this reason that we think that there is no isolated remedy to the problem of the excessive indebtedness of the Third World, and no neat financial prescription. The recurrence of indebtedness and its increase have to do with the overall functioning of the exploited and blocked societies, and thus, in the last analysis, with the very nature of the kind of society intended by their ruling élites.

IV. GENERAL CONCLUSION

For a better understanding of the manner in which technological and financial dependence works:

"Many cultural systems clearly do find ways of preventing subsistence scarcities leading to economic change. Class societies contain varying degrees of working-class poverty. Whenever significant poverty builds up within a rigid class society and is contained by social rather than environmental constraints, the development problem becomes a political one. The problems is to see how the poor are prevented from making the economic system respond to their unsatisfied needs; in other words, to see how the system is maintained at too low a level of environmental exploitation for the society which it serves."

R. G. Wilkinson
Poverty and Progress
(London: Methuen and Co. 1977)
p. 8

"The nation has not participated substantially in change except through an initial excess of boasting which has now turned into bitterness which cannot possibly lead to radical action; the slightest obstacle paralyzes it. The fact is that our revolution has so far been military: the change it has brought about has remained limited to the forms of power, whereas our ways have not been changed by it at all and it has scarcely touched our sciences, industries and trade."

Shibli Schmayyel
(on the Young Turk revolution)
Quoted by: R. Khoury
Contemporary Arab thought: the influence of the French Revolution on its social and political trends, (in Arabic), (Beirut: Dar Al Makchouf) p. 134.

Our inquiry into the origins of the indebtedness of the Third World has led us to constantly emphasize the sequence: desire for acculturation - transfer of technology - indebtedness. The desire for acculturation principally and initially manifests itself in the military sphere, where the overwhelming superiority of the industrialized countries since the 19th century has obliged the Third World to borrow Western technology. It then spreads gradually to the other spheres of the life of society, and it is in this way that the aspiration to the model of consumption of the industrialized countries becomes generally accepted. However, as we have seen, technological borrowing usually takes the form of the massive and indiscriminate import of the products of technology, and not of a global and sustained effort to acquire a command of technology. Whether they are military or whether they consist of capital equipment for the production of consumer goods, the equipment imported by the Third World is in no sense a transfer of technology. At most they constitute a transfer of productive capacity, the excessive cost of which is apparent only over a long period and blocks the dissemination of progress locally and the egalitarian and profitable insertion of the country in the circuits of international trade.

The real accumulation of capital which enriches society is that which lies in the capacity to produce productive capacity, and not in the expansion of the capacity to import productive capacities from abroad. In this sense the mechanisms for the "transfer" of technology from the industrialized countries to the countries of the Third World, as they have been used in practice since the last century, are precisely those which help the industrialized countries to develop even further their technological capacity, while the Third World becomes more and more dependent and lags farther and farther behind. Whatever capital is imported, the added value created in the exporting country far exceeds that in the importing country; the genuine spin-off effects take place in the country of origin of the equipment and not in the receiving country.

To talk about transfer of technology and transfer of resources, in respect of the current mechanisms of modernization, is thus a misuse of vocabulary. Technology is not transferred, it is acquired by the development of theoretical and practical knowledge and then it is produced in the form of productive capacity. The same is true of industrial capital, which permits the expanded production and which, unlike mercantile capital, cannot be imported. In this respect, capital and technology form a single conceptual notion. In an industrial society there cannot be capital without a command of technology, any more than there can be a command of technology without capital. The reason is simple: capital and technology are both the product of the work accumulated by the society and in the society. Trade in capital or trade in technology can of course help this process, in a more or less marginal way, when it takes place between two societies having relatively homogeneous levels of productivity (as in the massive use by the Japanese after the second World War of American industrial patents). On the other hand, the massive and uncontrolled importing of capital and technology produced in another society whose productivity is based on entirely different systems of production is not only incapable of supplanting the process of accumulation, but is in fact the main cause of the irreversible disruptions which create the structural dependence which is the basic feature of underdevelopment. Moreover, since capital is a "social relation between persons which is established through the intermediary of things" (Marx), any massive import of technological capital cannot fail to bring about the import of the production relations and, consequently, of the models of consumption which sustain them. The massive introduction of technological capital for the exclusive benefit of certain social groups and without some overall plan or national effort to acquire and master minimum levels of technological knowledge invariably leads to the paralysis of the positive spontaneous reactions the society might otherwise have had in order to adapt to changes in the economic and cultural environment.

Conversely, the purchase of technological capital, even through indebtedness, can be an important positive element in setting in motion a self-centered process of development, when it takes place within the framework of massive efforts to generate local technological know-how and when it is carefully planned and controlled.[1] For this reason, indebtedness in

(1) In order to hold one's own with the pioneers of industry - writes M. Usui - it is not enough to be a skillful negotiator, it is essential that those who organize productive operations should be increasingly aware of the needs for research, even if that only enables them to follow the current of change. The purchase of any given technology should thus be considered as an integral part of the company's policy of research and innovation. If the buyer does not adopt such a policy or if he does not move towards objectives which are deemed to be desirable then he will find himself very poorly placed to challenge the equity of any given technological transaction", from _Oligopoles, R-D et concession de licences - Réflexions en vue de définir les conditions d'une transaction équitable lors du transfert de technologie_, OECD Center for Development, July 1975, Special study No. 7, CD/TI (75) 11, p. 12.

itself is not necessarily a bad thing, as the experience of many countries shows: the United States, Canada, Australia and Japan, which in the 19th century built their technological development while having recourse to British capital. It is only where it is practised automatically and as a substitute for local efforts to generate savings and, accordingly, productivity, that indebtedness becomes the pivot of the mechanisms of dependence and technological backwardness.

In this respect the policy of the international financial institutions, as extended and amplified by the functioning of the local organs, is a basic element of the technological/financial dependence of the Third World. The global conception of external financing as the financing of projects using characteristic methods of evaluation has done much to link technological dependence to financial dependence. This is even truer in the case of the suppliers or buyers credits granted by the industrialized countries to the countries of the Third World for purchase of equipment. The close association between the mechanisms of external financing intended for the developing countries and the operations of the multinational corporations is, of course, well known;(1) it has to do with the very functioning of the external financing which we have described elsewhere (Chapter III) and there is no guarantee that recent attempts in certain international institutions to attenuate the direct presence of the MNCs (elimination of the Program of Industrial Cooperation in FAO);(2) will on their own be sufficient to break the main axis of their operations in the Third World, which consists of loans, assistance and direct investment. In this sense the functioning of indebtedness of the developing countries in the 20th century is the continuation of the experience of the 19th century and is based on the same logic. One is entitled to wonder, however, whether the successful cases of indebtedness in the 19th century can be reproduced with similar results, because of the ever widening technological gap which separates some industrialized countries from the majority of the countries of the Third World.

This brings us to the problems of the alternative models of development, which have generated an increasingly abundant literature in various circles in the industrialized countries,

(1) See S. George, <u>op.cit</u>., and E.H. Jacoby: "Les sociétés multinationales et le développement du Tiers-Monde - Une influence croissante dans le systeme des Nations Unies", <u>Le Monde Diplomatique</u>, July, 1976.

(2) See E. Jacoby: "Deux victoires a l'ONU contre les sociétés multinationales", <u>Le Monde Diplomatique</u>, September, 1978.

particularly since the cries of alarm of the Club of Rome on the evils of growth and the emergence of increasing numbers of ecological parties. Third World economists have shown surprisingly little interest in these alternative models, and in questions of alternative technologies (also known as "soft" or "intermediary" technologies), which often appear to be an attempt on the part of the industrialized countries to transfer modernization "on the cheap." This is doubtless due to the general attitude to the transfer of technology, the main feature of which is the confusion between the possession of capital goods and the means of producing them, and the belief that technology is a variable which depends on the disposition of capital and the manner of its appropriation.

The People's Republic of China, which had previously been an example of the alternative model, particularly in its autonomous efforts to achieve technological know-how(1), has just made a spectacular reversal of policy by opting for modernization geared to the massive import of technology-capital. It is clearly too soon to form an opinion as to the impact of this change on the evolution of the Chinese economy over the long term, and particularly as to whether this is a new phase in the fluctuations of Chinese socio-cultural policy or a change that is destined to last. Certainly, the mechanisms of external indebtedness are such that one is inclined to be sceptical about China's ability to eventually return to a self-reliant policy process of development. Leaving aside these questions, however, the current trends in China are evidence of the universal aspiration to achieve the model of consumption of the industrialized countries. For this reason we feel that the debate on alternative technologies in the Third World will continue to generate little response.

On the other hand, an analysis of technico-financial dependence and a critique of the local and international framework which sustains it is urgently necessary. In this sense it is not so much the legitimacy of the models of consumption themselves that needs to be challenged, as the validity of the ways in which the countries of the Third World have chosen to accede to those models, considered from the point of view of their local policies and also their international economic demands on the industrialized countries. Nor is it incorrect distribution of income as such that needs to be criticized, but the sterile use which is made, from the point of view of the command of technology, of the savings confiscated from the exploited segments of society by the dominant classes. Historical experience shows that, in the area of income distribution, models for access to industrialization can take various forms. A clear distinction must be made here between

(1) See in particular: China: Science walks on two legs. A report from "Science for the People",(New York: Avon Books, 1974); and S.R. Schram,(ed) Authority, participation and change in China, (Cambridge: 1973).

the problem of social morality and that of the command of technology, although the Keynesio-Marxist universe of developmental theories does nothing to facilitate that task.

Moreover, the vocabulary of the doctrines of alternative technology also seems inadequate, because the point at issue is not technical progress as such but the question of how to achieve access to that progress and a mastery of it, or at least to keep pace with it and its impact on social evolution in a more or less autonomous way. Technical progress cannot, of course, be divided into different levels of technology, because progress is primarily control of society by society and the autonomous capacity to influence its adaptation to the environment. If one accepts the categorization of technical progress according to technologies with differing costs, one is confined to a purely commercial situation governed by the logic of "capital" - clearly that of the most highly industrialized countries - and therefore to the cycle of trade conducive to underdevelopment in which commodities are exchanged for technology, with complete disregard for the socio-cultural aspect of the command of technology.

Successful modernization begins with "social" and "financial" calculations: in other words, by a consistant effort of society to enable the various social groups to react effectively to internal changes or to those imposed from outside. One is puzzled, in this respect, by the virtually complete lack of effectively applied research and development policies in the developing countries particularly when one considers the massive effort made by the industrialized countries, which spend 133 times more on research than the Third World;[1] the continued use of educational systems which are unable to generate technological capabilities is also puzzling. The absence of such capabilities in the fields of industrial design and engineering means that the countries of the Third World are doomed to technical stagnation; this absence is due not only to the inadequacies of policies of research and education, but also to the habits induced by systematic recourse to external indebtedness and to the MNCs, which provide technology, but only in the "packaged" or ready-made form - in other words, with the engineering included.

There is now an abundant literature on the need for "unpacking" of technology for the developing countries to be able to build a capacity for technological know-how which would reduce their external dependence; but the impact of this literature on the decision-makers in the sphere of Third

(1) See. M. Schiray: Tiers Monde et monde industrialisé, Notes et Etudes Documentaires, La Documentation Francaise, 29 March 1978, p. 128.

World industrial policy is virtually nil.[1] Instead, they are always looking for quick, short-term achievements, to the detriment of long-term national construction. This is why we always come back to the attitude of the dominant groups in policy-making, and why we feel it is urgent to fight the popular theories of development which obscure the analysis and place the problems in the wrong context. Our analysis of technological/financial dependence has enabled us to illustrate at length the way this process of concealment occurs.

Breaking the thousand and one links between technological dependence and financial dependence is a long business which involves upsetting large numbers of conventional notions about development. Yet only such a break with the past is capable of bringing about new types of planning, based as a matter of priority on an internal command of technology, and also new financial institutions which will mobilize savings in order to disseminate local productivity. It alone is capable of breaking the mechanisms of excessive profit of the MNCs and, therefore, the mechanisms of unequal trade which is reproduced, on an amplified scale, from century to century, as the technological gap between industrialized and Third World countries continues to widen. It is only in this framework that alternative models for development can begin to take shape.

As long as the mobilization of external financial resources is necessarily accompanied by "closed" technological imports, there is little chance of an internal accumulation of technology-capital capable of setting the developing countries on the road to technical progress. Once recourse to foreign capital is no longer closely tied to recourse to packaged technology, it will be a sign that the Third World is gradually emerging from dependence and underdevelopment. This is why any measures to combat the present mechanisms of indebtedness requires a revision of the functioning of the international financial institutions and also a revision of the nature of the collective demands made by the Third World for a new international economic order, since those demands, in their present state, can lead only to a deepening of dependence, even if they were only partially successful. In this respect it is for the intellectual élites of the Third World at long last to learn political economy, instead of trying vainly to grasp the secrets of the "magic arts" of the social sciences, the core of which is the economy of development and underdevelopment.

---

(1) See for example: Transfert de technologie et développement, under the direction of P. Judet, P. Kahn, A.C. Kiss, J. Touscoz, (Paris: Lib.Techniques, 1977); and "Le Transfert de technologies", Revue Tiers-Monde, Tome XVII, No. 65, January-March 1976.

(2) S. Andreski: Les Sciences Sociales - Sorcellerie des temps modernes, (Paris: PUF, 1975).

Chapter III

THE CONDITIONALITY OF DRAWINGS ON THE INTERNATIONAL MONETARY FUND

Abdelkader Sid-Ahmed

Introduction

The profound crises that have shaken the international monetary system in the last few years have aroused an increasing interest among the LDCs in its mode of operation and the possibilities of its reform. The 1972 session of the United Nations Conference on Trade and Development (UNCTAD) provided the forum in which the new interest could be displayed, and led to the agreement that the Third World should have an increasing say in international discussions on the reconstruction of the Bretton Woods system.

Before the LDCs began to take an interest in the matter, it is undeniable that little was written, with few exceptions, about international monetary management from their point of view. They were denied a voice when the problem of international liquidity arose, when a succession of crises hit the key currencies of the main industrialized countries and when a number of instruments were introduced after urgent international consultations. Not only were their interests completely disregarded during that period - they were scarcely mentioned at all. A specific example of this attitude is the fact that the key negotiations nearly always took place within the Group of Ten. Moreover, the LDCs were given virtually no part to play in the establishment of the special drawing rights scheme, and when they were eventually drawn in, it was in spite of the opposition (initially at least) of the developed countries.

The collapse of the Bretton Woods system in 1971 and the creation of the Committee of 20 on the reform of the international monetary system gave the LDCs the first chance they had had since the second world war to participate in the remodelling of the system. Their demands related to three points: i) the adaptation of conventional tax, monetary and exchange measures to meet their needs in the adjustment of balances of payments; ii) their international liquidity requirements, and the acceptability of the liquidity offered to them; and, iii) the monetary legitimacy of a link between the creation of international liquidity and development aid.

The purpose of this study is to examine the conditionality of drawings on the IMF, in other words, the terms on which conditional international liquidity is made available. The specific restrictions placed on the use of this liquidity involve a number of economic, social and political consequences for the LDCs which should be brought to light, especially as these consequences often doom the policies proposed by the IMF to failure, since they are more suited to the conditions prevailing in the developed than in the developing countries where the major imperative is not the adjustment of the balance of payments but development itself.

This study will therefore analyse the reasons for the failure of the IMF system of conditionality in the LDCs. It is hoped by the end of it to have demonstrated that the system in question is an integral part of the philosophy that lay behind the establishment of the Bretton Woods system for the benefit of the developed countries. The study will then review the conditions which prevailed when the present international monetary system was set up and which explain the anti-LDC bias that existed from the outset. As the aim of an international monetary system is to ensure that there is sufficient liquidity for all its members, it is necessary to study the characteristics of international liquidity in which conditionality is a major factor. The system of conditionality is the result of IMF rules and regulations and has been improved in recent years under the growing pressure exerted by the LDCs. The analysis will be completed by an inventory of the various types of conditional liquidity available to the IMF.

The second section will be devoted to an examination of conditionality in practice in the LDCs through the analysis of a number of test cases: Brazil, Chile, Colombia, Indonesia, Ghana, etc. The implementation of the IMF's stabilization programmes generally has the following effects: denationalization of the domestic system of production, high rates of export growth which favor devaluation, a fall in the growth and investment rates, and an increase in employment and under-employment, a temporary improvement in external equilibrium and higher external debt servicing as a result of over-borrowing to reduce the foreign exchange gap, which could have been bridged in other ways.

The failure of the Fund's programmes call for a number of explanations which form the subject-matter of the third section. Owing to various structural features in the LDCs, for instance, a devaluation of the exchange rate is seldom the best way to deal with the structural deficits from which they suffer. Moreover, the impact of devaluation on income distribution is apt to cause political problems which cancel out the supposed benefits of devaluation. The lack of non-discriminatory import controls means that the emphasis on devaluation as a means of reducing imports may cut down on imports that are necessary for development, and this is bound to have an adverse effect on the balance-of-payments situation and development prospects. Lastly, the structural changes which development entails are incompatible with the maintenance of relative price stability. The importance attached to monetary stability above all hampers the sectoral transfers of resources that are essential for development.

The factors listed above explain why it is indispensable to reform the system of conditionality. There does, in fact, seem to be a broad consensus nowadays on the fact that the corrective measures applied in the developed countries are not necessarily suited to the LDCs because of the internal and external structural problems with which they are confronted. There is also a fairly broad consensus on the fact that the liberalization of capital flows implicit in the Bretton Woods system is more in the interests of the developed than of the developing countries although it is the latter which have most need of liquidity.

It is obvious that the IMF is obsessed by monetary stability, which its senior officials regard as a prerequisite for sound development, and the absence of which is thought to be the main cause of balance-of-payments disequilibria. Hence, the fact that the letters of intent which accompany stand-by agreements emphasize control of local expansion of credit, public expenditure, taxation, wages and prices, trade practices and exchange rates, without making any distinction between the LDCs and the developed countries.

The IMF has nevertheless taken certain decisions with the aim of making more conditional liquidity available to the LDCs, as illustrated by the quota increases, the compensatory financing scheme and the other facilities accorded recently. But here too the financial assistance provided by the Fund is limited by the size of the quotas, the short-term nature of the agreements and the balance-of-payments orientation of its assistance.

The measures adopted at Kingston in 1976 were disappointing for the LDCs from that point of view, since a genuine reform should include:

i) a substantial increase in drawing rights;

ii) the abandonment of the Bretton Woods philosophy on the adjustment process.

The idea behind this is that a country should deal with disequilibria by making domestic adjustments, unless it is in a state of chronic disequilibrium, when a devaluation is necessary. However, this line of thought ignores the possibility that payment disequilibria may be caused by external forces which the country is unable to control and that an attempt at internal adjustment will simply correct them at the expense of its development.

iii) the increased participation of the LDCs in the creation of international liquidity;

iv) greater participation of the LDCs in the decision making process through bigger voting rights in the IMF and also through the guarantee that major decisions on the international monetary system will not be taken without their participation.

I. THE INTERNATIONAL MONETARY SYSTEM OF BRETTON WOODS AND ITS ANTI-LDC BIAS

The founders of the international monetary system of Bretton Woods intended to create a system that would give international trade stable rates of exchange and evade the dangers of competitive devaluation while escaping the deflationary rigidities of the Gold Standard in force before the second world war. The Bretton Woods system was very largely the product of ambitious Anglo-American plans during the war aimed at establishing a new and liberal international economic order that would do away with the economic evils of the 1930s - depression, the trade war and competitive devaluations - which were thought to have been among the causes of the second outbreak of hostilities. It was the results of those deliberations in the monetary field that were submitted in draft form to the historic Bretton Woods conference in July, 1944. Their ratification created the legal framework for a new international monetary institution, and was to shape the international monetary system for many years to come.[1]

The Anglo-American agreement that lay behind the creation of the Fund is the reason why no reference has been made in the Articles of Agreement to the specific problems of the LDCs or even in a general way to development. The United States opposed a proposal made by the Indian delegation in that respect,[2] which would have had the effect of differentiating the developing from the developed countries. Some writers countered the reproach implicit in that proposal by claiming that the distinction would have been pointless since article I (ii) of the Fund's Articles of Agreement states that it is the responsibility of the developed countries to "facilitate the expansion and balanced growth of international trade, and to contribute thereby to the promotion and maintenance of high levels of employment and real income and to the development of the productive resources of all members as primary objectives of economic policy". They added that there is nothing in the articles to prevent the Fund from adopting policies favourable to the LDCs.[3] This interpretation is not convincing because it is tantamount to denying that there are certain specific features in develop-

(1) On all these questions see: J.Marcus Fleming, "Developments in the international systems", Staff Papers I.M.F. (November, 1963), pp.461-471, and R. Triffin, "Evolution of the international monetary system: historical reappraisal and future perspectives", Princeton Studies in International Finance, (1964-No. 12).

(2) J.K. Horsefield: The International Monetary Fund 1945-1965 (Washington: I.M.F., 1969).

(3) G. Schleiminger "Developed and developing countries in the I.M.F.: cooperation or confrontation", Intereconomics (December 1970), p. 12.

ment policies that are appropriate for certain categories of countries such as the LDCs. Moreover, the senior officials of the Fund were soon to show that development was not its main objective. In 1946, the Executive Directors interpreted the Articles of Agreement in that sense. In their view, the functions of the Fund were limited to the grant of "temporary assistance to finance current balance-of-payments deficits in the framework of monetary stabilisation transactions". Economic development was purely incidental, and thereafter the Fund was to make quite certain that its assistance was used for purposes of short-term stabilisation and not for reconstruction or development.(1)

Apart from certain superficial changes, this interpretation of the Articles of the Fund was to determine its conduct in transactions involving LDCs, and the Fund's philosophy henceforward was that monetary stabilisation and restrictions were the best policy for promoting growth, and that inflation, not shortage of capital, was the major obstacle to development.(2)

It is clear therefore that the international adjustments of balances of payment was envisaged at Bretton Woods as the cornerstone of the economic process. As for the relevant policies and instruments, they were conceived solely in terms of the economic realities fo the developed countries, and this naturally had repercussions on the supply of liquidity available for the LDCs.(3)

A. Liquidity and conditionality

The term "international liquidity" (unconditional) is often used as a synonym for reserves,(4) defined as "the assets (of a country) which the monetary authorities can use, either directly or indirectly through the assurance of convertibility into other assets, to defend the rate of exchange when external payments are in deficit".(5) Conditional liquidity relates to the

(1) G. Maynard and G. Bird, "International monetary issues and the developing countries: a survey", World Development, vol.3, No.9 (September 1975),pp. 609-631.
(2) I.M.F., Report on the first ten years of the international monetary fund (Washington: 1956),quoted by Maynard and Bird, op.cit., pp. 612.
(3) Alexander Kafka, "Adjustment under the Bretton Woods code with special reference to the less developed countres", in: Jagdish Bhagwati and R.S. Eckans Heds (eds), Development and planning, essays in honour of Paul Rosenstein Rodan, (Cambridge: M.I.T. Press, 1973), pp. 210-238.
(4) F. Machlup and B.G. Malkiel (eds) International monetary arrangements: The problem of choice, (Princeton: 1964, International Finance Section.
(5) Group of Ten, Report of the study group on the creation of reserve assets (Ossola report), 1965.

possibilities of reserve borrowing among central banks (the so-called swap arrangements) or of drawing on the Fund.

Another and more functional interpretation of liquidity, or the "liquidity position" of a country, in the term used by Arndt,[1] is that it should provide a yardstick for assessing a country's capacity to finance a payments deficit without resorting to measures of adjustment. Thus, to the reserves held by a country, there must also be added borrowing possibilities, transfers in foreign exchange from commercial banks, commodity stocks that are traded on international markets, the degree to which the national currency would be accepted abroad in the event of a deficit and, lastly, the possibility of attracting foreign capital through variations in interest rates.[2] The most fruitful approach has been suggested by Kane, [3] who proposes defining the international liquidity of a country as the balance of its external assets, commitments, liabilities and lines of credit.

The LDCs have access to the conventional forms of liquidity and, like the developed countries, can draw on the IMF credit tranches, but their ability to finance balance-of-payments deficits without adjustment is far less than that of the developed countries, and especially the United States, which has the privilege of financing its balance-of-payments deficits by printing more dollars.

B. The LDCs' need for liquidity

A report by the Group of Ten states that "the supply of reserves should be large enough to allow the process of adjustment to operate satisfactorily".[4] The difficulty of gaining access to liquidity may be so great that the countries in deficit have to make more rapid adjustments than they would otherwise be called upon to make to meet their domestic economic objectives.

---

(1) H.W. Arndt, "The concept of liquidity in international monetary theory", Review of economic studies (October 1948)
(2) For further details see: John Williamson, "International liquidity: a survey", The economic journal (September 1973), No. 331, vol. 83, pp. 685-747.
(3) E.J. Kane, "International liquidity: a probabilistic approach", Kyklos, 1965.
(4) Report to ministers and governors by the group of deputies (Frankfurt: 1966) (known as the Emminger report) p. 8.

On the theoretical level, a number of studies have been made in the last few years on the demand for international liquidity (or reserves).(1) It is generally admitted by the authors that the reserves are held for the benefits they bring. They act, in fact, as a sort of buffer stock against sudden and undesirable adjustments in the balance of payments. The profit obtained from the reserves is thus equal to the cost of the forced adjustment which the country in question is thus able to avoid. While the reserves engender profits it may be assumed that they will be in constant demand, the maintenance of such reserves implies an opportunity cost equal to the real resources which could otherwise be acquired. In theory, therefore, the demand for reserves is functionally linked to the cost-benefit of maintaining them. The demand is a positive function both as far as the cost of adjustment is concerned and the probability that an adjustment will be necessary. What about the LDCs demand for liquidity? In this case too, a number of studies have been carried out.(2) The study by Clark concludes that the function of demand for reserves in the LDCs is similar in structure to demand in the developed countries.

The special vulnerability of the LDCs balances of payments therefore means that they require a higher level of reserves than the developed countries. The evidence to the contrary which Flanders puts forward concerning the instability of payments is not convincing because his conclusions are based on obsolete data.(3) The more recent data presented by Erb and

---

(1) See, <u>inter alia</u>, P.B. Kenen and E. Yudin, "The demand for international reserves", <u>Review of Economics and Statistics</u> (August 1965), p. 47; P.B. Clark, "The demand for international reserves: a cross-country analysis", <u>Canadian Journal of Economics</u> (November 1975), p. 3; Andrew D. Crockett, "Control over international reserves", <u>Staff papers</u>, vol. 25, No. 1 (March 1978), pp. 1-24

(2) See, <u>inter alia</u>, A. Kafka, "International liquidity: its present relevance to the less developed countries", <u>American Economic Review. Papers and Proceedings</u> (May 1968), p. 58; J.A. Frenkel, "The demand for international reserves by developed and less developed countries", <u>Economica</u>, vol. 41, No. 161 (February).

(3) M.J. Flanders, "The demand for international reserves", <u>Studies in International Finance</u>, No. 27 (Princeton, 1927).

Schiavo Campo as well as by Lawson (1) indicate on the average that the LDCs reveal a greater instability in their trade balances than the developed countries and that, all things being equal, their demand for liquidity is also greater. The cost of adjustment will therefore be higher in the LDCs since the development process is contingent on imports which are often impossible to reduce. A drop in the level of imports is therefore a far more serious matter for the LDCs than for the developed countries.

C. The supply of international liquidity and the LDCs

Williamson has noted that from the Genoa conference of 1922 until quite recently, more seems to have been written on the supply of reserves than on any other theme (in the area of international liquidity).(2) However, the mechanism by which reserves are made available has been given little attention in the literature on the subject, because most of the analyses have started from the premise that the supply of reserves should be considered as exogenous in origin. This is the assumption that underlies the provisions of the Fund's Articles of Agreement on the allocation of SDRs which imply that there will be a given volume of reserves from other sources and that the task of the Fund is therefore to supplement those sources in order to align the supply of liquidity with the global need for the endogenous growth of reserves which, under the Bretton Woods system, was considered to be "self-limited". It was argued that countries would hesitate to accept dollars beyond a certain point after which they would demand payment in gold, and that the United States itself would refuse to have an unduly heavy short-term external debt.(3)

The adoption of floating exchange rates - which made it possible to avoid undesirable variations in reserves - and the development of the international capital markets as a source of financing for balance-of-payments deficits increased the complexity of the problem, the control of international liquidity

(1) G.R. Erb and S. Schiavo Campo, "Export instability, level of development and economic size of less developed countries", Bulletin of the Oxford University Institute of Economics and Statistics (November 1969); C.W. Lawson, "The decline of world export instability - a reappraisal", op.cit. (February 1974).

(2) Williamson, "International liquidity: a survey", op.cit., p. 704.

(3) For the two opposing points of view, see C.P. Kindleberger, "Balance of Payments deficits and the international market for liquidity", Essays in International Finance, No. 46 (Princeton, May 1965); R. Triffin, Gold and the dollar crisis, Yale University Press, 1960.

and the relationship between conditional and unconditional liquidity. On the assumption that international liquidity is divided grosso modo into proper reserves and conditional borrowing (or drawing) possibilities, the expansion of the former will inevitably affect the degree of substitution existing between the two sources of liquidity.

Up to the beginning of the 1970s, the LDCs as a group were heavily dependent upon drawings from the Fund, and, with the introduction of the SDRs, the allocations of drawing rights represented a large amount of liquidity for them.(1)

D. The system of conditionality of the International Monetary Fund

The Fund's resources come from subscriptions by member States, based on quotas that were originally negotiated at Bretton Woods. The size of the quotas (2) was determined by criteria that took into account the levels of reserves, national income and foreign exchange as well as political considerations. At the time of Bretton Woods, the funds available amounted to $8,800 million. The voting rights of the IMF members are determined by the size of their quotas. The Articles of Agreement state that the Fund must be directed by a Board of Governors, each of whom represents a member State and by an Executive Board of Directors, who are elected by the members, five of them being nominated by the five members with the largest quotas and one by a country in surplus, while the seven others are elected by groups of member States which are not entitled to nominate Directors. The voting rights of the two groups are, in general, proportional to the size of the member's quotas. During the annual Assembly of October 1978, it was nevertheless decided that the number of Executive Directors nominated would be increased from five to six, as Saudi Arabia nominated a Director for the first time. The number of Directors elected remained at fifteen. Saudi Arabia acquired the right to nominate a Director under the terms of Article XII, section 3 (c) of the Articles of Agreement, by virtue of the fact that it was one of the two principal creditor members during the two-year period which came to an end on 31 July 1978. In decisions concerning access to the funds of the IMF, the vote benefits the countries in surplus. T. Hayter notes that, in practice, the Executive Directors play an influential part in the day-to-day operations of the Fund and in the

(1) S.D. Kresner: "The I.M.F. and the Third World", International Organization, (summer 1968), p.2.
(2) For further details see J.K. Horsefield, op.cit.

main decisions adopted.[1] The combined voting system has also increased the influence exercised by the major economic powers, notably the United States, over the activities of the Fund,[2] owing to the fact that the Fund is situated in Washington.

In 1942, Keynes put forward the idea of a "Clearing Union" giving automatic access to the resources of the Fund, which would have been three or four times greater than those finally agreed upon. Keynes believed that the Union's resources should consist of unsecured facilities, since it was easier to raise the ceiling than to increase subscriptions.[3]

In the solution adopted at Bretton Woods, the American position prevailed. The result was to limit the Fund's resources and to make access to them contingent on a number of conditions which were laid down in the Articles of Agreement. One of them, which is stated in Article V, section 5, can be interpreted very widely. It runs as follows:

> "Whenever the Fund is of the opinion that any member is using the resources of the Fund in a manner contrary to the purposes of the Fund, it shall present to the member a report setting forth the views of the Fund and prescribing a suitable time for reply. If no reply to the report is received from the member within the prescribed time, or if the reply received is unsatisfactory, the Fund may continue to limit the member's use of the Fund's resources or may (......) declare it ineligible to use the resources of the Fund".[4]

---

(1) T. Hayter, Aid as imperialism (Pelican, 1971), p. 35; Susan Strange, "I.M.F.: monetary managers", in: Robert W. Cox and Harold K. Jacobson, The anatomy of influence: decision-making in international organizations (Yale University Press, New Haven, Connecticut, 1973).

(2) Citing B. Tew, Cheryl Payer notes that the domination of the United States was so great that up to 1956 important decisions were, in effect, taken by the U.S. Secretary of the Treasury, and the Fund had no authority to negotiate drawing conditions. See Brian Tew, The International Monetary Fund, mimeo. 1969, p. 86, quoted by C. Payer, The Debt-Trap, p. 217.

(3) Robert W. Oliver, International economic co-operation and the World Bank (The Macmillan Press, 1975), pp. 50 and 130-134.

(4) See also article VI on transfers of capital and article VII on scarce foreign exchange.

Article VIII makes it compulsory for members to avoid restrictions on current payments, discriminatory currency arrangements or multiple currency practices, and to maintain the convertibility of the current account. However, Article XIX provides for transitional arrangements. From 1952 onwards, member States still resorting to such practices are required to consult the Fund, which may order them to refrain from them, in default of which they will be declared ineligible to receive resources from the Fund, or may even be expelled from it. This consultation procedure holds good whether or not the country in question is in urgent need of the Fund's resources. Consequently, despite the existence of these conditions, the Articles of Agreement in themselves do not afford a clear justification for the interference of the Fund with the domestic policies of member States. In this respect, the British point of view on the function of the Fund was incorporated into the articles of agreement to some extent. Its position was essentially that the Fund should provide more or less automatic access to its resources to help to solve balance-of-payments problems without resorting to severe deflation, and that it should not have any direct influence or control on the national policies of member States. The position of the United States was the Fund should control and examine all drawings and promote what it considered to be appropriate domestic policies.(1)

In 1966, in answer to a request for information from the Board of Governors the Executive Directors of the Fund interpreted the Articles of Agreement as meaning that the resources of the Fund are solely intended to provide temporary assistance for financing current balance-of-payments deficits as part of its monetary stabilisation operations.(2) The Fund thus adopted the United States point of view, and from then on considered that its main objective was not to grant additional and unconditional international liquidity, but to place exchange rates on a multilateral footing and to eliminate monetary restrictions.(3) Since 1949, the Fund has published annual reports on exchange restrictions and has brought pressure to bear on its member States to abolish restrictions and multiple exchange rates. At

(1) See, on this point, R.F. Harrod, The life of John Maynard Keynes (The Macmillan Press, 1951); W.W. Scammel, International monetary policy, 2nd ed. (The Macmillan Press, 1961); and T. Hayter, Aid as imperialism, op.cit., p. 38.

(2) IMF, Report of the Executive Directors and Summary of Proceedings (27 September - 3 October 1946), p. 106.

(3) Scammel believed that for the United States the multilateralisation of exchange rates was the Fund's major objective. See International monetary policy, op.cit., p. 163.

the beginning of the 1950s, the Fund defined its position more precisely: the use of its resources was to be considered as a means of overcoming temporary balance-of-payments difficulties through conditional short-term advances. At the time, the Fund was disquieted by some of the policies followed by member States and considered them to be a source of inflation (heavy investment and ambitious social security programmes). In 1951, Mr. Ivor Booth, Director of the Fund, informed the member States that the Fund's resources were available on certain conditions only. States should adopt programmes to control inflation and reduce exchange restrictions.(1) The Fund's annual report for 1955 stated that, while it was unlikely the Fund would refuse permission for drawings equivalent to the gold subscription of a member State (gold tranche or the first 25 percentage points of its quota), the later tranches would be subjected to increasingly strict conditions. In short, the conditions laid down for drawing on tranches became increasingly stringent as the country progressed from tranche to tranche. The Fund's policy is fairly liberal for the first credit tranche, and access to it is granted as soon as the member State has shown that it was making reasonable efforts to solve its problems. Requests to draw on the next tranche may be granted if the transactions are intended to support a far-reaching programme to establish and maintain the stability of a member State's currency at a realistic rate of exchange. The same criteria are applicable to the final tranches, when the member State must show that it is following or intends to follow the appropriate policies.(2)

Since 1952, ordinary drawings on the Fund have been subject to what are known as stand-by arrangements, which guarantee the borrower a line of credit for a given length of time. Whether or not the arrangement is made depends, of course, on a prior agreement between the Fund and the borrower State on the appropriate nature of the latter's domestic policies.(3) Later, the Fund was to require every drawing request or stand-by arrangement to be accompanied by a "letter of intent" from the

(1) Address to the annual meeting of the Board of Governors (September 1951). This statement coincides with United States pressure for the adoption of anti-inflationary policies in Western Europe.

(2) J. Gold, "...to contribute thereby to...development...: aspects of the relations of the I.M.F. with its developing members", Columbia Journal of Transnational Law (Fall,1971) p. 10.

(3) Emil G. Spitzer, "Stand-by arrangements: purposes and form" in: The International Monetary Fund 1945-1965: Twenty years of international monetary co-operation (Washington, I.M.F., 1969); Joseph Gold, "The law and practice of the I.M.F. with respect to stand-by arrangements", International and Comparative Law Quarterly (London, 1963), vol.12,pp. 1-30

member giving a detailed description of the policies it proposed to adopt.

By the end of the 1950s, it had thus become recognized that one of the principal functions of the Fund was to promote financial and monetary stability in its members although that function had not been envisaged in its Articles of Agreement. This function expanded with the elaboration of policies for drawing on credit tranches, since the purpose of those policies was to guarantee the "revolving" nature of the Fund's resources. The increasingly strict conditions attaching to the use of the later credit tranches was an essential feature of those policies.(1) Moreover, the Fund was able to act as lender of last resort, especially after the quotas were increased by 50 per cent in 1958.

E. The system of conditionality and the Fund's facilities

The Fund's realisation of the specific problems faced by the LDCs led it in 1963 to propose the creation of a compensatory financing facility (CFF) for the benefit of all its members. The facility is intended to enable countries that have experienced losses in export income to draw up to 25 per cent of their quotas with the Fund.(2) However, the drawings were submitted, inter alia, to a set of conditions that being specific were hard to test, namely, that the member should co-operate with the Fund(3) "in seeking solutions to the balance-of-payments problems".

Other decisions on drawing policies were taken after 1963 and modified to some extent the conditions imposed on the use of the Fund's resources. Conditionality was eliminated in practice when use of the Fund's resources did not go beyond the first

---

(1) J.K. Horsefield and G. Lovosy, "Evolution of the Fund's policy on drawings" in: J.K. Horsefield, *The International Monetary Fund 1945-1965*, *op.cit*.

(2) M. Fleming, R. Rhomberg and L. Boissonneault, "Export norms and their role in compensatory financing", *I.M.F. Staff Papers* (1963); J.C. Thornton, "Compensatory and supplementary financing as aid for development", *The Journal of Law and Economic Development* (1969).

(3) IMF, *Selected decisions of the Executive Directors*, third issue (Washington, D.C., January 1965), p. 42.

tranche.(1) The new factor was the introduction of various new "facilities"or amendments to those already in existence.

Listed in chronological order, the following facilities were either introduced to supplement the CFF after 1963, or else were enlarged:

1966: enlargement of the CFF
1969: financing of buffer stocks (FBS)
1974: the oil facility
1974: establishment of the extended facility
1975: further expansion of the CFF
1976: establishment of the Trust Fund
1977: supplementary financing facility or "Witteveen facility".(2)

As a result of these changes, the maximum drawing entitlement, which in most cases was expressed in terms of tranches (25 per cent of quota) was added, in the form of "floating tranches", to the ordinary tranches to enable the normal credit limit of 100 per cent of quota (equivalent to 200 per cent of the Fund's holdings in the currency of the country) to be exceeded.

Each decision leading to the creation or extension of a facility subjects drawings to certain specific conditions.(3)

Over the years, the "normal" ceiling for drawings on the Fund has been raised several times either through the "floating" arrangement referred to above or through the extension of facilities or additions to them as a percentage of the quota. In the last few years, an increasing number of countries have been tending to exceed the normal holdings of the Fund in their currencies (200 per cent of quota).

(1) IMF, Selected decisions of the International Monetary Fund, eighth issue (Washington, D.C., 10 May 1976). The decision concluded with these words: "The performance and time-limit clauses will be omitted from stand-by arrangements that do not go beyond the first credit tranche".
(2) "Access to the resources of the IMF is adapted to the financing needs of its members", I.M.F. Survey (10 December 1977), pp. 381-385; U. Sacchetti, "Reshaping the international monetary and financial arrangements", Banca Nazionale del Lavoro Quarterly Review (June 1977), No. 121, pp. 139-171.
(3) For further details of these facilities, see IMF, "Selected decisions of the International Monetary Fund", and in particular "How countries draw on resources of the Fund under the five tranches and under permanent facilities", I.M.F. Survey Supplement on the Fund (Fall 1976) and "Countries with payments need now use a variety of special purpose facilities", IMF Survey, September 18, 1978.

Abstract From: Financial Facilities of the Fund and Their Conditionality

Tranche policies

Reserve tranche
Condition - balance of payments need.

First credit tranche
Program representing reasonable efforts to overcome balance of payments difficulties; performance criteria and installments not used.

Higher credit tranches
Program giving substantial justification of member's efforts to overcome balance of payments difficulties; resources normally provided in the form of stand-by arrangements which include performance criteria and drawings in installments.

Extended facility

Medium-term program for up to three years to overcome structural balance of payments maladjustments; detailed statement of policies and measures for first and subsequent 12-month periods; resources provided in the form of extended arrangements which include performance criteria and drawings in installments.

Compensatory financing facility

Existence of temporary export shortfall for reasons beyond the member's control; member cooperates with Fund in an effort to find appropriate solutions for any balance of payments difficulties.

Buffer stock financing facility

Existence of an international buffer stock accepted as suitable by Fund; member expected to cooperate with Fund as in the case of compensatory financing.

Supplementary financing facility

To be used in support of programs under stand-by arrangements reaching into the upper credit tranche or beyond, or under extended arrangements, subject to relevant policies on conditionality, phasing and performance criteria.

Source: IMF Survey, September 18, 1978.

TABLE 1

Possible Cumulative Purchases

(per cent of quota)

	Present Position		With Supplementary Financing Facility	
	Tranche policy	Extended facility	Tranche policy	Extended facility
Reserve tranche	25.0	25.0	25.0	25.0
Credit tranches				
4 x 25	100.0[1]	--	100.0	--
1 x 25	--	25.0	--	25.0
Extended facility	--	140.0	--	140.0
Supplementary financing[2]				
1 x 12.5; 3 x 30	--	--	102.5	--
With extended facility	--	--	--	140.0
SUBTOTAL	125.0	190.0	227.5	330.0
Compensatory financing	75.0	75.0	75.0	75.0
Buffer stock financing	50.0	50.0	50.0	50.0
CUMULATIVE TOTAL[3]	250.0	315.0	352.5	455.0

(1) This limit may be waived by a decision of the Executive Board.

(2) In special circumstances a stand-by arrangement may be approved for purchase beyond these limits and the normal limitations under tranche policy; in such cases purchases will be made with supplementary financing. The amount of such additional finance will be quantified in relation to a member's need and the adequacy of its program.

(3) In addition, some members have used oil facility drawings. The average use by those members was equal to 75 per cent of quota.

Source: IMF Survey, September 18, 1978.

The Deputy Director-General of the Fund, Mr. William B. Dale, tried to give the impression, in a statement at the fourth UNCTAD session in Nairobi in 1976, that the creation of these facilities was proof of the interest taken by the Fund in the LDCs.

The real situation is rather different. First, Australia and New Zealand - both developed countries - made use of the CFF in 1976 and, secondly, the facilities were apparently not planned by the Fund itself, with the exception of the oil facility.(1) U. Sacchetti believes that the pressure exercised by the LDCs on the developed countries in the last ten years or so was partly redirected by the latter towards international institutions in the shape of proposals for the establishment of special arrangements(2) in the framework of institutions in which the developed countries retain the decision-making power.

F. The evolution and role of drawings on credit tranches and facilities.

The relative importance of drawings on the different facilities and on credit tranches can be measured in various ways. For instance, in 1976, drawings on the CFF alone (2,272 million SDRs) were almost as large as those on the ordinary tranches (2.5 billion SDRs). If the drawings on the first credit tranche are excluded, the volume of conditional drawings will be seen to lag far behind that of drawings on facilities and the first tranche. Again, at the end of 1976, current drawings other than those against ordinary credit tranches represented 76 per cent of total drawings. Lastly, and this is a fundamental point, only five LDCs went over the first tranche and made conditional drawings (those over and above that tranche). As a group, the LDCs used the net IMF credits up to 72,4 per cent of their total quotas, "of which 10.3 per cent were drawn in the ordinary tranches".(3)

The jump in drawings in the credit tranches in 1977 was mainly due to drawings by the United Kingdom (1 billion SDRs in January 1977) and South Africa.(4)

The increasing volume of drawings against the different facilities, particularly by the LDCs, can be illustrated by comparing the net credits (after repurchases) given under these

(1) Including, of course, the new Witteveen facility. However, this does not invalidate the argument, because the aim of the latter was to transfer part of the OPEC surplus to the developed market economy countries.
(2) See the Horowitz proposal to the World Bank. U. Sacchetti, "Reshaping the international monetary and financial arrangements", op.cit., p. 150.
(3) U. Sacchetti, op.cit., p. 150
(4) IMF, Annual report 1977, p. 52.

facilities with the total net credits granted by the Fund (in millions of SDRs). The data are approximate, and marginal errors may have been made because repurchases were taken into account in the calculations, but it is the general trend which is important.

TABLE 2

Total Net Credits and Net Credits under Facilities

(in million of SDRs)

Year end	Total net credits	Total net credits under "facilities"	B as a per cent of A
	A	B	
1963	1,061.7	76.0	7.2
1964	1,398.6	76.0	5.4
1965	2,959.7	87.3	2.9
1966	2,900.5	95.6	3.3
1967	2,292.9	261.2	11.4
1968	3,435.9	251.3	7.3
1969	3,698.5	226.5	6.1
1970	3,011.3	132.0	4.4
1971	1,113.2	146.3	13.1
1972	1,057.3	403.6	38.2
1973	992.6	473.9	47.7
1974	3,617.4	2,255.5	62.3
1975	7,314.6	5,193.4	75.1
1976	12,565.1	9,512.9	75.7

Source: IMF.

It will be noted that the percentages for 1974-1975 and, to a certain extent for 1976 as well, reflect gross drawings against the oil facility, but even if this is taken into account the trend is still clear: with the exclusion of drawings on the oil facility from columns A and B, the percentage was 47.9 in 1976.

It is the fact that the LDCs have made virtually no use of the higher credit tranches that has led some people to accuse the Fund of abdicating from its role as the watchdog of monetary and financial stability.

In actual fact, the LDCs endeavoured to evade the conditions imposed by the Fund which hampered them in choosing the development policy they themselve wanted by resorting to a number of facilities and, whenever they could, to the big private capital markets as well, in spite of the adverse effects on their level of external indebtedness.(1)

The role assumed by the private banks in development financing on the terms and within the time-limits set by the Fund is a major structural factor in the existing international economic order. In 1977, the LDCs' public debts as a result of their borrowings on financial markets (mainly commercial banks) amounted to 30 per cent of the total public debt as against 12 per cent in 1967.(2) These figures do not include their debts to private bodies not guaranteed by the host countries or short-term loans (with a maturity of not less than a year). Global estimates in the first category give a figure of 25 billion dollars (3) and a similar amount for the second category.(4)

The fact that the commercial banks gave the LDCs credit enabled the minority of LDCs with an average income to maintain their levels of imports and reserves irrespective of world economic trends resulting from the policies put into effect by the developed market economy countries, and hence to avoid the painful process of adjustment entailed by drawings on the higher credit tranches of the Fund. The marked development of capital flows from the Eurodollar market testifies to the importance of the role played by the commercial banks.(5)

(1) See W.H. Bruce Brittain, "Developing countries external debt and the private banks", Banca Nazionale del Lavoro Quarterly Review, No. 123 (December 1977), pp. 333-349; Paul M. Watson, Debt and the developing countries: new problems and new actors, Development Paper, No. 26, Overseas Development Council, (1978).

(2) Watson, op.cit., p. 35.

(3) The World Bank calculated the non-guaranteed debt at the end of 1976 to be 20-22 billion dollars. World Debt Tables: External Public Debt of L.D.C.s, Doc.EC-167/77, vol. 1 (31 October 1977), p. 47.

(4) With non-guaranteed bank loans for more than a year taken into account, the proportion of the debt owed to financial markets is over 40 per cent.

(5) UNCTAD, The external debt problems of developing countries. Private bank loans to developing countries, Doc.TD/B/AC.2/2 (Geneva, 20 June 1977); Irving Friedman, The emergency role of private banks in the developing world (New York Citicorp., N.A., 1977).

The medium-term loan commitments published by the banks rose by 19% in 1977, reaching a total of 34.1 billion dollars. The fact that this rate of growth is well below the rate for 1976 seems to indicate that the private banks have run out of steam as far as that which concerns the financing of the needs of the LDCs.

The average maturity of Euro-currency loans to all borrowers was nine years in 1973. In 1974 the global maturity was down to 8.1 years, while the average maturity dropped sharply to 5.5 years in 1975, rising slightly to 5.9 years for 1976. The shortening of maturities which may be observed in the averages occurs also when one considers the weighted average annual maturity applicable to borrowings by certain LDCs. For example, the weighted average maturity of borrowings made in 1973 by Brazil, Korea and Mexico was 11.9, 18.8 and 11 years respectively, against an unweighted average of 8.3 years for all other borrowers. In 1976 the weighted average of maturities applicable to the same countries fell to 7.1, 5.1 and 4.6 years.[1]

TABLE 3

Average maturity[a] of credits in Euro-currencies granted to the different groups of countries. (in years)

	1973	1974	1975	1976
Non-oil exporting developing countries	10.2	8.5	5.4	5.8
Oil exporting developing countries	9.8	8.0	5.6	6.3
Developed countries	8.3	8.0	5.7	6.2
Countries of southern Europe	9.5	8.3	5.5	5.3
Socialist countries of eastern Europe	9.0	7.7	5.5	5.3
Miscellaneous	5.6	5.0	5.0	5.0
Total	9.0	8.1	5.5	5.9

Source: UNCTAD Secretariat
(a) Weighted average for borrowings made within a country and for borrowings made within a group of countries.

The shortening of maturities of recent borrowings (despite the temporary improvement which took place in 1977)[2] is disturbing because it inevitably means that amortization payments

(1) UNCTAD, op.cit., p. 12.
(2) "International Banking and Capital Markets: main findings summarized", *IMF Survey*, 31 July 1978, p. 226.

on old and recent loans have to be concentrated in a short period. The UNCTAD Secretariat has also estimated that 78% of the unamortized borrowings made during the period 1973-1976 will reach maturity during the five years from 1977 to 1981.

The major role played by the commercial banks in the financing of the long-term development policies of the LDCs in a rapidly changing environment is reflected in the growing share of external profits in total bank profits during this decade. In the case of the United States, for example, the contribution of international operations to the total net profits of the twelve biggest American banks rose from 17% in 1970 to 48% in 1975.(1) And the contribution of the LDCs to bank profits is substantial.(2)

G. The spread of conditionality to the banking system: cooperation between IMF and the private banks.

In 1976 the Manufacturers Hanover Trust asked the IMF to study the possibility of setting up a formal system within which the private banks and the Fund would co-finance balance-of-payments deficits. Is this a step towards an expansion of the Fund's system of conditionality, which, in recent years, has come under pressure because of the appearance of other sources of financing? The answer is in the affirmative, because, as stated in 1977 by John Haley, the lending decisions of the commercial banks are closely linked to the operations of the IMF.(3) He noted that an informal procedure for coordination (parallel financing) already existed for certain countries. Under this system negotiations between international banks and borrowing States take place at the same time as those between the State and the Fund. The granting of the "private loan package" is made conditional on the results of the negotiations between the Fund and the borrowing State. Turkey in 1976-77 gave a perfect illustration of this type of existing coordination.(4) The commercial banks had made prior agreement with the Fund an essential condition for the granting of a large loan to finance the disequilibrium of the Turkish balance of payments. The Fund's views as to the appropriateness of the policies of the borrowing State greatly influence the banks' decisions. However, the accumulation of borrowings from the banks by certain LDCs in recent years makes the banks apprehensive about defaults; since they have no way of imposing "appropriate policies" on the borrowing States and

(1) Thomas H. Hanley; United States multinational banking: current and prospective strategies, New York: Solomon Brothers, June, 1976, p. 13.
(2) Bruce Lisman: "Loans to LDCs: who owes what to whom?", Drexel, Burnham, Lambert Newsletter, table 1, April 1977, New York.
(3) J. Haley: "Commercial banks and the IMF", International finance, 5 September 1977. Statement made by the vice-chairman of the Fund before the US Senate Subcommittee on international finance.
(4) Pamela Clarke, "Will the banks and the Fund make an example of Turkey", Euromoney, September 1977, pp. 16-23.

in any case are far less well informed about those countries than the Fund, the banks are only too happy to have the Fund apply the discipline which they themselves cannot impose.(1)

The information required by the banks concerns, inter alia, the past and present performances of the national economies, and data about the volume and structure of external debt.

The banks' demands are often presented in what has come to be known as the institutionalization of the "oil imports" loans of the LDCs - the only institution involved being the IMF.(2) This institutionalization of commercial loans to the LDCs was clearly defined by D. Rockefeller on the eve of the Annual Meetings in September, 1977.(3)

The increase in the number of bank loans made conditional on a prior agreement between the Fund and the borrowing State - Peru, Portugal, Sudan, Zaire, Egypt - indicates that, after several years of relative relaxation, the Fund's system of conditionality is now applied by the IMF itself but on behalf of the major Western banks.

---

(1) Henry C. Wallich: "The critical information gap", Euromoney, November 1977, p. 11.
(2) "The IMF wields sudden new power", Business Week, March 28, 1977, p. 86.
(3) "The problems that concern David Rockefeller", Euromoney, September 1977, p. 10.

II. THE SYSTEM OF CONDITIONALITY OF THE INTERNATIONAL MONETARY FUND IN PRACTICE: ITS RECORD AND AN INTERPRETATION.

During the fifties and sixties the Fund's activities mainly involved the implementation of stabilization programmes in Latin America. These programmes and the lessons which have been drawn from them have been the subject of great controversy.

A. IMF stabilization programmes in the LDCs.

Although the Fund publishes neither its reports nor the letters of intent addressed to it, the existence of the latter is well known and one can form an idea of what they contain.(1) Some of them have even been published by the countries involved, or as a result of public controversy as in the case of Peru or Egypt. Moreover, the Fund has regularly published articles in its "Staff Papers" and in "Finance and development" which give an idea of its attitude towards stabilization policies.(2)

1. The IMF stabilization programme: a model

As we have already seen, the field of IMF stabilization programmes goes well beyond anything envisaged in its Articles of Agreement. An early expansion of the Fund's activities involved the credit policies of the central banks, control of which was regarded as one of the best ways to solve balance of payments problems. The Fund's programme also goes into an immense amount

(1) A fictitious letter of intent with a good number of the regulations included in such a kind of document, is presented by J. Gold in The stand-by arrangements of the International Monetary Fund IMF, Washington D.C., 1970

(2) See, for example:
-"Have economists said their final word in the fight against inflation?", Finance and development n.3, 1963.
- U. Tun Wai: "The relations between inflation and economic development: a statistical inductive study", IMF Staff Papers vol 7, 1959-60.
- Gertrud Lovasy: "Inflation and exports in primary producing countries", IMF Staff Papers, vol 9,n 1, March 1968.
- Graeme Dorrance: "The effects of inflation on economic development", IMF Staff Papers, vol 10, March 1962.
- Hannan Ezekeil: "Monetary expansion and economic development", IMF Staff Papers, vol 14, n 1, March 1967.
- S. Kanesa-Thesan: "Stabilizing an economy: a study of the Republic of Korea", IMF Staff Papers, vol 16, n 1, March 1969.
- Omotunde E. G. Johnson: "The exchange rate as an instrument of policy in a developing country", IMF Staff Papers, vol 23, n 2, July 1976.
- I. Bhatia: "Inflation, deflation and economic development", IMF Staff Papers, vol. 8, 1960 - 61.

of detail about policies on matters such as taxation and incomes and sometimes even agricultural policies, not to mention the traditional concerns of the Fund with exchange rates and trade restrictions. In the view of the Fund, financial and monetary stability cannot be ensured unless these problems are taken into account: stability, according to the IMF, is thus the required condition for development.(1)

The letter of intent which accompanies the stand-by arrangement contains, in particular, the promises made by the borrowing State in order to receive the assistance of the Fund. This letter includes matters such as: expansion of domestic demand, recourse of the public sector to the banking system, deficit in the governmental budget level of foreign reserves, credit to the private sector, fiscal policy, foreign indebtedness (public or with public guarantee), elimination of trade and payment restrictions, etc. On some of these topics, specific quantitative ceilings are established; on some others, policy descriptions are included. In all cases, the obligation of prior consultations with the Fund is also included. When the State under consideration fails to meet the conditions laid out in the letter of intent, the Fund reserves the right to withhold drawings under the stand-by arrangement.

While it is evident that the details of each programme vary, the nature of the policies which the Fund wants to see applied does not change, it is uniform. This uniformity can be briefly described as follows:(2)

i. The abolition or liberalization of exchange and import controls.
ii. Devaluation of the currency.
iii. The implementation of anti-inflationary domestic programmes, including:

Control of bank credit, higher interest rates and also possibly an increase in reserves.

Control of the State deficit, reduction of public spending, an increase in fiscal pressure and higher charges by public enterprises, the abolition of consumer subsidies.

Control of wage increases.

The dismantling of price controls.

iv. A better climate for foreign investment.

(1) Graeme Dorrance: "The effect of inflation on economic development", IMF Staff Papers, vol. 10, n 1, March 1962.
(2) Cheryl Payer, The debt trap, op.cit., p. 33.

The area of the Fund's programmes which has come in for the heaviest criticism has been the anti-inflationary policies of point 3. While those policies are important they must nonetheless be analyzed in the light of the first two points if they are to be properly understood. The liberalization of exchange and import controls means the abolition of measures within the LDCs designed to save foreign currency - which is paradoxical in a critical situation which is precisely the result of the shortage of foreign currency. As we have already seen, this objective of liberalizing exchange and import controls is contained in the Articles of Agreement of the Fund.

The second point - the adoption of a realistic exchange rate - is a corollary of liberalization. The increased demand for foreign exchange caused by the liberalization of imports and the abolition of exchange controls drives the price of foreign exchange up and that of the national currency down (devaluation). The Fund sometimes agrees that progress towards the ultimate goal should proceed by stages. Here again the paradox is that, in order to prevent devaluations which would give an unfair price advantage to the country involved, the Fund, over the last few decades, has more often imposed devaluations than it has objected to their use. Legally the Fund has no competence to force a devaluation on a country with an overvalued currency, but the body of jurisprudence created by the Fund in this sphere deserves special attention.

> Overvaluation as such is harmful to the country practising it rather than to other countries. What is harmful to other countries is the reduction of imports, and perhaps of capital outflows, which the country having an overvalued currency is obliged to bring about in order to obviate a chronic payments deficit that would exhaust its reserves.(1)

From a formal point of view, the Fund is concerned only with exchange rates and exchange restrictions. But trade policies are so closely linked to exchange rate policies that the Fund has extended its competence to the sphere of "restrictions maintained for reasons of balance of payments" (restrictions on imports and even protective tariffs).(2) This explains why measures designed to liberalize trade often appear in stand-by arrangements.

(1) J. Marcus Fleming (Fund official): The International Monetary Fund, its form and function, Washington DC, IMF, 1964, p. 13, quoted by C. Payer, p. 35.

(2) The International Monetary Fund 1945-65: twenty years of international monetary cooperation, by Keith Horsefield, op.cit., vol.1, p. 469.

As C. Payer rightly observes, the Fund [1] is not empowered, either legally or formally, to dictate changes in the domestic policies of member States. In practice it does so in the majority of drawings beyond the first tranche. The anti-inflationary policies which it emphasizes fundamentally affect the sovereignty of States, as they involve the level and structure of public spending, taxation and credit policy. In practice, because of the emphasis on inflation, the Fund's "package" is known as the "stabilization programme".

It must be noted that the anti-inflationary policies are the necessary corollary of exchange rate stability - the prime objective of the Fund.

> Though the Fund is not entitled to object to a proposed devaluation because it is rendered necessary, for example, by a too inflationary domestic policy, this does not mean that the international system authorized by the Fund Articles is one in which countries are free to pursue whatever internal financial policy they please so long as they refrain from imposing restrictions but keep their external accounts in balance by continually developing their rates of exchange. On the contrary, as I pointed out earlier, it is an explicit purpose of the Fund not only to eliminate exchange restrictions but also to promote exchange stability. These two objectives, however, cannot be simultaneously attained unless countries so conduct their fiscal and monetary policies as to maintain a reasonable degree of international financial stability.[2]

Moreover, the Fund's hostility to inflation is strongly influenced by its impact on foreign investment. This point of view is clearly stated in the following passage from an article by the Director of the Financial Division of the Fund.[3]

> One of the differences between stable and inflationary economies is that investors can make reasonable estimates of future money costs and money receipts in the stable countries, while this is impossible once inflation is well underway. Further this uncertainty bears most heavily on foreign investors. All the chances in the lottery are stacked against them. International investment is in any event

(1) C. Payer: <u>op.cit</u>., p. 35.
(2) M. Fleming: <u>op.cit</u>., p. 9.
(3) Graeme Dorrance: "Rapid inflation and international payments", <u>Finance and Development</u>, vol.2,n 2, 1965, p. 67.

> likely to be more hazardous than domestic investment. With inflation, the hazards involved in movements of international capital are increased by the unpredictability of exchange rates. Not only are the net returns on investment in the developing country's currency unknown, but the returns in terms of the investor's currency are even more speculative. So it is not surprising that foreign investors tend to shy away from countries with extreme inflation, and that such countries tend to cut themselves off from access to resources from abroad.

Mr. Dorrance then goes on to describe the consequences of inflation:

> Strong inflation usually leads to the adoption of payments restrictions. Among the first candidates for restriction are payments on foreign capital... thus the almost inevitable exchange restrictions brought about by strong inflation do more than discourage capital from hastening development. They so frighten capital away, and even encourage repatriation, that measures designed to conserve foreign exchange may in fact dry up a country's resources and dissipate its reserves.(1)

A certain number of letters of intent actually include explicit conditions regarding foreign investment. The letter of intent addressed to the IMF by the previous government of Ceylon, and which was published in Colombo in 1970, contains the following clause: "review the moratorium on repatriations and adopt measures to improve the climate so as to attract official and private capital to Ceylon".(2)

Lastly, aid is in fact an important component of the Fund's stabilization package: first of all it serves to encourage the borrower country to abide by the conditions which, it is agreed, are necessary to the success of the package itself. The dismantling of exchange controls aggravates the shortage of foreign exchange, even when accompanied by the whole range of devaluations and stabilization policies. The purpose of aid, then, is often to finance the liberalization of imports. To sum up: the liberalization of exchange controls and import controls lies at the very heart of the Fund's stabilization programme and is in keeping with its Articles of Agreement. All

---

(1) op.cit., p. 69.

(2) N.M. Perera, Minister of Finance, Budget speech 1970-71, Department of Government Printing, Ceylon, 25 October 1970, p. 7.

the other components of the "package" - exchange rate adjustment, stabilization measures and the financing of the deficit through foreign aid - are merely measures needed to offset the predictable adverse effect of liberalization on the balance of payments. All these components are necessary. If one of them - for example, anti-inflationary measures - is missing, devaluation will be more pronounced. In other words, the system is logically interdependent and consistent with the basic objectives of the Fund.

2. Some actual cases of stabilization through the IMF programme in the LDCs.

a. Indonesia

After a trip to Indonesia in November 1964, a United States economic mission recommended the granting to that country of a five-year aid programme amounting to 390 million dollars, to which the United States would grant 233 million dollars. The mission had arrived in Indonesia precisely when the Indonesian government was in the midst of mounting economic difficulties.(1) The aid was made conditional on Indonesia's acceptance of cooperation with the IMF, which sent a mission to Jakarta to help the Indonesian government draw up a stabilization programme. In the opinion of the Fund the plan had to include a balanced budget, cuts in military spending, a policy of tighter credit, the devaluation of the rupee, the setting up of a system of multiple exchange rates (the first steps on the road to a single and stable exchange rate), and the abolition of price controls and public subsidies. The Indonesian stabilization plan prepared by Sutikno Slamet, former Executive Director of the IMF for Indonesia, was itself based on the Fund's philosophy: austerity in public spending, tight control of the money supply, an increase of between 400% and 600% in public charges, a de facto devaluation of the rupee, and the release of foreign exchange for an urgent import programme. The Fund and the Indonesian government could not agree, however, on the abolition of price controls.(2) This demand provoked a chorus of indignation: the Fund was accused of wishing to add to the sufferings of the people, while the stabilization plan was denounced as being contrary to the approach known as the "economic declaration", adopted in March 1963, according to which the rescue operation

(1) J.A.C. Mackie: Problems of Indonesian inflation, Ithaca, Cornell Modern Indonesia Project, 1967, pp. 39-40

(2) J.A.C. Mackie: op.cit., pp.39-40

was to be based on increased production.[1] The Fund's demands were interpreted as clear evidence of the dangers of dependence on foreign aid. President Sokarno declared that such criticism was a sign of profound economic patriotism[2] and in 1964 Indonesia left the IMF.

After the coup d'état of 30 September 1965 the official ideology radically changed its view of the role of foreign capital in economic development: emphasis was now laid on monetary measures designed to achieve stabilization, foreign borrowing and the need to attract foreign investors. A certain number of Indonesian economists trained in the United States challenged the idea that the production-based approach could resolve Indonesia's economic problems and that monetary measures should be rejected as being anti-patriotic and against the interests of the people. The idea that investment credits are not inflationary provided that they are linked to a growth of production is based on the unproven hypothesis that such a growth of production can keep pace with the increase in money supply. Even if such increases in production were to occur, their benefits would be swept away on the monetary tide unless measures were taken to reduce the money supply. In other words, it makes sense to embark on a productive effort only if stability has first been recovered through appropriate monetary measures.[3]

The conditions for complete cooperation with the Fund had thus been fulfilled. This school of thought became the official doctrine of Indonesia in July 1966, when the Congress adopted the new economic guidelines which abandoned the production-oriented approach. Those guidelines emphasized the need for a new code for foreign investment and the application of a drastic austerity programme. Over the short term all efforts should be concentrated on stabilization, infrastructure and export promotion. In September the Western creditors of Indonesia met in Tokyo to assess the new Indonesian plans. An agreement was reached on the principle of rescheduling the Indonesian debt, and the IMF announced its willingness to provide assistance to the country.

---

(1) Laksanakam Serempak Bentja, National Front Program, p. 16 quoted by B. Weinstein, p. 223.
(2) For more details on the conflict between the IMF and Indonesia, see: Bunnell: The Kennedy initiatives in Indonesia, pp. 308-441, Ph.D. dissertation Cornell University 1969.
(3) This group of economists included, *inter alia*, Mohamed Sadli, Ali Wardhana and Widjojo Nitisastro. For more details see: F.B. Weinstein, Indonesian foreign policy and the dilemma of dependence, *op.cit.*, p. 226.

The Indonesian recovery plan is contained in the regulations of 3 October 1966. The following main points are particularly worthy of note: a balanced budget, tight monetary policy, the end of public subsidies, raising of public charges, free play of market forces, simplification of export formalities, higher taxation.[1] The remarkable move, on 3 October 1966, was the transfer from the Central Bank to the open market, of the function of allocating foreign exchange as well as an important rise in the interest rates.

Lastly, the IMF limited public spending to a maximum of 10% of the national income, while at the same time imposing quantitative norms for the availability of bank credit. The last vestiges of the multiple exchange rate system were abolished in 1970. In order to complete the liberalization of the economy the major Western powers and Japan set up the Intergovernmental Group on Indonesia, which was to coordinate balance-of-payments assistance,[2] whereas the performance of the economy was assessed for the Group by the World Bank.

b. Chile

Inflation in Chile has grown virtually unchecked since the end of the 19th century. After the Second World War numerous stabilization programmes were set up, though their effects were at best ephemeral.[3] In 1963 and 1964 the Alessandri government tried to control inflation with the aid of the IMF (standby arrangements) and the IDA. The strategy applied was to keep earnings below the rise in the cost of living and to limit public spending. Its failure was evident. In 1963 and 1964 growth barely exceeded the increase in the size of the population; the rate of inflation in 1964 was 38%.[4] The year of the Frei government provided an opportunity to apply to Chile a stabilization scheme adapted to the conditions of a LDC. The first aim of the Frei government was to eliminate inflation which could not be eradicated by the purges applied by preceding governments.

(1) The new regulations on economic and financial policies, Jakarta, Department of information, 1966, and Bulletin of Indonesian economic studies, n 5, October 1966, pp.3-11. Also: B. Glassburgner: "Indonesian economic policy after Sukarno", in The economy of Indonesia: selected readings, B. Glassburner (ed.), Cornell University Press, 1971.
(2) G.A. Posthumus: The intergovernmental group on Indonesia, Rotterdam University Press, 1971.
(3) David Felix: "Structural imbalances, social conflict and inflation: an appraisal of Chile's recent anti-inflationary effort", Economic development and cultural change, January, 1960.
(4) T. Hayter, op.cit., p. 120.

Those in power had now realized that stabilization without growth was politically impossible. Although stability could be restored over the short term, it was nonetheless politically out of the question. Moreover, those in authority argued that boosting growth without stability would bring back Chile's old problems - particularly that of limited supply (agricultural and export difficulties). The Frei government claimed to take account of certain "structuralist" conclusions.(1)

In fact the Frei government shared the point of view of the monetarists, which was that the reason for the past failure of stabilization programmes had been the political inability of the governments then in office to carry them through. The originality of the Frei Plan lay particularly in the fact that it carefully determined the impact of readjustment by compensating the workers for rises in the prices of agricultural produce through a relatively liberal wage policy and a series of monthly devaluations of the escudo, the rate of exchange for which had been rising, in order to avoid sudden price increases. As far as growth was concerned, the Plan stressed the need for an expansion of copper exports by means of an agreement with the companies (the State providing, through foreign borrowings, the bulk of the financing), for industrial projects through the public body known as the Corporación de Fomento, and for agrarian reform. The result of this policy - which benefited from the high price of copper - was a reduction of unemployment, and, by means of fiscal, price and wage policies, what the fund described as a "profound redistribution of income". The redistribution of income actually went further than originally intended. This explains why some people viewed it as a triumph for the structuralist arguments; such a view is, however, exaggerated, as the 1967 drop in the price of copper partly accounts for the halt in the slowdown of inflation which had been taking place since 1965. In 1966 copper prices went up by 25% and the volume of exports by one third. Increases in the price of copper made up more than half of the increase in tax revenues. It is true that this experience does strengthen the structuralist argument whereby the difficulties of the LDCs are largely the result of fluctuations of prices and exports and the deterioration of their terms of trade, particularly in the fifties.

Like all governments trying to achieve stabilization, the Chilean government was to encounter the difficulty of stepping up investment. In 1967 the existing capacity of the private

(1) This point was the subject of an important controversy. IDA argued that this Frei Plan merely strengthened the conventional anti-inflationary policies of the Alessandri government, while others claimed that it was an embodiment of the analysis made by O. Sunkel: "Inflation in Chile: an unorthodox approach", <u>International economic papers</u>, n 10

sector was being fully utilized and new investment was needed to bring about expansion. In the opinion of the Government officials the limits of taxation had been reached and even exceeded. Thus, they proposed, as a way of boosting investment, that part of the adjustments in wages attributable to cost-of-living increases should be paid in the form of shares in the new industries built by the State. The government maintained that, given the choice between reducing the level of investment and cutting taxes in the private sector (thus encouraging investment), it was adopting the solution most likely to reduce the concentration of industrial power. This measure ran into opposition from the left, which saw in it a manoeuvre designed to lower the living standards of the workers by paying them with worthless bits of paper. In the political storm which followed, this policy was abandoned. In order to keep inflation down the government imposed in 1968 restrictions on public spending and on the expansion of credit, thus abandoning most of the "expansionist" aspects of the 1965 stabilization plan.

c. Colombia

Late in 1966 Colombia's relations with the international agencies reached a state of crisis. On 29 November the President of the Republic announced that he would not devalue the peso and that he was breaking off negotiations with the Fund. At the same time he announced that foreign exchange transactions were henceforth to be handled by the Central Bank and that import controls were being restored.

Since 1965 Colombia had been deep in economic trouble. A 365 million stand-by arrangement over one year had been signed with the IMF.(1) In November the government reached an agreement with the Fund on a series of measures which were supposed to lead to a more favourable investment climate without jeopardizing the country's long-term development objectives. These measures included, inter alia, the liberalization of imports, the regular adjustment of the exchange rate, the formation of a budget surplus through a squeeze on public spending, a ceiling on advances to the State from the Central Bank and tighter credit. Wage increases were to depend on increases in productivity. The IMF took the additional precaution of requiring Colombia to accept for one year certain balance-of-payments objectives. The Fund reserved its right to suspend or not to renew the stand-by arrangement if these latter objectives were not met.(2)

(1) Margaret Garritsen de Vries: The International Monetary Fund, 1966 - 1971: the system under stress, vol. 1, p. 358, IMF 1976.

(2) T. Hayter: Aid as imperialism, op.cit., p. 109

By autumn 1966 Colombia had fulfilled all the Fund's conditions concerning the limitation of the money supply, restrictions on public spending and wage increases, the blocking of credit for coffee production, the liberalization of imports and the devaluation of the currency for certain categories of merchandise. The only problem was that earnings generated by coffee exports were well below the levels expected, because of the reduction of the volume exported and of prices. Moreover, within the framework of the liberalization of imports, Colombia could not use the tied aid provided by IDA. Consequently the balance-of-payments objectives agreed upon with the Fund were not achieved. A joint mission of the IMF, the World Bank and the permanent mission of US IDA decided on the spot that a devaluation was necessary, and the Fund made that devaluation the condition for the renewal of the stand-by agreement. Colombia refused again. The New York commercial banks stopped their loans. The United States, to which Colombia had turned for help, made it known that no loan programme could be considered without a prior agreement between Colombia and the International Monetary Fund. In these circumstances President Lleras announced on television on 29 November 1966, that he was rejecting the devaluation advocated by the Fund and abandoning the policy of import liberalization.

It is interesting to note that there was almost unanimous criticism of the way the IMF had informed the Colombian government of its decisions and the offhand manner in which it treated national sentiment on the issue. According to some sources close to US IDA the hard line taken by the Fund was due to strong pressure from the United States and the World Bank. It was apparently the World Bank, in fact, which had put pressure on the New York banks to make them break off relations with Colombia.(1) The big question which remains is the reasons for such insistence on a devaluation which was clearly not necessary; it was felt more or less generally that Colombia's balance-of-payments problems could be overcome within the existing stand-by arrangement, which Colombia wanted renewed, if the commercial banks had not stopped their operations and US AID its aid programme.(2) Since the crisis was due to a drop in export earnings, the application of the compensatory finance facility set up in the Fund in 1963 was fully justified. This view was, moreover, shared by a number of IDA officials. From the political point of view the devaluation would have been extremely difficult in a country where the spectre of devaluation was highly unpopular

(1) T. Hayter: _op.cit_., p. 112.
(2) Lauchlin Currie: _Accelerating development, the necessity and the means_, McGraw Hill 1966. -Richard L. Maullin: _The Colombia-IMF disagreement of November-December 1966: an interpretation of its place in Colombian politics_, Memorandum R.M.-5314-R.C. Rand Corporation, 1967.

and had, in the past, given rise to general strikes. The arguments used by the Colombian government were the following: first, unless a government is politically strong, no economic policy can succeed; decisions concerning devaluation are seldom purely technical. Secondly, the remedy of successive devaluations did not seem to have proved its merits in the past as far as Colombia was concerned. Each one of them had caused price rises together with the consequential wage increases, but had not promoted exports, as the price of coffee was set outside Colombia, and there was little room for the diversification of exports.(1) Moreover, the existence of import controls - particularly those applied to luxury goods since 1945 - made it unlikely that the devaluation might lead to a reduction in imports.

According to Kindelberger the conflict could have been avoided because President Lleras was not opposed to a devaluation, but merely wished to define its timing and duration so as to minimize its economic and political repercussions.(2) Although they were recognized as being responsible for the attitude adopted by the IMF, the IDA and the World Bank decided to act as "mediators". In April 1967 an agreement was announced: it was a compromise between the positions of Colombia and the international agencies.

Colombia obtained a stand-by arrangement; it did not commit itself to the liberalization of import controls, so those controls remained in force. Colombia agreed to float the peso; it did not commit itself, however, on the exact extent of the float, which remained subject to controls. A basic agreement was also reached on a tightening of credit, but it did not contain specific norms about the money supply.

The Colombian case clearly illustrates what happens when the exchange rate is made the prime consideration, without regard for problems of long-term development or of supply as well as pressure for the application of policies which might have a bad effect over the long term.

(1) In December 1962 the peso was devalued by 34%; the following year the rate of inflation was 45%, compared to 6% during the five preceding years. See: United Nations Economic Commission for Latin America. Economic Survey of Latin America, 1964, New York 1966, p. 55; and Eduardo Wiesner Duran: "Las modificaciones del tipo de cambio y los niveles domésticos de precios", in La Nueva Economía, Bogotá 1966.

(2) C.K. Kindelberger: Liberal policies versus controls in the foreign trade policies of developing countries, AID Discussion Paper n: 14, Washington 1967.

d. Brazil

Like Indonesia, Brazil is considered to be one of the great successes of the Fund. After a heavy dose of stabilization policies applied by the military Government in the mid-sixties, Brazil recorded remarkable rates of growth for ten years. Before the military coup d'état of 1964, AID and the World Bank had stopped all loans or aid to the Goulart Government on the pretext that its economic and social policies (including, among other things, the redistribution of income in favour of the workers and the beginnings of land reform) were leading to "chaos", with soaring inflation rates and the likelihood of a default on the Brazilian debt. After the coup d'état, negotiations were reopened with international institutions. As in the case of Indonesia, two stages can be distinguished in the history of the Fund's relations with Brazil. The first ended with the 1964 coup d'état and the second began on that date and continues until now.

i. Relations with the Fund up to 1964

During the 1950s, Brazil achieved high rates of growth. However, this growth had its Achilles heel both economically and politically. C. Payer notes[(1)] that Brazil at that time exemplified "the inability of a democratic political system to withstand the difficulties caused by foreign exchange constraint".

The boom of the 1950s was based on two economic factors which were bound to be short-lived: the first was a chronic trade deficit, financed by external investment and borrowing, and the second was inflation. In the Brazilian context, every anti-inflationary programme had severe repercussions on production, especially in view of the important political implications of inflation. The reconciliation of the interests of the capitalists, the coffee planters, the middle classes and the urban workers through increases in the money supply made it possible to avoid the necessity of choosing with regard to the real distribution of resources.[(2)] The boom continued, inflation apparently provided the "fuel" to drive the machine, and the only contraints were the external account and the censure of creditor countries. All the stabilization programmes were brought to a halt for fear of a depression and political problems. Café Filho's attempt to put an end to inflation and satisfy Brazil's creditors by a drastic credit squeeze[(3)]

(1) C. Payer: The debt trap, op.cit., p. 146.
(2) Celso Furtado, Economic growth of Brazil, (Berkeley: University of California Press, 1963); Thomas E. Skidmore and Albert Fishlow, Politics in Brazil 1930-1964: an experiment in democracy, (Oxford University Press, 1967).
(3) Celso Furtado, op.cit., pp. 158-161.

aroused the hostility of industrial circles. The Minister of Finance had to resign and the credit restrictions were lifted. The new Minister launched a programme to reform the exchange system with the assistance of the IMF. This system would have left the coffee exporters with all their income intact, but Café Filho was unwilling for the State to sacrifice its control over the allocation of foreign exchange. Brazil's external indebtedness continued under the Kubitschek Government, but in 1958 it had to seek an agreement with the Fund on stabilization measures in order to be eligible for an American loan of $300 million. The President of the Bank of Brazil refused to accept the credit restrictions proposed for fear of a depression in the private sector. Moreover, the Kubitschek Plan to remove structural bottlenecks would have been threatened by the reduction of public expenditure recommended by the Fund. After several months of negotiation with the Fund, President Kubitschek broke them off and replaced the American loan by others obtained from private banks.[(1)] President Quadros inherited the crisis with the Fund and an external debt that was uncertain of being serviced and, because of this, was forced to accept the terms set by the Fund. The exchange system was modified, and foreign exchange auctions were replaced by a simpler system of dual exchange rates which, in the case of Brazil, was tantamount to a devaluation of the cruzeiro by 50 per cent,[(2)] an arrangement which was condemned by Vice-President Goulart. Inflation persisted in spite of the domestic credit restrictions and Quadros, who was criticized on all sides, abandoned the Presidency. His departure was interpreted in come circles as a victory for the economic pressure exercised by the United States, which had also been dissatisfied with Quadros' policy of non-alignment.[(3)]

President Goulart inherited a situation compounded of fifteen years of inflation and borrowing. The Ministers of Planning and Finance, Celso Furtado and Santiago Dantas, were made responsible for drawing up a stabilization plan in a development context. The aim of the Plan was to increase the growth rate of the economy and to carry out land and tax reforms while reducing inflation. Debt servicing amounted to 45 per cent of Brazil's income, and the rescheduling of the external debt became a matter of vital importance. Devaluation took place

(1) Thomas E. Skidmore, op.cit., pp. 174-182 and footnote 40, p. 386.
(2) New York Times (16 March 1961).
(3) New York Times (27 August 1961).

in January 1963 and subsidies in imports of wheat and oil were once again removed to satisfy the Fund. Restrictions on the budget deficit, on the expansion of credit and on wage increases completed the anti-inflationary programme.

However, this programme too ran into serious difficulties. The Government was unable to withstand the demands for wage adjustments, although this was the key factor in the stabilization plan and the prerequisite for the granting of external loans. The United States thereupon withdrew its offer of a loan of $398.5 million. With the rate of inflation at 100 per cent annually, and the passage of the new law on the repatriation of profits,[(1)] the United States became openly hostile. The subsequent announcement of the start of land reforms and the nationalisation of the oil refineries put an end to all hopes of aid and paved the way for the coup d'état of 1964.

ii. Brazil and the Fund after 1964

The avowed objective of the new regime was to restore order and efficiency to the economy.[(2)] A follower of the monetarist school - O. Campos - was put in charge of the Brazilian economy.[(3)] He established a three-point programme: to reduce the rate of inflation; to reimburse part of Brazil's external debt and to restore the level of reserves. He was obviously successful on all three counts. The rate of inflation was reduced to 40 per cent in 1966, a certain proportion of the external debt was repaid and reserves increased with the expansion of coffee exports. The main weapon of the new Government in achieving that result was deflation. Stringent credit controls were introduced, and the budget deficit was cut, while wage increases were kept well below the rise in the cost of living. Industry was severely affected and investment slumped although selective credit measures and fiscal incentives were adopted. Unemployment rose to alarming proportions, while real wages dropped by about 25 per cent in 1966. In order to encourage agricultural production, the State abolished price

(1) Under this law, the repatriation of profits was henceforth to be based on the capital originally invested in Brazil and not on the profits which had been reinvested locally instead of being repatriated.
(2) The IMF report for 1968 states: "In the middle of 1964, the Brazilian authorities put into effect a programme of policies to reduce the rate of inflation and lay the bases for stable economic growth", p. 77.
(3) See his contribution on this point in Latin American Issues: Essays and Comments, ed. by A.O. Hirschman, The Twentieth Century Fund, New York, 1961.

controls on food, thus making the poor living conditions of the urban workers even worse. Social questions were disregarded altogether.

The important United States programme of loans to the Federal Government was used to impose their exchange, tax and budgetary policies through the medium of the Multilateral Inter-American Committee of the Alliance for Progress. This aid was contingent on the results of an evaluation every four months of Brazil's performance.(1) The suspension of aid for six months in 1967 indicates that the evaluation was no formality, since at the time the United States and the Fund considered the restrictions imposed by Campos to be inadequate.

The suspension of American aid(2) was motivated by the replacement of Campos by A. Delfin Netto, who was no advocate of the Campos Plan but the spokesman for industrial circles in Sao Paulo, who were irritated by the restrictions on credit. It was nevertheless at that time that the Brazilian "miracle" began, with the progressive relinquishment of the Fund's orthodox remedies.

e. Ghana

The case of Ghana has many features in common with that of Indonesia. In the first stage, Ghana pursued a socialist-type course of development under the leadership of President Nkrumah, one of its main features being strong State control over the national economy. The direct involvement of the State in the system of production took place through the establishment of new public enterprises.(3) Nkrumah's main idea was that development represented a discontinuous process of structural transformation, in which the distortions created by the colonial

(1) Carlos Diaz Alejandro, "Some aspects of the Brazilian experience with foreign aid" in: Trade, Balance of Payments and Growth. Papers on International Economics in honor of C.P. Kindleberger, ed. J. Bhagwati and North, Holland, 1971), p. 452.

(2) Jerome Levinson and Juan de Onis, The alliance that lost its way (Quadrangle Books, Chicago, 1970), p. 209. See also A. Fishlow, "Some reflections on post-1964 Brazilian economic policy" in: A. Stepan (ed.), Authoritarian Brazil: origin, policies and future,(New Haven: Yale University Press, 1973), pp. 69 - 118.

(3) Tony Killick, Development economies in action: a study of economic policies in Ghana, (Lomdon Hememann, Nairobi).

economic structure based on primary production would be rectified. A big push was required to bring about the necessary transformation through the medium of a "massive planned industrial undertaking".(1) The effort that it entailed necessarily widened the gap between domestic savings and investment, especially at the beginning of the 1960s. In order to deal with the foreign exchange constraint, Ghana launched itself on a systemic policy of obtaining suppliers credits and loans from commercial banks, with the result that the external debt mounted rapidly.(2) In 1965, Ghana was no longer able to pay its debts, and the Fund was called to the rescue to reschedule Ghana's medium-term debt and provide financial aid. However, in view of the magnitude of the stabilization measures demanded, President Nkrumah broke off negotiations. In February 1966, he was overthrown by a military coup d'état.(3) The Committee of National Liberation was allergic to socialism and set as its first objective the restoration of "efficiency". The other main objectives of the CNL were as follows:(4)

- the rectification of the external imbalance;
- the halting of inflation;
- increased employment
- the return to a balanced budget.

On the advice of the Fund, orthodox monetary and tax policies were put into effect, public investment was cut back, and import restrictions were introduced while the accent was laid on the private sector. A number of public enterprises were returned to that sector while the others were reorganized, and over-employment in the public sector was reduced.(5)

---

(1) K. Nkrumah, _Africa must unite_, (International publishers, New York, 1972) (first published in 1963), p. 167.
(2) Ahmad Naseem, _Deficit financing, inflation and capital formation. The Ghanaian experience 1960-1965_, Weltforum Verlag, Munich, 1970.
(3) D. Rimmer, "The crisis in the Ghana economy", _Modern African_ Studies (May 1966); A. Douglas Scott, _Growth and Crisis: economic policy in Ghana 1946-1965_, Ph.D. thesis, (Harvard University, 1967).
(4) "Rebinding the national economy", (March 1966) _N.L.C._, Accra; "New deal for Ghana's economy" (July 1967), _N.L.C._, Accra.
(5) On the role of the Fund in this, see Ruth First, _The barrel of a gun: political power in Africa and the coup d'état_ (Penguin, 1972), pp. 169-224 and 376-407.

Although some external aid was given, the rescheduling of the external debt was a laborious process and entailed no fewer than three Conferences (1966, 1968 and 1970). In actual fact, its rescheduling added considerably to Ghana's burden.

TABLE 4

Financial Assistance to Ghana, 1966-71 (millions of cedis[a])

	1966	1967	1968	1969	1970	1971[j]
1. Contractual medium-term debt obligations (P+I)[b]	46	72	80	64	52	39
2. Negotiated medium-term debt obligations (P+I)[c]	5[h]	12	41	22	27	20
3. Debt relief (1-2)	41	60	39	42	25	19
4. Net credit from IMF[d]	58	26	15	-7	-32	-40
5. Gross long-term aid commitments[e]	28	69	89	79	73	n.a.
6. Gross long-term aid receipts[e]	14	14	61	71	75	54
7. Gross total assistance (3+4+6)	113	100	115	106	68	33
8. Actual debt service payments (P+I)[f]	24	19	36	30	30	35
9. Net total assistance (7-8)	89	81	79	76	38	-2
10. Net long-term aid (6-8)	-10	-5	25	41	45	19
11. External indebtedness[g]						
(i) medium-term	509				394[i]	
(ii) long-term	130				338	
(iii) total	639				732	

Notes:

a. Calculated throughout at ₵ 1.28 = $1.00

b. P+I signifies principal plus interest payments

c. As negotiated at 1966,1968 and 1970 debt conferences. Not all these payments were actually made, however, due to delays in completing bilateral agreements and various disputed items. Due to imperfect data these are order-of-magnitude estimates only.

d. Excludes use of Special Drawing Rights.

e. 'Receipts'differ from 'commitments' because of delays in utilizing the aid in question.

f. These figures relate to servicing of medium and long-term debts. They are derived from balance of payments data but, because of various inconsistencies in the data, are subject to substantial margins of error.

g. This excludes indebtedness to the IMF and various short-term debts. At the end of 1970 there were arrears on current payments of about ₵72 million and various other obligations (chiefly arrears on profit and dividend payments) amounting to about ₵70 million. The 1966 figures refer to the position as at 24 February 1966. The 1970 statistics relate to the end of the year.

h. Estimated actual payments in 1966.

i. Certain disputed debts have been excluded and arrears in certain other payments have been added.

j. Most of the estimates for this year are provisional.

SOURCES: Bank of Ghana balance of payments estimates and various unpublished sources.

Two years after the fall of Nkrumah, and after two reschedulings, Ghana was forced to pay the equivalent of 40 per cent of its original debt in supplementary interest as the price of the rescheduling. At the third conference on the Ghanaian debt in 1970, the Minister of Finance, J.H. Mensah, stated that because of the draconian conditions imposed on his country by its creditors, per capita income in Ghana had fallen from $261 in 1965 to $239 in 1969, and that 30 to 35 per cent of the population were unemployed.(1) In a statement made to The Guardian, Mr. Mensah said that "it was impossible to make any Ghanaian believe that public money should be used to pay debts rather than for the development of the country".(2)

B. The effects of the policy of conditionality of the Fund in the LDCs: balance-sheet and interpretation

The case studies described above show that the International Monetary Fund, like other institutions for which development is nevertheless a primary objective, emphasized in the 1950s and 1960s the need to achieve or maintain monetary and financial stability and the measures required to do so. Its stabilization programmes seldom bore fruit and their cost in most cases continued to increase while the private sector preferred to hold a watching brief. The main results of these programmes were usually recession and the emergence of political crises leading to a change of government and the abandonment of the programmes. The Fund has argued in return that the failure of a few programmes has often been attributable to a lack of will and determination in applying the monetary and financial stabilization measures, which continue to be the prerequisite for growth. Growth is therefore simply the outcome of the stabilization policies adopted once the price equilibrium disturbed by the actions of the previous government has been re-established.

1. The repercussions of the Fund's programme on the LDCs

A number of repercussions have been recorded, which are often common to all the countries concerned.

a. The fall of the economic growth rate

With a few exceptions, the stabilization programmes have led to a decline in the growth rate, which has sometimes dropped to zero, and on occasion to negative per capita income growth in periods of stabilization. Apart from the countries reviewed

(1) J.H. Mensah, "Some unpleasant truths about debt and development", Development Dialogue (Uppsala, 1973), N. 1,p. 16, and The state of the economy and the external debt problem (Ghana Publishing Corp., Accra, April 1970).
(2) The Guardian (19 July 1971).

above, this trend has been noted in other LDCs as well.[(1)] The fall in the growth rate is, as we have seen, politically untenable in the majority of cases because it reduces employment and enhances income inequalities.

b. The inefficacy of devaluation

Devaluations of the exchange rate cannot be a fitting response to structural balance-of-payments deficits. A number of experiences have shown that the price-elasticity of demand is usually low, and so is the price-elasticity of exports, when exports consist of one or two items, for which domestic consumption is no more than a small proportion of total production,

(1) On this point, see:
- A.D. Scott, "The role of the International Monetary Fund in económic development" in: Columbia Essays in international affairs: the Deans Papers, (Columbia University Press, 1967);
- S. Marley, "Inflation and stagnation in Brazil", Economic development and cultural change (January 1971), p. 19;
- I. Eshag and R. Thorp, "Economic and social consequences of orthodox policies in Argentina in the post war years", Bulletin of the Oxford Institute of Economics and Statistics (February 1965);
- Braun and L. Joy, "A model of economic stagnation: a case study of Argentina", Economic journal (December 1968);
- George Jackson Eder, Inflation and development in Latin America: a case history of inflation and stabilization in Bolivia,(Michigan University Press, 1968);
- Couriel y Lichtemsztejn, El F.M.I. y las crisis económica nacional (Montevideo, 1968);
- Rosemary Thorp, "Inflation and orthodox policy in Peru", Bulletin of the Oxford Institute of Economics and Statistics (August, 1967);
- Enrique Sierra, Tres ensayos de estabilizacion en Chilé (Editorial Universitaria, Santiago: 1969).

- Alejandro Foxtey, "Stabilization policies ans stagflation. The cases of Brasil and Chile", in World Development, Vol 8, p.887-912. 1980.

or when there are structural bottlenecks on the supply side.(1)

When domestic absorption is fairly considerable and supplies cannot be increased for structural reasons, devaluation is bound to have an inflationary effect on the devaluing country(2) and in the absence of controls, the same period is liable to favour imports that are not necessary for development. In the past, the LDCs have tried to overcome the difficulties caused by the unfavourable income and price elasticities for their major exports and essential imports by adopting a multiple exchange rate system. This enabled them to make distinctions between imports and exports with different price elasticities of demand and supply, in accordance with their importance for the development process, but this practice was condemned by the Fund.(3)

(1) Lance Taylor "Efeitos a curto prazo de desvalorização cambial sobre os economías semi-industrializadas. Um paso para frente, dois para tras", Pesquisa e planejamento económico, vol.8, No. 2, August 1978, pp. 425-437; C.A.R.N. Joyarajah, "Problems and prospects with respect to the international monetary system, implications of alternative exchange rate systems for developing countries", Bulletin, Central Bank of Ceylon (December 1969); R.N. Cooper, "Currency devaluation in developing countries", Essays in international finance,No. 86 (Princeton, June 1971); W. Konig, "Multiple exchange rate policies in Latin America", Journal of Inter-American Studies (1968), p. 10; René Patricio Villareal, "El desequilibrio externo en el crecimiento económico de México: su naturaleza y mecanismo de juste óptimo, devaluación, estabilización y liberación", El Trimestre Económico, vol. XLI (u), No. 164, p. 794.

(2) On this question, see Harold B. Dunkerley: "Exchange rate systems in conditions of continuing inflation - lessons from the Colombian experience" in: Development policy, op.cit., (ed. G. Papanek), pp. 118-174; G. Meynard and W. Rijckeghem, "Stabilization policy in an inflationary economy: Argentina" in: Development policy, op.cit.,pp.206-235; Carlos Diaz Alejandro, Exchange rate devaluation in a semi-industrialised country: the experience of Argentina 1955-1961, (Cambridge, Mass., 1965), pp. 2 et seq.; G. Corea, "The international monetary system and the developing countries", Staff studies, Central Bank of Ceylon (September 1971).

(3) M. de Vries, "Multiple exchange rates, expectations and experiences", IMF Staff Papers, (Washington D.C.: 1965), p. 12.

The liberalization of imports lessened the protection of local industry against imports of manufactures, and when combined with devaluation, can lead to the denationalization of the production system and the distortion of investment options, thereby weakening national planning.

Lastly, devaluation is apt to redistribute national income in favour of the affluent, and this, together with the abolition of price controls, increases the already considerable disparities between social classes.(1)

The emphasis laid on the reduction of the budget deficit entails cuts in public expenditure, especially on the programmes that are regarded as "non-productive" or of a "social nature", i.e. the social services, wages, housing, health, education and land reform. The Fund has seldom if ever viewed agriculture except from the angle of the supply of agricultural commodities and not in terms of a general improvement in rural living conditions.

c. The increase in unemployment and under-employment

The Fund's stabilization programmes tend to reduce the volume of employment in both the private and public sectors. In the latter, a number of workers have been laid off as a result of the credit restrictions, and fewer job opportunities have been created. In the public sector, pressure is also applied to reduce the work force. The World Bank, for instance, obtained from the Brazilian military government the promise of a reduction of about 70,000 workers in the railroads.(2) This sacrifice of employment to stability is particularly serious for the developing countries, which are already facing acute problems of under-utilization and of non-utilization of human resources.(3)

(1) Carlos Diaz Alejandro, op.cit.; Celso Furtado, Diagnosis of the Brazilian crisis (University of California Press, Berkeley, 1965); W. Beer, Industrialization and economic development in Brazil (Irwin, 1965); R.F. French-Davis, Políticas económicas en Chile: 1952-1970, Ceplan (Ediciones Nueva Universidad, 1973).
(2) T. Heyt: op.cit., p. 169.
(3) D. Morawetz: Employment implications of industrialization in developing countries", Economic Journal, Sept. 1976; No. 335, pp. 491-543.

d. <u>Redistribution of income in favour of export-related sectors</u>.

One of the basic ideas of the economists of the IMF is that inflation is caused most frequently by excessive demand and that measures must thus be introduced to liberalize the price system, which is severely affected by restrictive policies. Such measures are in fact intended to lead the economy to a natural balance of the price system, the objective being to bring about a contraction of internal absorption. The relative reduction of demand takes place through a smaller adjustment of earnings in the light of the inflation rate of the previous calendar year, a drop in public spending, control of the money supply and the devaluation of the national currency, which is a way of transferring income from certain parts of the internal sector to the export sector. Argentina after Peron's fall in September 1955, is a fine example of the application of such a policy, on the advice of the Fund and after the policy of industrialization and import substitution followed between 1943 and 1955. To put an end to chronic exchange rate crises the new production policy was encouraged by means of devaluations of the currency and the gradual elimination of price controls. Relative prices should reflect opportunity costs. In this case it was intended to increase the exportable output of the rural sector.[1]

The return to a price system which was closer to the social opportunity costs had considerable impact on income distribution; producers of exportable goods were favoured, while those sectors which produced for the local market were put at a disadvantage. Generally speaking the policy was carried out at the expense of urban wage-earners. The share of wages in the GNP dropped sharply from 41.8% to 37.7% for 1956-61, while real earnings had already begun to decline in the early 50s from their levels in 1948-49. The drop of wages in the share of earnings, and for the majority of the workers of real earnings, gave rise to the serious social and political difficulties which occurred in Argentina from the late 50s onwards and to a large extent accounts for the mediocre performance of the Argentine economy since that time.

(1) Carlos F. Diaz Alejandro: <u>An interpretation of Argentine economic growth since 1930</u>. Parts I and II. Yale University Economic Growth Center. Center paper No. 101, p. 168.

e. The drop in public investment and investment in general

The experience of a certain number of countries of the Third World makes it clear that expansion does not, in most cases, follow measures of stabilization and incentives designed to "reorient" the productive sector of the national economy. A decline in public investment, and of investment in general, seems to be a constant factor of such a policy. In Chile, for example, gross investment represented more than 10% of the annual GNP in 1955, the year in which the stabilization programme was applied; one year later, gross investment was well below 10% of the GNP.[(1)] At the same time, consumption increased its share of the GNP, thus showing how little downward elasticity this function has in the developing economies.

In the same way, there was a drop in public investment in Argentina during the above-mentioned period, from an average of 14.0% in the period 1950-55 to 12.7% between 1956 and 1963.[(2)] This reduction was due to the drop in tax revenues and in the savings of public enterprises, which were hit hard by measures of monetary restriction. In this way the budgetary deficit between 1956 and 1963 reached unprecedented levels, raising the rate of inflation in Argentina from 16% during the period 1943-1955 to 33% between 1955 and 1964.[(3)]

The budgetary deficit was made worse by the deficits of the public enterprises, but particularly by the periodic massive devaluations which caused wild fluctuations in relative prices.

f. The financial strangulation of small and medium enterprises and the denationalization of the national economy.

The credit restrictions involved in the programme of the Fund have as their first consequence the virtual stifling of small and medium enterprises, whose financial base makes it impossible for them to stand a chance against the subsidiaries of the multinational corporations.

(1) Enrique Sierra: Tres ensayos de estabilización en Chile, Editorial Universitario, S.A., 1969, p. 65.
(2) Consejo Nacional de Desarrollo. Plan nacional de desarrollo 1965-1969. Buenos Aires, 1965, Table 9.
(3) Richard Mellon: "Exchange policy: Argentine", in Development policy: theory and practice. Edited by Gustav F. Papanek, (Harvard University Press 1968) pp. 183 and 186.

This accounts for the close link which may be observed in the Third World countries between the strangulation or the absorption of small national enterprises and the denationalization of the national economies. Such a trend is moreover promoted by the periodic devaluations of the national currencies, which means that entire sectors of the local industry become available at bargain prices.

Towards the end of the 60s foreign investors were seen to be participating very strongly in the industrial sector of the countries of Latin America. In the most dynamic industries of that sector (which really determine the distribution of income) foreign participation was in most cases predominant. In Brazil, for example, out of 500 large manufacturing enterprises studied at the end of the sixties, 112 were subsidiaries of foreign enterprises which controlled 37% of the share of the sample considered.[1]

In Argentina more than half the earnings of the 50 principal enterprises of the country were derived in 1961-66 from the foreign-owned subsidiaries which had been favored by the "opening" in 1955.[2]

In Chile a study made in the sixties shows that 50% of the foreign subsidiaries occupied a monopoly or duopoly position on the national market, while 36.4% operated a system of oligopoly.[3]

The most serious of the findings of all these studies was that these investments were concentrated in the most dynamic sectors and that many of these subsidiaries had been formed from local firms which had been forced into bankruptcy or absorbed.

g. The aggravation of foreign debt.

It has been claimed that the Fund did not consult member-States as to the best way of reducing imports and strengthening their economic self-sufficiency, but that it taught them the best way to qualify for new credits.[4]

(1) F. Fejnzylber: Sistema industrial y exportación de manufacturas, análisis de la experiencia Brasilera. CEPAL. November 1970, p. 35.
(2) Aldo Ferrer: "El capital extranjero en la economía argentina". El Trimestre económico, No. 150, April-June 1971, p. 313.
(3) CORFO: Comportamineto de la principales empresas industriales extranjeras acogidas al DFL 258 Publication No. 9-A/70, Santiago.
(4) Inter alia: C.Payer: The debt trap, op.cit., p.46. "The international Monetary Fund and Indonesian debt slavery", in Remaking Asia: essays on the American uses of power, Mark Selden (ed), (New York Pantheon Books, 1974) pp. 50-70.

In actual fact, when a country finds itself in a situation of crisis because of its inability to service its debt, the Fund adopts a positive attitude by convening a conference with a view to rescheduling the country's external debt, if that country agrees to apply the economic programme elaborated by the services of the Fund.

For the debtor country the rescheduling of debt is actually preferable to "new aid", since the money intended for the immediate servicing of the debt can be used on other more urgent objectives. Apart from which, new aid is in most cases tied to purchases in the donor country. The problem is that the rescheduled debt still has to be repaid later on, while the interest due on the deferred payments is added to an already heavy burden of debt service. The country then finds itself once again potentially in a situation of chronic payments crises, alternating with apparently endless "salvage operations". A vicious circle has thus been achieved. Acceptance of the Fund's programme becomes the prior condition for subsequent debt relief, and the aid can never be fully repaid: the debtor country is increasingly subject to the will of the creditor country, while the burden of interest payments heavily mortgages any possibility of development. The examples of Ghana, Peru and Zaire illustrate this situation, as do the other cases analyzed previously. In such a situation, it is no exaggeration to say that the debtor countries are doomed to perpetual under-development. The cases analyzed fully reveal the close links between the World Bank, the United States IDA and the Fund, and their convergent views on the kind of policies which are suitable for the developing countries.(1)

These institutions advocate a liberal form of economic organization and compliance with the international rules of the game as defined by the Western countries. Their conduct is based on acceptance of the existing international order and the national framework of the capitalist economy. This explains why neither the Fund nor the World Bank are able to accept

(1) For a systematic treatment of this point, see:
- Andrzej Krassowski, The aid relationship, ODI 1968, ch.1;
- I Friedman, Some aspects of the economic philosophy of the World Bank (September 1968);
- R. Mikesell, Public international lending for development, Random House, New York 1966;
- E.S. Mason, Foreign aid and foreign policy, New York 1964;
- Harry Magdoff: The age of imperialism: the economics of US foreign policy, Monthly review press, 1969, ch. 4;
- E. Gmening: United States foreign aid in action: a case study, US Senate, Washington, 1966, pp. 102-114.

changes in the developing countries which run counter to the present pattern of international trade, or which call into question private investment and debt servicing. The principle of free enterprise and respect for the machinery of the market and also for private property (domestic and, above all, foreign) lie at the heart of the conduct of those institutions.

2. The failure of the IMF policies in the developing countries: an interpretation.

The Fund's efforts in the fifties and sixties were concentrated mainly in Latin America. It is therefore not surprising to learn that the first opposition to the programmes of stabilization came from a group of economists known as the "structuralists", most of whom belonged to the Economic Commission for Latin America (ECLA). In the opinion of the "structuralists" the deflationary policies of the Monetary Fund or their "monetary variant" did not eliminate the basic causes of inflation. The only way to do this and to restore stability was to make appropriate structural changes, including, inter alia, the development and the reorientation of production and a measure of redistribution of income. The origin of inflation in the developing countries should be sought, inter alia, in the inadequate growth of food supplies resulting largely from the rigid system of land tenure and the export of primary products.

The Fund's emphasis on the liberalization of trade and monetary and fiscal measures had proved to be unsuitable for the developing countries, on account of the structural problems confronted by them.[1]

(1) The main "structuralist" writings, apart from those already quoted, are:
- Dudley Seers: "A theory of inflation in under-developed countries based on the experience of Latin America", Oxford economics papers (June 1962);
- Raul Prebisch: "Economic development or monetary stability: the false dilemma", UN Economic Bulletin for Latin America, March 1961;
- ECLA, Inflation and Growth: a summary of experiences in Latin America, UN Economic Bulletin for Latin America, February, 1962;
- O. Sunkel: "El fracaso de las políticas de estabilización", El Trimestre económico, October, December 1963;
- David Felix: "Structural imbalances, social conflict and inflation: an appraisal of Chile's recent anti-inflationary effort", Economic development and cultural change, January 1960.
- Jorge Del Canto: "America Latina: desarrollo y estabilizacion economica", El Trimestre económico, No. 119, July-September 1958.

Weakness of price and income elasticities and thus of import demand for the commodities which make up the bulk of the exports of the developing countries is one of the main structural problems mentioned above.(1) This aspect also influences to some extent the situation of the balance of payments of those countries, due to the fact that the potential rate of growth of any developing country depends substantially upon actual demand in the industrialized economies and upon the rate of growth of those economies. In such circumstances, the realization of the development objectives ipso facto involves the deficit of the external balance.

Besides their long-term impact on the rate of development of the developing countries, fluctuations in the level of economic activity in the industrialized countries may be a source of short-term instability for prices and incomes in the developing countries. A short-lived boom in the industrialized economies may produce a steep rise in short-term demand for commodities; regardless of any monetary or fiscal policy applied, the prices for those commodities and the foreign currency earned by them in the developing countries will rise accordingly.(2) Conversely, an excessive supply of those commodities leads to a contraction of prices and earnings, thus giving rise to fiscal and other types of problems for the exporting countries. (3) This being so, currency devaluation cannot provide a suitable remedy for balance of payments deficits which are of a structural nature.

Moreover, although bad fiscal, monetary and exchange rate policies can severely handicap economic development, good policies in these spheres are not of themselves a guarantee of growth. In its early stages, economic development often involves substantial structural changes in the economy. These changes also often lead to short-term bottlenecks in supply, which can only be remedied by profound modifications of relative prices, which are usually incompatible with stable price levels.

(1) For recent econometric evidence see: - Constantile·Glazakos: "Export instability and economic growth: a statistical verification", Economic development and cultural change, vol. 21, nb. 4, part 1 (July 1973), pp. 670-679. C.S. Voivodas: "The effecto of foreign exchange instability on growth", Review of economics and statistics, August 1974.

(2) G. Maynard and G. Bind: "International monetary issues and the developing countries: a survey", op.cit., p. 613.

(3) UNCTAD:"Some aspects of international economic stabilization growth, inflation and international prices", Report of the Secretariat, Doc. TD/B/712/add.2, July 1978.

Emphasis on monetary stability is an impediment to the required structural transfers of resources. Experience shows that a certain degree of inflation is an unavoidable consequence of the mobilization of local resources through development policy.(1)

---

(1) Besides those concerning Latin America see, inter alia, the results of the econometric studies prepared for India and the Philipines: "The inflation problem in developing economies: India and the Philippines", The Indian economic journal, vol. 23, October-December 1975, n. 2, pp. 144-166.

III. REFORM OF THE INTERNATIONAL MONETARY SYSTEM AND THE DEVELOPING COUNTRIES

A succession of plans were drawn up from the beginning of the sixties onwards, culminating in the setting up, early in 1970, of the Special Drawing Rights which were intended to serve as one of the central pivots of a new monetary system.

The inconvertibility of the dollar made reform urgently necessary. In September 1972 the Governors of the Fund presented a report on the reform of the International Monetary System.(1) Previously on July 26, the governors had appointed a Committee on the Reform of the International Monetary System and Related Questions, consisting of twenty members, under the chairmanship of Ali Wardhana, the Indonesian Finance Minister. Twenty deputy members made up the Committee of Deputies, under the chairmanship of Jeremy Morse, of the United Kingdom.

This Committee was given two years to devise a new monetary system. The crisis of the Western economies, and consequently of the world economy, was to throw international economic relations into disarray. On this committee the LDCs had nine seats. Its terms of reference were worded as follows:

> "to grant the fullest attention to the interdependence between monetary reform and provisions which have been or might be taken between countries, particularly those relating to international trade, movements of capital, investments or development aid, which could have an adverse effect on the attainment of the objectives of the Fund enunciated in the present or modified Articles of Agreement"

These very broad terms of reference enabled the Committee of Twenty to take up the whole range of problems having a bearing on the international monetary crisis, including those of trade and financing. Yet the Committee refused to do this, and decided to limit the consideration of "non-monetary" problems to questions of trade or financial policy directly involving the adjustment of balance of payments.

This meant that from the very beginning of the negotiations, the idea of remodelling the international monetary system in the light of the needs of development was discarded, in the sense that the problems of commodity trade or the exports of the LDCs, which have a decisive influence on the state of their external payments, were excluded from the areas to be analyzed.

The negotiations therefore quickly focussed on the traditional topics: adjustment of payments, and asymmetry between surplus and deficit countries, for example. It was quite evident that, as far as the committee was concerned, reform should only take the form of arrangements assuring a mutual balance of payments between developed countries in a system which had been severely upset by the floating of the dollar. Reform should not, under any circumstances, concern itself with the state of relations between the developed countries and the LDCs or, consequently, with the directly related questions of financing and payments.

For this reason the Committee of Twenty proposed anything but a detailed scheme for a new monetary system.(1) Moreover, the committee accounted for its decisions in the following terms:

> "...because of present uncertainties related to inflation, the energy situation and other unsettled conditions, it is not appropriate to attempt to define the full details of all aspects of the system".(2)

With regard to the process of adjustment, the committee singled out certain procedures capable of bringing about a rapid adjustment and reducing the asymmetry between the principal reserve center, the United States and the other developed countries by means of a set of objective indicators (in particular, reserves).

But the committee ignored the asymmetry which exists between the developed countries and the LDCs in respect of their ability to finance their deficits through the structural elements mentioned above. Accordingly, no concrete measures were proposed by the committee on this matter.

A. A past attempt at reform: the Kingston agreement.

The work of the Committee of Twenty led, at the meeting of the Interim Committee in Kington in January 1976, to an agreement on certain amendments to the Articles of Agreement of the Fund, mainly having to do with exchange rates and gold.

---

(1) See the Committee's Outline of Reform, in the IMF document entitled: International monetary reform: documents of the Committee of 20, Washington DC 1974, and in the IMF Survey, supplement to vol. 3, n. 12, 17 June 1974.
(2) Ibid., preface of the Outline of Reform.

One of the few points in the agreement which were of any interest to the LDCs had to do with the increase of the IMF quotas. The developed countries had suggested that all tranches (equal to 25% of a country's quota) should be increased in the same proportion. Their purpose in so doing was to maintain the structure of conditionality applied by the Fund, one quarter of the increase continuing to be available under the conditionality of the first credit tranche, and the other three quarters being subject to a more severe conditionality. On the other hand, the LDCs wanted an increase in the amount which could be used according to the conditionality of the first credit tranche.

Agreement was finally reached on a 45% increase in each credit tranche, and, consequently, on a broadening of access to credit tranches from 100% to 145% of the existing quota.

It will be noted, however, that this measure was only temporary and came to an end with the entry into force of the new Articles of Agreement in 1978. The figure of 145% therefore does not apply to the new quotas.(1)

As far as that which concerns the use of the resources of the Trust Fund(2), it was decided that gold would be sold over a period of four years starting at the beginning of 1976 and that any profits made above the official price of 35 SDRs, would be made availabe to members with a low per capita income (less than SDR 300 per year), provided that the policies pursued by those members met certain conditions and that they were experiencing balance of payments difficulties.

These are the sole concessions made to the LDCs in the new international monetary system. In the opinion of the Fund the specific interests and problems of the LDCs are sufficiently taken into account in the framework of the CFF. The Fund does not in any case view its role as the transfer of real resources to development: rather it is

> "to supervise the international monetary system and provide temporary assistance to members to enable them to cope with their balance of payments problems. This is why the Fund has always emphasized three aspects of its policy on the use of its resources: non-discrimination among its members, the temporary nature of such use and the conditionality to which it is subject"(1)

---

(1) J.J. Polak: The Fund after Jamaica, (Washington, 1977).

(2) One of the major decisions taken at Kingston being the reduction of the role of gold and thus the cession of the gold assets of the Fund on the basis of market prices, the profits thus made were paid into the Trust Fund.

It can be seen therefore, in the light of the results concerning monetary reform, that the position of the Monetary Fund - and, through it, that of the developed market economy countries - remains basically unchanged on the problem of conditionality in access to the resources of the Fund. If one had any doubts on the matter, the speech made by Mr. Witteveen on 8 May in London at the Euromarket conference [(1)] would soon dispel them.

> "Conditionality consists of the requirement that a country making use of the Fund's resources do so in the framework of an economic policy program aimed at restoring equilibrium in its payments position. It is based on the simple premise that in most cases it is unwise and, in the end, not even reasonable to finance balance of payments deficits over a protracted period of time without taking corrective measures. I must stress, however, that there are circumstances in which less emphasis need be placed on adjustment, and this the Fund fully recognizes. Balance of payments disequilibria of a relatively small magnitude are a case in point - a case that has been accommodated by the liberal policy, in existence since 1955, relating to the use of the Fund's resources that does not go beyond the first credit tranche. Payments difficulties caused by downward fluctuations in export earnings which arise from circumstances substantially beyond the control of a country and which can be expected with reasonable confidence to be reversed in a relatively short period of time are another case in point. The Fund has accommodated this case by introducing in 1963 a special facility (the compensatory financing facility) to finance such needs with minimal conditionality. A third case in point - and the most dramatic - was that arising from the oil price developments of 1973-74. The Fund then considered that the payments deficits resulting from these developments had to be sustained and financed for a while, in order to avoid reinforcing the recessionary forces in the world economy. The oil facilities (for 1974 and 1975) with their limited conditionality were therefore set up.

(1) J. Witteveen: "Fund's conditional assistance promotes adjustment programs of members", IMF Survey, 22 May 1978, p. 145-151.

Apart from these special cases, the dominant feature of all other Fund lending is the degree of contionality that is attached to it... I have said before that conditionality consists of the requirement that a country making use of the Fund's resources do so in the framework of an economic policy program aimed at adjusting its payments position. Clearly, the specifics of such programs will vary depending on factors such as the causes and the severity of the payments problem and the structure and institutional framework of the country's economy. While, therefore, no two programs will look quite the same, there are some common desiderata: the payments objective should not be achieved by tightening restrictions on foreign trade or payments - indeed elimination of any newly introduced restrictions and, if possible the reduction of the more long-standing ones should be sought nor should it be achieved by merely depressing domestic demand temporarily without providing for a redirection of resources to the foreign trade sector; nor, finally, should it be achieved by resorting to foreign borrowing on a scale and in a form that may not be sustainable in the medium term. The rationale of these essentials hardly needs elaboration. Improvement in the payments position achieved by any of the above means cannot be enduring.

Given these desiderata, the broad objective of corrective programs is twofold. First, recognizing that balance of payments problems often reflect national overspending, the programs seek to ensure that aggregate demand for goods and services is brought into line with output. For regulating aggregate demand, the appropriate amount of domestic credit expansion is determined in the light of the likely increase in aggregate output...during the program period, the price and balance of payments targets, and an assessment of the likely demand for money. Limiting credit expansion to an amount that is compatible with the targets usually involves adjustments in government budgetary policy since bank-financed government deficits are often a primary cause of excessive credit expansion. In a number of cases this kind of demand restraint, taken by itself, would cause a reduction in growth and an increase in unemployment. In such cases, therefore, the program will also have to emphasize the establishment of an appropriate structure of relative prices - a structure that would encourage savings and investment and a redirection of investment as needed for the purpose of strengthening the international competitiveness of the foreign trade

> sector of the economy. The prices that are most often relevant to the adjustment program are the exchange rate, interest rates, and producer prices of certain key commodities.
>
> The performance criteria in programs supported by the Fund usually relate to the broadest possible economic aggregates that would suffice for the achievement of the objective of payments adjustment. The Fund avoids taking a view on the appropriate distribution of the burden of adjustment as between various sections of society....If we in the Fund attach as much importance to conditionality as I have said we do, we are conscience-bound to be constantly on our guard to ensure that its broad philosophy continues to be rational, realistic...
>
> One criticism is that Fund conditionality, with its emphasis on the role of demand restraint in dealing with payments problems, always compromises the growth objective unduly and is particularly inappropriate in the context of the current world economic situation which calls for more expansionary policies...But for countries with persistent domestic inflation and large balance of payments deficits, expansionary policies are not appropriate, even in the present world situation. They must give priority to bringing inflation under control and reducing their payments deficits to manageable proportions. In doing so, growth may appear temporarily to be sacrificed. However, if an appropriately restrained demand policy is combined with a realistic price structure, as I have already indicated, adjustment can go together with, and even lead to, stronger and healthier growth.[1]

This very long and very clear extract shows that the position of the Fund on the problem of conditionality and, consequently, on what constitutes a healthy form of growth, has not changed fundamentally, even if, under the pressure of circumstances, it was possible to introduce certain arrangements into the system.

Today the Fund is still convinced that stabilization policies are the necessary condition for healthy growth. In a recent article published in the IMF Staff Papers Reichmann

(1) Address by Fund Managing Director H. Johannes Witteveen delivered May 8 in London before the 1978 Euromarkets Conference on "Financing the LDCs: The Role of Public and Private Institutions.", IMF Survey, 22 May 1978.

and Stillson,[1] on the basis of an econometric analysis of the 79 stabilization programmes which have had the benefit of IMF stand-by arrangements in the upper credit tranches during 1963-1972, find that in seven of the 19 programmes which did not reach the desired results, the failure was due to extraneous factors. In the opinion of the authors, the other failures can for the most part be attributed to the failure of policies through the budgetary results. About half the programmes had been designed to slow down demand, and are thus based on credit restrictions. About one third of the programmes made previsionsfor recourse to the adjustment of exchange rates or the adoption of measures involving the liberalization of exchange rates and trade. The others dealt with various problems: the rescheduling of external debt and the temporary shortfall of foreign exchange earnings.

The problem is that the managers of the Fund and, through them, the developed market economy countries, are convinced that the Fund is only and can only be an institution dealing with monetary questions and not with development. This reasoning is hard to accept. The intention is not to finance develoment while neglecting the monetary aspects. The real issue, as the UNCTAD Secretariat observes[2], is whether:

> "international monetary cooperation is to stop short of the point at which it deals effectively with payments problems faced by developing countries and springing from the workings of the international monetary system, as well as from the very structure of developing economies. Clearly, IMF cannot successfully discharge its functions as an international monetary agency if it ignores or neglects the fact that developing countries have a special need for payments support. It should therefore, be recognized that meeting this need, far from causing the Fund to abandon its role as a monetary agency, would help it to fulfill that role".

Moreover, by helping the LDCs to overcome the difficulties which emanate from the unfavourable economic situation in the major developed countries, the Fund would not be encroaching on the prerogatives of the development agencies. It would, in fact, become "a mechanism, which is necessary but lacking at present, to offset the asymmetries between developed and developing countries in the balance of payments adjustment process

---

(1) T.M. Reichmann and R.T. Stillson: "Experience with programmes of balance of payments adjustment: stand-by arrangements in the higher credit tranches", <u>IMF Staff Papers</u>, Vol. 25. n.2, June 1978, pp. 293-310.

(2) UNCTAD: <u>International monetary issues: problems of reform</u>, Doc. TD/189, para. 60.

and to protect the latter from economic maladjustments in the former".[1] By granting loner-term loans the Fund would make a more effective contribution to international monetary co-operation.

The pressure which has been brought to bear through the Group of Twenty-four with a view to reforming the conditionality of access to the Fund's resources has continued since the Jamaica agreement. At the meeting of the Interim Committee in April 1977 in Washington the developed countries stuck to their basic position of principle, which is that strict conditionality is necessary. One small step has nevertheless been taken towards the demands of the LDCs in the form of the addition of the word "adequate". A clear definition of the concept of "adequate conditionality" has been provided by J. Witteveen: "I would describe adequate conditionality as conditionality that can ensure effective adjustment, so that...current account deficits can either be eliminated or reduced to amount that can be financed in a healthy way".[2]

As a result of pressures exercised by the LDCs and following a recommendation of the Interim Committee, the IMF reviewed in 1978 its policy on conditionality. In March 1979, a decision was adopted by the Executive Directors introducing a set of amendments of very little significance.[3] They basically refer to:

- extension of the stand-by arrangements up to "but not beyond" three years, and only "in appropriate cases"; the normal period remaining at one year.

- exclusion of phasing and performance clauses for stand-by arrangements that do not go beyond the first credit tranche.

- introduction of some flexibility for the revision of performance targets.

At the same time, it is very interesting to note the language used in connection with the three pharagraphs of the decision adopted by the Executive Directors which are in contradiction with the past practices of the Fund. Practices which, in fact, are not modified either by these three paragraphs - of a mere declarative nature - or by the contents of the other parts of

(1) UNCTAD, <u>ibid</u>., paragraph 60.
(2) <u>IMF Survey</u>, 2 May 1977, p. 135.
(3) <u>IMF Survey</u>, 19 March 1979.

the decision.

> "Stand-by arrangements are not international agreements and therefore language having a contractual connotation will be avoided in stand-by arrangements and letters of intent."

> "In helping members to devise adjustment programs, the Fund will pay due regard to the domestic social and political objectives, the economic priorities, and the circumstances of members, including the causes of their balance of payments problems."

> "The Managing Director will ensure adequate coordination in the application of policies relating to the use of the Fund's general resources with a view to maintaining the nondiscriminatory treatment of members."

But before the increasingly strong pressures on the IMF with regard to the developing countries, the IMF was nevertheless led to acknowledge that when the Fund assists the member countries to elaborate their adjustment program, the latter will take into account their political and social objectives at the national level of their economic priorities and of the situation in which they find themselves, including the reasons for their difficulties in the balance of payments.

At the April 1979 meeting, the Interim Committee furthermore decided to bring about some adjustments in the system of conditionality. In this way, the normal duration of the stand-by arrangement (which is one year) could be prolonged if the Fund considers that this extension is necessary to allow this country to successfully apply its adjustment program, it can in certain cases be extended to a maximum of three years. In the end, the Interim Committee approved the preceding decision of the Fund which expressed the desire of the latter to take into greater consideration, the political and social objectives of the developing countries as well as their economic priorities.

But these good intentions are contradicted by the subsequent paragraphs of the same decision and in particular Paragraph 7 which stipulates that "the Director-General recommends to the Executive Board to approve the demand for the utilisation of the general resources of the Fund in the credit tranche formulated by a member country when it has established that the program presented by the member country is consistent with the previsions and policies of the Fund.

The Fund therefore remains attached to the concept of "viability of the social and economic policies" that it has defined as the main objective of its system of conditionality and the industrialised countries hardly appear to be inclined to relinquish this formidable instrument of control and orientation of developing economies which constitutes this system. The veritable war conducted by the IMF against Jamaica, especially between 1979-1980, and to a lesser extent against Tanzania give evidence of this concern and thus the limitations of the reform of March 1979.[1]

Moreover, the IMF has decided to extend from eight to ten years the maximum duration of the repurchase period, provided for within the framework of the extended Fund facility. This decision was welcomed by the Ministers of the Group of 24 at their Hamburg session in April 1980.

Meanwhile the Group of 24 are of the opinion that these conditions could be further improved, particularly by a new extension of the repurchase period and the grace period.

The World Bank for its part has set up a loan "facility" intended to facilitate "the structural adjustment".[2] According to the World Bank, the aim of this facility is to provide assistance to member countries which are at grips with serious difficulties in balance of payments or those which in the future, are going to experience deficits impossible to manage and due to external factors.

The Ministers of the Group of 24 recommeded at the Hamburg meeting:

> "that the new facility should permit to increase the financial resources, that it should be adjusted with a low conditionality, that it should be distinct from the Fund and that it should be based on the program drawn up by the developing countries themselves. It also considers that the particular situation of each country should be studied, case by case, and not in a rigid manner, and that the facility should not replace other types of loans not linked to the projects or project-loans. The Ministers proposed that the real annual rate of interest of the transactions of the World Bank should be increased from 5% actual rate to 10%. They also earnestly recommended that the total of the loan programs should not be limited to 10% of the total of the bank loans -as envisaged at present by the management of the Bank".

As for the compensatory financing facility, it was the subject of slight modifications in 1975.

The inclusion of services for the "total export of goods" was rejected because "of the different techniques resulting from the absence of data" and few countries which would be the recipient (Jordan, Mexico, Turkey and Cyprus), but the compensatory amounts were greatly increased without modifying the fundamental philosophy

---

(1) For greater details see: Norman Girvan, Richard Bernal and Wesley Hughes; "The IMF and the Third World: the case of Jamaica, 1974-1978", Development Dialogue; 1980:2, pages 113 and 152.

(2) E. Peter Wright: "Les prets de la Banque Mondiale en faveur de l'ajustement structurel". Finances et dêveloppement, September 1980; pages 20 to 23.

of the facility [(1)]. The facility of compensatory financing provided an assistance of a total amount of 3.6 billion SDR's -Special Drawing Rights, during the period 1973 to 1976, of which 2.64 billion was for the developing countries but concurrently the accumulated deficit of the group of countries concerned during the same period on the basis of the revised IMF formula, amounted to 37.01 billion SDR's.

The drawings are modest in relation to the estimated deficits as well as in relation to the export earnings. The decision N°6224 (79/135) of 2 August, 1979, did not change the situation fundamentally: the ceiling of the outstanding purchases was increased from 75 to 100% of the quota of the member countries, the limit fixed at the equivalent of 50% of the quota for the purchases carried into effect during the period of 12 months was discontinued, the revenue issuing out of the remittances of workers abroad and tourism could now be added to the export earnings from goods in the calculation of the deficit. In 1970-1980, the drawings by virtue of this facility were increased to only 863 million SDR's.[(2)]

Besides the facilities, it is observed that, when necessary, the developing country exhaust their first credit tranche in the Fund, but it is not the same for the subsequent tranches at increasing conditionality. The developing countries in fact, feel reluctant to subject themselves to the Adjustment programs of the Fund- the Cairo outbreak of January 1978, illustrates the severity- and therefore do not mobilise the resources which they greatly need in this case. The increase in quotas in Jamaica, therefore, did not result in increased resources for the developing countries. The evaluation for the latter is consequently poor, concerning the access to the resources of the Fund. The only new developments which took place have been the creation of the Trust Fund and the modest extension of the duration of the programs of the Fund to take into account the difficulties of adjustment. Even the enhanced facility created in 1974 with a view to assisting the countries to overcome the structural difficulties in the balance of payments and presented as fulfilling the demands of the developing countries is not satisfactory even if it is only because of its limited duration (3 years maximum); more than ever, the planning of the system of conditionality of the large international financing organisations and greater participation of the developing countries[(3)] or the process of decision making in the latter, remains on the agenda of the North-South negotiations, as testified by the peripety which accompanied the PLO demand for adhesion to the IMF in September 1980.

(1) Goreux L.M. "Recovery of commodity prices is expected to show compensatory drawing this year". IMF Survey, 7 March, 1977, page 6 and JDA Cuddy: "Compensatory financing in the north-south dialogue: the IMF and Stebex Schemes". Journal of world trade law Vol. 13, N°1, January 1979, pages 66 to 76.

(2) IMF Annual report 1980. Page 87

(3) See the anxiety concerning this subject of a newspaper such as the Financial Times. David Tonge: "Third World bitterness towards IMF".
Financial Times. Jurek Martin: "Why the IMF fears the PLO challenge", 16.9.1980. Page 16

B. Recent conflicts between the Fund and the LDCs

The recent conflicts between certain Third World countries and the International Monetary Fund illustrate the continuity in the Fund's policy, the main pivot of which is the system of conditionality. These conflicts also illustrate the close link between the Fund and the private banks, as well as the role assigned to those institutions by the major industrialized countries. The conflicts which we shall now briefly examine, mainly concern Peru and Zaire. One could, however, add Turkey, Egypt, Jamaica, and in a different context, Mexico.

Discord between the Fund and Peru is not a new thing(1); the latest phase in their relations, and consequently the recent crisis dates from the profound change of policy applied by the Peruvian military Government to the national economy(2), the main component of which was nationalization. The nationalization of the mining sector, amongst others, turned the United States against Peru and cut off all access to external financing. These difficulties could have been overcome quickly as the price of copper and sugar were moving upwards at a reasonable pace or at least holding their own. In 1975, however, the price of copper, and in 1976 that of sugar, literally collapsed, while Peru had launched a grand programme of public investment and its external debt, more than half of which took the form of loans in Euro-currencies from the commercial banks, exceeded 5 billion dollars. Moreover 65% of the debt was repayable in five years and the debt service was assessed in 1978 at one billion dollars.

The drop in the price of copper and sugar was such that Peru had to quickly mobilize all external credit lines available to it. In 1977, therefore, the country's net international reserves showed a debit balance of one billion dollars, while the annual rate of inflation increased to 45%. In order to offset the social effects of inflation, the Peruvian State -like Egypt- had to subsidize the price of foodstuffs, which had already taken the full impact of the rise of international prices.

---

(1) On this point see, inter alia; Rosemary Thorp: "Inflation and orthodox economic policies in Peru", Bulletin of the Oxford Institute of Economics and Statistics, August 1967.
-T. Hayter, Aid as imperialism, op.cit., pp. 143-49.

(2) See, inter alia; S. Hunt: "Distribution, growth and government economic behaviour in Peru", in G. Ramis (ed.) Government and economic development, (Yale University Press 1971).
-C. Delgado: El proceso revolucionario peruano, (Mexico: Siglo XXI, 1972).
-R.C. Webb: Government policy and distribution of income in Peru 1963-1973, (Peru: Wilson School).
-INP, Plan nacional de desarrollo 1975-1978, (Lima 1975).
-E.V.K. Fitzgerald: The State and economic development: Peru since 1968, Occasional Paper n° 49, (Cambridge Univeristy Press 1976).
For more details on the expropriation of International Petroleum Corporation: IPC and its consequences, see:
-G.M. Ingram: Expropriation of US property in Latin America, (Praeger 1974).
-"Peru needs truth more than sympathy", Euromoney, (December 1977) p. 73.

With exports down sharply, a one or two year stand-by programme from the Fund could not cope with Peru's situation.(1) This programme, which was accepted by Peru in November 1977, provided for financing of SDR 90 million over two years, after long and very difficult negotiations. Peru had exhausted its first credit tranche from the Fund as well as SDR 114 million under the facilities and on the minimum conditions. The current payments deficit amounted to 1.2 billion dollars. Peru's needs were such that these credits would clearly fall far short of the level required and could not on their own enable Peru to meet the conditions set by the Fund. However, a 27% devaluation against the dollar had taken place in November 1977, with tighter fiscal pressure and a strict austerity budget.(2)

In February 1978 a Peruvian mission visited the main Western capitals looking for the necessary complementary financing - an immediate 260 million dollars over seven years. At the same time a Fund mission went to Lima to assess the first results of the programme.(3) Disaster then ensued. The budget deficit, which had been limited to 124 million dollars for the year,

(1) There can be no doubt that with the copper price at 55 cents per pound and the sugar price at 7 cents, no financial programme could on its own enable Peru to quickly reverse the situation. This point incidentally sheds much light on the ineffectiveness of the Fund's machinery for compensatory financing.

(2) "Peru: back to crisis", The Economist, 18 March 1978,p. 77.

(3) Under this plan Peru undertook to reduce its current deficit from one billion in 1976 to 850 million in 1977, 400 million in 1978 and 150 million in 1979. Over four years the balance of payments, in terms of the GNP, was to drop from 8% to 1%. Internal inflation was to be brought down from 40% in 1977 to 20% in 1978 and less than 10% in 1979. The deficit of the public sector was to be quickly eliminated through a sharp reduction of spending and higher taxes, whereas the expansion of credit was to take place within very strict limits. The float of the sol against the dollar, which had begun in November 1977, showed a depreciation of about 50% for the national currency by February 1978, with an exchange rate of 145 sols to the dollar against 80. See: "Peru crisis: rescheduling is on the way," Euromoney March 1978, p. 26.

had already been exceeded by the end of February. To compensate for this the Peruvian authorities proposed a new devaluation of the sol as well as increases in retail prices. The Fund remainded intractable, and decided, early in March, that "Peru was no longer eligible for its financing under the stand-by arrangements of November 1977".(1) The international banks, led by Manufacturers Hanover, got the message and, on 10 March, against the advice of the European banks, changed their mind about the projected loan of 260 million dollars.

President Bermudez of Peru condemned the extreme rigidity of the Fund, finding that its programme was unsuited to the conditions in Peru, regretted the failure of the private banks to produce a solution and stated that the United States had vastly reduced the chances of a return to democracy in Peru.(2)

In May 1978 the Chase Manhatten Bank informed the Central Bank of Peru that the 750 million dollars of financing intended for the copper smelting project of "Southern Peru"(3) would be made conditional on the adoption of a law granting certain advantages to the exports of that company, 54.3% of whose capital was owned by Asero, Inc.(4)

In the circumstances new negotiations had to be held with the Fund in June, as Peru had now virtually stopped payments altogether, despite the emergency loan of 85 million dollars granted, out of solidarity, by four Latin American countries (Venezuela, Brazil, Argentina and Mexico). The Fund wanted a new and immediate depreciation of the sol, from 155 to 200 to the dollar. Peru found these new demands excessive and in any case impossible to carry out immediately. The budget deficit was to be reduced from 55 billion sols to 28 billion. Peru argued that anything below 50 billion would cause major political and administrative chaos. The Fund wanted severe credit restrictions on the private sector: these restrictions could not fail to bring about hundreds of bankruptcies, with long lines of unemplyed. As it was, the considerable depreciations of the sol had already

(1) Peru's debts, "The IMF refuses to ease burden", Financial Times, 16 March, 1978.
(2) "How Peru's president views the IMF and the banks", Euromoney, March 1978, p. 28.
(3) In 1976 a consortium of banks headed by Chase had agreed to finance this project.
(4) The purpose of the law was to prevent Peru, now short of hard currency because of the bank blockade, from compelling Southern-Peru to make its payments to the State. See: New York Herald Tribune, May 31, 1978.

lowered to a great extent the standard of living of most of the social classes of Peru. Whereas the earnings index had stood at 114.1 in 1973, it was now down to 74.1 in 1977.[1] In the past two years real earnings were generally thought to have dropped by about 28%, even before the ending in May 1978 of subsidies for items of prime necessity and the consequent doubling of the price of bread and tripling of the price of fuel oil. Unemployment and under-employment were reported to be up 50% in the previous few months, while the part of the population living at the levels of subsistence rose to 40%.[2]

It is hardly surprising that, in the circumstances, the situation began to be extremely tense from June onwards: the occupation of the mines by the army and popular riots against price rises were only some of the manifestations of the crisis. An agreement between the parties was eventually reached in August; its terms are as follows:

- The budget deficit for 1978 would be kept at the level of that for 1977: 72 billion sols, or half of its value in real terms. This implied an increase in fiscal pressures and the price of consumer goods. The sol would continue to be devalued in small doses to reach a parity of 200 sols to the dollar (against 165 in August 1978 and 80 in June 1977).

- Interest rates were readjusted upwards, the current bank rate being fixed at 23.5% for the major industrials.[3] The letter of intent signed between the Peruvian Government and the Fund, which was published in September showed that the government had been obliged to accept the following clause, whereby it virtually disowned the whole of the policy pursued by the Alvarado administration and the emphasis which that administration had placed on public investment and State control over the key industries:

---

(1) Hugh O'Shaughnessy: "Peru's struggle with the world monetary fund", Financial Times, June 29, 1978.
(2) "Peru: the breaking of a revolution", The Economist, September 1978, p. 70.
(3) Nicolas Asheshov: "Peruvians welcome accord over credits with IMF", Financial Times, 12 August 1978.

> "The policies followed in the past, which sought to increase consumption through subsidies and wage increases, have proved to be incompatible with sustained economic development and have thus not been able to guarantee a regular improvement of the well-being of wage-earners".

It then became known, in November 1978, that many enterprises of the industrial sector were to be sold, in keeping with the new economic policy of the Armed Forces régime. A few days later the Minister of the Economy, Mr. Javier Silva Ruete, told the Annual Conference of Executives that the national and international private sector would be able to associate itself with the State in the "strategic" sectors, which had previously been a State monopoly.

The case of Peru is a good illustration of the American position, as expressed in February 1977 by Arthur Burns, then Chairman of the Federal Reserve Board. In his statement Mr. Burns had urged the commercial banks to make their future loans to the LDCs conditional, without any exception, on compliance with the IMF packages. Otherwise those banks could not expect the FRB or the United States government to compensate them in case of default.(1)

Peru is not an isolated case; other recent examples make it clear that the Fund's attitude towards that country is not an isolated attitude.(2)

One of the major lessons to be learnt from the Peruvian example is that nowadays there are very few LDCs which could hope to get financing from private banks if they do not fulfill the performance criteria of the Fund: ceilings on domestic credit and public debt, inter alia. It is significant that the new facility set up under the name Witteveen Facility carries exactly the same conditions as earlier facilities.(3)

Zaire, Jamaica, Gabon, Egypt, Turkey, Sudan and Zambia are, besides Peru, the LDCs which are in open or latent disagreement with Monetary Fund over the scope and the nature of the measures which should be taken to remedy the existing situations. In most cases, the devaluation imposed by the Fund is the measure which encounters most opposition, as the countries in

(1) Quoted by Michael Hudson: Global fracture: the new international economic order, (Harper, November 1977) p. 153.
(2) This is true although the IMF has recently shown yet again that there was room for broad variations in its assessment: consider, for example, the benevolent treatment it granted to Egypt, compared to the policy of genuine strangulation which it imposed on Peru.
(3) "A more waspish, less waspish IMF", The Economist, June 24, 1978, p. 86.

question feel it does more harm than good. The failure of Zaire's 42% devaluation in 1976 - a failure which was recognized by the Fund itself - can only console them on this point.(1) Yet here again, after battling the Fund for months on end, Sudan had to resign itself to a 20% devaluation of the Sudanese pound in June 1978.(2)

The relative mildness shown by the Monetary Fund in previous years towards Zaire did not prevent it from applying to that country in June 1978 a shock therapy which some bankers today think is the finest possible course of action. As is well known, that shock therapy consisted, inter alia, of imposing a genuine protectorate on Zaire, by the appointment to the key posts in the economy and finances of Zaire of representatives of the Fund (including one supervisor with the governor of the Central Bank of Zaire) and the virtually total denationalization of the Zaire economy. This practice takes the Fund right back to the practices of the 19th century which had accompanied the Ottoman Debt or the Egyptian Debt. The following passage taken from a recent article by Dr. I. Friedman, Vice-President of Citicorp, is significant evidence of the new approach of the international financial community.(3)

> Zaire is a fascinating case study in this respect because of its unique and precedent-setting character. Zaire had fallen into arrears by 1975 on payments to private banks and official lenders. It was also widely assumed that what was done by the official lenders would guide the private lenders. A Paris Club was called and re-scheduled the official debt. What about the private debt?
>
> The international banking community was truly at a crossroads - over 100 banks of many nations were involved. Re-scheduling would have been technically easy and readily understood. In the process, however, Zaire might well have lost its creditworthiness with many private banks and done

---

(1) "Zaire: an object lesson in rescheduling", Euromoney, March 1978, p. 37.
(2) For the history of the crisis with the Fund, see: "The sick men of the euromarkets", Euromoney, March 1978, pp. 10-15. -"Sudan, you're rocking the boat", Euromoney, March 1978, p. 31. -"Sudan: IMF talks end in disagreement", The Middle East Economic Digest, 5 May 1978, p. 40. "Sudan devalues currency by effective 20%", Financial Times 10 June 1978.
(3) Irving S. Friedman, "Country risk: the lessons of Zaire", The Banker , February 1978, pp. 29 and 30.

so for years. The banks' level of tolerance for risk was too low by 1976-77 to assume that rescheduling would be followed by new loans. Zaire drastically needed new bank credits to revive its economy. Funds from official sources were simply much too small or too slow.

After much discussion among the banks concerned, it was decided to try to help Zaire re-establish its creditworthiness with private banks. Of key importance would be major changes in economic policy and management. An IMF standby in the higher credit tranches would help in the process of re-establishing confidence in Zaire in the private financial world, because it would indicate international scrutiny, endorsement and monitoring of Zaire's economic situation and policies. Repayment of arrears to banks would demonstrate that Zaire gave the highest priority to honouring its debts with private banks - as in fact many developing countries already were - but which was being questioned in many circles, particularly in the lending countries like the United States. In addition to reforms in the monetary, fiscal, and balance-of-payments areas, Zaire also undertook major changes in the real economy, including the return of certain economic entities like plantations to previous owners, re-organisation of the management of river and railroad transportation, improved pricing policies, and strengthening personnel in government.

These policies were intended to make it possible for Zaire to revive its economy and begin again to benefit from its rich resource endowment and diversified productivity, which was the essential ingredient in servicing all past and future external debt to all lenders. It was an experiment for both Zaire and the private banks. It was analogous to a bank dealing with individual borrowers in trouble by helping them create healthy conditions which would enable them to go forward after the 'work out' process had been successfully completed. The approach borrowed heavily from experience with corporate borrowers. It also borrowed heavily from my experience in the IMF and the World Bank. Given the reforms in the various areas of the economy which I have just mentioned, it is believed that the new credits will be used efficiently and productively by Zaire.

Thus, Zaire is not only a case of how to judge the creditworthiness of a country, but also an international policy question of how to re-establish today the creditworthiness of a country which has lost its creditworthiness and thus greatly eroded the foundation for continuing growth and stability in the future. The emphasis is likely to be not on changing the financial terms of outstanding debt, but on the economic management of the country.

GENERAL CONCLUSION

The least that one can say, at the end of this study, is that the IMF's record in the LDCs is less than brilliant. Wherever the Fund's package has been applied the situation has only worsened. For example, in the case of Brazil, which is one of those for which outstanding success is claimed, the truth is that the "Brazilian miracle" made its appearance only with the arrival on the scene of Delfim Netto, spokesman for the industrialist circles and whose first measure was to relax credit. In the case of Indonesia the miracle has not yet happened and all the Fund's programmes have so far failed to bring about the "take-off stage" for the economy of a country with one of the lowest per capita incomes in the world and demographic projections which are hardly reassuring.(1)

The World Bank's report for 1978 refers, in its study of the Indonesian economy, to the growing gap between domestic production and the demand for food.(2)

On the other hand the therapies applied by the Fund have severely jolted countries such as Ghana, Argentina and Chile, to mention only a few. The case of Ghana is particularly illustrative, because, even after a decade of application of the measures advocated by the Fund, the country has still not recovered the prosperity it formerly had during the fifties, and which justified its nickname of Gold Coast.(3)

This is inevitable if the Fund's package is applied indiscriminately to countries seeking to draw on its resources without regard to the conditions peculiar to each of them The same package is thus indiscriminately applied to the United Kingdom, Italy or Egypt. The implementation of the same instruments has given rise to the same results whatever the country involved and whatever its specific historical features. Yet the economic, social and political impact of credit restrictions, for example, simply cannot be compared in the case of a country like the United Kingdom, and one like Egypt. The former has a mature economy with a substantial per capita income; a slowdown in the rate of growth of such an economy does not jeopardize its development along similar lines in the future. A devaluation of the national currency, for example, may be good for such an economy, which usually has an autonomous capacity for the production of capital goods; devaluation, in this case, may increase the level of employment in the country and global income, assuming that leakages on imports can be contained.

---

(1) W.A. Henna: "Indonesian projections and the arithmetic of anxiety", American Universities Field Staff Reports, Southern Asian Series 22 no. 3, March 1974, pp. 1-11.

(2) IBRD: Annual report on the Indonesian economy, April 1978.

(3) M. Dickson: "Ghana, a country that has lost its way", Financial Times, 11 December 1978.

In an LDC, however, any devaluation immediately upsets the investment capacity of the country, and, accordingly, its prospects for development, which, as is universally recognized, has the highest priority.

An analysis of the various individual experiences of the application of the Fund's programme makes it possible to define a typical series of consequences: slowing down of global rate of growth, a drop in public investment and in total investment, lower employment levels, worsening of disparities in income, denationalization of the national economy and the short-term mortgaging of the country's import capacity by means of the repatriation of funds in order to pay the amortization and interest on foreign capital. In such a system the debtor country can only remain essentially in debt. The levels of its rate of growth and its rate of investment affect its long-term development prospects and, accordingly, its capacity to make external payments. Recourse to indebtedness is then the only remaining alternative to relative stagnation. Interest payable under debt servicing and profit to foreign investment have the combined effect of gradually mortgaging the country's capacity to pay, leading it to bankruptcy.

Whatever progress has been made in the Fund in recent years, with the establishment of various facilities has not - despite their undisputed value - fundamentally altered the situation. The fact is that the whole philosophy of adjustment needs to be revised if machinery appropriate to the situation and the specific problems of the LDCs is what is really wanted, within the framework of the reform of the international monetary and financial system. Unfortunately, international monetary reform has not introduced substantive changes in the basic elements of the international monetary system. More than ever before, changes are needed in the economic system whereby the developed countries - through the Monetary Fund and the other international institutions - reserve the right to control and monitor, on a permanent basis, the domestic economic, financial and social policies of the LDCs. Through the conditionality of drawings the LDCs find themselve obliged to make a burdensome contribution to the world problem of adjustment, while the world economic situation, for most of them, is an exogenous variable which generally governs the levels of their financial earnings and, accordingly, of their level of economic activity. The deep recession which has spread in recent years from the developed countries to the whole of the world economy, and which has been characterized in particular by a wave of protectionism, has made the contribution of the LDCs to the process of world adjustment an even greater burden for them.

There is a major contradiction between the commitments accepted by the developed countries in the various international fora, in respect of the need for a transfer of real resources to the LDCs and the burden which is imposed on them-the consequence of which is the sacrifice of development.

The repeated failures of the United Nations General Assembly to deal with the problems of the New International Economic Order are significant. The United States, United Kingdom and German representatives have been totally opposed to the possibility of having discussions on monetary matters in the context of Gobal or North-South negotiations. In their opinion, it would have the effect of interfering with the activities of bodies such as the IMF and the World Bank, where the voting power of the industrialized countries makes it possible for them to protect their own interests.

The problems recently encountered by a certain number of LDCs such as Peru, Zaire, Sudan or Jamaica, in having acces to the resources of the Fund, clearly indicate that the Fund's traditional approach still persists. This is all the more paradoxical because, as Reichmann and Stillson have referred to above, in 29 cases where the Fund's stabilization programme had been put into effect, inflation declined in only seven cases.(1) Are such meagre results worth the social and political costs which they entail? There is still a huge gap between the solem recognition by the developed countries of the need for a new monetary and financial order and the positions which those same countries adopt in actual practice.

---

(1) Thomas M. Reichmann and Richard T. Stillson: "Experience with programs of balance of payments adjustment: Stand-by arrangements in the higher credit ranches, 1963-72", <u>IMF Staff Papers</u>, vol 25, N°2, June 1978.

Chapter IV

THE EXTERNAL INDEBTEDNESS OF THE DEVELOPING COUNTRIES TO INTERNATIONAL PRIVATE BANKS

Samuel Lichtensztejn
José Manuel Quijano

Introduction

This study is concerned with the loans made by private international banks to the developing countries, and analyzes the modalities of such loans as well as the repercussions on the Third World of the strengthening of this financial link. This is by no means a new phenomenon in the economic history of the developing countries, but it is now undoubtedly assuming greater importance in their current external financing. The expansion of private bank credit has, in fact, led to significant changes in international relations, expecially since the early years of the 1970s.

We would begin by drawing attention to the increasing scale of the financing transactions with private banks which are extending their geographical sphere of action and embarking upon new activities. The existence of this expanded process of lending on a world scale does not mean the fragmentation of the markets. On the contrary, the trend is towards increasing concentration, on the side of the lender banks and of the borrower countries alike. One aspect of the trend is the difference in the cost and accessibility of loans for the developing countries compared with other groups, and the disparities of treatment among the developing countries themselves.

The process known as the "privatization of the public external debt" of the developing countries is characterized by the adoption of a new modus operandi by the international financing system, in terms of maturities, interest rates and destination of funds. In the last instance, such modalities made the time profile for the external debts of the developing countries even more inflexible and added to the burden placed on their balance-of-payments by debt amortization and servicing.

When a conventional evaluation of external indebtedness is made, the analytical criteria are those of solvency and payments capability. From this point of view, the limits and conditions for external debts and new loans would be determined in the light of the present and future balance-of-payments situation. However, the growing influx of private bank credit into the developing countries cannot be dismissed as a spontaneous upsurge of demand or as the outcome of a sudden desire on the part of bankers to contribute to solving the problems of the deprived countries. Once any conceptions of the problem as a matter for international co-operation is discarded, its complexity still defies explanations based exclusively on commercial considerations, i.e., the need to comply with the conditions of a capital market. This is tantamount to recognizing that although an analysis of the external debt problem of developing countries must take into account their real and potential payments capacity, a comprehensive evaluation of it must be on a higher plane.

The concern felt about the need to adopt a broader approach to the financial relations established between the governments of the developing countries and the big private international banks can be epitomized in two major questions. First, to what extent are the lending banks able and anxious to influence the economic policies and development strategies of the debtor countries (and particularly the most important of these). Second, to what extent have the transnational corporations operating in the developing countries become the driving force behind private external financing and the ultimate recipients of its benefits (even when a debt is directly contracted or guaranteed by a government)? The assumption underlying both of these lines of inquiry is that the privatization of external indebtedness intensifies the processes of internationalization and economic concentration (in production, trade and finance).

This study is divided into three chapters in accordance with our general thinking on its objectives and orientation. The first chapter gives a short account of the growing external indebtedness of the developing countries to private international banks from three points of view: its historical dynamic (development), its quantitative dynamic (expansion) and its operational dynamic (concentration). The second chapter describes the way in which the private banks conduct their loan operations in terms of the main formal conditions imposed, namely, maturities, cost and destination, while the third chapter makes a critical analysis of the effects of external indebtedness to the system. This aspect is examined from two points of view: the traditional or balance-of-payments approach and a broader approach, which measures the extent to which development policies are conditioned and assesses the real beneficiaries of the debt process. Finally, some country case studies are cited to illustrate the points we wish to make.

I. THE DYNAMICS OF EXTERNAL INDEBTEDNESS TO THE PRIVATE INTERNATIONAL BANKING SYSTEM

The history of the process

The period prior to the 1929 world depression was a golden age for the private international banks in their financing of the developing countries. At that time foreign banks played a prominent part in the placement of securities and other portfolio operations, notably, the English banks that specialized in the placement of foreign bonds, the French industrial and commercial banks, the old issuing houses of Paris, the four major German banks and the branches of American banks. If investment in colonial territories is excluded, Latin America was the preferred area of operation for those banks. Of the 107 branches of American banks throughout the world in 1926, 61 were to be found in Latin America.(1) Up to 1914, the region's public debt to foreign banks was US $3.3 billion, or 30 per cent of the total foreign investment made in the region.(2)

This situation changed after the 1929 crisis, and the links were not renewed until some years after the institution of the new international order that emerged in the aftermath of the second world war. In 1955, for example, of the estimated total of $8 billion for the developing countries' medium- and long-term debts, the major proportion came from official bilateral and multilateral loans. The bulk of the private financing came from suppliers' credits and the proportion increased constantly. In 1960, Latin America, which accounted for nearly half the external debt of the developing countries, did not owe more than 14 per cent of its total debt to private banks.(3) The foreign branches of United States' banks in that year were in virtually the same position as in the pre-war period.(4)

(1) Xavier Gorostiaga: _The international financial centers in the underdeveloped countries_ , (Mexico: Instituto Latinoamericano de Estudios Transnacionales, 1978), table 4, p. 32.
(2) United Nations, "The external financing of Latin America", (E/CN.12/649/Rev.1), December 1964, pp. 16-17. (Spanish text)
(3) Inter-American Development Bank, "Latin America's external indebtedness: current situation and prospects", May 1977, table 4.
(4) X. Gorostiaga: _op.cit_.

Although there were no fundamental changes in this pattern during the early years of the 1960s, the conditions were already being created that would open the way to the active involvement of private international banks in the developing countries in general. First came the decolonization and political independence of the new countries of Africa and Asia - which led to the transformation of the former government subsidies and transfers into bank loans - followed by the inclusion of these new nations in the private international financial and commercial network. Secondly, there was the process of opening up to the outside world, which was furthered in Latin America by the stabilization policies introduced under the auspices of the Internaitonal Monetary Fund.[1] The directives given facilitated the movement of goods and capital, thereby enabling increasingly close relations to be established with the international banking system. The opening of more interbanking connections and the more generalized use of bank and government guarantees in commercial operations also illustrated the dynamic effect exercised by the existence of favourable conditions for obtaining loans from the international banking system.

Even so, it was not until the end of the 1960s that the privatization of the external debt of the developing countries began, a process which was to reach spectacular heights after 1973. This process was closely connected with the growth of the Eurodollar market, which took 12 years to reach the net figure of \$57 billion in 1970, but in the last 8 years alone rose to over \$400 billion.[2] Created midway through the 1950s with the dollars which flooded in as a result of the United States balance-of-payments deficit, strengthened by the growth of that deficit as a by-product of the Vietnam war, and fed by the heavy investment of the oil-producing countries in the first half of the 1970s, the Eurodollar market took a leading place in the flow of international financing.

Its expansion was originally confined to the traditional financial centers of the developed countries, but then led to the formation of new international financial centers in some of the developing countries. In fact, when the United States monetary authorities began to control the flow of funds out of the country, the American banks began to operate in the European market (London, Zurich, Luxemburg, Lichtenstein).

---

(1) Samuel Lichtensztejn: "On the orientation and role of stabilization policies in Latin America", Economía de América Latina, (CIDE: September, 1978) pp. 27-30.

(2) In gross terms, the amount rose from \$115 billion to \$700 billion between 1970 and 1978.

Subsequently, the increasing activities of those centers were shared with the banks of the European Economic Community and Japan and with banks in other parts of the world (Netherlands Antilles, Bahamas, Bermuda, Grand Cayman, the Virgin Islands and Panama in the Caribbean; Lebanon, Bahrein and Abu Dhabi in the Middle East; Hong Kong and Singapore in Asia; Liberia in Africa and the New Hebrides in Oceania).

To place this spectacular growth of private international banking in its proper context, we must look at the internationalization of production and the current crisis of the capitalist system.

It may be claimed, in a sense, that the internationalization of the financial capital was paralleled by the internationalization and concentration of the contemporary system of production. The subsidiaries of United States concerns which were active in Europe and other parts of the world were wanting capital, and this led to the development of international financing. It was this correlation between the growing need for capital accumulation on the one hand, and the expansion of the financial markets (Euromarket and offshore banking centers) on the other, which explained why most of the resources increasingly available went initially to the industrial rather than to the developing countries.

Although the nature of the internationalization process did not change in essentials, the current crisis has nevertheless altered its motive force and modes of adjustment. The tremendous increase in private bank loans to the Third World countries has coincided with the most serious depression experienced by the main industrial market-economy countries and the capitalist system as a whole since the end of the last war. Capitalism in the 1970s is characterized by monetary disequilibria, inflation, underemployment and a decline in the growth of investment, after almost 25 years during which it was believed that the spectre of such crises had been exorcised for ever.

Many different explanations have been found for the crisis that has marked the last few years and its relationship with the financial expansion described above. Some circles, for instance, have stressed the influence which they believe certain factors to have had, such as the rise in the price of oil and the growing disparity between real wages and productivity in the industrial countries (as a result of union pressure). However, there is now an increasing consensus that these factors succeeded the crisis and, although they actually sparked it off, they were not the original cause of it. The most penetrating studies of the economic crisis base their interpretation on the structural problems of productive accumulation, its sequel as expressed in the collapse of the world monetary system established at Bretton Woods and the fierce competition that has broken out among the major developed nations.

Some writers believe that all this coincided with the "long cycle" of depression into which capitalism was plunged, followed by the "long cycle" of expansionism, which extended from the end of the second world war to midway through the 1960s. For others again, the crisis is the tangible result of the decline of United States' hegemony and the readjustment required to establish a system of international relations. In any case the crisis, which is rooted in the process of real capital accumulation, undoubtedly encouraged the formation of a huge surplus which was then used by banking and financial circles. The restructuring and expansion of the financial centers and the international financing system are thus the outcome of the need to invest the available surplus for which there was no immediately accessible productive outlet. The transfer and financial reallocation of these resources was facilitated by the climate of inflation and perpetual exchange rate modifications. In the circumstances the big banks began to turn their attention to the developing countries, which had hitherto been relatively neglected.

Perhaps the most remarkable feature of the international financial markets has been their ability to act without the constraints of national markets. As the new financial centers were very largely the result of the bankers' desire to evade controls, the new degree of freedom they enjoyed enabled them to create more and more financial surpluses by continually juggling debits and credits, virtually without the need to maintain reserves. Consequently, old debts gave birth to new and even bigger debts. This endogenous process of reproduction in the international financial market, which was increasingly dissociated from the levels of liquidity for transactions, thus became associated with inflation, rising interest rates and speculation.

This situation has fanned the fears of a widespread financial crisis, which are fed by memories of the period immediately preceding the great depression of 1929, and are referred to in a number of documents and statements. The bankruptcy of two American banks, and of the Herstatt bank in the Federal Republic of Germany, has done nothing to dispel the general disquiet. Nevertheless, the international private system has not lost its powers of adjustment and its flexibility, although this does not mean that it is free of all contradictions. It has been seen therefore that the private international banks have taken over many of the functions which used to be the province of the International Monetary Fund, and that it is greatly to the interest of the private international financial community - despite permanent monetary instability and "institutionalized" inflation that the Euromarket and other international markets should continue to expand without restraint.(1)

Growth of the external debt to private international banks

The total external debt of the developing countries grew at an ever-increasing pace during the early years of the 1960s and this trend has been even more marked since the beginning of the present decade. Since the second half of the 1960s, the debt to private sources (at current prices) increased at a faster rate than the debt to official sources. At the same time, the Third World accounted for an increasing share of international credit operations. According to World Financial Markets published by the Morgan Guaranty Trust Co., the developing countries represented 9.3 per cent of transactions of over one year in the Euromarket in 1970, 30 per cent annually between 1971 and 1974 and 51.2 per cent annually between 1975 and 1977.

---

(1) The periodical International Currency Review, referring to the concern often expressed by Dr. Witteveen, former Director of the International Monetary Fund, about the lack of controls in the Euromarket, suggested that: "his tendency to refer to this utterly fundamental fact during his last year at the helm of the IMF may explain why his contract was not renewed and why he was replaced by an optimistic French bureaucrat", Vol. 10, No. 5, pp. 28-29.

TABLE 1

The growth of the external debt of developing countries, 1955-1976
(In annual percentages)

	Current prices	Constant prices deflated by: Import prices	Constant prices deflated by: Export prices
Period 1955 - 1960	14.8	13.5	14.7
Period 1960 - 1965	16.5	15.6	16.3
Period 1967 - 1972	16.8	10.8	12.6
Official sources	13.3	7.7	9.3
Private sources	22.7	16.7	18.3
Period 1973 - 1976	21.0	7.6	9.1
Official sources	15.7	2.9	4.3
Private sources	26.8	12.7	14.3

SOURCE: World Bank study of May 1977, quoted by Helen Hughes in "The external debt of developing countries".

If we analyze the expansion of the debt in constant prices, we shall see that the total debt of the developing countries is growing more slowly, with the result that the sharp upswing in the debt to private sources has not altogether offset the declining tempo of growth in official external financing. It is suggested therefore that the total indebtedness of the developing countries has not increased, substantially in the last few years since their external debt as a proportion of GNP rose from 16 to 18 per cent only between the years 1972 and 1976.

The important fact, however, is the extraordinary growth of loans from private international banks. This reached such proportions that the share of the debt to private banks in the total public external debt of 94 developing countries increased from 7.5 to 27.6 per cent between 1970 and 1976. If we take into account solely the private sources of financing the debt to banks,during the same period and for the same number of countries, expanded from 26.2 to 65.3 per cent of the total. (see Table 3)

TABLE 2

Public external debt of 94 developing countries(1)

(In billions of dollars)

Year	Official Sources		Private Sources			
	Bilateral	Multilateral	Suppliers' credits	Banks	Other(2)	Total(3)
1970	27.82	7.84	7.50	3.93	3.52	51.76
1973	42.53	12.80	10.00	13.85	5.58	85.94
1974	48.72	15.64	11.34	19.36	6.47	103.18
1975	55.18	19.35	12.17	28.19	7.30	123.52
1976	62.41	23.36	13.58	42.22	8.78	152.42

SOURCE: Prepared from UNCTAD secretariat data based on World Bank figures, "External indebtedness of developing countries: A statistical note", (TD/B/C.3/148), Geneva, 23 October 1978.

(1) Disbursed and contracted for more than a year
(2) Mainly bonds
(3) The figures may not add up to the totals owing to unallocated flows, rounding, etc.

TABLE 3

Public external debt of 94 developing countries

(In percentages)

Year	Official sources: Bilateral	Official sources: Multilateral	Private sources: Suppliers' credits	Private sources: Banks	Private sources: Other	Total
1970	53.7	15.1	14.4	7.5	6.8	100.0
1973	49.4	14.8	11.6	16.1	6.4	100.0
1974	47.2	15.1	10.9	18.7	6.2	100.0
1975	44.6	15.6	9.8	22.8	5.9	100.0
1976	40.9	15.3	8.9	27.6	5.7	100.0

SOURCE: Prepared on the basis of Table 2.

The acceleration in the growth of the developing countries' external debt to private international banks will no doubt assume even greater dimensions if other loan components, which are not usually included in the published figures, are also taken into account. We refer, in particular, to loans made to the private sector of the debtor countries which are not guaranteed by the respective governments. Information on external indebtedness generally relates only to public debts or those that are publicly guaranteed, so the loans granted to developing countries are actually being underestimated.

It is difficult to make calculations in this respect because of a number of methodological obstacles and the impossibility of obtaining full information on certain countries.(1) However, some data may help to give a rough idea of the scale of unguaranteed debts in the developing countries. In Table 4, for instance, it is estimated that the unguaranteed debt as a proportion of the guaranteed debt averaged 29 per cent at the end of 1976 for 85 developing countries. From the information available, there seems to be a high positive correlation between a country's level

(1) The main obstacles which are usually recognized as preventing more realistic estimates from being made are the lack of information on debts of less than a year, on the volume of debts contracted by the private sector in the developing countries and on debts for military expenditures.

of income and the extent of its unguaranteed debt. It will be seen later that a similar correlation can be found between income level and the share of private international banking in debt financing. It may be argued therefore that a high proportion of unguaranteed operations is connected with bank credits and loans, which would increase still further the scale on which this kind of financing is extended to the developing countries. The figures for Latin America, which are given in Table 5, confirm this assumption, if the country groupings are taken as representative of a country scale by level of income.

TABLE 4

Unguaranteed external debt of 85 developing countries. Disbursements at the end of 1976 (In billions of dollars)

	Public debt and publicly guaranteed debt	Unguaranteed debt (estimates)	Unguaranteed debt / Guaranteed debt
Total for 85 developing countries	157.0	45.5	29%
- more than 1136 dollars per capita	47.6	31.0	65%
- between 281 and 1135 dollars per capita	65.6	12.2	19%
- under 281 dollars per capita	43.8	2.3	5%

SOURCE: IMF, Survey, 5 June 1978, p. 173.

TABLE 5

Unguaranteed external debt of the non-oil exporting Latin American Countries. Disbursements at end of each year

(In billions of dollars)

	Public debt and publicly guaranteed debt	Unguaranteed debt (estimates)	Unguaranteed debt / Guarnateed debt
Argentina, Brazil and Mexico:			
1974	20.2	16.9	84%
1975	24.8	21.0	84%
1976	33.8	26.4	78%
1977	41.0	28.0	68%
Chile, Colombia, Peru and Uruguay:			
1974	8.4	2.9	35%
1975	9.3	3.1	33%
1976	10.0	3.5	35%
1977	12.0	4.0	33%
Other Countries:			
1974	3.0	0.0	0%
1975	3.9	0.4	10%
1976	4.9	0.7	14%
1977	6.0	no data	no data

SOURCE: ECLA estimates on the basis of a number of sources (E/CEPAL/1061), 7 February 1979, p. 85.

The Concentration of debtor countries

The number of countries involved in the phenomenon of private debt contracting by the Third World is actually relatively small. The concentration of external debts to private sources holds good both for bank loans and for the placement of bonds on international financial markets. This means that a very significant proportion of the developing countries remains on the margin of the debt privatization trend. The move towards concentration has taken place along three converging lines: by number of countries, by geographical region and by level of economic development.

a. The historical composition of bank loans by non-OPEC developing countries shows unmistakably that they were highly concentrated. (see Table 6) Two-thirds of the private international bank loans granted were taken up by five countries, and three-quarters of the total was channeled to ten countries. OECD data for 1977 confirm the continuity of this structure.(1) It is worth adding that the degree of concentration is even higher for loans from United States banks.

When the degree of concentration is calculated for all developing countries, including members of OPEC, the figures drop slightly although they still remain at a high level. Five countries account for half the loans and the first ten represent two-thirds of the total debt. As in the previous case, the degree of concentration rises when the analysis centers on loans from United States banks.

Mention should also be made in this chapter of the placement of bonds by Third World countries in the main international capital markets (Eurobond market, United States, Japan and Switzerland). As there is considerable participation by banks and financial agents in these markets, it is interesting to see how far the trend towards concentration noted in relation to bank loans is reflected here as well.

It will be found that very few countries have had access to this type of financing, that, in the majority of cases, they are the countries that took the bulk of the bank loans. Brazil and Mexico, for instance, accounted for 64.7 per cent of the total placement of bonds by non-oil exporting developing countries in 1977. In 1978 the percentage for the two countries was 49.7 per cent, while Argentina, Taiwan, Malaysia and Panama increased their shares. Thus, with few exceptions, the same countries are in the lead for this type of international private financing as well.

b. If we now analyze the concentration by geographical region, it will be found that Latin America is the main destination for private international bank loans. According to World Bank data, elaborated on by the UNCTAD secretariat, in 1976 Latin America accounted for 57 per cent of the debts contracted with private banks by 94 developing countries and three countries in Southern Europe. In that same year, Africa accounted for 14.7 per cent, the Middle East for 3.5 per cent, Southern Asia for 0.3 per cent, Eastern Asia for 13.4 per cent and the three countries of Southern Europe for 10.9 per cent.

c. Lastly, the concentration can also be studied from the standpoint of economic development level, measured in terms of per capita income.

(1) OECD, Financial Market Trends (various members).

TABLE 6

Concentration of the external debt with private international banks as of 30 June 1976
(In percentages)

Developing countries not members of OPEC				Total Developing countries			
Private international banks		United States banks(1)		Private international banks		United States banks (2)	
1.Brazil	25.6	Mexico	26.2	Brazil	20.9	Mexico	22.0
2.Mexico	23.4	Brazil	25.1	Mexico	19.1	Brazil	21.1
3.So.Korea	5.5	So.Korea	6.8	So.Korea	4.5	So.Korea	5.7
4.Argentina	4.7	Argentina	5.0	Argentina	3.8	Venezuela	5.2
5.Peru	3.7	Taiwan	4.9	Indonesia	3.6		
Five first countries	62.9		68.0		51.9		58.2
6.Philippines	3.5	Philippines	4.7	Venezuela	3.5	Taiwan	4.1
7.Taiwan	3.4	Peru	2.9	Peru	3.0	Philippines	3.9
8.Colombia	2.2	Colombia	2.9	Philippines	2.9	Indonesia	3.8
9.Thailand	1.9	Thailand	1.9	Taiwan	2.8	Algeria	2.9
10.Chile	1.3	Chile	1.5	Algeria	2.2	Peru	2.4
Ten first countries	75.2		81.9		66.3		75.3

SOURCE: World Financial Markets (Morgan Guaranty Trust Co.), December, 1976.

(1) Including banks in Belgium, Luxembourg, France, West Germany Italy, Netherlands, Sweden, Switzerland, United Kingdom, Canada, Japan, United States, and branches of United States banks in the Bahamas, Cayman Islands, Panama, Hong Kong, and Singapore.

(2) Banks in the United States (including branches, agents and subsidiaries of foreign banks in the United States) and branches of United States Banks abroad.

On this basis, it will be seen that the countries with the highest relative income, including the oil-exporting countries, have a high absorptive capacity for bank loans. As Table 7 indicates, the rise in the percentage participation of the oil-producing countries up to 1973, its decline and subsequent recovery up to 1976 are partly reflected in the index of loans to the countries with the highest relative income. Meanwhile, although this does not constitute a really definite trend, the middle-income countries seem to be losing ground to the least developed countries in the distribution of bank funds, although the latter's degree of participation is still very small. The slight increase noticeable for these countries in the Table is no doubt due to the participation of certain countries such as Indonesia and Zaire which, despite their low per capita income, have oil and strategic minerals.

According to United States Federal Reserve Bank data, the distribution of United States bank loans shows an even stronger degree of concentration. The non-oil high-income countries (between $500 and $2000 annual per capita income) received 77 per cent of the loans, the middle-income countries (between $200 and $500 annual per capita income) took 20 per cent while the low- per capita income countries (under $200) had 3 per cent.(1)

Taken as a whole, the trend towards the bunching of loan recipients in the financial market is consistent in certain respects: banks lend more to a few developing countries, especially those which have made relatively greater economic progress or have a dynamic export base (such as the existence of an oil surplus can give a country). The statements made by bankers confirm this view while throwing more light on it. To take one example, in explaining the concentration of loans, the Senior Executive Vice-President of the Fidelity Bank of Philadelphia, Charles S. Ganoe, said that the principal Third World debtors of United States banks "are countries classified by the World Bank as of high or medium per capita income, characterized by being growth economies with an expanding industrial base and by having very close economic and *political* ties with the United States" (author's italics)(2) As the President of the

(1) Federal Reserve Press Release, June 1977.
(2) Charles S. Ganoe: "Loans to LDCs: Five Myths", *The Journal of Commercial Banking Lending*, November, 1977,

Hanover Manufacturers' Directory also said recently: "loans given through the international capital market have, in fact, been very large and highly concentrated; in the case of non-oil exporting countries, they have been highly selective".[1]

The facts show that the Third World market has split into big groups: the more advanced countries, which international bankers, using various criteria, classify as "good clients", and the less advanced countries which cannot easily obtain bank credit. In a tacit international division of credit, banks are increasingly participating in the financing of the first group, while suggesting to the World Bank and Monetary Fund that they should see to the needs of the second group of countries. Commenting on this, a member of the United States Council of Economic Advisors asserted that "relatively few banks have carried the bulk of the loans and relatively few developing countries with high income levels have had access to this source of financing. At the same time, official development financing has been increasingly slanted towards the poorer developing countries...".[2]

TABLE 7

Distribution of loans disbursed by private international banks to 94 developing countries grouped by income level[a]

(In percentages)

	1970	1973	1974	1975	1976
1. High-income countries ($801 and over per capita)	68.7	72.7	69.9	66.8	70.0
2. Middle-income countries ($301 - $800 per capita)	24.7	19.0	20.5	21.6	19.8
3. Low-income countries (under $300 per capita)	6.6	8.3	9.6	11.6	10.2
	100.0	100.0	100.0	100.0	100.0
Non-oil-exporting countries	80.9	76.3	85.0	83.6	80.8
Oil-exporting-countries	19.1	23.7	15.0	16.4	19.2

SOURCE: UNCTAD secretariat on the basis of World Bank data "External indebtedness of developing countries. A statistical note" (TD/B/C.3/148), 19 September 1978.

(a) Gross national product per capita(in current dollars)in 1975.

(1) Graham Perrett: "The international capital market and the international monetary system",*Finanzas y Desarrollo* Vol. 15, No. 4, December 1978.

(2) Marina V.N.Whitman: *Bridging the gap*, Finacorp, 1978.

Concentration of lending banks

Various studies and the data available suggest that an increasing number of international banks are engaged in lending to developing countries. For example, it is estimated that 605 banks were concerned with lending to the developing countries between 1971 and 1973, and their number is likely to have become still higher in the last few years. Of these banks, 475 are located in OECD member countries (137 in the United States, 107 in the United Kingdom, 57 in France and 31 in Japan), and 110 are in more than 20 countries of Africa, Asia and Latin America. As P.A. Wellons has said, "the countries where the institutions are domiciled is not necessarily the same as the countries where the loans are decided and the capital originates."(1) Thus,of the 475 banks in the OECD countries, 157 are under the control of a bank or banks in another country (usually itself an OECD member).

However, a fairly sizeable proportion of the Third World's external debt was owed to a group of major banks, mainly of American origin. Towards the end of 1975, two-thirds of the private external debt of those countries came from loans granted by United States banks, and, what is even more important, nearly 40 per cent of the debt was accounted for by only six of those banks.(2)

(1) P.A. Wellons: "Developing country borrowings on the Euro-dollar market", _Etudes du Centre du Développement_, Paris, 1977, pp. 60-61.

(2) Miguel S. Wionczek (Director): _Estudios del Tercer Mundo_, "The extreme indebtedness of the developing countries", vol. 1, No. 2, June 1978, pp. 39-40. United States banks have continued to play a predominant role although there is evidence that Japanese and German banks in particular are expanding their business. As a index of this process, it may be noted that, of the 300 biggest international banks, United States banks dropped from 96 to 80 between 1971 and 1975, while Japanese banks increased from 46 to 52 during the same period. Nevertheless, banks under United States control still seem to do a large proportion of their business with the developing countries. It should also be remembered that of the 874 branches of transnational American banks, 641 (73%) were in the developing countries in 1975, while of the 2641 non-American transnational banks, the proportion in the developing countries was less than 50%. See X.Gorostiaga, _op.cit_.

Information furnished by the Morgan Guaranty Trust Co. indicates that the hegemony of the American banks in bank loans to the developing countries not members of OPEC amounted to 65 per cent of those countries' total external private debt towards the end of 1976. The banks' participation was highest in the non-oil producing countries of Asia and Africa (72.6 per cent) and next highest in their Latin American counterparts (63.6 per cent).[(1)]

The trend towards the concentration and internationalization of bank lending is inspired by a variety of factors. As already pointed out, it reflects the cycles of capitalism at the present time in which a phase of expansion and intensive capital accumulation is immediately followed by a crisis in which the main need is to use the surplus accumulated for some financial purpose. In the circumstances, control over capital in general became increasingly dependent on the control exercised over the well-springs of credit. This gave rise to what we might describe as the "artificial reproduction" of external debts and credits. Debts led to fresh debts and, by the same token, assets originated other assets.

The dominant role of the financial markets led to fierce competition and thus contributed to the formation of banking corporations or transnational concerns, veritable giants which centralized capital on a world scale and battle for profits at every level in which these leaders of financial capitalism are involved.

The internationalizing of banking was naturally associated with an increase in the scale of the international profits made by the big banks. The privatization of the external debt of the developing countries formed part of the process, although some bank executives try to minimize the importance of the transactions and gains made by the major banks in their operations with the Third World.[(2)]

(1) World Financial Markets, December, 1976.

(2) Irving S. Friedman, Senior Vice-President and Senior Advisor for International Operations of Citicorp has said that: "a recent study made by the Reserve City Bankers Association indicated that many of its members were not significantly involved in international loan transactions. Much of this business in the United States is handled by a relatively small number of banks, although at least 15 of the 20 principal banks are involved and in competition...The total amount of loans from United States banks to developing countries, taken as a whole, is probably less than 5% of the (total) loans of those banks...Consequently, the total loans made to developing countries amount to less than one year's profits for the banking system", The emerging role of private banks in the developing world, Citicorp, 1977.

From the information available, it appears that the five principal United States banks with the highest profits from international lending operations, listed in accordance with the level of profits made in 1975, are: Citicorp., Bank of America Corp., J.P. Morgan & Co., Chase Manhattan Corp., Manufacturers Hanover Corp., and Chemical N.Y. Corp. These five accounted for 77.9 per cent of the total profits from international operations accruing to the 13 principal United States banks.(1)

It should also be borne in mind that international loan operations carry considerable weight in the total profits made by banks. The figures available indicate that the international gains of the 13 principal United States banks amounted to 34.2 per cent of total profits in 1973 and 47.7 per cent in 1975,(2) and it is estimated that roughly 75 per cent of the profits of United States banks in 1976 came from their foreign operations.(3)

Although there is no information on the incidence of the gains obtained from loans to developing countries in total profits, there is good reason to believe that it has become fairly significant, partly because of the weight which loans to these countries has now assumed in total international lending. Table 8 indicates that the developing countries and member countries of OPEC accounted in 1977 for more than 40 per cent of the international loans made by three of the principal United States banks. Again, the margin and commission charged by the big banks over and above the interest rates on loans to developing countries are higher than in the case of loans to industrial countries, as we shall see in the next chapter.

It is logical to suppose therefore that, as loans to developing countries account for a substantial percentage of the total international transactions of the major banks and as in addition a high proportion of their total gains derive from their lending operations, the developing countries represent an important and expanding source of profit

(1) Salomón Brother: "United States multinational banking: current and prospective strategies", Euromoney, September, 1976.

(2) "The 75 most active lead managers in the Euromarket", Euromoney, September, 1976.

(3) Miguel S. Wionczek: "The external debt of the less developed countries and the Euromarkets: an impressive past, an uncertain future", Comercio Exterior, Vol. 27, No. 11, (Mexico: November, 1977).

for the big banking corporations in proportion with the Third World's ranking as a borrower. It need only be remembered that Citicorp. informed its shareholders that its operations with Brazil alone had yielded 13 and 20 per cent of its total profits in 1976 and 1977 respectively.(1)

TABLE 8

International loans made by three of the principal United States banks, year-end 1977

(Millions of dollars)

	Citicorp		Bank of America		Chase Manhattan	
		%		%		%
Developing countries	11,100	37.0	6,080	32.0	5,610	33.0
OPEC	3,000	10.00	1,710	9.0	1,360	8.0
Industrial countries	15,300	51.0	10,450	55.0	9,520	56.0
Centrally planned countries	600	2.0	760	4.0	510	3.0
Total	30,000	100.0	19,000	100.0	17,000	100.0

SOURCE: Prepared from data in "International banking: a survey - Competing onshore", The Economist, 31 March 1979.

However, the increasing scale of their operations places constraints on the competition between the big banking consortia. When the concentration of loans reaches a certain level, mechanisms are required to raise profits and lessen risks. The result has been the inception and development of banking syndicates and "clubs", (2) which are essentially co-operative mechanisms for specific transactions.

(1) CIDE: "Brazil: the critical conjuncture of a model", Economía de América Latina, No.1 (Mexico: September 1978).

(2) In Europe, the principal banking "clubs" are the Associated Banks of Europe Corporation (ABECOR), Europartners, European Banks International Company (EBIC) and Interalpha.

The most familiar device is the syndication of bank credits, especially since the early years of the 1970s, when it coincided with the Euromarket boom.

There are several advantages which this type of organization can offer its members. In the first place, it allows them to reach very high loan levels that are consonant with the demands often made by public bodies and enterprises. Secondly, it distributes the risks so as to prevent a critical situation from arising in the event of a default. Risk-sharing thus becomes a source of strength, since a joint commitment by banks in different countries presents a solid front to discourage the outbreak of disputes with debtor States. Thirdly, loan fragmentation makes for the transfer and endorsement of debts to other banks; in other words, it encourages the recirculation of debts. Fourthly, it increases the profitability of loans through additional commissions for administration and partipation (these questions will be discussed later). Lastly, these devices make it possible for the big banks to operate in certain cases simply as the organizers of financial projects, in other words, they sell their services as project-finance engineers.

Looked at from the standpoint of the developing countries, syndicated loans enhance their dependence on a handful of major international banks, since it is these which usually operate as the organizers and leaders of the syndicates.

Trends during the next decade

The latest figures (1977 and estimates for 1978) indicate that the flood of private bank loans into the developing countries, which was at its height in 1974-1976, is now easing slightly. According to OECD data,[1] credits granted by private United States banks and Eurobanks to Third World countries rose by 29.7 per cent in 1976 over the previous year, but increased by only 11.1 per cent in 1977.

The decline is confirmed by World Bank data for Latin America. The total debt of the non-oil-exporting countries of Latin America increased by 11.9 per cent in 1977 as against 28.0 per cent in 1976. Estimates for 1978 indicated that it grew by a little over 10 per cent. These figures show that the indebtedness of the Third World countries is now increasing at a more moderate pace.

(1) Financial Market Trends, various numbers.

TABLE 9

Projection of the outstanding medium-term and long-term debts of the developing countries[1]
(Billions of current dollars)

Source	1975 Amount	1975 %	1976 Amount	1976 %	1977 Amount	1977 %	1980 Amount	1980 %	1985 Amount	1985 %
Public	44.4	34.7	51.4	32.7	61.9	31.6	99.4	36.9	186.3	34.8
Private	83.5	65.3	106.0	67.3	134.0	68.4	169.5	63.1	349.8	65.2
Total	127.9	100.0	157.4	100.0	195.9	100.0	268.9	100.0	536.1	100.0

SOURCE: International Currency Review, vol. 10, No. 5, prepared on the basis of data from the International Monetary Fund and World Bank.

(1) Countries with a per capita product of over $250 in 1976 (includes Southern European countries but not the oil-exporting countries).

However, the tendencies forecast suggest that indebtedness to private sources will continue unabated in the future.

Table 9 shows that the projections made on the basis of World Bank and IMF data forecast a similar percentage for the private debt in 1985 as the total debt in 1975. If these projections are realized, this will mean that halfway through the next decade the developing countries will have approximately two-thirds of their debt contracted to private sources. This also seems to be the view of bankers themselves.

II. MODALITIES OF THE DEVELOPING COUNTRIES' DEBT TO BANKS

This is a consensus that the privatization of the developing countries' external debt has coincided with a change in the terms and conditions of the loans granted. Between 1969 and 1975 there was a marked decline in the coefficient or concessional element of the developing countries' debt. This is true of all the operational conditions (maturity, period of grace and rate of interest), which demonstrates that the deterioration in lending terms was correlated with the expansion of private loans which took place throughout those years. In other words, the hardening of the terms on which private bank loans were granted had an adverse effect on the terms of the external debt as a whole.

TABLE 10

Average terms of the total external financing extended to 84 developing countries and Latin America

	84 developing countries		Latin America and the Caribbean	
	1969	1975	1969	1975
Maturity (years)	18.0	15.3	14.0	10.4
Grace period (years	5.0	4.5	3.6	3.1
Interest (annual percentage)	5.4	6.7	6.7	7.5
Concessional element (percentage)	29.0	20.0	18.0	11.0

SOURCE: World Bank reports, 1977 and 1978.

Debt maturities

Up to 1972 the loans obtained in the Eurocurrency market -an important source of the developing countries' debt to private banks - had maturities of 5 to 7 years. From 1972 to 1974, as a result of the trend of development in that market, the average maturity was extended to 10 to 12 years. Roughly 75 per cent of the loans to the developing countries were for more than 7 years. It was at that time that Brazil, for instance, succeeded in obtaining some loans with a 15-year maturity.

After 1974, however, the average period was shortened again to between 5 and 7 years. Loans with a maturity of over 10 years became virtually unobtainable until 1977.

TABLE 11

Maturities of loans in Eurocurrencies

(In percentages)

	1974	1975	1976	1977	1978 (second half)
Industrialized countries	100.0	100.0	100.0	100.0	100.0
1 to 3 years	3.2	8.0	5.5	1.2	3.1
3 to 5 years	11.6	36.7	27.5	10.6	5.3
5 to 7 years	30.6	39.0	54.1	63.0	11.0
Over 7 years	50.7	8.1	4.4	19.0	75.8
No data	3.9	8.1	8.5	6.2	4.7
Developing countries	100.0	100.0	100.0	100.0	100.0
1 to 3 years	1.9	5.7	2.3	3.9	2.6
3 to 5 years	13.6	62.9	53.6	19.5	3.8
5 to 7 years	18.5	24.1	30.6	63.8	25.9
Over 7 years	62.5	5.0	4.7	8.6	65.3
No data	3.6	2.2	8.9	4.2	2.4

SOURCE: E/CEPAL/1061, 7 February 1979, based on World Bank data.

Of the countries in debt to the Eurocurrency market, it was the developing countries which were hardest hit and bore the brunt of the deterioration in the maturities allowed. Between 1973 and 1975, the average period was reduced from 12 to 7 years for Algeria, from 12 to 6 1/2 years for Brazil and from 9 to 5 years for Peru. An extreme case was that of Mexico, which up to 1976 was given loans at maturities that were less than half those it had obtained three years earlier

It is only recently that there has been some extension of the amortization period, which has made it possible for certain countries to obtain new loans with a 10-year maturity. In all cases, however, loan maturity was longer for the industrialized countries than for the developing countries.

The reduction of maturities led to a concentration of debt over the relatively short term, and this altered their profile. The UNCTAD secretariat estimated that three-quarters of loans outstanding for the period 1973-1976 had to be repaid between 1977 and 1981 and that nearly half of them had to be re-imbursed between 1977 and 1979. The balance-of-payments effect of this variation in maturities is obvious and, as we shall see in due course, exerted serious pressure on the developing countries.

Interest rates and cost of loans

The interest rate levied on commercial bank loans is mainly determined by two indicators: the London interbank offer rate (LIBOR) and the rate for top category banks in New York (the prime rate). In both cases, the rates are applied to short-term loan operations of not more than 6 months.

In recent years, the interest charged on private loans to the developing countries has tended to raise the cost of external financing. This is stated in the light of the trend taken by the rate of interest and of other elements which must be taken into account in bank transactions such as the risk spread or margin, commission, fees, etc.

With regard to interest rate plus spread, the average rates prevailing since the expansion of the Eurocurrency market in 1972-1973 were a good deal higher than the rates recorded earlier. In spite of the market fluctuations, the prevailing trend is upward. More recently, the annual rate of interest plus the risk spread seems to be averaging 10 to 11 per cent (see Table 12). Moreover, with the roll-over practice adopted for Euro-loans, based on a six-monthly revision of interest rates, the upward trend has been largely instrumental in raising the cost of loans. The formula, which was suitable for converting short-term funds into medium-term and long-term loans, creates unstable conditions involving a high risk of loss.

TABLE 12

Interest rate plus risk spread of Euroloans[1]

(In annual percentages)

	1967-1971	1972	1973	1974	1975	1976	1977	1978	1979[2]
Non-oil-exporting developing countries									
Interest		5.86	9.32	11.20	7.62	6.13	6.30	9.34	12.4
Risk spread	____	1.50	1.19	1.19	1.68	1.71	1.50	____	____
	7.34	7.36	10.51	12.39	9.30	7.84	7.80		
Average for all countries (interest rate plus risk spread)			10.20	12.14	8.94	7.69	7.50		

SOURCE: UNCTAD secretariat, TD/AC.2/2 of 20 June 1977. The data for 1977-1978 have been estimated on the basis of International Financial Statistics and, for January 1959, Financial Market Trends, No. 8.

(1) Annual average of LIBOR at six months, plus the weighted average of the spread.
(2) January.

Thus, there may be a very significant variation in the amounts which the developing countries are required to pay as interest. The publication Latin America Informe Semanal [1] states that :

> "...the sharp rise in the floating rate (LIBOR), which has risen from the level of 7 per cent halfway through the past year to nearly 12 per cent at the present time...has, at a stroke, increased the interest payments to be made by Brazil this year by $660 million and those of Mexico by about $500 million.

The situation is made worse for the developing countries by the fact that the annual rate of interest plus the risk spread charged is usually a quarter to a half a point above the average terms set for all countries operating in the Eurocurrency market. Even when the risk tends to be reduced, as in 1977, not all the developing countries benefit from this. L'Observateur of OECD, in March 1978, stated that the spread was reduced by under 1 per cent at the end of 1977 for recipient countries of the first rank. Of the developing countries, only Venezuela, Iran and Malaysia were able to operate at that level. Consequently, neither Algeria, or South Korea or any of the other countries were in a position to benefit from the reduction. Brazil, for example, continues to operate with a margin of 1 7/8 to 2 1/8 per cent.

We must add to this the commission fees charged, which are usually omitted from the international loan cost studies made by private banks. This "front charge", as such fees are described in banking circles, is an additional burden which has become part of normal loan practice. Its significance can be measured by the fact that its level is almost equal to the cost of the risk spread.[2] It may even be

(1) "Euromonedas: el recurso sin lîmite", Latin America Informe Semanal, Vol. 1, no. 1, 4 June 1979, p. 3

(2) "Latin America's External Indebtedness: current situation and prospects", Inter-American Development Bank, May, 1977, p. 25 (Spanish text): "The spread on the rate of interest has been as high as 2.5 per cent in some cases, and this, together with other charges, has raised the real cost of the loans to more than 4 per cent of LIBOR".

higher since, for reasons of market prestige, some lenders prefer to increase the commission payable - whose existence and amount are often unnoticed - while lowering the risk spread, which is reported internationally.

The rise in the overall cost of private international bank loans has undoubtedly increased the burden which interest payments (even without the commission fees) represent for total external debt servicing by the developing countries. According to UNCTAD, between the years 1970 and 1976, the proportion of interest in the external debt servicing of 97 developing countries expanded from 30.5 to 38.8 per cent. It is illuminating that the added weight of interest charges should coincide with an increase in the proportion of interest paid to private banks. In 1970, the developing countries channelled 14.8 per cent of their total interest payments abroad to private international banks. In 1976, of the $7 billion paid by 97 developing countries under the head of interest, 39 per cent ($2.7 billion) went into the coffers of the private banks.

The situation is much worse in Latin America and the Caribbean. As a result of the region's increasing indebtedness to private international banks and the higher cost of loans, the proportion of its interest payments in its external debt servicing as a whole rose by 25.5 per cent in the period 1966-1969 to 40.1 per cent in the years 1974-1977.

---

(1) Fred A. Jaspersen: "Perspectivas de deuda externa y crecimiento econômico de Amêrica Latina", Revista Monetaria, (CEMLA: January - March 1978) pp. 56-57 (Spanish text).

TABLE 13

Commission fees charged on international loans made by commercial banks(1)

Type of Fee	Estimated Cost
1. Commitment fee	
Payable on that portion of the loan which has not been made during the drawdown period	0.5 per cent annually
2. Participation fee	
Fee payable to the banks in the syndicate	0.625 per cent at the opening or withdrawal of the credit
3. Management fee	
Fee payable to the managing bank or agent	0.375 per cent on the amount of the loan and $10,000 annually

SOURCE: Samuel Bandele Falegan: "¿Por qué Nigeria se abstiene de solicitar préstamos al Euromarcado?", Endeudamiento Externo de los países en desarrollo, (Mexico: Colegio de México and Third World Center for Economic and Social Studies, 1979) pp. 477-478, (Spanish text).

(1) Based on a Eurobank proposal to Nigeria with a 7 year maturity, 2 years of grace and a spread of 1.625 per cent annually over LIBOR.

Destination of loans

All the publications on this subject refer to the serious obstacles encountered in attempting to establish the destination of the bank loans made to the developing countries. When the problem is approached from the institutional point of view, emphasis is laid on the continual under-estimation of the credits granted to the private sector, it can be seen that the bulk of the funds is taken by public or semi-public enterprises or companies, whether directly concerned with the production of goods and services or connected with financial activities. It must be remembered in this respect that the real guarantees which certain banks and public concerns in the developing countries are able to give have ensured that certain loans have been contracted by those bodies with a view to their use by others or by the central government.

TABLE 14

Destination of bank loans to developing countries

(In percentages)

	Eurocredits (1)	Placements by 119 United States banks (2)
Public Sector	90	93
a) Semi-public bodies	55	
- general	(3)	
- Central Banks and exchange houses	(12)	
- financial sector	(12)	
- extractive industries and information	(17)	
- public utilities	(5)	
- transport	(5)	
Private Sector	8	7
Unclassified	2	

SOURCE: P.A. Wellons: *Les emprunts des pays en développement sur le marché des euro-dollars*, (Paris: 1977); and Federal Reserve Bank Release, January 1978.

(1) Based on Euromarket loans of the order of $11.5 billion between 1971 and 1973.
(2) Based on the balance, as of 30 June 1977, of placements of over a year for the value of $26 billion.

If it is clear that judgements on the institutional destination of the external debt to private international banks have to be relative, it is even more difficult to reach a conclusion on the economic destination of the loans made. As Wellons has aptly pointed out:

> "It is difficult to determine from most of the information published, the destination of Euroloans and their impact. Since loans to project free funds that are committed to other uses, all loans to governments have implications for the national budget. Numerous loans made to public sector recipients may also help to improve the balance of payments by increasing the reserves."(1)

All these considerations demonstrate that, instead of following statistical indicators, the way to deal with this problem is to make a critical analysis of its global effects. This entails the formulation of a hypothesis on the impact produced by the policy of the private banks on the functioning and strategies of the developing countries, which is to be the subject of the next chapter.

---

(1) P.A. Wellons: <u>op.cit.</u>, pp. 36-37.

III. CRITICAL ANALYSIS OF THE EFFECTS OF EXTERNAL INDEBTEDNESS TO THE PRIVATE INTERNATIONAL BANKS.

The analysis of the consequences of the indebtedness of the developing countries to the private international banks prompts certain observations about the approach used. In most cases, indebtedness has been analyzed mainly from the standpoint of its effects on the net balance and structure of the balance of payments of the debtor countries. It cannot be denied that the first impact which is noticed and calculated is precisely that which the amounts of debt and debt servicing have on external flows.

This kind of approach corresponds, moreover, to the kind of immediate concerns of both the lenders and the governments of the debtor countries with regard to the disbursement and payment of the transactions agreed. In other words, judgements about solvency and capacity to pay have been continually associated with the analysis of trade flows and the external financing handled by the lender countries.

This evaluation of the impact of external debt is necessary and has been constantly enriched - to the point of extreme sophistication - through the elaboration of new formulas designed to give more reliable indicators of the real capacity to pay of the debtor countries. While this methodology is both necessary and inevitable, it is also evident that it is inadequate.

On the one hand, when it is used in isolation it may lend weight to the belief that the only conditions which restrict or open access to the loans of the private international banks are strictly financial in nature. This supposition seems to have won a privileged place in many studies which emphasize the banks' relative lack of interest in the purpose of the loans, the facilities for processing them, the absence of commitments or letters of intent about features of economic policy, etc. Yet this lack of interest is more apparent than real. A more thorough analysis shows that the banks are not indifferent to the characteristics of the economies to which they extend loans, the kind of policies pursued by governments, the main features of the social and political situation, etc.

The logic behind the functioning of the private international banks - particularly as their invested capital has risen, with the consequent need for greater control over the economies of the debtor countries - has caused the notion of "risk per loan" (as a unit of analysis) to be superseded by that of "country risk". In this shift from one concept to another, the conditions for each operation tend to be replaced by conditions affecting development strategies, which in turn implies a much more searching scrutiny of economic, social and political affairs. The international private banks have not, in this way, come to replace the International Monetary Fund (or have done so only transitorily) but they have become an instrument which strengthens the control which the Fund has wielded in the postwar period, and which has been detrimental to the levels of autonomy of the developing countries and conducive to a new international division of labor.

Constant reference to the guidelines and criteria on which international private banks base their lending policies may also give the impression that theirs are the only interests which influence those policies. There is no doubt that bank profits are a prime objective of lending policy. However, it is essential to consider those banks as an expression of financial and industrial capital and their profits as a variable of the return on that capital at the international level. In this way one can see why it is true that not all business deals are equally acceptable, even if their rate of return for the bank is high. Since international private banks are able to support the transnational corporations engaged in production or trade, their purpose has to be seen as the attainment of the highest possible levels of profits for each transnational complex as a whole.

From this point of view it is the role of the bank, on the one hand, to make high profits, and, on the other, to act as a lever to help transnational capital penetrate the developing countries. This latter process does not readily lend itself to empirical expression. First of all because it may operate indirectly, in the form of external loans to the public sector. Moreover its influence is relative, since it is exerted within a flow of funds in which access to international loans may vary according to conditions on the national credit markets. An analysis along these lines requires a macro-economic view of the effects of external indebtedness.

In other words, the critical evaluation of the effects of the indebtedness of the developing countries to the international private banks has to take place at four levels: a) the compulsory, traditional balance-of-payments approach; b) the relationship between external debt and the restructuring of the international division of labor; c) the less common but equally necessary factor of the effects of that indebtedness on the strategy and economic policy of the

the developing countries; and d) the impact of the big private banks on the processes of concentration and denationalization of productive capital.

External debt and balance of payments

Consideration of the effects of external indebtedness on the borrowing countries tends to focus on its effects on balance-of-payments adjustments. Studies on the subject usually base this kind of analysis on two major themes: a) the relationship between import capacity and external credit, and b) the magnitude of the debt service burden.

With regard to import capacity, it is logical to presume that external credits have made it possible to maintain imports of goods and services. This is particularly evident in the non-oil-exporting developing countries, which have suffered from constant and increasing upheavals in their foreign trade, mainly as a consequence of the sharp fluctuations of prices for their exports and losses due to unfavorable terms of trade. This phenomenon has become more pronounced since the mid-sixties. Between 1973 and 1978 alone, it is estimated that the non-oil-exporting developing countries ran up a current account deficit of some 188 billion dollars.(1)

If one analyzes the weight of external debt in relation to imports of goods and services, one realizes that it has come to play an increasingly important part in sustaining external purchasing capacity. It thus becomes clear that, between 1973 and 1976 inclusive, about 20% of the 571 billion dollars' worth of goods and services imported by the developing countries depended, directly or indirectly, on access to external credit. The Latin American countries seem to have been even more heavily dependent on such credits. The ratio between inflow of foreign capital (in all forms) and imports of goods and services rose from 8% in 1965 to 28% in 1971 and an annual average of 40% during the period 1972-1975.(2)

---

(1) According to UNCTAD information published in 1977 (quoted in the study - "The development of international debt", p. 44, published in Internationale Verschuldung, Schulthess P. Verlag, Zurich, 1978) the current account deficits already recorded are the following (in billions of dollars): 12.2 (1973); 30.5 (1974); 41.4 (1975); and 28.4(1976). The projected deficits for 1977 and 1978 are36.3 and 38.9 respectively.

(2) Robert Devlin: "El financiamiento externo y los bancos comerciales", Revista de la CEPAL, 1st half of 1978, pp. 85-86.

Import possibilities have been made even more heavily dependent on external debt by the current magnitude of the servicing of that debt. The destabilizing effects which such payments have on the debtor countries have been increasingly recognized; in fact for many developing countries the payment of earlier debts begins to herald the need for future indebtedness. It should be borne in mind that, according to certain estimates, by 1980 1.5 out of every 3 dollars lent to the developing countries will go on debt payments. By 1985, 2 out of every 3 such dollars will be spent in this way.(1)

For different reasons, among them the inflexibility of the private banks when it comes to altering the terms of debt, and the caution and fears of the lending countries at the thought that the financial markets might fall into disrepute, the fact is that those debt service payments are becoming a relatively fixed component of the policies of the debtor countries. As a result, balance-of-payments adjustments attributable to the pressure of debt servicing are unloaded on the trade balance. Then either in the form of import restrictions or intense promotion of exports, the developing countries are eventually driven towards lower levels of basic consumption or to a general economic slowdown. In these circumstances one can see how policies designed to benefit the balance of payments begin to fit into a process in which the country's economic and social development strategy is at stake.

The problem has become more serious as indebtedness to the private international banks has risen. The relatively unfavorable terms on which loans are granted leads, as we have seen, to a paradox: the more debt servicing one pays, the less one's debt is amortized, in relative terms. (see Tables 15 and 16). While the servicing of private bank debts doubled its share of total debt servicing, rising from 14.6% to 30.6% between 1970 and 1976, the rate of amortization of that debt dropped to less than half in the same period. But amortization will begin to weigh heavily in the next few years.

The vulnerablility caused by this pressure to pay can be recorded in numerous indicators. First of all, it has reduced the function formerly performed by reserves. They, as their name suggests, acted in certain critical situations, to finance external flows, both commercial and capital. Nonetheless, while the developing countries in 1967 had reserves equivalent to one third of their external debt,

(1) Miguel S. Wionczek: "El endeudamiento externo de los paises en desarrollo", <u>Estudios del Tercer Mundo</u>,Vol.1, No. 2, June 1978, p. 39

TABLE 15

External debt service disbursed for 94 developing countries

(In billions of dollars)

Years	Debt servicing from official sources	%	Debt servicing from private bank sources	%	Debt servicing from other private sources	%	Total	%
1970	2.70	46.8	0.84	14.6	2.23	38.6	5.77	100.0
1973	4.43	40.3	2.66	24.2	3.91	35.5	11.00	100.0
1974	5.16	38.3	4.27	31.7	4.03	30.0	13.46	100.0
1975	5.83	39.6	4.19	28.5	2.70	31.9	14.72	100.0
1976	6.56	38.3	5.24	30.6	5.31	31.1	17.11	100.0

SOURCE: UNCTAD Secretariat with data from World Bank "External indebtedness..." *op.cit.*

TABLE 16

Amortization of external debt for

94 developing countries

(As % of debt balances)

Years	Amortization of debt from official sources in terms of the balance of official debt	Amortization of debt from private bank sources in terms of private bank debt	Amortization of debt from other private sources in terms of the balance of other private debts
1970	4.9	15.5	14.3
1973	5.0	13.9	16.9
1974	5.1	14.7	15.8
1975	4.6	8.1	17.1
1976	4.3	6.6	16.5

SOURCE: UNCTAD Secretariat with data from World Bank "External indebtedness..." *op.cit*.

ten years later it barely amounted to one tenth of it. Reserves then failed to perform their function of providing overall coverage of the external flows of the most heavily indebted countries. For those countries, which were acutely dependent on a flow of new loans, reserves were reduced to the role of guarantees or collateral for the loans. Worse still, those reserves were gradually formed at the expense of the indebtedness itself: in other words, the international private banks also made loans in order to establish a body of reserves for the payment of their own loans.

Secondly, debt servicing absorbs an increasingly large share of the exports of goods and services of the developing countries. The situation of certain medium- or high-income countries whose indebtedness has become accelerated is particularly delicate. (see Table 17)

TABLE 17

Ratio of external debt servicing for 84 developing countries

Service ratio[1]	1973	1974	1975
	(Number of countries)		
10% or less	56	63	60
Between 10% and 20%	22	18	16
Over 20%	6	3	8

SOURCE: World Bank, 1977

(1) Servicing of public debt in respect of exports of goods and services not attributed to factors.

The fact that there is a great majority of Latin American countries among those with the highest debt service ratios is attributable to the extensive nature of their access to the private capital markets. In recent years the situation of countries which already had a high debt service ratio has become more critical: in the case of Peru, for example, debt service ratio amounted to 46.3% in 1978. At the same time, certain countries which had not been among those which used a high proportion of hard currency derived from exports to pay off external debts now began to do so. This is true of Brazil, which came close to the top in 1978 with a ratio of almost 40%, while Bolivia's ratio in that same year approached the threshold of 30%. (Table 18 provides data for 1975)

TABLE 18

Developing countries with the highest debt service ratio in 1975

1. Uruguay	45.9% (a)
2. Chile	28.4% (a)
3. Mexico	25.9% (a)
4. Egypt	25.7%
5. Peru	23.8% (a)
6. Argentina	22.0% (a)
7. Sudan	21.3%
8. Sri Lanka	20.3%

SOURCE: World Bank, 1977.

(a) The figures for these countries in 1976 are the following: Uruguay - 34.1; Chile - 34.5; Mexico - 37.1; Peru - 21.8; and Argentina - 18.3.

Most of the developing countries have suffered intense destabilizing pressures on their balance of payments as a result of mounting external debt servicing. It is generally felt that this phenomenon has grown worse with the expansion of lending by private international banks. However, certain studies, proceeding from an empirical basis, claim that those debt service payments have been fairly stable when measured in constant prices. (see Table 19)

TABLE 19

Debt service of 75 non-oil exporting developing countries

Debt service (billions of dollars)	1973	1974	1975	1976
Current prices	8.8	9.7	11.6	13.8
1970 prices[a]	6.4	5.1	6.2	7.0

SOURCE: World Bank quoted in IMF Survey, April 9, 1977.

(a) Deflated with export prices.

These figures uphold the opinions of those for whom the magnitude of indebtedness and debt servicing is only relative, since it is argued that international inflation depresses the real value of external liabilities and payments. Reasoning of this sort can lead one to the extreme of claiming that, in an inflationary climate, external debt is more beneficial to the debtors than to the creditors.

This attitude, which really amounts to saying that external debt is not, after all, such a great burden on the balance of payments, has been thoroughly refuted by several authors.[1] In particular, they have pointed out that it is a grave error to deflate debt and debt servicing by the export or import price index. It can be shown that the real value of debt servicing is affected by three things: a) changes in the future flow of payments (mainly interest); b) changes in the social value of currencies; and c) the need for domestic sacrifices (lower consumption now or in the future) to obtain foreign exchange. On this basis it cannot be claimed that there is a real reduction of the impact of indebtedness. In fact there is every reason to sup-

(1) Carlos Massad and Roberto Zahler: Inflacion mundial y deuda externa: el caso de la deflactación impropria, (Santiago de Chile: CEPAL, July 1977).

pose that "in certain circumstances the effect might be that of increasing the weight of debt".(1) We may thus safely conclude that external debt service payments of the developing countries are a basic factor in the dislocation of their balance of payments, and that, in recent years, the contracting of debts to the private international banks has tended to aggravate those imbalances.

External debt as a "national risk": a new modality for evaluation.

Further critical analysis of external debt necessarily involves a reference to the new modality for evaluation which the international private banks have introduced in recent years. The criteria applied by lending banks in judging the conditions which a potential borrower must fulfill to qualify as a "good client" have evolved significantly. The change in criteria has gone well beyond the concept of solvency and its assessment in purely financial terms and has now led, basically, to a global evaluation of the country involved ("country risk"). This phenomenon implies that relations of indebtedness to the private international banks have now reached the stage where they distinctly influence fundamental aspects of the autonomy of the borrowing country.

During the sixties it was generally believed that lenders relied mainly on rates of indebtedness as a means of deciding whether to extend credit to an applicant. One important ratio which was extensively used initially was that based on the number of years worth of exports which were owed to external lenders. In this respect a critical indicator was the point at which external indebtedness exceeded the value of three years worth of exports. Consideration was also given to the amount of foreign exchange available and an estimate was made of how many month's worth of goods and services could be bought with that foreign exchange. The margin of security was defined on the basis of an amount not lower than three months of imports. Later on it became increasingly common to use the ratio of external debt servicing to exports of goods and services ("debt service ratio"). It was felt that a ratio not exceeding 20% entitled the lender to be reasonably confident of getting his money back. Above this rate there lay a critical zone in which credit applications were rejected or subjected to certain conditions.

(1) C. Massad and R. Zahler: *op.cit.*, pp. 1,5 and6.

In actual fact, long before the expansion of external indebtedness to international private banks, the method of evaluation had already become quite complex and involved much more than following mere financial indicators. The conditions which the International Monetary Fund imposed on compensatory loans above the first tranche of the quota were for many years used as benchmarks for private internationalcredit. In other words, the private international banks participated, indirectly, in loans or refinancing for countries in balance-of-payments difficulties as long as those countries, which were usually underdeveloped, made certain commitments to the IMF which necessarily affected their macro-economic policies and their development strategies.[1]

The economists Duff and Peacock have pointed out that until the end of 1976 the private banks were still relying on the information made available and the judgement provided by the IMF.[2] These authors note that the main

---

(1) This point was already being emphasized in 1967: "The IMF's relations with the United States and European banking systems, as with the international institutions (World Bank, Inter-American Development Bank, etc.) have been described more than once. The Fund acts like an inspector whose job it is to give or withhold his endorsement. If its judgement is negative, the country is virtually regarded as a dangerous debtor and is made subject to credit restrictions. The endorsement of the IMF is thus decisive in the foreign banking world; the presence of high IMF officials in private United States activity is therefore highly suggestive". Samuel Lichtensztejn: El FMI y la crisis economica internacional, (Uruguay: Librería de Cultura Universitaria), (in collaboration with Alberto Couriel).

(2) Duff and Peacock: "The experience of the international banks with loans to the developing countries", The Banker, reproduced in Dos Bancos, year 1, No. 2, (Bueno Aires, Argentina: June 1977).

indicators were the ratio of debt servicing to exports, the level of international reserves and the level of per capita income. A study by the Export-Import Bank in December 1976[1] of the criteria applied by 37 United States banks with international business found that many of them lacked systems for the evaluation of the global or country risk they incurred by granting a loan. Consequently a large number of private banks thus studied were found to be lending to the developing countries on the basis of meagre or conventional methods of forecasting. There could have been several reasons for this; for example, some of the banks were operating with lower guarantees than those considered advisable by the financial market, in an attempt to circulate the large amount of liquidity which they had accumulated. Also, credits were being granted within the framework of a broader stragegy of financial capital than that applicable to the granting of a loan on which timely reimbursement is expected.

Nevertheless, in the mid-70s a shift began to occur and the subject of lending criteria was taken very seriously in banking and financial circles. There are several reasons for this renewed interest on the part of banks in methods for the evaluation of their external loans: severe imbalances in the balance of payments, inflation and the international crisis, the enormous difficulties involved in securing an adjustment by commercial means, etc. There can be no doubt, however, that the magnitude of the loans granted and the external debt accumulated in the developing countries were crucial to this reconsideration of procedures and criteria for evaluation.

---

(1) Quoted by Richard S. Weinert: "Why the banks did it", <u>Finacorp</u>, San Pablo, Brazil, 1978.

The first expression of this phenomenon was the definition of new indicators for the proper estimate of the flow of foreign exchange.(1)

Secondly, it was suggested that statistical indicators be scrapped and replaced by dynamic analyses of flows and resources and even of the economic policies followed. The conclusions to be drawn for any given year from the service charges on external debt were now regarded as less important. This meant that two borrower countries might not be treated alike even though their debt service burdens were similar, while two countries with unequal liabilities might not be accorded proportionally different opportunities for access to the financial market. In this way,as noted in September 1977 by Ishan Kapur of the Division of External Finance of the IMF, the main criteria of the private banks began to include the average growth of the gross national product in recent years, the expected flow of exports, the country's export policy and the expected growth of debt servicing from current foreign exchange earnings.(2)

---

(1) Duff and Peacock suggest, for example, the following indicator for the proper assessment of the flow of currencies:

$$IFD = \frac{RA + AEN + LC + CE + IE}{SDPP}$$

RA = short-term assets, normally consisting for the most part of reserves.

AEN = net assets or liabilities in foreign exchange in the hands of private banks.

LC = loans granted to a country and still not used, including lines of bank credit

CE = positive or negative foreign trade balance

IE = net balance of service account.

SDPP = debt service (interest and repayment of loans).

(2) Ishan Kapur: "Fondos en eurodivisas para los paises en desarrollo", Finanzas y Desarrollo, Vol. 14, No. 3, September 1977, p. 32 and following.

Lastly, this was followed by the analysis of the country risk, an assessment of the global functioning of the Third World countries in the economic and financial, political and social spheres - the culmination and synthesis of the changes in the working methods of the private international banks. It is clear that the IMF and the World Bank were carrying out and still are carrying out their studies on the overall functioning of the developing countries. In the opinion of the bankers, however, the analyses prepared by those bodies can serve as a complement to the banks' own studies of their potential clients but cannot be a subsitute for them:

> "Banks can take advantage of the existence of outside expert sources of information and judgement - the various national official agencies dealing with foreign countries and the multinational agencies like the IMF, World Bank, regional development banks, U.N. agencies, OECD, the European Economic Community (EEC) agencies, and so forth... None of these sources, however, can be used effectively unless the private bank has its own capability to make judgement assessments.[(1)]

What, then are the main criteria which the big banks have started using to assess the situation of a country? Pancras J. Nagy contends that the "country risk" is to be understood as the possibility that a loss might be incurred by granting an international loan because of events which, at least to some extent, are under the control of the government of the borrowing country.[(2)] From that point of view, the concept of "country risk" is associated with the capacity for management not only in economic affairs but in all spheres of government activity.

The idea that the country must be "well-managed" is the key to determining its creditworthiness. But the question arises as to what bankers understand by "proper management". The answer is complex, and allowance must be made for different shades of emphasis. The "country risk" has been linked to the possibility of the occurrence of certain events which can be classified in three categories. On the one hand, there are the political risks involved in wars, occupation by foreign countries, rioting in the streets, internal ideological differences, conflicts of economic

(1) Irving S. Friedman, <u>op.cit.</u>, p. 49.

(2) Pancras J. Nagy: <u>Country risk, how to assess, quantify and monitor it</u>, (Euromoney Publications) p. 13.

interests, etc. On the other hand there are certain social risks associated with civil wars, uneven distribution of income, trade union militancy, religious divisions, antagonism between social classes, etc. Lastly there are the economic factors, including the decline in the growth of productivity, rapid price rises, a drop in exports, an increase in imports of food or energy, etc.

All of these elements are qualified and quantified and go to make up the picture of the situation and help monitor developments. The ordinary observer would usually attach little or no significance at all to facts which may become important in banking practice. This seems to be the case, in particular, with certain political evaluations. For example, in the opinion of Nagy, one particularly common myth is the belief that political stability is, in itself, a positive factor in obtaining bank credits. As he sees it, much more weight is attached to the anticipated ability of the potential successor government to run the country than to the political stability of the regime currently in power: "For example, the fact that the regime of Señora Perón was inherently unstable did not necessarily increase the "country risk" of Argentina".

The present government is thus as important as its potential successor, and the existence of a "well organized extremist group with a chance of coming to power" is one of the elements which bankers tend to take very seriously when forming a judgement about a country applying for a loan. Nagy distinguishes between various categories, among them the possibility that the "extremist group may come to power through elections" or "through a coup d'état because they are well-armed and/or led by capable and unscrupulous men and/or are receiving outside support.[1]

A change of government or a coup d'état - which, in the terminology of "country risk" are elegantly known as "changes in the identity of the borrower" - even includes the possibility that the "country may be occupied by a foreign power". This analysis also allows for the possibility that the forces which might take over the government may be inclined towards nationalizations ("indigenization"), or, on the contrary, that they may pursue the same kind of policies as the government in applying for the loan.[2]

(1) Nagy, op.cit., p. 55 and following.
(2) Nagy, op.cit., p. 59 and following.

Another observation which emerges from these evaluation methods is that an ironclad military regime, with technocrats trained in monetarism and put in charge of the economy, may not offer all the guarantees required by the lending bankers:

> "...Even when countries are headed by authoritarian regimes supported by an able technocratic team, there are important limits to their freedom of action. Such governments are not only limited by the inherent characteristics of their countries, such as low output or poor natural resources, but are often victims of their own past actions - e.g., excessive nationalism discouraging foreign capital inflows, technology and technicians; disturbed political and social conditions encouraging capital flight; emigration of skilled people; inheritance of weak or inadequate entrepreneurial skills; and earlier promises creating unrealistic expectations of consumption, employment and income distribution."(1)

Another interesting feature of this line of thinking is the importance which bankers attach to the expectations that Third World governments can arouse among the people. This is certainly related to the studies made by political scientists and sociologists in the United States in recent years, according to which many of the instances of "violence" which occur in the Third World countries (that is, political conflicts or more or less widespread popular discontent) are the result of the "false expectations" generated by their own governments.

The foregoing shows the importance which bankers attach to political aspects, which they evaluate on the basis of patterns which are ideologically consistent, though not dogmatic or rigid. The same kind of thing happens in certain spheres of economic evaluation. Of course,such analyses expose the myth of the belief that international monetary reserves are a basis and a component of confidence for new debts:

> "Borrowing externally to increase reserves, as in Brazil and Turkey, is quite different. The increased debt is in a sense a charge against reserves, and in that sense the net international position of the country is not fundamentally improved. These are not savings from past surpluses to meet future contingencies."(2)

(1) I. Friedman, op.cit., pp. 29 and 30.
(2) I. Friedman, op.cit., p. 23.

A more significant aspect of economic evaluation is what is usually known as "good management" of countries and the appropriate use of loans. In actual fact, this concept is not defined very explicitly in the documents which refer to it, though it should, on the whole, be interpreted as the application of what is regarded as the right kind of economic policy. Under this method, countries which fulfill the recommendations of the IMF score high marks. It is not difficult, for example, to conclude that a country is "well-managed" whenever its economic polices coincide with the traditional precepts of the IMF. Even so, it would be a mistake to think that monitoring and follow-up of the developing countries are, because of this identity of aims, left solely to the IMF. In fact the opposite is stated quite explicitly:

> "...acceptance of IMF conditions and the mere fact of being under IMF supervision do not necessarily mean that a country's 'country risk' has improved, because countries do not always comply with the conditions they have accepted. This is a fact which the commercial banks often neglect."(1)

As we shall see later, the literal interpretation of this position has meant that, in some cases (Peru, for example) the private international banks have operated openly, despite the well established belief that the banks lack the personnel and the experience to act as global managers of the financial markets and coordinators of economic policies. The fact that in the case of Peru since the experience of 1976, the banks have once more started to operate behind the IMF may well confirm these limitations. Even so, an important fact still remains: the private banks have formed and developed their own methods for appraisal and their own personnel for the economic, social and political auditing of Third World borrowers.

External debt and the international division of labor.

According to the information available, the loans extended by the international private banks to the developing countries have been used mainly for the financing of the public budget and for certain investment projects. In this latter sphere, in recent years, the bulk of financing has been concentrated in the extracting and manufacturing industries, public services and transport and energy, with particular intensity since 1974.

(1) Nagy, op.cit., footnote, p. 96.

Although the vice-president of Citicorp, in his "canons for borrowers", recommends that they "maximize the use of borrowings from private banks for export-oriented activities"(1) few projects financed by the banks have been directly associated with export.(2) Although it is not possible to seek a direct relationship between the intended purpose of the debt and foreign trade, it is commonly recognized and emphasized that major debtor countries are noted for their increasing exports of manufactured products or of certain highly coveted raw materials.(3) The influence of external debt on foreign trade is based not so much on its financing as on the forces and needs which such debt generates, and which eventually lead to the adoption of models of export or exposure to foreign sources.

In a number of underdeveloped countries this influence has precedents and deep historical roots, particularly with regard to the extraction and production of the raw materials needed by a developed and industrialized world. We shall shortly be considering some recent instances which illustrate the way the private international banks try to recover or consolidate the transnational control of stragegic sources of raw materials. In this part we are concerned with an analysis of a new phenomenon which, in the opinion of some authors, has a profound impact on the link between the Third World and the advanced capitalist countries: the relationship between external debt and the export of manufacturers.

To begin with, it should be noted that the encouragement of the export of manufactured goods cannot be regarded as a project - either explicit or implicit - of the private banks for all the developing countries. Such a sweeping judgement could hardly be valid for such a broad range of countries with such different levels of development. There can be no doubt, however, that the objectives of the private international banks include that of starting the export of certain manufactured goods in some of the developing countries.

(1) I. Friedman, op.cit., p. 75.
(2) P.A. Wellons, op.cit., pp. 88-90.
(3) Jean-Marie Parly: "Financement international du dévelop- pement", Revue Economique, Vol. 29, No. 6, November, 1978, p. 990.

This question is relevant to the international crisis of the past few years. On the one hand, in recessive stages, the procedure of external credit has made it possible to some extent to maintain the developing countries' imports of capital goods. In some cases, as we have seen, it has even augmented their import capacity.(1)

On the other hand, long-term banking business with the developing countries cannot be based on "compensatory loans" patterned on those of the IMF. In other words, it cannot be based on the objective of providing transitory remedies for balance of payments imbalances or constantly financing a country's import capacity. The needs of the banks, and also of the transnational corporations, both productive and commercial - particularly at a time of critical difficulties in the accumulation of capital - seem to be moving towards the shifting or re-deployment of certain manufacturing activities to the periphery of the industrial system. Of course this strategy, which has been pursued by certain developing countries, brings in foreign exchange with which to pay the debt service charges and thus makes it possible to incur further debt.

The foregoing considerations mean that external debt is a lever to bring about certain changes in the international division of labor. The private banks would be highly involved in the promotion of these changes and in

(1) "Commercial bank credits to the developing countries were of benefit to the industrialized countries in a number of ways. They provided their private financial sectors with a relatively new source of growth and profits and also helped maintain external demand for their exports during the recession". David C. Beek: "Commercial bank lending to the developing countries", FRBNY Quarterly Review, Spring 1977, pp. 1 and 2.

financing during the transitional phases.[1] From the point of view of the major bankers the central countries would in future keep their monopoly over the capital-intensive industries which require sophisticated technologies, while the most advanced countries of the Third World would engage in those industries or parts of processes which are relatively labor-intensive. North-south trade flows would no longer be characteristically an exchange of manufactured goods and raw materials: the trade in various kinds of goods would now become predominant.

If we consider the international trade figures produced by the World Bank[2] it becomes clear that the percentage of manufactured goods in the total exports of the developing countries has grown, particularly in the past few years. Towards 1978, manufactured goods accounted for about 25% of the total exports of merchandise of those nations. In 1965, on the basis of constant 1975 prices, only seven countries had exports of manufactured goods worth more than 500 million dollars in their balance of payments. By 1975 the number had risen to fifteen, nine of which exported manufactured goods worth more than 2 billion dollars annually.

Trade in manufactured goods produced in the developing countries is, however, highly concentrated in a small number of countries. 45% of the total of manufactured goods exported by the underdeveloped countries and by the three least developed countries in southern Europe come from South Korea, Taiwan, Hong Kong and Spain. If one adds to those countries Mexico, Brazil, Yugoslavia, Portugal, Singapore,

(1) "Closely related, the developing country often depends on one or a very few primary products for export earnings, which fluctuate widely and unpredictably with changes in world business conditions. There is a chronic incentive or pressure to acquire capital from abroad. In addition, major time lags are involved, in turning increased savings, whether from domestic income or capital flows into increased productive capacity and increased diversified exports - especially manufactured goods. These involve structural transformations in the developing countries - a painful and time-consuming process at best. The diversification of exports and, more particularly, building of export capabilities in manufacturing is the key element in this process of change", I. Friedman, op.cit., p.10.

(2) World Bank: World Development Report, 1978, p.10.

Greece and India (this latter having a declining share in the exports of manufactured goods of the Third World), the eleven nations mentioned represent 80% of the total of manufactured goods exported by the developing countries.

The World Bank emphasizes, moreover, that in recent years, Malaysia, Colombia, Turkey and Thailand have significantly increased their foreign sales of manufactured goods. If one now compares the nations which have absorbed a high percentage of the total debt from private sources and those which account for a high percentage of Third World exports of manufactured goods, it will be seen that, with some exceptions, they are virtually the same countries. This observation demonstrates the essential link between external debt and the new international division of labor advocated by the big banks.

TABLE 20

Developing countries: Growth of manufactured exports, 1970-85
(Average annual percnetage growth rates, at 1975 prices)

	1970-75	1975-80
Clothing	20.3	8.3 [a]
Textiles	17.8	6.2 [a]
Chemicals	16.5	13.0
Iron and Steel	10.7	14.5
Machinery and Transport Equipment	20.3	17.3 [b]
Other	10.2	10.0
All Manufactures	14.9	12.2

SOURCE: World Bank, World Development Report, 1978, pp.28-29.

(a) Assuming that the present quantitative restrictions will be implemented fairly strictly and extended up to 1985, an annual growth of 4 per cent in the volume of clothing exports and of 3.5 per cent in textiles is projected. It is also assumed that the quality of these products will be upgraded somewhat, raising the projected real annual growth to 5.5 per cent in clothing and 4.5 per cent in textiles. These growth rates are applied to the actual exports of 1976, which were about 30 per cent higher than in 1975, to give the projected growth rates of clothing and textile exports for 1975-85 that are shown in Table 20.

(b) Over one-half of developing countries' exports of machinery and transport equipment to industrialized countries consists of electronics - Exports of these and other electronics products, such as office equipment and calculators, and especially electronic components, are mostly organized by transnational firms.

Although the great increase in the export of manufactures is limited to the 15 countries mentioned above, certain distinctions have to be made between them. When one breaks down manufactures, it becomes evident that the highest annual average growth rates of exports between 1970 and 1975 were to be found in garments, machinery, equipment and textiles. But the World Bank projections for 1975-1985 indicate that the high rates will occur mainly in machinery and equipment, iron and steel and chemicals.

If these projections should prove correct, exports of manufactures between 1975 and 1985 will tend to be concentrated in those sectors, and, for that reason, will reach only the most advanced of the developing countries, such as Brazil, Mexico, South Korea and Spain. This, in any case, seems to be the view of the international bankers, since the highest percentages of total Third World debt to the big private banks is concentrated in those countries.(1)

This is a subject of great significance which, apart from anything else, illustrates the different interests involved in the principal developed capitalist economies and, more particularly, in the United States. Only in this way can one explain the fact that, while the banks now appear to be the most solid defenders of free trade, the industrialists of the advanced countries (especially those producing in the same sectors as competing Third World manufactures) and the workers are demanding a resurgence of protectionsim.(2)

---

(1) For an analysis along these lines see: Isaac Minian: "Rivalidad intercapitalista e industrializacion en el subdesarrollo. Notas para un estudio sobre la division internacional del trabajo", Economía de América Latina, CIDE, Mexico City, No. 2, March 1979.

(2) An intense debate is going on in the United States on the risks involved in the new international division of labor promoted by the big banks. Many analysts of the subject are clearly concerned, as can be seen from the opinions quoted here. Albert Fishlow, of Yale University, has pointed out that:

> "...the problem of debt is, in the last resort, a problem of trade. The devloping countries will be able to repay the loans and interest to the banks if they successfully apply a program of substantially increased exports. Yet the world's leading capitalist economy, the United States, is faced with a mounting deficit in its trade balance, and a free trade regime capable of absorbing the increasingly competitive exports of manufactures from the developing countries now seems more remote than ever.

(cont'd.)

This is obviously not the place to discuss the fate which awaits the exports of manufactures of the developing countries. But it is necessary to highlight the part played by the big international private banks in this relative shift in the international division of labor - a part which, in various Third World countries, has meant a radical change in the development strategies applied in previous decades. One should not forget, moreover, that these new versions of an outward-looking growth have been accompanied, in those countries, by military dictatorship which, in the last analysis, have proved indispensable as a means of reducing domestic consumption, drastically cutting back real earnings and reconverting the industrial structure for purposes of export.

---

footnote 2 of preceding page continues:

> The industrialists and workers in the advanced economies are not interested in rising volumes of imports. _It is the banks which now emerge as the new champions of free trade and increased access to markets_".

Albert Fishlow: _Debt remains a problem_, (San Pablo, Brazil: Finacorp, 1977). (Our emphasis). More recently the New York Times has gone so far as to state that:

> "...the private banks are actually making the foreign economic policy of the United States without any public debate or the vigilance of elected representatives...these private loan agreements require the guarantee of favorable access of the borrowers' exports to markets, so that they may acquire foreign exchange...in a parody of 19th-century British colonialism, the United States could become a captive market, by becoming the victim of extremely shaky debtors...the supreme irony is that while government organs remain passive, foreign policy is gradually being compromised".

J. Zwick and R. Goeltz: "United States banks are interfering in foreign policy", _The New York Times_, 18 March 1979, p. 14F.

<u>External debt, economic policies and development strategies.</u>

At the risk of omitting other aspects, the analysis of the influence of the international private banks on the economic policies and development strategies of the countries of the Third World can be based in general on the following points:

a) A knowledge of the extent to which the international private banks have supplanted the IMF in the setting of conditions for the developing countries.

b) An enquiry into the differences and similarities between the conditions imposed by private bankers and those of the IMF, and the levels of demands in each case.

The situation is not identical for all the borrowing countries in the Third World. Generally speaking, however, one can say that, on the basis of their relations with the international private banks, the Third World can be divided into three groups of countries:

- countries which have obtained credit from the international private banks and which make amortization and interest payments within the prescribed time limits;

- those which have borrowed large sums of money from private bankers and which, for various reasons, apply for new loans. When this happens, the private banks and/or the IMF, before extending new credit, set as a condition that the current economic policy be carried out more thoroughly;

- countries which have borrowed large sums of money from private bankers and which, for various reasons, apply for new loans while they are in the midst of processes of reform (agrarian reform, nationalizations, stepped-up state participation in the economy, etc.). In these cases, before new loans can be approved, the private banks and/or the IMF insist that there should be a change of economic policy and, consequently, of development strategy.

The last two situations mentioned here are without a doubt the most frequent and the most interesting for our purposes in this part of the study. A reading of the specialized literature shows that there is a close relationship between the weight which external debt acquires in any given country and conditions imposed on that country to ensure that its economic policy and development strategy should be carried out more thoroughly or changed. The axis around which these adjustments revolve is closely linked to the implementation of policies or programs of stabilization. But these guidelines, the purpose of which is to attack inflation and achieve basic balance and lay the foundations for an improvement of the country's economic and financial situation, are barely the tip of an iceburg. The fundamental purpose of these policies - and this is the point which we propose to illustrate - is to keep certain economies increasingly tied to international business and to promote monopolistic control by transnational financial capital. In the last analysis it is an attempt to curtail the degree of autonomy of states and to restrict the decision-making capacity of governments.

In the Third World over the past 20 years, there is an abundance of examples to confirm this point. It is both unnecessary and tedious to review all the cases, because the objectives and procedures have, with varying shades of emphasis, been similar. Instead we have taken a few examples from the more recent past, to illustrate the type of conditioning which is coming into being between the developing countries and the private international banks. To begin with, we can mention the difficulties of Gabon in meeting its debt service payments within the prescribed time limit in 1977. As reported by Euromoney(1) this situation caused "...some anxiety among the bankers...". Meanwhile, the government of Gabon was looking for another short-term loan of 300 or 400 million francs. A "team of advisers" was then set up, consisting of bank creditors; it analyzed the state of the economy of Gabon and reported back in 1977. With the "suggestions" of the team and the IMF, the government of Gabon drew up a stabilization plan which, amongst other things, contained the undertaking not to raise the external debt during 1978 above 2 million dollars, and also made provision for a drastic cut in the public spending programed for 1976-1980.

In 1975 it was the turn of Zaire to find itself unable to pay its debt service charges. The operations of the private banks in Zaire bring to light certain elements of crucial importance, such as the coordinated efforts of the private banks and the IMF, the link between the private banks and direct foreign investment and the clash of intersts between those same big transnational banks, despite their attempts to present the borrowers with a united monolithic front.

---

(1) "Gabon in the nick of time", Euromoney, March 1978,p.26.

After calling for the intervention of the IMF, the private banks offered a new line of credit of 250 million dollars, over five years, on condition that Zaire undertook to pay at the prescribed time the service charges of the earlier debt[1] and, moreover, that it should agree to a stabilization plan - the essence of which was as follows: restrictive monetary and fiscal policies, freedom of prices and of foreign movements, administrative reorganizations in certain areas, and "the return to their former owners of certain economic entities such as the plantations". These demands were actually designed to bring about "major changes in the economic policy and administration of Zaire".[2] It will be readily understood that the criterion of the "well-managed country" to which we referred when discussing the "country risk", really came into its own.

It should also be noted that some banks, fearing that Zaire should be faced with the real impossibility of paying all its creditors, hastened to seek a separate agreement with the government of that country. This was the case with Manufacturers Hanover Trust Company and the Export-Import Bank. On August 9, 1976 two other banks, Citicorp and the Bankers Trust Company, took legal action in a New York court to prevent the accused from obtaining priority reimbursement of their loans to Zaire.[3]

The case which, without a doubt, attracted the most attention and on which the greatest amount has been written, is that of Peru which was under severe pressure in 1976 from the big international banks in their attempts to influence its domestic politics and steer its economy in a certain direction. In the Peruvian case one clearly perceives the determination of the bankers to bring about a change in the economic policy and the development strategy started by the government of Juan Velasco Alvarado in 1968. It is clear also that external credit was used as an instrument for the support of certain moderate military factions against other factions which, in the opinion of the

(1) It is important to note that, whereas Zaire managed to renegotiate and reschedule its debts with official creditors, the private banks rejected this solution.
"Zaire's external debt with the private banks has been treated as being essentially separate from the debt it contracted with official lenders".
I. Friedman: "Country risk: the lesson of Zaire", The Banker, February, 1978, pp.29-31

(2) I. Friedman: op.cit.

(3) Wellons, op.cit., p. 130.

bankers, were further to the left. Relations between the bankers and Peru were also influenced by their intention of severing the links between that country and the socialist bloc, particularly in connection with military supplies.

A little background information might be helpful at this point. The Peruvian nationalist process which began in 1968 gave rise to profound changes. One third of the usable land, particularly that belonging to the big sugar and cotton agro-industrial enterprises, was expropriated and for the most part turned into cooperatives. Moreover, as a preamble to the constitution of social ownership and administrations based on self-management, labor communities were set up in the manufacturing industry, mining and fisheries. About 40 industrial enterprises ceased to be foreign-owned, besides the International Petroleum Corporation, which had been nationalized from the beginning. The fish-meal processing plants, the mining enterprises of Cerro de Pasco (one-third of mining output), railroads, electricity, telephones, cement, paper pulp and part of the banking system were all nationalized.

Finding its path blocked by the official financing agencies, Peru obtained considerable loans from the private international banks (more than 800 million dollars in 1972 and 1973 alone) to finance its investment projects.[1] The deposits of oil and the copper mines were, at least to begin with, sufficient guarantee for the big banks.

In 1976, however, the situation became critical for Peru. One year before, Morales Bermudez had become president, and a conservative trend became noticeable. The Peruvian economy, which had moved along at a good pace during the early years of the reforms begun in 1968, now found itself facing serious problems: inflation, a heavy deficit in its trade balance, a drop in the reserves of the Central Bank, etc. The big international banks made no secret of their fear that Peru might not be able to cope with its weighty debt service burden.

(1) The fact that the private banks gave their backing despite the blockade of the official agencies was no mere coincidence. According to certain sources, the Velasco government, convinced that it would need the financial support of the big private banks:

> "...fervently sought to curry favor with Chase and presumably, with the rest of the financial community - its assets acquiring five and a half times their market value and three times their book value".

Barbara Stallings: "Privatization and the public debt: US banks in Peru", NACLA, Vol. XII, No. 4, July-August, 1978. A corrected and enlarged edition of this study is entitled "Peru and the US banks: privatization of financial relations". Our references are to the second edition.

A) The first talks. - Early in 1976 the Peruvian government felt that, in order to meet its external obligations and the deficit in its balance of payments, it needed another external loan of at least 400 million dollars. The choice was between the IMF and the private international banks. Since the undertaking to be given to the Fund necessarily included a Letter of Intent which was unacceptable to major sectors of Peruvian society and the government itself, the Peruvians sent missions to New York and London in April and May respectively to negotiate with the private banks.

The first attempt was clearly fruitless. The bankers had more than one grudge against the Peruvian government. First of all they were disturbed by the proposal made by highly placed Peruvian officials for a joint moratorium on the debt of countries of the Third World.(1) The publication Business Latin America(2) recalled that the debt moratorium for the Third World was :

> "...a pet de la Flor (the foreign minister) proposal that did nothing to endear Peru to international lenders".

Early in 1976 the international bankers felt that the political situation in Peru was unstable, and that leftward-leaning civilians and military controlled key posts in the cabinet and the administration. There could be no doubt that a purge of the radical elements would be viewed with favor by the international financial community.

As far as we know, there is no proof that the international bankers, in their first talks with the Peruvian missions, raised the possibility of removing the more reform-minded military and civilians from office. On the other hand, there can be no doubt that the package of "stabilizing" measures which the international banks demanded would necessarily involve curtailing the power of those sectors which defended the reformist thinking of the military movement of 1968, or, quite simply, removing them from office alto-

(1) According to the Quarterly Economic Review, Peru-Bolivia, No. 2, 1976:

> "...matters can hardly have been helped by the... minister's public suggestion of a joint moratorium on debt repayments by a group of Third World countries..."

(2) Business Latin America, August 4, 1976.

gether.[1]

The private bankers' insistence that the state should reduce its interference in the economy in order to make way for more active participation by private enterprises was designed specifically to block the spread of socialism and state nationalization.[2] In order to get its international loans the Peruvian government had to abandon its aim of setting up a powerful state with a leading role, through its economic participation, in accumulation, production and marketing.

While pressing their case for more favorable treatment for private initiative, the bankers reminded the Peruvian missions of the Marcona Mining Company, which had been nationalized and which had challenged the amounts set by the government to compensate it for its expropriation, as well as the case of Southern Peru Copper Corporation, which was involved in litigation with the government over charges of tax evasion. The nationalization of Marcona had been decreed in 1975. (By way of reprisal, the traditional purchasers of Peru's iron ore in Japan suspended their orders.) Moreover, an earlier governmental decision required that at least 50% of iron ore exports should be shipped in Peruvian-flag vessels - a grave blow to "Marcona Carriers" a subsidiary of Marcona registered in Panama - which had previously shipped Peruvian iron ore. In December, 1975 the new Peruvian government recognized the right of Marcona to compensation for the nationalized mines. Protracted and difficult negotiations then began. Early in 1976 when talks began between the Peruvian government and the private banks,

---

(1) "The bankers ultimately accepted the Peruvian position, reasoning that if a crunch were to come, General Jorge Fernandez Maldonado and the left-wing faction of the government might come out on top and lead Peru back towards a radical nationalist position. It seemed safer to support the Morales government, with its new rightist tendencies, than to risk such a leftist outcome. One New York banker involved in the negotiations put the point very clearly. He said the 'main reason' for the loan was 'to perpetuate Morales Bermudez in power', since the banks considered this the best bet for getting their money back". Barbara Stallings, _op.cit._, p.238.

(2) As far as the development strategy is concerned, one of the pillars of the so-called Peruvian revolution consisted precisely of consolidating a solid State participation in the economy by means of the Publicly Owned Enterprises (EPS). The Peruvian project involved, in its first stage, in 1975-76, 63 publicly-owned enterprises (EPS) "in the

(cont'd.)

the banks:

> "...made it clear that a satisfactory agreement with Marcona was one of the conditions which they set for granting the loans requested by Peru." (1)

Lastly, in order to get money from the private bankers it was necessary to adapt oneself to a "stabilization plan" proposed by the bankers themselves; its main measures included the following:

1. devaluation of the local currency;(2)

2. reduction of public spending and improvements in the system of taxation to increase state revenues;

3. liberalization of prices; wage controls.

---

footnote 2 of preceding page continues:

process of formation", operated by "management committees" in which the workers controlled one third of the seats. All in all, according to the project, there were to be 454 productive units, and for the extension of the area of public ownership, an investment of 1,323.5 million dollars would be needed.

(1) Latin American Economic Report, Vol. 4, No. 41, 22 October 1976.

(2) With reference to devaluation, <u>Business Latin America</u>, of July 7, 1976, noted:

> "...the move is aimed at regaining the confidence of international bankers who had made devaluation a condition for considering Peru's request for new credits and debt renegotiation".

And the <u>Quarterly Economic Review, Peru-Bolivia</u>, No. 3, 1976, had this to say:

> "...Devaluation was one of a series of measures announced in May and June in order to improve the balance of trade and payments position to stimulate domestic investment and to reduce the fiscal deficit. The Central Bank has been trying to encourage foreign bankers to provide US $400 million this year in addition to normal financing...and the measures are intended primarily to restore international financial confidence".

Similar views are to be found in the Chase Manhattan journal <u>International Finance</u>. See, for instance, the issue of 14 June 1976.

B) The loan. - On July 26, 1976 it was announced that the loan had at last been granted to the Peruvian government, but that it was to be divided into two parts. The second part would be paid several months later and would be subject to the strict application of the conditions imposed by the bankers. The total operation, for a loan of 400 million dollars, involved bankers from the United States (210 million dollars), Europe (80 million), Japan (35 million), Switzerland (35 million) and Canada(30 million).

The big banks decided to go ahead without bringing in the IMF, but, so as to make sure that the conditions would actually be met, they set up a steering committee whose job it was to keep a very close watch on the progress of the Peruvian economy. Six big international banks made up this committee: Citicorp, Chase Manhattan, Bank of America, Manufacturers Hanover, Morgan Guaranty Trust and Wells Fargo. The loan was granted for five years, and with an interest rate with a spread of 2.25 points over LIBOR.

C) The fulfillment of the conditions. - There is no doubt that the demands of the bankers were met, at least partially.

- On July 1, 1976 the sol (Peruvian currency) was devalued by 44%; this decision was followed by a package of measures along the lines indicated by the stabilization program. When announcing the measures in front of the television cameras, the current Minister of Economy and Finances, Luis Barua Castañeda, said at the beginning of his speech:

> "The country has a limit to its capacity to incur debt. And we must take great care with this limit - and that is not all: the sources of international financing are already beginning to limit our use of resources".

- Between July and August 1976 the Prime Minister, Jorge Fernandez Maldonado, the Minister for Foreign Affairs, Miguel Angel de la Flor, the Minister of Agriculture, Enrique Gallegos, and the Director of the National System of Public Enterprises, Angel de las Casas, all resigned from their posts.

---

(1) Business Latin America, August 4, 1976.

- Publicly owned enterprises - a decisive part of the strategy defined in the first phase of the Peruvian revolution were also to be placed in jeopardy. At the end of July, General Cesar Rosas Cresto, on becoming director of SINADEPS instead of Angel de las Casas, declared that the public enterprises were more inefficient than private enterprises. In November the 63 EPS in the process of formation were reduced to 23, and the overall project, which included the socialization of a total of 454 enterprises, had been cut back to 60.

- At the same time the State enterprise PESCAPERU was divided into two main sections: the processing of fish would remain in the hands of the state but the fisheries themselves would revert to private hands. The employees of PESCAPERU would have 90 days to acquire the company's ships. The second choice would be open to the former owners of the vessels, who would have vouchers which they had received from the government at the time of expropriation. The bankers interpreted the return of PESCAPERU to private hands as the "beginning of the shift from leftist policy."

- On August 12 the Peruvian government cancelled the provision whereby 50% of Peruvian iron ore had to be carried in Peruvian-flag ships and, 3 days later, announced that an agreement had been reached on compensation for Marcona: 37 million dollars in cash, and 22.4 million for the shipping of iron ore by Marcona Carriers.(1)

The action taken by the banks in Peru in 1976 brought to light certain novel elements which clearly illustrated the greater functions performed by financial capital at the international level. On the one hand the private banks themselves began to participate in the elaboration of a stabilization plan and also in the monitoring of its execution. On the other hand, the banks identified with the interests of the foreign direct investment companies which had been upset by the measures adopted by the Velasco government.

We do not claim that the course of events which had begun in 1968 in Peru substantially changed direction solely as a result of the intervention of the international bankers. There is no doubt that certain forces within Peru were moving in that direction, and that the economic difficulties of 1975 left the government with very slight room to manoeuvre. What does seem certain, however, is that the international private banks took advantage of Peru's difficulties

(1) Latin American Economic Review, Vol. VI, No. 41, 22 October 1976.

to influence its economic policy and development strategy, and, besides that, to effect changes in the political life of the country and secure more favorable conditions for foreign firms which were in the midst of negotiations to settle outstanding disputes with the government.

D) In 1977, Peru's balance of payments problems continued. The government turned once again to the international financial community for loans. But this time the big banks refused to enter into direct negotiations and insisted on the participation of the International Monetary Fund. This was a most significant change. The IMF, which had been dislodged from the scene a year before, was now being called in to mediate the relations between the private banks and the Peruvian government. What led the big banks to take this step?

Barbara Stallings mentions three types of factors which could have influenced the bankers to demand the intervention of the IMF. First of all, differences of opinion among the bankers themselves. In the direct negotiations of 1976 between Peru and the big banks, two important private institutions - Bankers Trust and Continental Illinois - refused to participate in the steering committee and to extend new credit to Peru. The executives of these two institutions felt that the banks were taking serious economic and political risks by acting directly, imposing a stabilization plan and various measures which affected the development strategy of the Peruvian government.

Secondly, the bankers considered that, by working through the IMF, they would achieve a more neutral image, put to use their experience of direct negotiations with Third World countries and thus meet the wishes of the Federal Reserve, which favored negotiations through the Fund over

(1) "For a private bank to police the actions of a sovereign government puts it into a difficult position. International agencies have a more neutral role and are better suited for this", declared Alfred Miossi, Executive Vice President of Continental Illinois. Another banker, Harvey D. Shapiro, an executive of one of the institutions which made up the "steering committee", said: "I don't think the banks can play the role of appearing to intervene in the affairs of the country. Whether they like it or not, it could be considered Wall Street imperialism". Quoted by Barbara Stallings, op.cit. p. 243.

direct negotiations between private bankers and the governments of the developing countries.[1]

Thirdly, in the light of certain fundamental political changes which reduced the danger that Peru might shift further to the left, the intervention of the IMF would make it possible to impose a much more detailed and restrictive stabilization plan than that demanded by the bankers in 1976.

From then on, the IMF recovered its functions as an intermediary and guarantor of operations between the international financial community and the State of Peru. In the case of Peru the big private banks recognized, implicitly, that direct negotiations entailed risks (political, economic) which could be avoided, at least in part, if the operation was to be conducted through an international institution with a more neutral image. It also appears that several banking executives reached the conclusion that the Fund had had greater experience and was better prepared to impose restrictive conditions on the developing countries. In actual fact the main objectives pursued by the private banks in the case of Peru had been achieved in the 1976 negotiations - removal of "leftward-leaning" high officials, a reversal of the program of publicly owned enterprises, acceptable compensation for Marcona, etc.

Once the course of Peru's development stragegy had been altered, the intervention of the IMF in 1977 became a necessary instrument to spell out precisely the economic policy which fitted the new strategy.

<u>External debt, oligopolistic concentration and economic denationalization</u>.

The penetration of the international private banks in the developing countries, as has repeatedly been said, cannot be view exclusively in terms of profits extracted by means of the expansion of highly lucrative investments. The interaction between financial investments and productive and direct commercial investments is a key to the dynamics of transnational capital. To some extent this is the result of the mergers and other organic linkages between capi-

(1) "We need to develop the rule of law in this field", stated Arthur Burns, director of the Federal Reserve in February 1977 - "and the only instrument for this is the IMF. Unless we have the rule of law, we will have chaos". Quoted by Barbara Stallings, *op.cit.*,p.244.

tal which occur within countries and through its international expansion. On the other hand, however, this phenomenon is the fruit of the cycles which are characteristic of the capitalist system's chronic inclination towards instability.

The formation of a financial-industrial capital which gradually comes to function at the international level raises new questions which must be considered in any analysis of external debt to the big private banks. As has already been pointed out, the management of such debt in the developing countries has been highly responsive to the treatment extended to foreign capital as a whole. So much so, in fact, that their demands as leaders are usually accompanied by those which they make as spokesmen or shareholders of other foreign investment enterprises.

The relationship between banking capital and industrial capital has been extensively dealt with in theoretical analysis; it is generally regarded as not lending itself readily to empirical proof. In this part of the study we shall try to show, on the basis of the experience of certain Latin American countries, that external debt, particularly in the most advanced developing countries, creates conditions which are conducive to the concentration and denationalization of industrial capital.

A) The process which began in Chile in September 1973 has a number of interesting aspects which bear out the hypothesis of the role of external debt in the concentration of capital and in economic denationalization. A combination of various factors in Chile helped give particular significance to access to the international market. First of all, it should be noted that the depression of the domestic market, which was caused by the policy of stabilization, meant that it became extremely important to be able to obtain more credit. Secondly, articles 14,15 and 16 of the Law of International Exchange authorized the free and direct entry of external credit, from 1976 onwards. Lastly, the financial market for Chilean enterprises had obviously become fragmented. As noted by J.E. Herrera and J. Morales, in Chile there are:

> "...two separate financial markets: the domestic market, with prohibitive interest rates, which applies to the great majority of small- and medium-enterprises which have to finance their operating capital needs in this way, and the external market, with reasonable interest rates based on the conditions in the international capital markets. In actual fact, as is logical, the possibilities of

> external credit are not equally open to all kinds of enterprises. Once again it is the big enterprise which can directly obtain an external loan or do so indirectly through a bank guarantee".(1)

In a supplement on Chile published in July 1978, the periodical Euromoney confirms this reasoning when it points out that:

> "...those few investors who have access to external long-term credit have secured substantial competitive advantages which tend to distort the internal allocation of resources over the short term".

In this situation, which was made even worse by the vigorous application of policies favoring the external sector, the small and medium industrial and commercial enterprises found themselves in great financial difficulties, to the point where their very survival was severely threatened. The authors referred to above, report that out of a total of 1500 limited liability companies and thousands of personal enterprises a mere 514 private enterprises absorbed the total volume of external credits which entered Chile between July 1976 and December 1978. They go on to add that 70 enterprises, controlled by about ten national or foreign economic groups, obtained more than half of that external credit.(2)

---

(1) J.E. Herrera and J. Morales: La inversion financiera externa en los modelos hacia afuera: el caso de Chile, 1974-1978. CIEPLAN, May 1979, p. 64. Shortly to be published by ILET.

(2) "...the form and conditions under which the internal productive apparatus is projected towards the external economy, in the commercial and financial spheres, reflects the high degree of concentration existing in the national pattern of property ownership, and on the other hand the conditions under which this projection occurs stimulates and promotes the process of contentration itself..." Herrera and Morales: op.cit., p. 65.

B) As another interesting case we have chosen that of the external debt of Brazil. With one of the largest debts of the Third World (and one cf the highest debt service ratios) this semi-industrialized country has accumulated international financial liabilities amounting to some 40 billion dollars, and direct investments and reinvestments of not less than 15 billion. It could be said that the growing magnitude of external debt has been crucial to the contemporary dynamism of the Brazilian economy. The close association which has been maintained between this debt and productive international investments is a key factor. To some extent one may say that the functioning and expansion of the transnational corporations in the various spheres of production have brought into being the conditions for a strong boost to external debt.

First of all it is necessary to emphasize the imbalance in the commercial sphere. A survey made by CACEX (Office of External Trade) in 1974 showed that 115 international corporations accounted for about one-third of total Brazilian imports (excluding oil), and had a trade deficit of more than 2 billion dollars - almost half of the trade deficit for the Year.(1) According to those same official sources, 19 of those corporations accumulated a trade deficit of 661 million dollars in 1977. This high rate of imports of the foreign enterprises was influenced by the acquisition of mass produced or standard capital goods used by subsidiaries in keeping with the technological and investment policies defined by the parent companies, and the conditions provided by certain domestic situations.

Secondly, some consideration must be given to the operations of remittances. The sending of profits and other outflows based on the relationship between the foreign subsidiary and the parent company rose by 18% annually during the sixties. There can be no doubt that this factor of pressure on the balance of payments makes the need for debt, which is generally incurred by the state, all the greater.

The CACEX survey shows that in 1974 the same foreign enterprises were directly responsible for 11% of the external debt generated in that year. This indebtedness, peculiar to the system of subsidiaries of transnational enterprises, is attributable to various factors. Some are related

(1) Quoted by Regis Bonelli and Pedro Malan: "Los limites de lo posible. Notas sobre el balance de pagos e industria en los años 70", Pesquisa e planejamento, August 1976, p. 364.

to productive activities, such as programs of investments and imports, etc. , while others are financial in nature: financing agreements with the parent companies, internal credit restriction, interest rate differentials in favor of external credit, overpriced currency, etc.

It is on this basis that we may affirm that the same logic of functioning of foreign investments in Brazil and its dominant role in the strategic sectors leads to conditions which are likely to boost the external debt not only of the private sector (which already accounts for 38% of the total debt) but also of that controlled or guaranteed by the State itself.

In recent years, external debt has expanded for basically financial reasons. On the one hand the classical "domino" effect applies: the need to pay off old debts leads the borrower into new debt. On the other hand, however, are the repercussions of the distortions of the domestic capital markets and the spread of speculative practices. In the opinion of some, the greater part of the external capital entered the country in the form of loans which were used particularly to satisfy the corporate need for working capital. It has even been argued that these loans were responsible for 75% of the increase in the country's external debt.(1)

The main reason which led to the demand for external financing which was then converted into Brazilian currency before being used, was the difference between the high rates of interest on the domestic market and the more moderate rates available internationally (on account of the overvaluation of the exchange rate in Brazil). Rather than inadequate savings and domestic credit, the forces which fuelled that quest for external financing had their origins in the extraordinary profits to be made on the capital markets.

The foreign banks played a fundamental role in this process. Government authorization to make "transfer loans" by which the banks served as an intermediary between the foreign lender and the borrowing enterprise in Brazil - known as Resolution 63 - was the mechanism which made possible this external debt of financial origin. According to some accounts, the Euromarkets financed virtually all the loans made under Resolution 63.(2) By 1973 the loans referred

(1) Jose Eduardo de Carvalho Pereira of IPEA, quoted by Movimento, 21 August 1978.

(2) P.A. Wellons, *op.cit.*, p. 322.

to were shared equally between the investment banks, and the commercial banks (including the Bank of Brazil).

According to Wellons[1] the investment banks were the instruments through which the foreign banks maintained their presence in Brazil. The foreign banks have managed to take over one-third of the investment banks, and they are prominent shareholders in others. A mere fifteen institutions held 70% of the total foreign loans of the investment banks. The majority of these banks are members of a financial conglomerate or have foreign shareholders. There can be no doubt that foreign banks have penetrated the Brazilian financial system and are highly involved in the management of the loans on the international markets.

Transnational banking corporations and transnational direct investment corporations are responsible for driving Brazil more and more deeply into external debt. Through their better and wider access to foreign financing sources they have also increased their economic control in critical situations as well as obtained additional benefits from the traditional restrictive credit measures, adopted in such circumstances.

C) A recent study on the Mexican economy in the period 1970-75[2] shows how the concentration of capital and the denationalization of the big Mexican private enterprises took place during a phase of depression and by means of control of the local financial market and of access to the international financial market. This enquiry enables us to see how - in a specific case and at a specific time - the transnational investment corporations joined forces with the transnational financial corporations.

First of all, and by way of background to this case, we should recall that since the end of the sixties and the beginning of the seventies, the Mexican economy has entered a depressed phase of the economic cycle which has taken the form mainly of a drastic decline in the level of capacity utilization by the industrial enterprises. This process coincided with the beginning of strong inflationary pressures, something which had been unknown in Mexico for more than a decade. In this context the Mexican administration of the time was faced with two serious problems which in

(1) P.A. Wellons, op.cit., pp. 329-340.

(2) Jose Manuel Quijano: "Concentración desnacionalización y crédito. El caso de México 1970-1975", CIDE mimeo - to be published in Economía de America Latina, No. 3, October 1979.

the opinion of many analysts were unrelated, but which, from our point of view, turned out to be the two sides of the same coin: the relative decline of private investment and domestic inflation.

To cope with the dual problem,the government had recourse to contrary measures of economic policy. The government followed an intense policy of public investment to halt the decline in private investment; but at the same time the Bank of Mexico, at the end of 1972, began to have recourse to credit restrictions and higher domestic interest rates. According to official declarations, the first policy was designed to maintain the level of economic activity, and the second to combat inflation.

It is in this context that one should analyze the effect of access to domestic credit and to external indebtedness on the concentration and denationalization of industrial capital.[(1)]

The tight credit policy started in 1972 posed two fundamental questions: 1) How were small and medium-sized enterprises affected during the depressed phase, and to what extent was it evident that a concentration of capital was taking place? 2) How did the big and very big Mexican enterprises fare in comparison with foreign enterprises?

(1) The information used in the research of Jose M.Quijano comes from three main sources: a) the annual tax declarations of the enterprises were made available by the Secretariat of Economy and Public Credit of Mexico; b) the information on foreign enterprises by the National Registry of Foreign Investments in Mexico; c) the information on public and private external debt by the Bank of Mexico and the Secretariat of Economy and Public Credit. In order to make the data comparable, two homogeneous sample surveys were made of 23,291 Mexican enterprises and of 1,249 foreign enterprises; these sample surveys consisted of all the enterprises which had submitted their tax declaration during all the years of the period. The Mexican and the foreign enterprises were grouped in four layers, depending on the level of their annual income: small, medium, bit and very big. An enterprise was regarded as being foreign if 25% or more of its equity was under foreign control.

The findings of the study were roughly as follows:

- The small and medium Mexican enterprises greatly increased their demand for credit between 1970 and 1972. This higher level of indebtedness was the result of an increase of inventories, the extension of credit to clients (on the one hand, as a means of increasing sales, and, on the other, as a consequence of arrears in payments), the drop in the rate of utilization of installed capacity and the lower rate of self-financing (due to profit levels lower than those of larger enterprises).

- In this period the greater indebtedness of the small and medium Mexican enterprises was attributable to their access to the local credit market. Tables 21, 22 and 23 show the meagre percentage of the total credit on the international market which was obtained by those enterprises. Access to external credit rises as one considers the bigger enterprises.

TABLE 21

Private Local Manufacturing Enterprises

Average indebtedness on the local and external markets, for 5 years.

LEVEL		CREDIT
1	Local	94.8
	Foreign	5.2
2	Local	89.1
	Foreign	10.9
3	Local	84.6
	Foreign	15.4
4	Local	70.9
	Foreign	29.1

SOURCE: Jose Manuel Quijano, *op.cit.*, on the basis of the Secretariat of Economy and Public Credit of Mexico.

TABLE 22

Debt of Local Enterprises - Manufacturing Sector - Accumulated on the Local and Foreign Markets
(Millions of pesos)

Year		1969	1971	1973
Level				
1	Local	6,846	9,287	9,915
	Foreign	255	808	454
2	Local	5,985	7,533	8,286
	Foreign	814	1,005	901
3	Local	5,714	9,626	9,020
	Foreign	977	1,247	2,105
4	Local	13,062	16,372	24,050
	Foreign	5,568	5,612	9,538

* In 1969, 1971, and 1973, rate of exchange 12.5 pesos to dollar.
** Sample of 23,291 enterprises

SOURCE: Jose Manuel Quijano, op.cit., on the basis of data of the Secretariat of Economy and Public Credit of Mexico.

TABLE 23

Debt of Foreign Enterprises - Manufacturing Sector - Accumulated on the Local and Foreign Financial Markets.

(millions of pesos)

Year		1969	1971	1973
Level				
1	Local	483	782	502
	Foreign	773	763	551
2	Local	810	822	971
	Foreign	853	842	1,090
3	Local	1,098	1,425	1,233
	Foreign	726	1,326	1,331
4	Local	3,987	5,410	6,450
	Foreign	4,662	5,609	10,795

* In 1969, 1971, and 1973 exchange rate of 12.5 pesos to the dollar.

** Sample of 1,249 enterprises.

SOURCE: Jose Manuel Quijano, op.cit., on the basis of data of the Secretariat of Economy and Public Credit of Mexico

- With the tight domestic credit policy started in 1973, the very big enterprises both Mexican and foreign, greatly increased their participation in the total volume of credit, which rose from 51.9% in 1969 to 58.3% in 1973. At constant prices the credit obtained in 1973 by the small and medium enterprises fell drastically, there was a slight decline for the big enterprises and only increases for the very big enterprises.

- In the case of the very big enterprises there is clearly a division between the sources of financing. The private enterprises of the country become heavily indebted abroad while absorbing a high percentage of local credit. Meanwhile the foreign enterprises had massive recourse to the credit obtained on the international financial market.

- As the tight credit policy remained in effect throughout 1974 and 1975, the big Mexican enterprises turned more and more towards the international market for finance. In this process there does not seem to be any significant difference regarding access to the international credit market between the very big Mexican private enterprises and those of foreign origin. There were, however, clear differences in the conditions. Table 24 shows that while the foreign enterprises tended to incur long-term debt, the very big Mexican enterprises went in for short-term credits of less than one year.

- This difference of conditions between the two groups of enterprises is reflected in the interest payments and in the magnitude of financial costs. Between 1969 and 1973 the increase in total interest payments was over 70% for the Mexican enterprises, whereas it came to 59% for the foreign enterprises. If we now look at the financial costs - the debt servicing (amortization and interest) Table 25 shows an increase of 124.5% for Mexican enterprises, against 70.2% for foreign enterprises, over the same period.

TABLE 24

% of Private Indebtedness of Foreign and Local Enterprises (1970 - 1975)

Total private debt to foreign sources	
Foreign enterprises	41.5%
Local enterprises	58.5%
Total private debt to foreign sources. Long term.	
Foreign enterprises	76.0%
Local enterprises	24.0%
Total private debt to foreign sources. Short Term	
Foreign enterprises	29.2%
Local enterprises	70.8%

SOURCE: Data provided by the Economic Indicators of the Bank of Mexico and the Head Office of the Secretariat of Economy and Public Credit.

TABLE 25

Increment in cost of finished production, raw materials, wages and financial costs, manufacturing sector.

(%)

	Foreign Increment 1969-73	Local Increment 1969-73
Cost of finished production	55.0%	60.0%
Raw materials	44.3%	66.2%
Wages	93.7%	69.6%
Financial costs	70.2%	124.5%

SOURCE: Jose Manuel Quijano, op.cit., on the basis of data from the Secretariat of Economy and Public Credit of Mexico.

- The tough conditions of external credit were to be the reason which drove many Mexican entrepreneurs into association (partial sale) with foreign capital. The National Registry of Foreign Investments, recorded a total of 4,137 enterprises 25% or more of whose equity was foreign-owned. Of that total, 1,771 had actually been set up between 1970 and 1975. This means that 42.8% of the enterprises with foreign participation of 25% or more were registered in the period being analyzed. Since the period in question was one of recession, in which there was no evidence of a major flow of direct investments, this phenomenon reflects the partial acquisition of established Mexican enterprises and not the construction of new industrial plants. This concurs, moreover, with the findings of Newfarmer and Muller: three out of every four United States subsidiaries established in Mexico in 1971 and 1972 acquired a Mexican enterprise which was already in business.

One may, therefore, conclude that, in a semi-industrialized country like Mexico, and during a depressed phase, the terms on which external credit was granted by the international private banks to the private enterprises of Mexico laid the foundations for a more thorough denationalization of the industrial set-up of the economy. In this way, for an economy of medium development such as that under consideration, the depressed phase of the cycle shows two simultaneous capital-concentrating processes at work: a) a first one which, through domestic credit, affects the country's medium and small enterprises and b) a second process which, through international credit, affects the country's very big enterprises while favoring the foreign enterprises. The case of Mexico and the cases of Chile and Brazil demonstrate how closely external debt is linked to the penetration of transnational direct investment capital into the underdeveloped countries.

Some theoretical reflections

This study has aimed at organizing the large amount of information available on the external debt of developing countries and examining as far as possible its short and long term effects. But there has not been any deliberate intention to explore its theoretical ramification.

Such an exercise would have encountered several obstacles, notably the little information on the economic destination of the loans. Banking "secrecy" and government reservations very much limit the availability of such elements of judgement. Most researchers would agree that critical studies on external debt, as in general studies on contemporary capitalism are deficient and seldom theoretically treated.

These final conclusions are expressed within such limits, but with the aim of seizing the theoretical meaning of some of the conclusions of this study.

The dynamics and importance of the external debt of the Third World with private international banks imply three main ideas: a) the overwhelming role of "financial capital", understood as a merging of various interests; b) the functioning of this financial capital as something going beyond the traditional or classical approach (linked to the merging of fractions of capital, with the incorporation of intensely conditional elements at the level of the functioning and direction of nation states); c) the structural meaning acquired in the present crisis of this financial internationalization of capital, as a counterweight to any conjunctural or circumstantial view of this historic phenomenon.

In general, the treatment of Third World external debt has been submitted to criteria according to which it consists of an accumulation of deficits, forcibly arising out of the balance of payments deficits of these countries. From this point of view, external indebtedness, as a financial flow cancelling disequilibria in merchandise flows, tends to constitute the central objective of these studies. Undoubtedly, descriptive methods tend to support this type of approach. But when the effects of these relations are examined, it emerges that the objective studied is on a more transcendent level of social relations: the pattern of international accumulation and its dominating sectors. Debt - loan capital - under this approach, emerges as an external or epiphenomenal expression of its underlying substance - its articulation with productive capital. In spite of this, the internationalization and financial domination tends to operate in the last instance as an advancement of the internationalization of productive capital. Thus, beyond their forms and mechanisms, loans and debts are part of a capitalist function, based on international and monopolistic conditions in which capital accumulates and reproduces. From this angle, international debt yields to "financial capital" since this description better demonstrates the character of financial relations in which the articulation of capital and the complex unity of management are involved. The change of emphasis, as we have pointed out, does not cancel but makes relative the value of certain aspects such as solvency or the borrowers' capacity to pay.

If financial capital is retained as the key to understanding the indebtedness relations between banks and governments, this does not imply admitting that its present conceptualization corresponds exactly to certain currents of thought at the beginning of the century. Nor that the key argument consists in deciding in which parts of this capital reposes the control over the entity described as "financial capital". It emerges that little developed facets in the classical concept of financial capital are fundamental aspects of the cohesion and elucidation of levels of control within and between capitalist complexes.

This refers more specifically to conditionalities and degrees of subordination between these complexes and the power range of States. External debt has been shown to be a lever to alter or strengthen certain inherent functions and directions in State machinery. Economic policy and development strategies have been directly under the influence of indebtedness problems. It also could be argued that the power of financial capital and its capacity of expansion progressively lead to the adaptation of the apparatus of maximum coercion - the State - to its own strategic interests. There is not, in our view, the possibility of substituting one power by another. But it is possible to include State power as part of the power of "financial capital" - to convert into a general interest the specific interest of this capital.

This would not involve, as happened at the beginning of the century, the State managing tariffs or various mechanisms of commercial protection. It is the entire economic policy and the direction of the nation that are involved in the restructuring aimed at and needed by financial capital.

As the expansion of the international system of private banking loans took place above all in the 1970's, it can be thought that this phenomenon translates the impact of an economic and financial crisis (fall in the dollar, increase in the price of oil, decline of the IMF, etc.). If normal conditions of the cycle were restored, the present financial hypertrophy and psychosis would recede, reducing things to a circumstantial and transitory problem. However, this judgement seems based on wishful thinking, rather than reality. To start with, because the phenomenon can be perceived before the start of this crisis. Financial capital can be perceived in the historical origins of internationalization and the tendencies for the monopolistic functioning of capitalism. It is already present in the first World War, and does not necessarily coincide with the critical phases of the system. Projections carried out show that indebtedness and increasing interference will continue into the future.

Finally, the historical antecedents and forecasts confirm the actuality of financial capital as a concept implicit in the structural functioning of present day capitalism. In the final analysis, the phenomenon of multinational companies, the importance of financial policies in main countries, the gravitation of "monetarist" currents of thought and other events can only be interpreted from the perspective of the expansion of international "financial capital" on a world scale. In other words, as part of a long-term trend, and not a stage in a cycle.

Principal Conclusions

1. In the 1970's, the external debts of developing countries and their governments have become increasingly private. Between 1970 and 1976, for 94 developing countries, the participation of international private banking in total public debt of those countries almost quadrupled, rising from 7.5% to 27.6%.

2. Loans of private banks have been concentrated on a limited number of developing countries, with only 10 accounting for two-thirds of Third World debt to international banks.

3. A small number of major international banks control a high percentage of the credit operations of Third World countries. Financial transactions and earnings on loans to those countries have increased and have a considerable weight in their total operations on an international level.

4. This process is accompanied by a worsening of concessional terms of indebtedness: a tendency to an increase in interest rates (plus commissions) and the reduction of maturities.

5. Most developing countries have been subjected to intense pressures on their balance of payments, as a consequence of the increasing burden of debt service (in particular interest payments). This phenomenon has been aggravated with the expansion of loans of private international banks.

6. Private banks - simultaneously with the increase of their loans to Third World countries - have developed their own methods of evaluation and auditing teams to examine the economic, social and political situation of borrowers. There has been a significant change in criteria of evaluation. The concept of solvency, the strictly financial measure of capacity to pay, has been overtaken by an overall evaluation of the country as a whole ("country risk").

7. The major private banks, through their transacting with developing countries have moreover become levers to operate certain transformations in the international division of labor. Their interest is confirmed because the more advanced developing countries concentrate on developing certain labor-intensive industries without altering the industrial monopoly of the central countries by setting up more technologically intensive interest.

8. Private international banks have been the active protagonists of the conditioning of the economic policies and development strategies of developing countries. Although in most cases private banks have seconded the activity of the IMF, they have sometimes taken a leading role and intervene on their own initiative in the internal affairs of developing countries, whether in the establishment of stabilization programs or in the control of their execution.

9. The external debt of Third World countries is closely linked to the penetration and functioning of direct productive investment by the transnational. In certain countries, and especially during the downswings in an economic cycle or recessions encouraged by economic and especially financial policies, external debt unleashed or deepened processes of concentration and denationalization.

Chapter V

MULTILATERAL DEBT RENEGOTIATION EXPERIENCES

Gonzalo Daniel Martner

It tinkles no more
your little golden coin?
Your treasure box,
before it is shattered by time,
empty shall remain? *

Antonio Machado. Proverbios y cantares.

---

*Ya no suena/ tu monedilla de oro?/ tu alcancia,/ antes que el tiempo la rompa/ Se ira quedando vacía?

Introduction

This study aims at presenting some of the more significant features of debt rescheduling experiences of the Third World countries in recent decades.

In the present international financial situation, the external indebtedness of developing countries has become a burden restricting the growth potential of many of them. The expansion of external debt, and the deterioration of the international economic and financial situation in a context of high liquidity and a particularly fragile international monetary system, has highlighted the importance of rescheduling the external debt of developing countries. These operations are presented as an alternative to breaking the bottleneck of financial charges linked to foreign indebtedness and to reducing international risks of any suspension of payments.

The characteristics of acute external indebtedness situations will be examined as well as the variables determining debt servicing capacity. Situations leading to debt rescheduling operations in the light of various experiences will be examined: types of rescheduling and the institutional framework for these operations. Finally the concrete cases of Chile and Turkey will be studied. The Chilean case offers a good example of the interrelation between style of development, external indebtedness and pressures exerted through debt renegotiation.

The second, will illustrate the trends and most recent modalities of indebtedness and resheduling.

I. The process of indebtedness

Generally speaking, external indebtedness is not so much the total liabilities of a country but a continous flow of new loans and outflow of foreign exchange to service previous debts (amortizations and interest). Positive debt management implies contracting new loans which are greater than the service of accumulated past debts. This results in a balance, or net transfer, the financial counterpart of a transfer of real resources.

Indebtedness must be considered as a "roll over" procedure, involving "debts to pay debts". The limits to this process in relation to debt service are described below.

Under the hypothesis of a constant annual amount of indebtedness, the net increase of resources for the debtor country (through the generation of a given capacity to import) will decrease over time, to reach the point at which debt amortization payments will equal the amount of new loans. From this point the constant rate of new borrowing will continue but will be offset exactly by repayments of previous borrowing, the net addition to the debtor's own resources on capital account being zero. The interest payments on the unchanged outstanding debt will be a net subtraction from the debtor's own current resources, to meet the foreign exchange which will have to be generated.

The outer limit will be reached earlier with higher interest rates and shorter maturity periods for the loans. This limit can be delayed by extending grace periods and amortization periods and lowering interest rates. With long term loans, the debtor will have to remit foreign exchange flows over a long period after having ceased to receive net resources.

With variable capital flows, i.e. in a situation far closer to the real process, the outer limit will occur earlier if new indebtedness is reduced -by the decision of the debtor country, or for reasons of creditors' good will arising from market conditions or any other type of consideration (e.g. political). If the level of indebtedness increases, the outer limit will occur later as soon as new loans for higher amounts provide more resources than those required for the repayment of previous loans. (For mathematical formulae, see Annex II).

Of course, debt service capacity is determined by all operations generating foreign exchange, beyond the relationship between new debt and service of previous debts. Debt service can only be ensured if there is an increase in exports of goods and services, a reduction of imports, a net positive flow of direct foreign investment, and the use of reserves or resort to additional indebtedness as described above.[1]

---

(1) H. Bitterman, The Refunding of International Debt (North Carolina: Duke University Press, 1973).

However, it is necessary to emphasise that debt service is ultimately linked to the performance of national output, whose levels are difficult to forecast. There will always be a high level of uncertainty in relation to the exact debt service capacity of a country in the medium and long term.(1)

II. Situations conducive to the reorganization of external debt: the experience of recent years.

Circumstances in which reorganization of debt of a given country takes place can be generally described by putting forward a certain number of hypotheses but they cannot be unequivocally and automatically identified. However, the analysis of debt rescheduling experiences of developing countries within the global indebtedness framework reveals elements and trends, which yield significant conclusions.

Certain quantitative data will be given on these experiences derived from a study by Pierre Dhonte.(2)

A. On the relationship between the debt outstanding (stock) and the gross National Product, the sample established by Dhonte, including 69 "developing countries", indicate that for

---

(1) For present forecasts of short and medium term (according to varius econometric models) see: -G.B. Smith "The external debt prospects of the non-oil exporting developing countries: and econometric analysis". Overseas Development Council, monograph N°10 (October 1977). -G. Feder: "Economic growth, Foreign loans and debt servicing capacity of developing countries World Bank Staff Working Paper N°274 (1979).

(2) P. Dhonte: "Describing External Debt Situations: A Roll Over Approach", IMF Staff Papers, (1975:1).

1969, this reached an average of 16%, but exceeded 18% for one quarter of the countries concerned. The ratio between debt outstanding and current exports reached 86% for three-fourths of the countries sampled, but was far higher for a few countries.

At the same time, in the countries in the sample involved in rescheduling (13 countries) in the year previous to the renegotiation (t-1), there were no high ratios between debt outstanding and GNP compared to the sample as a whole. Only in 4 out of the 13 countries did this ratio exceed 18%. However, in 9 out of the 13 countries the ratio between debt outstanding and exports exceeded 86%, a most significant feature in the identification of characteristics of countries which have rescheduled their debt. (see Table I)

Table I: Thirteen Renegotiation Cases: Values of Indicators of the level of indebtedness

(in per cent)

Country	Year of Renegotiation (t)	Debt Outstanding / Gross National Product (t-1)	Debt Outstanding / Trend Exports of Goods and Services (t-1)	Debt Outstanding / Trend Exports of Goods and Services (t-4)	Growth Rate of Debt Outstanding (t-7tot-1)	Growth Rates of Exports of Goods and Services (t-7tot-1)
Argentina	1962	16.4	179.4	121.1	15.3[1]	3.5
Brazil	1961	18.0	165.5	98.7	12.2	-0.2
Chile	1965	16.5	147.3	110.8	15.1	6.6
Egypt	1966	28.4	146.6	95.3	20.5[1]	7.6
Ghana	1966	25.2	141.3	39.4	58.4	-0.2
India	1968	13.6	287.2	180.4	15.5	3.4
Peru	1968	15.7	69.1	35.7	12.3	8.2
Philippines	1970	4.9	32.2	26.5	17.5	4.0
	1959	9.9	100.9	84.2	9.9	0.9
Turkey	1965	11.1	153.4	158.3	6.9[1]	6.9
Uruguay	1965	8.8	65.1	73.5	12.2[1]	7.9
	1966	28.5	122.3	98.6	21.3	17.0
Yugoslavia	1971	9.4	42.8	62.0	1.9[2]	14.3[2]

SOURCE: BIRD, IMF and local sources, Quoted by P. Dhonte, <u>op.cit.</u>, p. 183.

1. t-6 to t-1.

2. 1966-70

B. The average annual rate of growth of debt outstanding, for the 69 countries, reached 17.5% between 1965 and 1969, in contrast to the rate of growth of exports which was only 7.3% per annum. Countries renegotiating showed various growth rates for debt outstanding, but only 3 of the 13 analysed showed higher rates than the average for the 69 countries. The growth rates of exports are not uniform either in renegotiating countries, while the ratio between accumulated debt and exports also grew in ten of these countries between t-5 and t-1, a rate not above that of the average for the 69 countries.(see Table I)

It can thus be concluded that renegotiations imply a high level of indebtedness but do not constitute examples of particularly sizeable increases in indebtedness in relation to export capacity in the period preceding renegotiation. (see Table I)

C. From the point of view of flows, indebtedness could be measured by the ratio between current services on foreign debt and current export income. The average of this ratio for the 69 countries was 8.1% in 1970, while only nine countries went above 15%; in 1965 the corresponding figures were 5.7% with only 5 countries going above. For the 13 countries renegotiating, 8 showed ratios below 15% in the year preceding the operation, but only 3 in t-4. (see Table II) Thus, generally, but not systematically, the debt service ratio of countries renegotiating is high, and tends to increase in the period immediately preceding the renegotiation.

D. But this indicator only measures current debt service payments, and does not include payments to be made in the near future. Over a period of 5 years for example, debt service ratio can change substantially, and not in a uniform manner. In order to avoid this problem, an attempt has been made to substitute current payments for payments programmed for the future. These obligations can be expressed as the average over a chosen period or as a sum of debt service payments discounted over the period, itself divided by current or trend values of exports. Thus in a sample of 27 countries which have not renegotiated their debt, the average of annual payments to be made over the following 15 years (including amounts not disbursed) at the end of 1970 was divided by 1969 exports. The resulting average ratio was 19.3%, considerably higher than the previous ratio of 9%. This reflects the programming of payments on loans not yet disbursed and the ending of grace periods over previous loans.

In contrast, in cases of renegotiation it has been observed that the average debt service repayments from 1 to 15 years is lower than current payments for reasons described below. The ratio of projected debt service payments to exports in t-1, was (except in the case of India) lower for the 13 countries renegotiating than for the average of the 27 countries sampled, so that renegotiating countries appearing as having high debt service obligations at the time of renegotiation, did not appear as such in a longer term perspective.(see Table II)

Table II

Thirteen Renegotiation Cases: Values of Debt Service Indicators

(In per cent)

Country	Year of Renegotiation (t)	Debt Service / Trend exports of goods and services (t-4)	Debt Service / Trend exports of goods and services (t-1)	Debt Service[1,2] / Exports of goods and services (t-1)	Debt Service[1,3] / Debt[1] (t-1)
Argentina	1962	11.9	20.1	--	--
Brazil	1961	19.6	36.9	--	--
Chile	1965	24.6	21.1	10.5	53.3
Egypt	1966	2.7	12.6	--	--
Ghana	1966	6.2	33.7	10.3	73.4
India	1968	12.2	20.5	19.4	41.8
Peru	1968	5.8	10.7	7.8	62.4
Philippines	1970	6.8	4.0	3.5	75.7
Turkey	1959	--	21.5	--	--
	1965	20.4	19.6	13.4	53.6
Uruguay	1965	5.9	6.0	6.0	75.0
Yugoslavia	1966	10.8	16.2	9.2	70.3
	1971	11.9	8.5	4.6	74.5

SOURCE: See Table I

1. On DRS-reported debt, including undisbursed.
2. 1-15 year average
3. Discounted 1-15 years.

E. Also, the ratio of the sum of discounted debt service payments on accumulated debt is a good indicator of the distribution over time of debt service obligations. If debt service payments were equal in the 15 future years, this ratio would be 50.7% with a discount rate of 10%. The greater the concentration of payments in first years, the higher the ratio, and inversely. It can thus be inferred from the above that payments in the first years following renegotiation are characteristically higher than those made in latter years when the ratio in question is above 50.7%.

For the 27 countries in the sample, the ratio was 55.5% on the average, without any major divergences. In the case of the renegotiating countries the average was around 60%, reflecting serious problems of "bunching". (see Table II) This explains the paradox that these cases showed high debt service ratios in contrast to the ratios of the average of 15 years of debt service payments to exports.

F. It is useful to link disbursements to import levels, which give a good indicator of the degree of dependence of the level of economic activity on external loans, as well as indirect costs associated with the indebtedness process. In the sample examined here, the ratio of disbursements to imports for the 69 countries averaged around 13.1% in 1969, while one quarter of the countries reached a ratio of 19%. Renegotiating countries received a high level of disbursed foreign loans in the year previous to renegotiation, while 8 of the 12 countries had a disbursement/imports ratio near to or above 20%, a ratio which had been increasing over previous years. (see Table III) Thus it cannot be argued that indebtedness crises generally originate in a sudden interruption of new loans.

G. On the other hand, the net transfer of resources by indebtedness related in each period to the volume of imports constitutes a useful element of measurement of the benefits and drawbacks of indebtedness in relation to external equilibrium and on the degree of dependence of the continuation of the process of transfer of resources.

In the sample of 69 countries, the ratio of net transfers to imports averaged 5.9%, though it was above 9.5% for one quarter of the countries. Renegotiating countries received substantial transfers in the years previous to the renegotiation. (see Table III)

Table III

Thirteen Renegotiation Cases: Values of Indicators of Disbursement and Net Transfer

(In per cent)

Country	Year of Renegotiation (t)	Disbursements / Imports[1] (t-1)	Net Transfer / Imports[1] (t-4)	Net Transfer / Imports[1] (t-1)	Debt Service / Disbursements (t-1)	Debt Service / Debt Outstanding (t-1)
Argentina	1962	33.2	17.1	17.9	46.1	13.3
Brazil	1961	45.5	16.7	14.9	67.3	26.6
Chile	1965	27.9	26.1	8.4	69.9	15.8
Egypt	1966	29.9	13.9	20.0	33.0	11.0
Ghana	1966	34.0	21.5	13.2	61.2	29.5
India	1968	31.1	35.4	17.2	44.7	8.1
Peru	1968	16.5	12.0	6.9	58.0	18.4
Philippines	1970	6.9	5.0	3.4	50.5	14.9
Turkey	1959	--	--	--	--	--
	1965	28.1	19.5	9.5	66.3	13.9
Uruguay	1965	6.5	4.9	--	100.0	9.5
Yugoslavia	1966	49.2	25.2	33.0	32.8	18.7
	1971	5.5	11.9	-1.9	135.4	20.1

SOURCE: See Table I

1. Imports of goods and nonfactor services.

In the same order of ideas, another significant indicator is the ratio of payments for debt service to disbursements, expressing the proportion in which disbursements for new loans are used for the payment of debts established at a given period. The higher this ratio, the higher the level of disbursements required to ensure a given net transfer. As has already been pointed out, setting aside short term movements within annual flows, the value of this long term ratio depends on the rate of growth of disbursements and on the terms of loans (which are at present difficult to successfully treat statistically). For the 69 countries, the average value of this ratio is 69%, while for one fifth of the countries the ratio was above 100%. Renegotiating countries however did not show particularly high ratios, compared to remaining countries.

Only in half of the renegotiating countries did the ratio show signs of growth. (see Table III) In so far as renegotiating countries have not shown high growth rates for indebtedness, it would be hoped that the moderate value of the debt/disbursements ratio would result from an indebtedness contracted on favourable terms. In reality, taking the ratio of debt service on debt stock as indicator of terms of loans, it appears that at the moment of renegotiation countries in question had not contracted debts on very favorable terms. Thus, except in the case of India, the ratio of debt to debt outstanding is in excess of the 11.3% average for the 69 countries. (see Table III) However, the average interest (ratio of interest payments on debt outstanding) paid by renegotiating countries was between 3% and 6%, showing that they were mainly concessional. The high ratio of debt service to total debt existing in these countries, reflects large amortization payments as a proportion of total debt - part of the debt "bunching" problems of these countries. So that the moderate ratios of debts to disbursements can be explained by a substantial level of disbursements, reflected by the ratio of disbursements to imports. This fact is linked to the frequent recourse to medium term credits.

To sum up, renegotiation is resorted to by heavily indebted countries actively using external loans, not only to finance maturing obligations, but also to ensure a net transfer. Their debt service obligations are high and growing, while the demand for capital inflows (disbursement/imports) is high, even though debt accumulated on unfavorable terms (disbursements/accumulated debt) and in spite of its high level, continues growing faster than exports.

While a satisfactory "roll over" ratio is maintained (debt service/disbursements) it is the sign of growing external indebtedness rather than a cautious policy on terms for new credits.

If the objective of these countries is to maintain a high level of net transfers in the following years, they must increasingly obtain new loans insofar as past indebtedness conditions have resulted in a "bunching" in the maturing of these loans. On the one hand, a policy ensuring high net transfers under these conditions will soon lead to a level of indebtedness which cannot be maintained due to bottlenecks in offers of credits or in absorptive capacity.

On the other hand, in general, the total of debt service programmed to be repaid over a long period (15 years) is not excessive, so that it can be hoped that the most immediate maturities can be postponed to later dates by a renegotiation, which could eliminate the probability of a suspension of payments in the short term, but would strongly affect capacity to face obligations over a longer period, which explains why renegotiations take place frequently in the majority of countries using this mechanism.

Thus experience indicates that debtor countries trying to maintain a balance between the magnitude of their indebtedness and conditions to which it is subject, as well as to maintain a relationship between growth of its external indebtedness and growth of exports, will not be obliged to renegotiate their debts. When this balance is broken, debt repayments problems seem probable and give an incentive to seek a negotiated revision of debt service payments.

However, there is nothing automatic about the decision to renegotiate payments. There are renegotiations which take place without urgent payments problems, as well as different situations regarding the imminence of a suspension of payments.

Creditor countries, or creditor organizations in general, are not guided by single criteria,[1] but adapt general policies to countries or regions affected by serious debt service problems.[2] Ways in which these policies are manifested in a number of cases will be set out below.

(1) Private banking experts distinguish three types of situation which can give rise to debt renegotiation (See D.Duff and I. Peacock: "Refinancing of sovereign debt", The Banker, January, 1978).
The first is a situation arising from political events, i.e. the decision of a given debtor country not to cancel debts for overriding political reasons. These situations have not arisen in the recent past, though there are historical precedents at the beginning of the century and between the two world wars.
The second is the suspension of payments for reasons of economic need, a situation reached when earnings from exports, actual or potential, are below essential imports (food and oil) plus debt service and when there is no prospect of obtaining new capital flows.
The third possible situation, is when there are less extreme economic difficulties forcing a renegotiation, but when there is little or no possibility of paying debts promptly and totally.

(2) The most outstanding cases are Indonesia and Ghana, which though similtaneously facing the same debt service problems with the same creditors benefit from very different renegotiation conditions.

III. Types of renegotiation

Debt renegotiations have in most cases been multilateral since it is assumed that this approach ensures an "equitable" treatment, and increases the scope for creditors to relieve the financial situation of the debtor country, thus reducing the risk of a default which could have a major negative impact on international capital movements and harm interests of creditors. For debtor countries, multilateral procedures avoid the implication that one country is interfering in the internal affairs of another - accepting the conditioning of its economic policy implied in any renegotiation - as it is assumed that the former is the result of an "international consensus". This procedure can also eventually increase the negotiating capacity of the debtor country.

Between the 1950's and now, the number of nations involved in multilateral debt renegotiations is fairly small. Renegotiations have been repeated several times for a number of countries: for the 40 renegotiations which have taken place, India has renegotiated nine times; Chile, Ghana and Indonesia, four; Argentina, Turkey, Pakistan and Peru, three times.

TABLE IV

Renegotiations Since 1956

Country	Year	Country	Year
Argentina	1956 1962 1965	India (cont'd.)	1974 1975 1976 1977 1978
Brazil	1961 1964	Indonesia	1966 1967 1968 1970
Cambodia (now Kampuchea)	1972 (Two separate agreements, one in January and one in November)	Pakistan	1972 1973 1974
Chile	1965 1972 1974 1975	Peru	1968 1969 1978
Ghana	1966 1968 1970 1974	Turkey	1959 1965 1978
India	1968 1971 1972 1973	Sierra Leone	1977
		Zaire	1976 1977

SOURCE: World Bank, 1979.

On the other hand, types of direct debt relief can be as follows:

- converting loans to be repaid into grants
- reduction of amortization or interest payments
- reprogramming over time of these obligations (transfers are postponed, a grace period being usually granted)
- consolidation as a rescheduling of maturities, funding of arrears or of future payments, as they fall due, or principal interest on loans previously granted by the same public creditor or group of creditors. The refunding applies to a number of outstanding credits to which the revised terms apply. The consolidation may involve the cancellation of outstanding credits and the substitution of a new credit instrument with a new schedule of interest and maturity and it may be total or partial.(1)
- Refinancing, which in OECD and IBRD terminology describes loans through which an official body "takes over" credits previously extended by private lenders providing new credits after the debtor country reimburses the original loan. This term also describes operations carried out by private international banks, i.e. the granting of loans to be used to cancel debts, being essentially an accounting operation. However, the moment when normal "rolling over" of existing credits becomes refinancing it is not always apparent. Insofare as banks participate in new "rolled over" loans in accordance with their own profitability criteria (judging the terms granted this implies adequate earnings in relation to risks), such new loans are not refinancing. This implies that financing is a restructuring of a debt contracted in less favourable conditions and terms than those which lenders would have granted for a normal portfolio loan. Lenders only participate in refinancing operations because they are "locked in" or subject to political or other pressures.

  Refinancing is necessary in two types of situations: in the case of "excessive debt" when a government can have such a high level of indebtedness that refunding in the market at commercial rates becomes difficult or impossible; or when total debt can be maintained at acceptable levels, but since the maturity structure of the current years is inappropriate the "roll over" process in the market becomes impossible.

(1) See H. J. Bitterman: "The refunding of international debt" op.cit., pp.77-107; and G.K. Helleiner: "Alternative solution to the external public debt problem of the LDCs", report to an expert's meeting, (Mexico: 1977).

In fact, debt renegotiation usually takes the last two forms. But recently, there have been debt reorganisation operations on behalf of the "least developed" countries. Following initial discussions of the problem at the Conference on International Economic Co-operation in Paris in 1977, several creditor countries took positive measures. In November 1978, the UNCTAD Secretariat stated that leading industrialised creditor countries had announced plans to convert 6.2 billion dollars of outstanding debts into grants. This "retroactive terms adjustment" is estimated to have involved a saving of annual debt service of about 300 million dollars.

IV. Present institutional arrangements for debt renegotiation

A. The Paris Club

The Paris Club debt renegotiations consist of meetings between a given debtor country and its principal creditors inside an informal and exceptional framework, which has neither a legal organization nor a secretariat.(1) It started in the 1950's when the main European currencies were not convertible. Its initial objective was to design a multilateral system of payments between European countries for transactions with Latin American countries. Some of the latter had been accumulating unpaid debt service, which led to the first multilateral renegotiations.

This body has considered indebtedness situations and restructured payment arrangements with Argentina (1956, 1962, 1965), Brazil (1965, 1964) Chile (1965, 1972, 1974, 1975), Peru (1968, 1969, 1978), Indonesia (1966, 1968, 1970, 1974), Zaire (1976,1977). Countries taking part are the main creditors of the country whose debt is under review, their number varying from 5 to 15. Some of these countries take part as observers. The IMF and the World Bank take part in Club meetings as observers, as does the OECD and the major regional development banks.

Despite their informal character, debt renegotiations are subject to certain norms:

- the weight of the project debt service of the renegotiating country must be seen by creditors as sufficiently significant to consider that without relief the country would tend to default on its undertakings. Frequently, countries examined have been either late with payments or have suspended them. Thus renegotiation takes place in a very exceptional situation.

---

(1) The site of these negotiations can vary: when France convenes the meeting it takes place in Paris; when The United Kingdom calls a meeting, it takes place in London. Other meetings have taken place in The Hague.

- All governments of participating creditor countries agree to bilaterally negotiate on the basis of the same or similar repayment terms (collectively fixed in a minute of agreement), although they usually leave the fixing of the interest rate to the discretion of each government;

- Only private suppliers' credits assured by specialized agencies of creditor countries (generally as from 6 months maturity) were initially considered in the renegotiations, in the sense that government loans are not supposed to constitute a factor of difficulty for the fulfilling of undertakings, given their concessional terms. However, later on, official export credits and concessional development loans were included on a case-by-case basis;

- Debt relief must not be directly associated with development aid, since the Paris Club approach is to address short term payments difficulties, excluding any perspective on long term development financing needs;

- Once rescheduled, debts should not be renegotiated again. On occasion, this requirement has proved inapplicable;

- The Paris Club generally imposes on a debtor country a stabilisation programme under the auspices of the IMF (through a stand-by agreement with this organisation) as well as a system of control and supervision of future indebtedness. Limits to new medium-term credits are often fixed.

The procedure generally used in the meetings is described in the following text:

> "At the first session of each meeting the creditors typically meet among themselves to discuss their various attitudes to the requested relief. When the creditor countries have broadly settled on a common stance, a session is held in which the debtor country's representatives make a presentation covering the events leading up to the crisis and the current economic circumstances of the country, and proceeding to an explanation of their request for debt relief. The representative of the IMF usually makes a statement explaining the Fund's interpretation of the current situation and views regarding the measures that will have to be adopted by the debtor to overcome its difficulties. On occasion the representative of

the World Bank has also been requested to present the views of the Bank on the current economic problems and prospects of the debtor country.

After a session in which the debtor country's representatives respond to questions raised by the creditors, the creditors again meet among themselves to agree on a common set of proposals to be presented to the debtor. A final session is held in which the debtor and creditor meet to draw up an agreement containing the terms of relief to be recommended by the creditor representatives to their governments and statements on policy measures the debtor will take. This understanding takes the form of Agreed Minutes which set out *inter alia* the type of debt to be included, the percentage of debt service which will be relieved, the consolidation period and the repayment terms. Usually the moratorium interest rate is not specified in the Agreed Minutes but is expected to be settled in the subsequent bilateral agreement; the rate of interest is expected to accord with the individual creditors' domestic commercial rates. However, at least in one case the Agreed Minutes suggested a maximum rate of interest.(1)

It is necessary to emphasize that the main limitations of debts resheduling within the framework of creditor clubs are the absence of concern about the global growth perspectives and the restrictive character of the debt under consideration.(2)

---

(1) UNCTAD Secretariat, "Present Institutional Arrangements for Debt Renegotiations", TD/B/C.3/AC.8/L3, February 1975.

(2) At UNCTAD V in Manila, the G 77 proposed the creation of an ad-hoc commission for debt renegotiation in the Paris Club. Industrialized countries proposed the intervention of a "mediator" to defend the interests of developing countries but refused to give the same degree of powers as the President of the Paris Club. Negotiations failed.

B. Aid co-ordinating group

The "Aid Co-ordinating groups" have incorporated this problem more extensively, and for this reason their evolution has come up against various obstacles. It is no accident that these bodies originated in acute financial crises rather than the search for a deliberate policy.

Aid Co-ordination groups (consortia and consultative groups) are informal mechanisms, which periodically bring together main creditors and donors of certain developing countries with actual or foreseeable financing difficulties affecting external debt service. In general these groups are organised by an international institution (World Bank, OECD) on the request of countries wanting financial aid.

The first aid group was set up when India's financial crisis broke out in 1958, in view of the difficulty of ensuring short term debt service and the financing of imports of industrial goods provided for in the second five year plan. India needed an agreement with its creditors to meet immediate obligations, but the basic problem was to finance the latter years of the development plan.

Creditor countries (Canada, F.R. Germany, Japan, United Kingdom, United States) guaranteed the foreign exchange necessary to carry out the second development plan, after an examination of the "reasonable" character of its needs. The World Bank co-ordinated the Creditors, maintaining the ad-hoc and provisory character of the group. In 1960, the group became an "aid consortium" to examine the Indian economic situation twice a year, the progress of the plan, and evaluate external aid needs, as well as aid commitments.

The similarity of Pakistan's financial problems led to an extension of the mechanism. But the repetition of the operation gave rise to reservations of the group faced with the prospect of a generalisation of this type of approach. This system was in fact extended, but with lesser goals.

At the start of the 1960's many developing countries achieved independence, thus posing the problem of new links specially financial links with former colonial powers. The Co-ordination of so-called aid did not however take place inside consortia, since this implied definite commitments for participating creditors. But at the same time, the aid problem began to lose its bilateral character. Co-ordination of aid continued under the auspices of the World Bank, while in 1960 the OECD established the Development Assistance Committee.

The problem of extending the mechanisms of creditor's groups, called upon to not only guarantee the service of external debt but also foreign exchange needed to finance development plans, is explained by the innovation such plans presented from the point of view of industrialized countries' interests, of the respective situation of creditor countries. In particular, the United States and the U.K. sought to share with the other European countries the burden of aid considered necessary. Aid was unequally distributed "as a result of past political and commercial relations"(1) and as a consequence of varied conditions in which it was granted. Hence the formation and extension of aid groups presented a certain interest to creditors, permitting the adjustment of the aid burden.

But in fact, the existence of these groups is always linked to balance of payments problems and to the service of public or public guaranteed debt. In this sense, aid is linked to the problem of external debts management and its refunding in limited circumstances. But in contrast to what happens with creditors. clubs, activities of consortia and consultative groups include problems arising from estimated deficits in balance of payments. However, creditors make no commitments, while they can exercise significant influence on the development options of the recipient countries. Hence the limited character of such groups from the latter's point of view. As emphasised by a high World Bank official" probably the most important service rendered by the aid groups to participants is the opportunity for frank exchanges of information, ideas and comments", while he indicates that "from the point of view of the beneficiary country, there is the risk that with donors meeting collectively they can exercise an excessive degree of influence on policies in exchange for promises of aid".(2)

Thus consortia and consultative groups have served as fora for renegotiating terms of industrialised governments' loans in the case of India, Pakistan, Indonesia and Turkey. Though their terms have generally been concessional they sometimes resemble those granted by the Paris Club -as seen in the case of Turkey recently.(3)

The initial approach of the group, i.e. to engage the creditor countries' governments in development finance programs, has been broadly transformed penalizing the real resource transfer to peripheral countries.

---

(1) J.C. Goodman. "Co-ordination de l'Aide. Tout Commenca par une crise" Nouvelles et Opinions sur le Développement, N°1 Janvier, 1979.

(2) R. J. Goodman, op.cit. p.3.

(3) Moreover, Indonesia renegotiated its debt with the Paris Club and a creditors' consortium. See A.C. Cizukas "International Debt Renegotiation, lessons from the Past" op.cit. 203-206

V. Conditions of multilateral debt renegotiations

Table V summarizes the main characteristics of debt renegotiation as regards financial conditions granted to debtor countries until 1976 (more recent information is not available).

TABLE V

CONDITIONS FOR RENEGOTIATION 1961-1976

	Number of renegotiations	%
A. Proportion of restructural indebtedness (in %)		
50-or less	8	25
50-60	2	6
60-80	16	50
100	6	19
B. Amounts restructured (in millions $) (1)		
Less than 50	3	11
50 to less than 150	12	45
150 to less than250	5	19
more than 250	7	26
C. Consolidation period (2)		
Less than 2 years	12	43
2 to less than 3 years	9	32
3 to less than 4 years	2	7
4 or more years	5	18
D. Grace periods and maturities (3)		
Less than 6 years	5	18
6 lo less than 10 years	10	36
10 years or more	13	46

Source: IMF, on the basis of minutes of the rescheduling agreement.

(1) only includes rescheduling until 1974.

(2) excludes 4 renegotiations in which consolidation periods were determined.

(3) excludes 4 renegotiations in which repayment periods were not specified in the minutes of agreement.

In half of the operations 60 to 80% of indebtedness was restructured. In recent years, however, cases in which less than 50% of debt is rescheduled have occurred (case of India).

Although amounts rescheduled have tended to increase, reflecting the general increase in indebtedness, they do not generally exceed $250 millions for each rescheduling.

The consolidation period (time in which rescheduled debts expire) seldom exceeds three years. This was particularly the case in the 1970's when the period exceeded four years only in one-fifth of the cases.

Grace periods and maturities granted by creditors have remained stable: in half the cases, they exceeded ten years, and in 36% they were between 6 to 10 years, while they were less than 6 years in 18% (1)

These conditions are not satisfactory for affected countries. As pointed out by the World Bank, they have led developing countries to judge that multilateral renegotiations of their debts by the Paris Club are too limited since they only apply to part of their debt. They consider that the repayment periods are too short, and in most cases, ill-adapted to the particular situation of the debtor country.(2)

These rescheduling conditions are explained by the desire of the creditors to submit debtor countries to stabilisation plans (generally under the auspices of the IMF) and to closely control their execution, as a condition of any future debt relief that may be needed. These objectives would be more difficult to achieve with longer term debt rescheduling agreements.

In the case of Indonesia for example, negotiations with creditors lasted four years, before yielding a more global solution. Debts to be cancelled by the end of 1967 were first spread out over an 11 year period at the end of 1966.(3) Present debt rescheduling and its conditions thus permit creditors to exercise a sometimes extended control over the internal economic policy options of debtor countries.

---

(1) For more details, see the following IMF documents which summarize the minutes of agreement of renegotiations: "Multilateral Debt Renegotiations - Experience of Fund members" August 5th 1971 and 20th September 1974. "Avoidance and resolution of debt servicing difficulties", 23rd September 1976.

(2) World Development Report, 1979.

(3) See P. Dhonte, La Dette des pays en voie du développement (La Documentation Française, 1979).

VI. Study of significant cases

The official participation of creditor States has been a predominant feature of debt rescheduling. The bulk of sums rescheduled have comprised officially guaranteed suppliers' credits. When repayment difficulties arose, State credits guarantee organizations took them over. The other major components were official bilateral loans in the case of consortia. Many factors led to priviledged if not exclusive state participation of creditor industrialised countries in the rescheduling process. Chile will be studied as a typical case -since it also points out the indissociable character of the style of development and excessive indebtedness, as well as the dependency links it involves.

On the other hand, in the past years there have been important changes in the external debt structure of Third World countries. In 1973-1977, private bank credits, represented 36% of these countries' debt, while it was only 10% in 1969/73, the proportion of private debt increasing from 32 to 73%- a 40% annual growth rate.

Also, suppliers' credits have in most cases fallen in both absolute and relative terms, while official loans have been consentrated on least developed countries with very limited access to capital markets. The external financing of developing countries has undergone major qualitative transformations, parallel to structural changes taking place in international financial mechanisms. However, there will still be room for the significant participation of state bodies of creditor countries in negotiations but the roles of the various financial entities involved are being redistributed and becoming more complex. Private banks are acquiring an increasingly more determining role in the management of international liquidity.

This implies the transformation of multilateral debt rescheduling mechanisms as has been seen lately in the cases of Zaire, Peru and Turkey. The case of Turkey will be analysed to illustrate such actual trends and problems.

A. The Case of Chile

Chile has had more frequent recourse to the renegotiation of its external debt than any other Latin American country. It did so in 1965, 1972, 1974 and 1975, and its current level of indebtedness is higher than ever before.

This country has had a long history of difficulties with external debt, largely due to persistent and high rates of inflation and to recurrent deficits in its trade balance financed by external indebtedness.

Immediately after achieving its independence at the beginning of the last century, Chile began to have recourse to external indebtedness, through the floating of bonds in Great Britain, which was then the leading economic power of the world. Reimbursement of these first bonds stopped in 1826. In 1840 Chile's debt was rescheduled. A moratorium was decreed on the whole of its external debt between 1880 and 1884, and there were later successive reschedulings. Later on, Chile became heavily indebted on the United States bond market until the depression of the thirties, payments of interest and amortization being suspended in 1930. In subsequent years, when its bonds were being traded at low prices, Chile found it preferable to use its foreign exchange holdings to repatriate the bonds rather than make the scheduled payments. In 1935 the accumulated total of the debt was rescheduled over a period of 30 years, with rates of interest of between 0.6% and 2%. This arrangement was later challenged by the creditors, and when the matter was re-examined in 1948 interest rates were raised.

It can therefore be seen that ever since independence the trend towards excessive external indebtedness has been inherent in the Chilean mode of development and in the nature of its relations with the world economy. The opening of the saltpeter cycle late in the last century consolidated an economic structure based on the export of single mineral raw materials (saltpeter and later copper) as the country's main productive activity, and ended whatever chances there were of ever stablishing a dynamic industrial capitalism with a national character in Chile. This factor made the rate of growth of the national product highly vulnerable to the movement of prices of its mining exports, thus giving rise to a succession of balance-of-payments crises, and crises in the country's capacity to service its external debt.

Later on, with the advent of the process of import substitution after the crises of the thirties and the second World War -a process common to most of the Latin American countries- the pattern of large external debt still continued.

The massive use of imported inputs in the newly created industry compelled Chilean industrialists -including the biggest one of all, the State, which through its Corporation for the Promotion of Production, set up dozens of basic industries -to have recourse to lines of credit made available by the suppliers of those inputs. Suppliers credits thus made up the bulk of the external debt. At the same time, although industrialization was based on the replacement of imports -which initially lowered the ratio of imports to product- the rate of growth of imports tended to exceed that of national industrial production, paradoxically in fact, when one considers what the process of substitution is supposed to achieve.

This process was moreover accompanied by the entry into the local economy of subsidiaries of transnational corporations which were reluctant to reinvest their high profits in the economy of Chile -hardly a surpriseing attitude when one considers its chronically high inflation rates and economic instability.

TABLE VI

Chile: Current Sources and Use of Foreign Exchange

	1950	1951	1952	1953	1954	1955	1956	1957	1958	1959	1960
I. Current Sources	331	419	511	383	447	538	527	445	430	498	563
A. Exports of goods and services (1)	325	409	496	370	436	521	517	429	388	473	532
B. Income on capital						2					
C. Private grants			1	1	1	1	1	2	15	10	13
D. Other services	6	10	14	12	10	14	9	14	27	15	18
II. Total Uses											
E. Income on foreign capital	58	67	67	44	52	81	98	53	55	58	65
1) Profits and dividends of I.D.	50	57	54	32	39	70	86	38	40	38	46
2) Interest on loans	8	10	13	12	13	11	12	15	15	20	19
F. Amortization and depreciation of foreign capital	25	25	62	30	94	69	53	68	90	122	78
G. Outflows of national capital			9	8	1	6	6	1	12		4
H. Errors and omissions	9	- 7	- 17	- 17	1	16	- 10	- 32	25	8	46
I. Other services	11	10	16	19	19	22	33	19	15	20	25
J. Import of goods	234	332	355	328	320	361	359	410	389	387	507
K. Freight, insurance and other transport	34	47	51	46	49	45	49	54	49	52	63
L. Travels	7	8	7	5	5	5	11	15	13	14	67
M. Grants	1	1	1	2	3	2	1	1	1	1	

Continued on next page

(1) Excluding other services

TABLE VI (cont'd.)

Uses of % of current sources	1950	1951	1952	1953	1954	1955	1956	1957	1958	1959	1960
E/I	17.5	16.0	13.1	11.5	11.6	15.1	18.6	11.9	12.8	11.6	11.5
1/I	15.1	13.6	10.6	8.4	8.7	13.0	16.3	8.5	9.3	7.6	8.2
2/I	2.4	2.4	2.5	3.1	2.9	2.1	2.3	3.4	3.5	4.0	3.3
F/I	7.6	6.0	12.1	7.8	21.0	12.8	10.0	15.3	20.9	24.5	13.9
G/I			1.8	2.1	0.2	1.1	1.1	0.2	2.8		0.7
H/I	2.7	-1.7	-3.3	-4.4	0.2	3.0	-1.9	-7.2	5.8	4.0	4.4
I/I	3.3	2.4	3.1	5.0	4.3	4.1	6.3	4.3	3.5	4.0	4.4
J/I	70.7	79.2	69.5	85.6	71.6	67.1	68.1	92.1	90.5	77.7	90.0

SOURCE: ECLA and IMF figures

Ever since the fifties, therefore, there had been a large outflow of capital in the form of income from foreign capital, particularly through remittances of profits and dividends generated by direct foreign investment. This income amounted to 17.5% of current foreign exchange earnings in 1950, 15.1% in 1955 and 11.5% in 1960. (see Table VI)

These factors caused recurrent pressures on the balance of payments, to which one should add the instability of foreign exchange earnings from exports (mainly of copper ore), while greatly inflating the volume of external indebtedness. External public debt rose from 322 million dollars in 1953 to 542 million dollars in 1960 (equivalent to the value of annual exports). Meanwhile, the servicing of that debt rose from 50 million dollars (about 10% of annual exports) in 1956 to 78 million dollars (approximately 15% of exports) in 1960.

These factors explain why, between 1961 and 1964, part of the Chilean external debt was bilaterally refinanced, the funds needed to meet rising payments thus being derived from new credits. For example, in 1961 and 1963, credits of 30 million dollars were granted to refinance purchases previously contracted in the United States. After the 1960 earthquake, the United States' financial agencies granted credits of 110 million dollars, while the United Kingdom refinanced credits worth two million pounds sterling.

1. The 1965 renegotiation

In 1965 a renegotiation of Chile's external debt took place. This event coincided with the coming to power of the leader of the Christian Democrats, Eduardo Frei, who enjoyed official United States support. This support was part of the stepped-up program known as the "Alliance for Progress" which had become the official policy of the United States and was viewed as an alternative to the prospects of radical change which the Cuban revolution had opened up for the continent. This Alliance was designed to promote certain structural changes, including agrarian reform, and also major financial support from the industrial centers for the "promotion of development".

Despite the great importance of the participation of the European creditors and Japan, the renegotiation of the Chilean external debt in 1965 can therefore be explained to a large extent by the "goodwill" of the United States authorities towards the recently enthroned Christian Democrat government which, with its project for reform based on "revolution in freedom", was the best guarantee of United States interests in Chile, while its political model was invoked as an example for the rest of Latin America.

These points become more significant when one remembers that the structure of Chilean debt at the time was not particularly unfavorable. While the level of indebtedness was certainly high - the ratio of accumulated debt to exports was 147%, while the usual level for developing countries was in the region of 80-90% - the rate of growth of debt compared to that of exports (15.1% and 6.6%) was not abnormal; the debt service ratio was not on the rise, there were no problems of "bunching", the ratio of debt servicing to disbursements was normal and the terms of indebtedness were not particularly unfavorable as the ratio of debt servicing to total debt was 15.8%, close enough to the 11.3% recorded in most of the developing countries.

The difficulties encountered thus lay more in the chronic trade deficit (see Table VII), in high outflows of capital - which took the form of a ratio of net transfer to imports which fell from 26.1% in t-4 to 8.4% in t-1 - while reserves showed a marked decline. The amount of the annual drop was equivalent to about one third of imports. This explains the failure to meet certain payments and the fact that the Chilean government started negotiations late in 1964 with its creditors, finding them favorably disposed, for the reasons given above.[1]

(1) "The balance-of-payments deficit had to be resolved on a permanent basis. This would be done by renegotiating the external debt servicing, doubling copper output and quadrupling industrial exports". From R. Ffrench-Davis: Politicas economicas en Chile, 1952-1970, (Santiago: 1973), p. 54.

TABLE VII - Part I

Chile Foreign Trade
(1960 - 1964)

	1960	1961	1962	1963	1964
Exports	534.4(30)[a]	531.2(29)	568.4(29)	584.7(29)	676.8(31)
Imports	-642.3	-726.9	-680.7	-666.8	-712.8
Trade Balance	-107.9	-195.7	-117.3	-82.1	-36.0
Total capital inflow	139.2	260.2	210.4	234.5	296.9
a) investment	77.8	75.0	62.4	38.9	64.6
b) loans utilized	54.0	171,4	208,3	227,3	240,5
Total capital outflow	-116,8	-156,9	-176,8	-213,5	-242,3
a) net profits;transfers; payments of interest on debts	-38,2	-58,0	-77,7	-85,5	-95,6
b) amortization of loans	-46,2	-72,6	-69,8	63,1	-88,5
c) depreciation	-32,4	-26,3	-29,3	-64,9	-57,2
Net capital flow [b]	22,4	103,3	33,6	21,0	55,6
Reserves	-59,0	-191,0	-234,5	-264,0	-238,7

a The numbers in brackets indicate the price of copper in that year, in U.S. cents
b Omitting minor autonomous capital flows.

-cont'd-

TABLE VII - Part II

Chile Foreign Trade
(1965 - 1969)

	1965	1966	1967	1968	1969
Exports	776,4(36)[a]	977,7(47)	985,9(48)	1,032,2(52)	1.306,3(65)
Imports	-716,6	-888,3	-909,2	-954,2	-1,086,8
Trade Balance	59,8	89,4	76,7	73,0	219,5
Total capital inflow	244,4	369,5	355,7	581,6	792,2
a) investment	67,6	93,8	149,4	142,2	137,6
b) loans utilized	237,9	258,3	227,7	438,8[c]	639,4[c]
Total capital outflow	-282,2	-370,9	-435,9	-486,4	-725,9
a) net profits; transfers; payments of interest on debts	-116,4	-171,6	-204,1	-208,3	-243,9
b) amortization of loans	-91,6	-109,4	-122,2	-135,2	-244,9
c) depreciation	-74,2	-89,9	-109,6	-142,9	-246.1
Net capital flow[b]	-37,8	-1,4	-80,2	-95,2	-3,3
Reserves	-182,9	-66,1	-91,5	-37,7	-219,8

a The numbers in brackets indicate the price of copper in that year, in U.S. cents
b Omitting minor autonomous capital flows.
c Increase due to loans for the expansion of copper output negotiated under "Chilenization" agreements

SOURCE: Chile, National Planning Office (ODEPLAN), Antecedentes sobre el desarrollo chileno 1960-1970, Santiago de Chile, 1971. Also Inter-American Committee of the Alliance for Progress (CIAP), Domestic Efforts and the Need for External Financing for the Development of Chile, April 1972, Table V-6.

The renegotiation involved the external debt servicing for 1965 (242 million dollars, or about 40% of foreign exchange earnings, paid on official or publicly guaranteed credits) and 1966 ($275 million).

Besides the European members of the Paris Club, the meeting in the French capital was attended by the United States, Canada and Japan, while the IMF, the World Bank, the Inter-American Development Bank and the OECD were there as observers.

As a way of providing the creditors and the IMF with substantive guarantees, the Chilean government proposed restrictions on the indebtedness of the Central Bank, a stabilization program to bring down inflation and, lastly, limits on the number of suppliers' credit arrangements entered into.[1] The successive measures which were to be adopted would be reported to the IMF, which would then inform the creditors.

In this way, on 24 February 1965 a memorandum of agreement was drawn up for the renegotiation of the debt. The agreement concerned 70% of payments to be made in 1965 and 1966 for the amortization of the principal on suppliers' credits guaranteed by the State of Chile and the official agencies of the creditor countries with maturities longer than six months incurred before 31 December 1964, and on specific inter-governmental loans. For the amounts falling due in 1965 there was to be a grace period - coming immediately after the period of consolidation, which lasted one year in this case - so that payments were scheduled from 1 January 1968 to 31 December 1972. For the amounts originally owed in 1966 a similar grace period was allowed: payments were now to be made between the beginning of 1969 and the end of 1973. This meant that $135 million which originally fell due in 1965 and $162 million in 1966 were postponed and payment extended over 5 years from the end of the grace period referred to above. Interest payable on the earlier obligations was kept at the rate originally agreed upon, while variable rates were applied to consolidate credits.

A non-discrimination clause was also granted whereby if more favorable terms than those contained in the memorandum were granted to any creditor (including non-participating creditor

(1) Chile undertook that:
"...the new suppliers' credits for the public sector, authorized after February 28, 1965, with a term greater than 180 days and less than eight years will not at any time before January 1, 1967, exceed actual repayments made by Chile after February 28, 1965, net of any refinancing obtained on such payments. The same norms will apply to private suppliers' credits authorized after February 28, 1965, with a term greater than 180 days and less than five years. In addition, for private credtits with a term of more than five years and less than eight years, new authorizations during the period mentioned above will be limited to the amount of repayments inclusive of refinancing on such credits."

countries) they had to be extended to all participating creditors. A "goodwill" clause was also established, saying that the participating countries would be prepared to review the development of the situation of the debtor country at a later date with a view to providing future debt relief. At the same time it was agreed that Chile would repay without delay all outstanding payments.

The memorandum of agreement included provision for strict monitoring of the evolution of Chile's external debt by the IMF (in the form of monthly reports), which would make the necessary information on the matter available to the creditor countries. In this context, the IMF agreed to grant a stand-by credit of 36 million in 1965. Simultaneously, the United States treasury granted 16.1 million dollars in a trade agreement.

Immediately after the meeting of the Paris Club the respective bilateral agreements, providing additional short-term debt relief, were signed. For example, while the majority of the creditors restructured 70% of the debt, the Ex-Im Bank consolidated 75.4% of the principal involved in 1965 and 72.8% in the following year. The Export-Import Bank of Japan, for its part, refinanced 100%; Canada 88% in 1965 and 77% in 1966; West Germany 70% of the principal and the additional interest, while also granting new loans.

As for the modalities of the restructuring, most of the creditors extended new loans to the government or the Central Bank in amounts equivalent to the deferred payments. In the cases of the United States, Belgium and Holland, the Central Bank repaid 30% of the principal and the creditor debited the consolidated credit for the remainder.

The result of the renegotiation was that payments for the amortization of the debts covered were reduced to 46.2 million dollars in 1965 and 46.9 million in 1966.

On the other hand, United States commercial banks granted a 4-year credit of 45 million dollars, probably in order to restructure short-term debts not included in the agreement.

As can be seen, this debt renegotiation was influenced by the positive attitude of the creditors. They took part in the debt renegotiation in a frame of mind which was greatly influenced by extra-economic factors, while orthodoxy in financial management was guaranteed by the participation of the International Monetary Fund.

However, when the renegotiated amounts began to be remitted in 1968, amortizations rose by 27 million dollars in that year and by 57 million in 1969 and 1970. The consolidation had not incorporated the long-term credits granted by the multilateral agencies and, in general, by governments. To this should be added a substantial rise in external indebtedness starting in 1968. (see Table VIII)

TABLE VIII

General External Debt of Chile
Nominal series, 1966 - 1977
(Millions of dollars)

Year	I General External Debt	II Gross Reserves	III General External Debt, Discounting Gross Reserves (I - II)
1960	746	119	627
1961	1.010	104	906
1962	1.255	106	1.149
1963	1.469	114	1.355
1964	1.635	131	1.504
1965	1.781	182	1,599
1966	1.852	234	1.618
1967	1.908	200	1.708
1968	2.201	288	1.913
1969	2.689	433	2.256
1970	3.123	505	2.618
1971	3.196	290	2.906
1972	3.602	271	3.331
1973	4.048	401	3.647
1974	4.774	535	4.239
1975	5.263	427	4.836
1976	5.195	816	4.379
1977	5.434	871	4.563

Column I: General External Debt - net ordinary outstanding external balances on 31 December of each year, taking into account: traditional external debt, i.e., the debt of the public sector and the publicly guaranteed debt of the private sector. Debt to the IMF. The external debt of the direct private sector (deferred coverage). The financial credits of the private sector, Decree 1272 (Art.14,15,&16) and the short-term lines of credit to the monetary system(Central Bank, commercial Banks & the State Bank)
Column II: Gross Reserves of the Monetary System: All the assets of the monetary system (Central Bank & commercial banks) on 31 December of each year. In this series the value of gold included in the international reserves has been corrected by the average buying price at the close of the London market in December of each year. Mutual credit arrangements have also been treated on a net basis.
Column III: General External Debt discounting Gross Revenues: refers to the net debt position of the country with regard to external creditors (Columns I - II).

Virtually the whole of the indebtedness is attributable to the copper companies (of United States origin) which made massive use of external credits to finance their expansion programs to the amount of 469 million dollars, and, on the other hand, to the public sector. The central government, the decentralized agencies and the State enterprises relied mainly on suppliers'credits and other external sources to finance their operations and public investment projects, for a total amount of 435 million dollars.

The structure of the debt was upset by the fact that additional indebtedness was concentrated in medium-term suppliers' credits and other credits concluded on commercial terms. For example, while in 1967, 67.5% of the debt had a maturity of over 15 years, by 1970 this proportion had dropped to 60.5%. The Central Bank alone reduced its indebtedness by 30 million dollars.

In this way both the increase in the debt and the changes in its structure helped bring about a significant rise in debt servicing. Despite the large increase in the price of copper and also in the level of output, which led to a 31% increase in the volume of exports, the debt service ratio rose from 12.5% in 1967 to 17.5% in 1970. Debt servicing also rose, from 124 million in 1967 to about 230 million in 1970. (see Table IX)

TABLE IX

Chile: Debt Service Ratios, 1967-73
(In millions of U.S. dollars and percentages)

	1967	1968	1969	1970	1971	1972	1973
Exports of goods and services	996	1,035	1,316	1,314	1,153	1,007	1,443
Scheduled debt service payments	124	205	236	230	248	495	512
Actual debt service payments	124	205	236	230	198	129	162
Debt service ratio (2:1)	12.5	19.8	17.9	17.5	21.5	49.2	35.4
Actual debt service ratio (3:1)	12.5	19.8	17.9	27.5	17.2	12.8	11.2

SOURCES: Central Bank of Chile and Development Corporation

R. Ffrench-Davis, who was at the time an official of the Central Bank, explains this phenomenon in the following way:

> "Another problem which persisted throughout those years was the absence of control over external indebtedness... Gross external indebtedness rose faster than it had in the previous few years. The paucity of national savings encouraged public and private enterprises to have recourse to foreign capital; on the other hand, the excellent state of the balance of payments opened the doors of international credit to Chile. The concrete result was greater gross indebtedness, which the country did not need... Unfortunately, the problem was not properly understood, and no decision was taken to establish strict regulation of the movement of foreign capital."(1)

The rise in the price of copper on international markets brought in resources with which to service the debt, but the situation remained precarious because of the possibility of wide fluctuations in the volume of exports.

This happened early in the seventies, at the beginning of a political process which challenged the interests of foreign capital and the dominant local groups and called for an overall review of Chile's relations with the capitalist world.

2. The 1972 renegotiation

Chile entered 1971 with external public debt amounting to more than 150% of the total value of exports for 1970 and about 30% of the national product for that year and double the total for 1965. Commitments for payments in 1971 and 1972 amounted to 248 and 495 million dollars respectively.

The expansionist policy adopted by the Popular Unity government, which sought to make use of idle productive capacity by means of an increase in demand generated by higher wages, led to an 8% increase in imports in 1971; at the same time, the sharp fall in the price of copper on international markets (from 61 to 50 cents a pound) caused a drop of 14% in earnings derived from exports of goods and services and a trade balance deficit of 122 million dollars. Payments of interest on external debt rose from 69 million in 1970 to 86 million in 1971, so that the current account balance showed a deficit of 257 million dollars.

(1) R. Ffrench-Davis, *op.cit.*, p. 107.

As far as the capital account is concerned, it changed from a net flow of private capital of 12 million in 1970 to a reverse transfer of 113 million in 1971 - a reflection of the financial blockade to which the Popular Unity regime was subjected and which we shall later consider in greater detail. Moreover, the net flow of official capital dropped by 150 million dollars from its 1970 levels. This means that the external debt virtually failed to grow in 1971. (see Table VIII)

In order to counteract this negative balance-of-payments situation, the escudo was sharply devalued on the brokers' market (where unofficial transactions were conducted) in July 1971, and, to a lesser extent, on the official market in December.

Import restrictions were tightened up at the same time. Even so, the balance of payments in 1971 showed a deficit of 355 million dollars. The impact of that deficit on the level of reserves was partly softened by default on a payment of 50 million dollars; nonetheless, by the end of 1971, reserves were down to 38 million dollars, a drop of 305 million. This situation could not fail to lead to a renegotiation of Chile's external debt. Before we consider the 1972 renegotiations operation, however, we should complete the picture by describing the financial blockade to which Chile was subjected.

3. The financial blockade

Once the National Congress had approved the law nationalizing the copper companies, in the middle of 1971, the President of the Republic was empowered to set the amount of compensation due to the foreign companies, after the deduction of what was regarded as the excess profits previously repatriated by those companies. This decision set in motion a series of threats and reprisals from the United States government, particularly after the announcement by S. Allende that 774 million dollars, representing excessive profits, would be deducted from the total amount of compensation; this meant that the copper companies would not only receive no compensation at all, but that they would actually owe the State of Chile 360 million dollars.

The companies replied that "the issue was no longer simply between the companies and Chile but between Washington and Santiago". In a meeting between the representatives of six companies with operations in Chile (Anaconda, First National City Bank, Bank of America, Ralston Purina, ITT) and Secretary of State Rogers, the latter pointed out that "the Nixon

Administration was a 'business administration' in favor of business and its mission was to protect business".[1] He also expressed his concern at the possibility that the Chilean case might create a domino effect on other Latin American countries unless the United States took strong action. He mentioned the application of an informal embargo on spare parts and materials for Chile and stated that the government would try to amend the Hickenlooper Amendment and eliminate all aid to Chile as long as the expropriated companies did not receive compensation.

Even before the Popular Unity coalition came to power, however, the big multinational companies had tried to provoke a military takeover through the murder of the Commander-in-Chief of the army by an extreme right-wing group. After the failure of that attempt the White House and the National Security Council of the United States drew up a strategy consisting of two facets: a prolonged economic confrontation and the gradual collapse of the State of Chile. In the economic sphere the tactics used consisted of the promotion of an international financial blockade, through the ability of the United States to put pressure on the international financial organs and on countries to which Chile was in debt. This policy was carried out without further thought, as the United States administration clearly felt the same way as H. Kissinger, who said: "I don't see why we need to stand by and watch a country go communist due to the irresponsibility of its own people".[2] A succession of events then followed:

- from July 1971 onwards the Ex-Im Bank rejected any credit for Chile and suspended guarantees on loans;

- The State Department promptly instructed its representatives in the World Bank to reject any credit for "countries which expropriate foreign property without compensation".

---

(1) United States Senate, Multinational corporations and United States foreign policy, part 2, pp. 975-979. Quoted by J. Petras and M. Morley: "The United States and the overthrow of the Allende government", Monthly Review Press, New York, 1975.

(2) Statement to the Committee of 40, mentioned in the New York Times, 11 September 1974.

It is not surprising that this was followed by a steep decline in United States aid to Chile, and also in that of the multilateral organs under its influence.

TABLE X

Aid to Chile from the United States
and the multilateral institutions under its control
(millions of dollars)

	1968	1969	1970	1968-70	1971	1972	1973	1971-73
U.S. aid	57.9	35.4	18.0	111.3	1.5	1.0	0.8	3.3
Food program	23.0	15.0	7.2	45.2	6.3	5.9	2.5	14.7
Military program	7.8	11.7	0.8	20.3	5.7	12.3	15.0	33.0
Ex-Im Bank	13.4	28.7	--	42.1	--	1.6	3.1	4.7
World Bank	--	11.6	19.3	30.9	--	--	--	--
IDB	16.5	31.9	45.6	94.0	12.0	2.1	5.2	17.3

SOURCE: official sources as reported in J. Petras and M. Morley, *op.cit.*, pp. 166-167.

According to an official of the Inter-American Committee on the Alliance for Progress (CIAP), the United States employed a number of tactics in an effort to hold up IDB loans to the Allende government.

> The U.S. had the opportunity in the IDB to hold up loans. The pressure could go through different channels: (1) veto power. But the problem was to use a more sophisticated way of holding up loans; (2) either by using the power you have in the subcommissions of the Board - the technical way; (or) (3) the political way - calling the director of this department and telling him what you think. At least the last two methods were used.

A similar situation prevailed in the World Bank which did not make a single loan to the Allende government despite the fact that a number of detailed projects were submitted for consideration. In one instance, an appraisal mission to Chile to evaluate a fruit-processing plant project (part of the agrarian reform program and considered crucial in improving Chile's balance of payments situation), was cancelled at the request of the State Department.(1)

(1) Quoted by Petras and Morley, *op.cit.*, pp. 94-95.

In October 1971, a congressional subcommittee inquired of Treasury Under-Secretary Walker as to what the U.S. position within the World Bank or the Inter-American Development Bank would be in response to a loan request from the Allende government:

> I would put it within the context of an expropriation of property in which there has been absolutely no indication up to this time that the compensation will be adequate or timely. On that basis if a loan to Chile were to come up today in the Inter-American Development Bank or the World Bank - the World Bank has a rule and they would not lend to Chile under these circumstances, but the IDB has no such rule - there is no doubt in my mind what Secretary Connally's instructions of Mr. Constanzo (U.S. executive director) would be...(1)

- Kennecott and Anaconda took legal action against the Chilean government. All deposits in the accounts of the principal Chilean state agencies in the United States were seized. Those companies instituted proceedings to seize the Chilean copper which had been exported to various European countries. Merchandise for the Chilean Copper Corporation in the hands of shippers was sold.

- The United States private banks cut back on their financing of Chilean imports, from 220 million dollars in November 1970 to 88 million in 1971 and 32 million in November 1972. In previous years five major banks with their headquarters in New York (Chase Manhattan, Chemical, First National City, Manufacturers Hanover and Morgan Guarantee) had granted credits to the copper companies. These banks, particularly Chase Manhattan and Chemical, whose privileged links to Anaconda are well known, were the most hostile: they totally suspended credits.

The reduction and suspension of lines of credit, combined with the technological rigidity which prevented an immediate shift to other suppliers, caused effects which, in the short term, were difficult to overcome. It was extremely difficult to replace industrial stock and, consequently to maintain levels of activity, as 50% of the capital equipment came from the United States, while in some key com-

(1) Quoted by Petras and Morley, op.cit., pp. 94-95.

panies the proportion of American-made equipment was 100%.(1)

Moreover, the financial blockade, together with the trade balance problems due to the low price of copper severely limited Chile's ability to service its external debt.

In 1971 commitments under the servicing of official debt amounted to 248 million dollars, or 21.5% of exports; the negative prospects for the next two years and the foreign trade situation caused the suspension of most payments early in November 1971. Chile then requested a meeting with the members of the Paris Club to renegotiate its debt. This took the form of four meetings between representatives of Chile and of twelve creditor countries (Belgium, Canada, Denmark, West Germany, France, Italy, Japan, Netherlands, Spain, Switzerland, United Kingdom and the United States). Of these, the United States was the main creditor. From the outset it tried to impede the renegotiation, making it conditional on a "stand-by arrangement" with the IMF which could not fail to run counter to the program of changes undertaken by the Popular Unity government, which rejected the proposal.

The Economist Intelligence Unit assessed the problem as follows:

> "Chile has opposed such an agreement on the grounds that it means sacrificing autonomy in internal economic policy. Such an agreement would certainly lay down norms concerning wages and prices policy. And this would almost certainly mean an end to the present domestic expansion in Chile, a curbing of government expenditure and credit, and an insistence upon movement toward trade liberalization and devaluation. The political implications of such policies, enforced from the outside, would be extremely embarrassing for the administration."(2)

---

(1) For information on the modalities of the United States blockade, the reader should consult, in addition to the work by Petras and Morley already referred to, S. Bitar: Las relaciones economicas entre Chile y EE.UU. en el periodo 1971-1972, (Caracas: 1975) and E. Farnsworth, R. Feinberg, E. Leeson: Chile, el bloqueo invisible, (Buenos Aires: 1973).

(2) Economist Intelligence Unit, Quarterly Economic Review of Chile, no. 1, March, 1972. Quoted by Petras and Morley, op.cit., p. 116.

As an alternative, Chile proposed a declaration of intended policy in the field of external financing designed to provide guarantees for its creditors. It included an undertaking concerning the handling of the balance of payments, limits on the authorization of new external credits with maturities of between one and eight years, and, lastly, payments of arrears in current payments and previously renegotiated amounts. At the same time Chile undertook to provide its creditors with regular information, through the IMF.

The Fund from its side, granted loans of a total of 148 million dollars under normal allocations of drawings rights and compensation for reduced export earnings, which it could not refuse to do.

The second obstacle encountered by Chile was the question of compensation for the expropriations and that of the debts assumed by the government after its takeover of the copper companies. This was resolved through the decision of the Chilean government to acknowledge all the debts incurred by the public sector -directly or by guarantee- to guarantee "fair compensation for any nationalization in keeping with Chilean and international laws", and to carry out direct negotiations to promptly resolve the problems related to the question of compensation.

The creditors accepted the guarantees offered by Chile, and a memorandum of agreement was signed on 19 April 1972, providing for the refinancing of 70% of the amortization and interest of officially guaranteed commercial credits of more then one year, and loans guaranteed by the governments of the creditor countries with the exception of loans of more than 40 years of duration and those connected to previous renegotiations. The period of consolidation involved extended from 1 November 1971 to 31 December 1972, with a grace period of one year. The Chilean request for an extension of the period of consolidation until the end of 1974 was turned down.

According to an IMF document:

> "The service payments renegotiated in these agreements amounted to US$129 million, 70 per cent of which (US $90 million) was refinanced or rescheduled at rates of interest ranging between 5 per cent and 6 per cent. The remaining 30 per cent (US $39 million) was to be

paid by Chile upon, or shortly after, the conclusion of the bilateral agreements. The service payments due to the United States, subject to renegotiation under the provisions of the Paris Club Agreement also amounted to US $129 million. With 70 per cent of this amount eligible for rescheduling or refinancing, the full implementation of the Paris Club multilateral debt renegotiation would have potentially provided Chile with US $181 million in debt relief. In fact, Chile obtained in 1972 a substantially larger effective relief on the service payments covered by the Paris Club Agreement for two main reasons: (1) no bilateral agreement was signed with the United States in 1972 and therefore no payments were made to this country and (2) a substantial part of the downpayments due by Chile under the bilateral agreements concluded with other countries were postponed to 1973, as some of the agreements were signed late in 1972 or early in 1973. Taking into account these factors, the effective debt relief that Chile ultimately obtained in 1972 amounted to US $243 million or close to 95 per cent of the service payments covered by the Paris Club Agreement.(1)

The United States attitude is consistent with the tough line taken by the authorities of that country. It was significant that the United States delegation was made up of experts not from the State Department, but from the Department of the Treasury, who, according to the Washington Post, were more inclined to "keep Chile's feet to the fire" in connection with the expropriations of the copper companies, considering that "progress in the one field is tied to progress in the other". Officials of the Central Bank of Chile found that Britain and Germany tended to side with the United States, whereas France seemed to adopt a wait-and-see policy, and Italy and Spain were favorably disposed towards Chile.(2)

In 1972 Chile also renegotiated various payments outside the context of the Paris Club, involving longer deadlines and amounting to a total of 198 million dollars, with relief for 1972 coming to 40 million dollars. The major part involved 145 million dollars to private banks by the end of 1976, the refinancing being granted with an interest rate equivalent to the London inter-bank rate at 90 days, plus banking commissions. Other special negotiations were carried out with private European banks and the government of Norway.

---

(1) I.M.F. Multilateral Debt Renegotiations - Experiences of Fund Members, 1971 - 74, September 20, 1974.
(2) Farnsworth, Feinberg and Leeson, Chile, el bloqueo invisible, op.cit., p. 78.

In this way the highly compromised debt servicing capacity of Chile compelled its creditors to renegotiate its debt, or to risk a default, which would have been contrary to their interests. Strong pressure from the United States failed to halt this operation but did ensure that its terms and conditions were much harsher for Chile than in 1965, providing relief only over the very short term.

Chile thus paid in 1972 one quarter of the original payments (129 out of 495 million), the reduction being equivalent to 28% of that year's imports. Nevertheless, the problem was postponed rather than resolved. And at the two meetings which the government of Chile held with the Paris Club in 1973, the creditors were reluctant to agree to any renegotiation at all. Meanwhile, the military coup d'état of September 1973 changed the situation for the creditors, as the new regime came to power precisely with the intention of openly favoring their interests.

4. The renegotiations of 1974 and 1975

Late in 1973 the situation was as follows: out of the 367 million dollars originally due in 1973 only 162 million had been paid. The difference results from refinancing agreed in 1972 with the private banks, 46 million produced by the signing of the bilateral agreement with the USA (which had been systematically denied to the previous government) and 271 million dollars of unfulfilled payments.

The problem lay not so much in the structure of the debt or its size, but in the weight of the debt servicing of late payments and the interruption of some of those payments in 1973. Originally Chile was supposed to remit a total of 434 million in 1974 plus 271 million for late payments. Even assuming that copper prices stayed where they had been, debt servicing would still have amounted to 30% of exports; moreover, the grace period granted in 1972 came to an end at the end of 1974. The balance-of-payments situation became critical and forced the Chilean government to ask for a meeting with the members of the Paris Club in order to renegotiate part of the debt servicing for 1974 and 1973, a total of 867 million dollars. The non-renegotiable portion was estimated by the Chilean government to be 383 million dollars, with 484 million subject to discussion.

This renegotiation was broadly favored by the attitude of the United States towards the new military regime. All financial boycott measures were suspended and a large amount of official aid was granted to Chile. The situation was summarized as follows by one United States official:

> "It is fair to say that we took a different view on terms and conditions of rescheduling with the new regime. For example, we were trying in the previous debt rescheduling renegotiations with the Allende regime to use that as leverage for some progress on the investment compensation issue. The new regime said, "Yes, that's no problem, we will start negotiations tomorrow to eliminate unjust things Allende government attempted to impose."(1)

The Pinochet regime set in motion a policy of unconditional support for United States interests, thus restoring the "international creditworthiness" of Chile. The expropriated copper companies obtained compensation according to their wishes. In this way, between September 1973 and March 1974, Chile obtained offical credits from multilateral institutions totalling 468.8 million dollars, in sharp contrast to the volume of loans obtained by the previous government from those same sources.

The first step in the renegotiation was that of obtaining an agreement with the IMF for a stand-by loan, which included the application of a program of stabilization. In the light of the ultra-liberal outlook of those in charge of the Chilean economy, this did not give rise to major difficulties.

On 25 March 1974 an agreement was therefore reached on the consolidation of 80% of the payments of amortization and interest on commercial credits officially guaranteed before the end of 1973 and governmental loans with a duration of less than 40 years, except those involved in previous renegotiations. The period of consolidation in question covered the years 1973 and 1974, with a two-year grace period and payments staggered from the beginning of 1977 to the middle of 1983. The remaining 20% was paid in the following three years in portions of 5% for the first two years and 10% for the third.

In addition, in the light of the high debt service projected for 1975 (460 million dollars) the door was left open for an examination of those payments in 1975. On 5 July 1975 a new agreement was reached, consolidating 70% of liabilities under officially guaranteed commercial credits incurred before the end of 1973 and the official loans incurred before that date which had not been previously renegotiated.

(1) Quoted by Petras and Morley, op.cit., pp. 141-142.

A grace period of 2 years and a repayment period of 7 years were granted: the outstanding 30% (of debts) was cancelled in 10% annual portions between 1975 and 1977. The operation was subject to the implementation of a stabilisation plan at the basis of a stand-by agreement with the IMF. Thus, conditions granted in the last two reschedulings for Chile were more favourable than those granted in 1972 or even in 1965.

The case of Chile thus shows that renegotiation operations are closely linked to the general policy of the main creditor countries towards the debtor country, and that considerations of a purely technical nature are relegated to the background. Chile had its debt renegotiated under three different political regimes and the treatment it received on each accesion depended on its degree of political dependence on the principal creditor, the United States, which did not hesitate to pursue a policy which was at times openly interventionist.

B. The Case of Turkey

The Turkish case illustrates various processes associated with external indebtedness and its renegotiation. Turkey has had to face various mechanisms for resolving its payments crises. Actually, it has become a test case.

Its inability to service its external debt,[1] arising out if its chronic current account deficit, has lasted for about 25 years. Imports have usually exceeded exports by some 50%, sometimes more than 100%. This situation has worsened considerably in recent years. Furthermore, the budget has registered permanent deficits, monetary creation and inflation have reached high levels, while the Turkish lira has been generally overvalued, thus feeding the trade deficit.[2]

The industrialization model established though permitting fairly high growth rates (3.5% to 4% on per capita GNP in the long term) has induced high average and marginal propensity to import, since nationally produced products incorporate a significant proportion of imported inputs. Thus, almost all imports are associated with the industrial sector. At the same time, exports have consisted mainly of agricultural and mineral products, even though manufactured products have increased their relative shares in recent years.[3]

Moreover, the massive economic aid received by Turkey since the 1950's from the United States and other NATO countris has been tied, as could be expected, to strategic considerations arising out of geopolitical considerations, Turkey being a key component of the Western defense system in the Mediterranean area, the Balkans and Asia Minor. U.S. and European aid has consisted of grants (including military aid), soft loans to finance development projects and imports of consumer and intermediate goods needed for the regular functioning of the economy.

---

(1) The Ottoman Empire became heavily indebted in the past century, facing various payments crises. See the study of G. Corm: "L'endettement des pays en voie de dévelop-pement: origines et mécanismes".

(2) H. Bitterman "The Refunding of International Debt", *op. cit.*, pp. 136-137.

(3) See OECD's "Economic Surveys: Turkey" (Paris: November, 1978).

TABLE XI

Approximate Turkish Public Debt Outstanding, Including Undisbursed and Debt Service Payments, 1956-76

(Millions of Dollars)

	Outstanding principal	Debt Service
1956	249.0	
1957	241.1	11.5
1958	250.1	10.0
1959	363.6	8.9
1960	864.8	49.3
1961	813.0	172.4
1962	910.5	98.7
1963	941.4	83.0
1964	1,039.6	76.8
1965	1,198.9	147.8
1966	1,324.5	120.0
1967	1,562.5	106.4
1968	1,743.7	103.1
1969	1,979.4	134.1
1970	2,691.6	171.5
1971	2,970.7	163.0
1972	3,253.9	226.4
1973	3,669.6	206.9
1974	4,100.7	229.9
1975	4,390.7	245.9
1976	5,466.5	273.1

SOURCE: World Bank

The growth of official guaranteed debt is shown in the table.XII.

1. Renegotiations in 1959 and 1965.

Turkey's foreign debt grew fast throughout the post war period. Following the drop in economic activity after the Korean War boom in the 1950's, there was a sharp fall in export earnings, resulting in serious debt servicing problems. However, Turkey's suppliers continued to grant sizeable short term credits, despite serious reimbursement difficulties, made possible thanks to the support of official credit insurance agencies in the creditor countries.[1]

(1) See indicators on the factors leading to renegotiations in Tables II, III and IV, in Chapter II.

Meanwhile, Turkey joined the OEEC, predecessor of the OECD. The OEEC organized an international conference which resulted in the renegotiation of 320 million dollars worth of Turkey's commercial debt (i.e. 100% of the supplier's credits, including amortizations and interest, representing 37.4% of its total debt). A multilateral agreement was thus obtained on 12 May 1959, in consultation with the IMF. The IMF imposed a stabilization program and a devaluation of the Turkish lira. The agreement had several unusual features: it included non-insured private credits, terms were more favorable than those granted by the Paris Club and compensatory loans were associated to debt relief, linked to the balance of payments deficit, and granted on concessional terms by OEEC countries and the U.S. Payments were phased over 12 years, in progressively increasing amounts, with a 3% interest rate with no grace period.

However, Turkey continued facing balance of payments deficits and debt service difficulties. In 1962, a consortium to aid Turkey was established within the framework of OECD and in 1965, member governments granted Turkey debt relief (some preferred to grant compensatory credits rather than direct relief).

This operation included renegotiations of debts previously renegotiated and the recognition of balance of payments loans as a factor of debt relief. It should be noted that both approaches had been, in principle, rejected by the Paris Club. Moreover, it was accepted that the various creditor countries practiced different relief terms, with a minimum consolidation of 60% of the principal of credits consolidated in 1959 (to be orginally paid between 1966 and 1967), with a 4 year grace period for each annual total. In the minutes of the agreement, Turkey was enjoined to carry out a development policy with financial stability, based on long-term financing.

2. Renegotiations in 1978/79.

The rapid deterioration of the current balance of payments in recent years (see Table XIII),and the emergence in 1977 of an acute external payments crisis arose from the worsening of terms of trade, the drop in demand for Turkish exports, the decline in remittances by Turkish workers abroad and the pressure on internal demand, and thus import demand.(1)

(1) The structural characteristics of Turkish industrialization continue to be the origin of this phenomenon. See: The Banker, January 1978 which states that:

"... Certain structural problems within Turkish industry are causing particular concern at present. At least one arises from the concentration of industry in the hands of...large conglomerates. Because of their western outlook, they have largely

TABLE XII

Turkey: Balance of payments

(millions US $)

	1970	1971	1972	1973	1974	1975	1976	1977
Trade balance	-360	-494	-678	-769	-2,245	-3,337	-3,169	-4,044
Exports	588	677	885	-1,317	1,532	1,401	1,960	1,753
Imports	948	-1,171	1,563	2,086	3,777	4,738	5,129	5,797
Balance of services net	188	372	670	1,253	1,525	1,458	868	618
Remittances from emigrated workers	273	471	740	1,183	1,426	1,312	982	982
Interest payments	-48	-60	-62	-59	-103	-124	217	-360
Profit transfers	-33	-36	-35	-35	-71	-36	-83	-116
Tourism, net	4	21	44	78	42	46	-27	-65
Other, net	-8	-24	-17	86	231	260	213	177
Balance of current operations	-172	-122	-8	484	-720	-1,879	-2,301	-3,426
Debt Service principal	-146	-125	-130	-77	-156	-147	-119	-214
Non-monetary capital operations	512	472	450	510	415	725	654	1,732
Private sector	92	72	82	129	146	403	263	1,229
Public sector	420	400	368	381	269	322	391	503
Global balance	194	225	312	917	-461	-1,301	-1,766	-1,908
Errors and Omissions	-24	121	-295	35	22	25	-15	-220
Monetary movements	-170	-346	-17	-952	483	1,326	1,781	2,128
Reserves variations	-236	-345	-235	-728	431	417	112	560
IMF	66	-1	-116	--	-8	301	149	14
Other	--	--	334	-224	60	608	1,520	1,554

SOURCE: OECD, 1978.

This situation was partly faced in 1977 by net capital in-flows ($500 million), but the rest had to be financed by using reserves ($560 million) and by an increase in indebtedness through short-term Euro-issues, bank advances, etc. However, Turkey could not meet its commitments abroad and had to request the aid of the IMF and of the OECD consortium.

Foreign debt totalled almost 7 billion dollars, comprising a substantial share of "soft" long-term government loans whose services did not pose any special problems. However, most of the debt towards private creditors consisted of short-term deposits in convertible Turkish lira amounting to some 2 billion dollars. These commitments negatively unbalanced the structure of external indebtedness and posed serious repayments problems.

At the beginning of 1978, when the People's Republic Party led by B. Ecevit came to power, the Turkish government adopted a stabilization program and signed a stand-by agreement with the IMF in April of that year. This put $450 million at Turkey's disposal phased over a two year period, conditioned by periodic examination of the development of the economy. This program includes "classic" measures: a 23% devaluation of the Turkish lira, with a unification of exchange rates, a restrictive budgetary policy, a reduction of Central Bank issues, and reduction of imports. The external deficit diminished as a result, but the growth rate also fell (to half of the 1977 rate), as well as the average use of the industrial capacities (to 50%), and the highest unemployment rate in the OECD (reaching 20%).(1)

At present, Turkey faces a group of creditors closely co-ordinated amongst themselves i.e. the OECD consortium, the IMF, private banks and commercial suppliers. In May 1978, the 14 members of the OECD Consortium consolidated Turkey's debt service obligations for a 6 to 8 year period, on terms more similar to those of the Paris Club, as development loans as well as publicly guaranteed short- (i.e. less than one year, an unusual practice) and medium-term credits.(2)

From then on, bilateral agreements have been concluded with Austria, Belgium, France, West Germany, Italy, Japan, Norway, Sweden, the United Kingdom and the United States, usually with 2 to 3 years grace periods.

---

outstripped the ability of domestic ancillary industries to meet their needs. The imported content of their products is quite high. Cetin Tokcan, General Co-ordinator of the Eczacibasi Holding Company estimates that 33 per cent of its recent TL 1 billion investment in a new sanitary ware plant at Bozoyuk was imported. (In general the figure probably ranges between 25 per cent and 40 per cent."

(1) See M. Munir: "Struggles to avoid a long recession", <u>Financial Times</u>, November 13, 1978

(2) A.C. Cizaukas: "International Debt Renegotiation: lessons from the past", <u>World Development</u>, (1979:7), pp. 199-210.

Also, 14 OECD countries in May 1979 agreed to place at Turkey's disposal $900 million dollars worth of credits to finance urgent import needs. However, the countries mentioned demanded that Turkey arrive at an agreement with the IMF for the third tranche of the stand-by credit negotiated in 1978.(1) Once the agreement was reached, additional US $55 million were extended.

The negotiations with the IMF involved two particularly controversial problems: devaluation and the "re-ordering" of the traditionally extensive public sector. The first devaluation of March 1978 was followed by a 46.6% devaluation on July 11,1979. Contrary to its traditional practice, the Fund agreed to the establishment of multiple exchange rates to favour essential imports. A few months before, the Turkish government had opposed a 30% devaluation requested by the IMF, but finally had to give in.

The right-wing opposition accused the government of capitulating to the Fund. On the other hand, the Turkish State has played a considerable role in development since the 1930's. The armed forces also control several industries (as, for example, an automobile factory in association with Renault). Hence the resistance to the demand of the IMF to reduce the role of the public sector.(2) But the Turkish government, with a view to avoiding deep recession, has maintained that it cannot fulfill the conditions that the IMF is trying to impose whilst private international banks do not grant new credits. At the same time, private banks were awaiting the green light from the IMF.(3)

A "letter of intent" from the Turkish government was submitted to the IMF in mid-1979. This contained the commitment to cut the growth rate provided for in the development plan: reduce public sector expenditures; contain wage increases within "reasonable" limits;increase prices charged by state entities in deficit; reduce government subsidies to agricultural products; check internal consumption and boost exports. The main object was to reduce galloping inflation (70% in 1978) which was 25% in the first four months of 1979.(4) On July 19, 1979, the IMF approved a one-year stand-by loan equalling $327.5 million to Turkey, paving the way for at least an additional $1.57 billion in aid (corresponding to three quarters of the current deficit) from Western countries and commercial banks. The new credit replaced the one that had been arranged in 1978.(5)

(1) Se The OECD Observer, (1979:98)

(2) See Le Monde, "Turquie: une democratie chaotique", 28 June 1979.

(3) Euromoney of September, 1977 states:
"...The recent concern over the deficit and shortage of foreign exchange has led most bankers to sit it out and wait for the IMF to move in first. Because of their confidence in the dynamism of the Turkish economy, most bankers say they will gladly arrange medium-term loans to Turkey as soon as possible after an IMF agreement, but the spreads are likely to be high..."

(4) Le Monde, 13 June 1979

(5) International Herald Tribune, 20 July 1979.

The negotiations with 221 commercial banks or financial institutions were even more complicated, given the links with the IMF's "green light". They set out the norm that "private debts must be punctually met to preserve credit worthiness for subsequent loans".[(1)] A certain number of banks representing 90% of the accumulated debt with this type of creditor (2.200 million dollars in convertible lira deposits) accepted the refunding requested by Turkey. The seven banks co-ordinating the negotiation were Barclays, City Bank, Chase, Deutsche, Dresdner, Morgan Guaranty and Union de Banques Suisses. In July 1979, Turkey and a group of international banks signed a new medium-term loan for \$407 million and agreed to reschedule \$429 million of short term debts of the Central Bank. On 22nd August 1979, Turkey held a meeting with 200 private creditor banks to agree on the rescheduling of 2 billion liras in convertible deposits.

Finally, late payments in the form of non-guaranteed suppliers' credits were rescheduled. A difficult task, due to the high number (90.000) and the variety of suppliers involved. The terms discussed were similar to those for guaranteed suppliers' credits.

But the size of the problem and the impressive volume of external debt -\$12 billion at the beginning of 1979 with half maturing in the short term, as well as the persistent external desequilibrium, will certainly involve Turkey in new negotiations in the near future. The members of the Aid Turkey Consortium of the OECD decided that "it would be appropriate to provide for the additional refunding or rescheduling of Turkey's debts".[(2)]

The case of Turkey shows present trends in indebtedness and the problems it involves. In spite of extensive official bilateral aid favoured by Turkey's geopolitical situation, the recurrent external deficit obliges it to resort to short-term private bank loans to avoid bankruptcy. Their terms have a negative impact on debt service capacity. Hence the increasing need for more frequent and sizeable renegotiations of payments commitments -including those previously renegotiated with four types of creditors (OECD, IMF, private banks and suppliers' credits) which alternate the granting of financial resources as a function of the level of conditioning attained in Turkish economic policy, the IMF being the organization determining the "credit worthiness" of Turkey,

---

(1) J.C. Friedman, <u>The emerging role of private banks in the developing world</u>. Citicorp, 1977, quoted by P. Bhonte, <u>La Dette des Pays en Développement</u>, op.cit., p. 52.

(2) OECD, Press Release, July 26, 1979.

over its government and giving or withdrawing its green light according to how events develop.[1]

As pointed out by J. Juruna "this evolution presents certain similarities with the situation prevailing in the 1950's. There was an alternating movement between private commercial banks and international credit institutions: The IMF and the World Bank created conditions in certain countries enabling them to contract credits from private banks: when the level of indebtedness becomes a major risk for commercial banks, international institutions intervened again to allow these countries to initiate another cycle of indebtedness".[2]

It is perhaps not foolhardy to say that this scenario is beginning to occur frequently in various Third World countries, or will do so soon, taking into account recent developments both in the volume of indebtedness and in its composition, and institutional mechanisms.

But it is hard to imagine greater operational integration between private banks and the IMF in debt refunding. Until now, the Fund has preferred to give financial information only circumstantially on a case-by-case basis to private banks so as to avoid debtor countries distorting the statistics they supply to it[3]; the World Bank however, has carried out jointly financed

---

(1) Euromoney states in its issue of September 1977: "Will the banks and the Fund make an example of Turkey?":

"Yet the banking community admits that the real test of the unwritten agreement between the IMF and the international banks is still to come. Will they show a hard front to countries borrowing to finance balance of payments problems. Turkey may provide that first test case.

The ground is strewn with obstacles... David Rockefeller days: "a comercial bank that tried to impose conditions on a sovereign nation would soon be in a lot of trouble". In Turkey's case, many of the banks concerned are outwardly adamant that they will not lend to the politically troubled country until the IMF has imposed a hard line over the country's finances, or until the Turks have forestalled the IMF by taking these measures themselves. Neither will the banks attempt to impose conditions on Turkey".

(2) J. Juruna, "Le Fonds Monetaire et les Banques Privées. Le Gendarme du Grand Capital". Le Monde Diplomatique, Oct. 1977.

(3) Sidmon, H. "Les thérapeutiques de redressement économique du FMI", l'Expansion, October 5, 1979.

projects with private banks[1]. Thus the IMF points out that: "The participation of Fund staff in meetings between the debtor country and private creditors and the role which such staff could play depends on the circumstances of each case, with due attention to the maintenance of confidentiality of relations between the Fund and the member country.[2]

Flexible relations tend to develop, giving the IMF the role of last resort for creditors in case of financial crisis, through the acceptance of stabilization programmes, aimed at re-establishing the debt servicing capacity of debtor countries.

VII. Conclusion

Every time the equilibrium is ruptured between the size of a given country's indebtedness and the conditions to which the latter is subject on one hand, and the growth in indebtedness and exports on the other, a situation arises which can necessitate debt rescheduling. Rescheduling is by definition an exceptional situation. It is a revision of the conditions according to which external financial resources have been obtained; which is justified because, taking into account the factors determining debt servicing capacity, it is evident that obstacles have emerged in the flow and continuity of the external financing process in its varios phases. Refunding sanctions the manifest disfunction of this process, based on the present structure of international economic relations.

But refunding, as it has taken place so far, is only a temporary solution to financial crises with two sides:

a) The correction of the disfunction mentioned is faced with recessional logic, since usually its realisation is conditional to the adoption of stabilisation plans promoted by the IMF. These are conceived to bring about measures centred on financial variables, with little attention to their internal structural origins, or exogenous factors influencing them. The most frequent result is a loss of dynamism of national economies, manifested in a drop in investment, employment, gross national product levels, in a deterioration in income distribution and the capacity to import, and thus a decline in the capacity to break structural bottlenecks only possible with self-sustaining growth[3]. *It is not surprising, as pointed out above, that there are recurrent breaks in the financial flow of external finance.

---

(1) R. R. Horstein. "CO-financing of Bank and Aid projects" <u>Finance and Development</u>, January 1977.

(2) IMF "Avoidance and resolution of debt servicing difficulties", September 23, 1976.

(3) See A. Sid Ahmed, "Conditionality of drawings on the IMF" CID, Paris 1979.

* To this should be added the inadequacy of debt relief terms (interest and amortization period).

b) Refunding operations expose countries to significant losses of independence. First, as just mentioned there is severe conditioning of economic policies which amongst other factors, leads to the denationalisation of the economies of affected countries, the final result being the expansion of the operating area of transnational capital. Second, various refunding efforts have revealed that global or concentrated political pressures are exercised inside these operations. In fact, they constitute an area of confrontation and if they resolve short-term problems, they are not directed towards the solution of structural problems of third world economies even when they do not actually work against them by breaking the dynamism of growth.

ANNEX Analytical Relations of the process of indebtedness

Analytical Relations of the process of indebtedness

The process of "roll-over" indebtedness will be examined assuming equilibrium in the trade balance, so as to determine the impact on the balance of payments, based on the analysis developed by Bitterman.[1]

A constant annual amount of disbursements, without grace periods and with uniform annual amortizations is assumed. Though this may be a simplification, it facilitates the understanding of the indebtedness mechanism.

With:

P=the amount of the principal of each annual loan
i=annual interest on accumulated debt
n=number of years for amortization by means of identical annual amounts
m=year in which payments equal the amount of new loans, i.e. when the net transfer of resources is interrupted, the central variable to be determined.
R=total remittances to the lenders, equivalent to the total payment of debtors in the year m
P/n=annual amortization of each loan.

a) In the year m, total amortizations will be mP/n. The accumulated amortization at the end of year m will be

$$\frac{P}{n} + \frac{2P}{n} + \cdots + \frac{mP}{n} = \frac{mP}{n} \cdot \frac{(m+1)}{2}$$

Accumulated debt will be

$$mP - \frac{mP}{n}\frac{(m+1)}{2} = \frac{2nmP - m^2P - mP}{2n}$$

(1) H. Bitterman, "The refunding of international debt", op.cit. pp 244-249.

Table I

Cycle of Loans at Annual Amount of P: Years in which Receipts of Interest and Annual Amortization (Equal Annual Payments) of Principal Will Equal New Principal Loaned, with No Grace Period on Principal (Interest Rates Percent per Annum).

n	0.5	1.0	1.5	2.0	2.5	3.0	3.5	4.0
5	4.93	4.85	4.78	4.70	4.63	4.56	4.49	4.42
10	9.73	9.45	9.19	8.92	8.66	8.41	8.16	7.93
15	14.40	13.81	13.24	12.68	12.14	11.62	11.13	10.66
20	18.96	17.93	16.94	16.00	15.11	14.28	13.50	12.79

n	4.5	5.0	5.5	6.0	6.5	7.0	7.5	8.0
5	4.35	4.28	4.21	4.15	4.08	4.02	3.95	3.89
10	7.70	7.47	7.26	7.05	6.85	6.66	6.47	6.30
15	10.22	9.80	9.41	9.04	8.70	8.37	8.06	7.78
20	12.12	11.51	10.95	19.43	9.95	9.51	9.11	8.73

For example, a country can be assumed to contract debts of 100 million dollars a year for 10 years, with linear amortizations over ten years and a 6% interest rate on the accumulated debt. As can be observed in Table II, at the end of the seventh year, total debt service will equal the amount of indebtedness. After the tenth year, amortizations will equal new loans, so that total debt will reach $550 million indefinitely with an annual interest charge of $33 million.

b) interest will be paid on the total loans, minus interest on the sums amortized until the beginning of year m, so that total remittances in this year will be

$$R = \frac{mP}{n} + iPm - iP\,\frac{m(m-1)}{2n} \quad \text{Then} \quad 2nR = 2mP + 2imnP - im^2P + imP$$

c) it has been indicated that year m is when R equals P. Hence $2nP = 2mP + 2imnP - im^2P + imP$. By successive transformation the following general formula results:

$$m = \frac{2 + i(2n+1) = \sqrt{4(1+i) + i^2(2n+1)^2}}{2i}$$

Thus the following table can be constructed, to reflect the moment at which disbursements equal remittances according to different interest rates and amortization periods.

Table II

Interest Cost and Amortization of a Succession of Loans of $100 Million Annually and Amortization in 10 Years, No Grace Period (Millions of Dollars).

Year	Loans outstanding in January	Interest payments	Amortization	Loans outstanding at end of year
1	100	6.0	10	90
2	190	11.4	20	170
3	270	16.2	30	240
4	340	20.4	40	300
5	400	24.0	50	350
6	450	27.0	60	390
7	490	29.4	70	420
8	520	31.2	80	440
9	540	32.4	90	450
10	550	33.0	100	450
11	550	33.0	100	450
12	550	33.0	100	450

This can be graphically represented: assuming a country contracts debts of 100 million dollars a year for 10 years for an indefinite period, at 5% interest, similar to the amortization rate for each annual disbursement. Graph I is obtained.

Annual Capital Imports and Debt Service, with Constant Annual Borrowing.

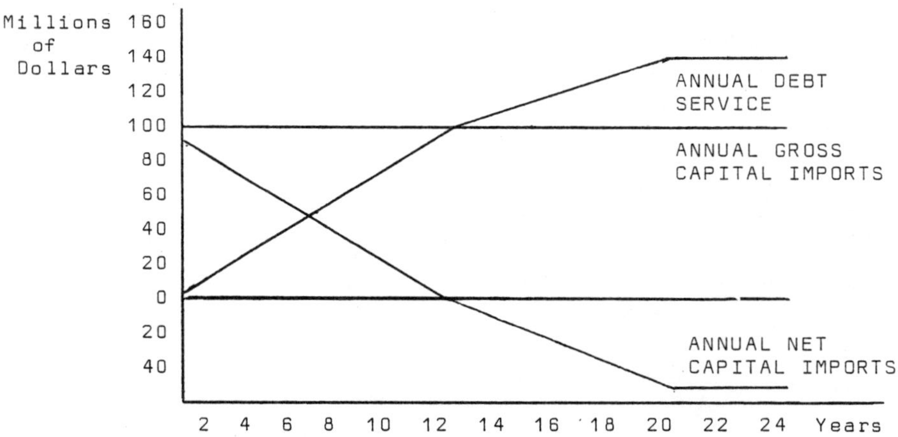

The progressive drop of net annual capital imports under a constant annual indebtedness situation is observed, with identical amounts each year.

In order to give the analysis more precision, debt can be considered as a variable of economic policy, depending on the growth rate of disbursements and on the terms of loans[1].

The indebtedness programme, defined by total flows in the period $t(GF_t)$, with a constant growth rate (C) from an initial disbursement ($GFo = X$; $GF_t = (1+C)^t X$) without grace period, with identical annual amortizations (with T as the amortization period), with an interest rate (i) on the debt accumulated at the beginning of the period (or at the end of the previous period $D_t - 1$), with A_t as the flow of payments for amortizations during the period t. I_t is the flow of payments for interest in the same period, DS_t is the sum of A_t and I_t. NF_t is the net transfer defined by $N_t = GF_t - A_t - I_t$. Debt accumulated in Period 0 is nil. $D_t - 1$ is the sum of the non-amortized parts of disbursements between 0 and t-1.

Considering the case in which the total amortization period has expired, $t > T$ we obtain:

$$D_t - 1 = \frac{X(1+C)^t}{TC}\left[\frac{T-1}{C} + \frac{1}{(1+C)^T}\right]$$ i.e. the sum on non-amortized parts (between o and t-2)

$$A_t = \frac{X}{TC}\left[(1+C)^t - (1+C)^{t-T}\right]$$ i.e. the flow of amortization payments in t

$$\frac{NT_t}{GF_T} = nt = (1-\frac{i}{C})\left[1 - \frac{1}{TC} + \frac{1}{TC(1+C)^T}\right]$$ or net transfer.

Thus for $t > T$, when amortization period has expired, the net transfer, objective of efficient indebtedness, is a constant which is positive if the growth rate of disbursement is higher than the interest rate. When this interest rate is given the transfer grows, as C grows, (the growth rate of disbursement) or T, the amortization period grows.

---

(1) See P. Dhonte, "Describing External Debt Situations", op. cit. pp 183-184.

Chapter VI

TOWARDS AN ALTERNATIVE POLICY FOR THIRD WORLD INDEBTEDNESS

J. C. Sánchez Arnau
Gonzalo Daniel Martner
Abdelkader Sid-Ahmed

TOWARDS AN ALTERNATIVE POLICY FOR THIRD WORLD INDEBTEDNESS

An alternative policy aimed at solving the external indebtedness problem of developing countries should be based on two types of considerations. First, there must be determined and systematic action by Third World countries within present international financial structures. The present system of conditionality of drawings on the IMF and other sources of finance must be questioned. New sources of financing must be placed at the disposal of the Third World which can stimulate the self-centred growth of their economies.

We shall put forward proposals appearing necessary in this context, such as the increase of IMF quotas, the increase in SDR allocations, the transformation of compensatory facilities, the easing of access conditions to long-term capital markets for certain developing countries, the creation of a special refinancing system and the transformation of the institutional framework for debt renegotiation.

Secondly, there is a need to question the development ideology underlying consumption and technology models at the origin of excessive Third World indebtedness. This implies insisting on the need for the major transformation of the economies of developing countries and the introduction of new planning methods. But this can only become continuous and consistent if there is a change in the position of the Third World in the international system, i.e. the creation of a New International Economic Order.

I. The need to transform international financing systems

The payments restrictions and the recessions which have afflicted many LDCs over the past few decades may be partly blamed on the failure of the international monetary system to provide the LDCs with adequate liquidity.

This observation leads us to propose a certain number of reforms, the purpose of which is not stability at any price, but rather development above all else.

A. Reform of the system of conditionality

At the eleventh meeting of the Group of 24, in Washington, August 1975, the ministers agreed to "recognize that the LDCs will need a considerable amount of assistance with their balance of payments" and emphasized that the IMF would be responsible for providing most of it. They drew attention in particular to the need to modify the Fund's policies for action and its procedures in order to cope with the situation. In particular the "ministers were definitely of the opinion that the conditions which traditionally accompany drawings on the Fund are no longer appropriate, since they allow the burden of adjustment to fall on the developing countries". They therefore urged the Fund to revise its policies for action so that they would be able to meet the new and exceptional needs of the developing countries. "For that purpose" they called for an increase in the amounts available under the Fund's tranche policy.

In January 1976 the Group of 24, meeting in Kingston, confirmed their earlier demands for a substantial broadening, on a permanent basis, of access for the developing countries to the credits of the Fund; they also recommended "the immediate addition of two credit tranches under the same conditions as the first tranche". Lastly, the ministers "are convinced that the conditions governing the use of the Fund's resources in the higher credit tranches are excessive at the present time and that they should be made more flexible". In October in Manila the ministers of the Group of 24 took up this point again and "took note that very few developing countries have used the resources of the Fund beyond the first credit tranche, that only two countries have had recourse to the extended facility of the Fund, because of the limited amount of resources available under these facilities and the excessively strict conditions applying to their use". In April 1977 in Washington, the ministers of the Twenty-four called again for "a revision of the conditions on the use of the Fund's various credit facilities because they are so rigorous that members have been discouraged from having recourse to some of the Fund's resources which were available to them". In Mexico City, in April 1978, the ministers of the Twenty-four "considered that the strict conditionality attached to drawings of the higher credit tranches and the extended facility should be modified in the light of the fact that the developing countries have so far made very limited use of those facilities". A facility for long-term financing for the benefit of the LDCs was moreover to be studied by the Development Committee. The reason for this latter proposal is the failure of the Fund's policies on the financing of the balance of payments.

The attitude of the IMF despite the meaningless modification introduced to the system of conditionality in March 1979, is that long-term loans to the LDCs (development finance) should be used on specific projects and should be allocated independently of the short-term situation of the balance of payments. The non-tied and unconditional loans of the international institutions are only available over the short term. This position derives from the idea that the process of adjustment of the balance of payments differs little in the LDCs and the developed countries - whence the clear and basic distinction established between the process of development and the process of adjustment of the balance of payments.

These differences between the developed countries and the LDCs over the functioning of the process of balance of payments adjustments are not taken into account in the Fund's Articles of Agreement. Moreover, the arrangements which have been worked out in respect of payments do not recognize that in many cases an imbalance in payments might be due not to an excess of demand nor even to modifications of the structure of demand or to an increase in productivity, but to fundamental rigidities, which can be eliminated by further or accelerated growth and the diversification of the productive structure. Since the Fund's resources are not available over the long term, these countries are then unable to make the necessary adjustments and the resorption of the deficit can be achieved, in the circumstances, only at the price of high unemployment and the disruption of the development process.

With regard to the fluctuation of export earnings, the necessary measures should therefore make a distinction between those cases in which the shortfall is attributable to the country itself and those in which it is the result of circumstances beyond its control. These latter include, inter alia, a slow-down of the world economy linked, for example, to internal measures taken by the major industrialized countries, one of the first consequences of which is reduction of demand for imports from the LDCs. In this later case, the problems affecting the economies of the LDCS are caused by an imbalance in the market economies. One can hardly expect the LDCs to apply costly adjustment measures to their economies while they are in no way responsible for the situation with which they are confronted.(1) Lastly, at their ministerial meeting in September 1978 in Washington, the Group of 24 once more raised the question of the conditionality of the Fund. They

(1) UNCTAD Document DT/188, para. 20.

expressed "concern at the multiplicity of performance criteria and some other forms of conditionality that inhibit access to Fund resources by member countries". They therefore "urged the Executive Board of the IMF to set appropriate guidelines and establish other institutional procedures related to the use of the Fund's resources, especially in the upper credit tranches, in support of economic adjustment programmes. In this context they were of the view that the guidelines should be designed so as to limit the performance criteria only to relevant macroeconomic variables, paying due regard to the growth considerations of the member countries and their prevailing economic and social situations".(1)

The fact is that the whole philosophy of adjustment needs to be revised if machinery appropriate to the situation and the specific problems of the LDCs is what is really wanted, within the framework of the reform of the international monetary and financial system. Unfortunately, international monetary reform has not introduced substantive changes in the basic elements of the international monetary system. More than ever before, changes are needed in the economic system whereby the developed countries -through the monetary Fund and the other international institutions- reserve the right to control and monitor, on a permanent basis, the domestic economic, financial and social policies of the LDCs. Through the conditionality of drawings the LDCs find themselves obliged to make a burdensome contribution to the world problem of adjustment, while the world economic situation, for most of them is an exogenous variable which generally governs the levels of their financial earnings and, accordingly, of their levels of economic activity. The deep recession which has spread in recent years from the developed countries to the whole of the world economy, and which has been characterized in particular by a wave of protectionism, has made the contribution of the LDCs to the process of world adjustment an even greater burden for them.

The question arises as to what LDCs can do to escape from the many traps which the IMF and its managers have placed in their way to control their evolution or economic independence. But first, it should be noted that the representatives of many developing countries in the Fund bear a great responsibility for the persistence of these factors. The constant acceptance of the "logic of the Fund", efforts made to escape from confrontation with industrialized countries, and the passive acceptance of substantive decisions on the international financial and monetary system, normally adopted on the fringe of the Fund (in the Group of Ten or the increasingly frequent "summits" of industrialized countries) and frequently against the interests of the LDCs, are some of the indications of what we have in mind. Logically, this is only a reflection of the present structure of international power, but it can be questioned whether efforts to modify it are not less than they could be.

So long as this situation is unchanged, the international financial system will not change either. But nevertheless there are ways of making this system more compatible with the interests of developing countries. Thus, one of the most important battles to be fought is to modify the conditionality of the Fund. Its central role as a factor conditioning the autonomy and economic policies of LDCs, makes it the obvious target for major effort.

(1) IMF Survey, 2 October 1978, p. 307.

B. Quotas and access to IMF resources

For each member country of the Fund, the quota plays a capital role in the determination[1] of its subscription to the Fund, the drawing rights it can obtain under current operations and the Fund's special facilities,[2] the number of votes it can have and the percentage which it receives of any allocation of special drawing rights. So far there have been seven general reviews of the Fund's quotas.

Despite these increases, the quotas of the developing countries are still too low when compared to the magnitude of their needs and the nature of the problems which they face. In this respect it should be noted that at the end of their fourteenth meeting, held in Washington in April 1977, the ministers of the Group of 24 found that a general 100 per cent increase in quotas at the seventh general revisions of quotas was desirable.[3] This suggestion was reiterated at the sixteenth meeting of the group in Mexico City in April 1978. The participants at that meeting moreover called upon the Fund:

> "to re-examine the criteria on which the allocation of quotas was based, with a view to rationalizing them and making them better suited to the economic position of the developing countries".[4]

A partially positive reply was given, because an agreement on a 50 per cent increase in the quotas, bringing the Fund's resources to 58.6 billion SDR, was adopted at the Annual Meeting of the Fund in September 1978.[5]

But the inadequacy of such a measure was recognized by the IMF's Managing Director, when he pointed out that he was "perfectly aware, given the extent of balance of payments needs, that the amounts and structures of quotas should be re-examined".[6]

The volume of quotas is also linked to the voting rights of member States. Each member State has 250 basic votes, plus a supplementary vote for every 100 SDRs of quota.

Except in very specific cases, all the decisions of the Fund are taken by a majority of votes. In the case of the second amendment, special majorities have been reduced, though the expulsion of a member State still requires 85 per cent of the total votes.

The developing countries have 33.16 per cent of the votes - a percentage which with the entry into force of the seventh quota review represents only ten points more since 1945, whereas the number of developing countries' members of the Fund has risen from 27 to 101. Moreover, the increase which took place from the fifth to the sixth review involves only the oil-producing developing countries and is still completely out of proportion to the important role which those countries have acquired in the functioning and replenishment of the monetary system.

---

(1) "Quotas govern subscriptions, drawing rights, votes", IMF Survey, 17 April 1978, pp. 121-125.
(2) IMF Survey, 2 May 1977, p. 137.
(3) Communiqué of the Group of 24, Article 19, April 1978.
(4) Rolf M. Jeker: "Voting rights of less developed countries in the IMF", Journal of World Trade Law, vol. 12, No. 3, May-June 1978, p. 218.
(5) IMF Survey, 2 October 1978, p. 305.
(6) Speech by Jacques de la Rosière to CNUCED V. Finances et Développement, Vol. 16, No. 3, September 1979.

As a result of this situation, the developing countries have regularly denounced the inadequate and inequitable character of voting rights and of their distribution in the Fund[1] and demand full and effective participation for the developing countries in all phases of the process of decision-making on the formulation of a durable and equitable monetary system, and adequate participation for the LDCs in the work of all organs related to reform and in particular to the Fund's Board of Governors.[2]

These arguments are reinforced by the fact that for major decisions to be adopted within the Fund, qualified majorities are required, which give the right of veto to the small number of industrialized countries with major individual quotas and voting power.

C. Special drawing rights and the LDCs

In the light of the mounting difficulties of the international monetary system, the idea of creating supplementary liquidity in the form of special drawing rights came to be conceived. The objective was to provide the international monetary system with a source of liquidity which would be independent of the United States balance of payments situation and also of the production of gold and the behaviour of the speculators.[3]

In September 1974 some 9,315 million SDRs had been allocated, only 2,348 million of them going to the LDCs. On the average, each industrialized country had received 441 million SDRs whereas each LDC had received only 27 million.[4]

The value of this form of liquidity for the LDCs lies, inter alia, in the unconditional way in which it may be used and in its low cost, at least until 1974 (1.5%).

On account of these advantages the LDCs proposed a certain number of improvements to the SDRs, in the form of certain critical comments.

(a) The share of LDCs in the allocations of SDRs is too low, since it depends on their quotas in the Fund.[5]

(b) The scheme of the SDRs is incomplete as it does not include a durable and deliberate link between the creation of liquidity and development aid.

(1) United Nations General Assembly resolutions 3201 (S.VI) and 3202 (S.VI), second part, paragraph 1 (d). Declaration and Action programme on the establishment of a new international economic order (May 1974). Conference on international economic co-operation: Relevant aspects of international monetary reform, Document submitted by Iran, on behalf of G.19, p. 10, as well as the various communiqués of the Group of 24.
(2) United Nations General Assembly Resolution 3201 (S.VI)(1.d).
(3) F. Machlup: Remaking the international monetary system, (Baltimore: Johns Hopkins, 1968).
(4) G.K. Helleiner: "The less developed countries and the international monetary system", Journal of development studies, April-July 1974, p. 10.
(5) C. Sinha: "International Monetary System and the SDR scheme" in: International Monetary System, Indian economic conference Pahre 1969, Bombay Popular Prakashan 1970.
D. Bhattacharya: "The special drawing rights and the developing countries", Revista internazionale de Scienze economiche e commerciali, Milan, 21 August 1974, pp. 716-727.
R.G. Hawkins and C. Rangeraja: "On the distribution of new international reserves", Journal of Finances, September 1970, p. 25.

At all its meetings, the Group of 24 has called for setting up a link between the allocation of SDRs and the granting of financial resources to the LDCs, as well as new allocations of SDRs. A favourable reply has been forthcoming on this last point, as the Annual Meeting of the Fund, in September 1978, decided, on the proposal of the Interim Committee, to double the present volume of SDRs through new allocations.(1)

D. Reform of the facilities of the Monetary Fund and the duration of loans

Among the Fund's various facilities, the Compensatory Financing Facility (CFF) is the one which has given rise to the sharpest criticism and the largest number of proposals for reform. In general the CFF has been criticized in three areas:

(a) The method used to assess shortfalls in export earnings.

(b) The inability of a short-term financing facility to resolve essentially long-term problems.

(c) The ineffectiveness of the CFF as a short-term measure.

The CFF is ineffective even in the short term(2) because: 1) The quotas limit drawings, and the volume of resources available through this facility is insufficient. 2) The CFF applies only to situations in which there has been a drop in export earnings due either to price reductions or to a drop in volume. It does not, however, apply to situations in which payments difficulties are the result either of a rise in the price of imports, or of bad domestic harvests leading to increased imports of foodstuffs. 3) Since the drawings are supposed to be repaid after three or five years, it is taken for granted that the drop in export earnings will have been followed by a boom in those earnings.

But the harshest criticism levelled against the CFF scheme is that it ignores the most basic and long-term problems facing the LDCs: worsening of the terms of trade, concentration of exports in one or two products, and outmoded structures for production and trade. Only long-term financing can help resolve these problems. Yet the granting of such financing is incompatible with the Fund's Articles of Agreement.

This is another area in which the ministers of the Group of 24, at their various meetings, have made a number of specific proposals. At the meeting in Paris in June 1975, the "ministers recognized the need to improve the facilities of the IMF. They stressed the need for a liberalization of the compensatory financing facility so as to include services in the coverage of current account transactions, to ensure that to the extent possible, shortfalls in export earnings should be offset at the precise moment at which they occur, and that such compensation should take account of the movement of import prices, and to prolong the period of repayment. The ministers have also emphasized that as far as floating with the gold tranche was concerned, drawings under the buffer stock financing facility should enjoy treatment equal to that applied to drawings under the compensatory financing facility, and that the IMF should be empowered to make direct loans to buffer stocks, whether they are organized by producer-consumer groups or by producer groups alone, with the appropriate guarantees provided for the interested members of the IMF" (paragraph 10 of the communiqué).

(1) IMF Survey, 2 October 1978, p. 305.
(2) G. Corea: "The international monetary system and the developing countries", op.cit.

When, in September 1978, they saw that no reply had been made to their demands on this point, the Twenty-four dealt with the matter again at length, in paragraph 25 of the communiqué of their ministerial meeting in Washington.

As part of the efforts to stabilize the current account of developing countries, the ministers emphasized the need to strengthen the compensatory financing facility by adopting the following measures:

(a) the limit on outstanding drawings under the facility should be increased from 75 to 100 per cent of a member's quota. Drawings in any 12-month period should be increased from 50 to 100 per cent;

(b) the repayment period should be lengthened from the present three to five years to one of five to seven years;

(c) countries should be given the choice of basing the calculation of their shortfalls on their total receipts from merchandise exports or the combined receipts from merchandise exports and services;

(d) in the calculation of shortfalls, account should be taken of the increase in the price of imports;

(e) increased import volume resulting from climatic or other factors beyond the control of the country concerned should also be taken into account in calculating the shortfalls;

(f) drawings under the facility should not be subject to any credit tranche conditionality.(1)

In 1979, some of these grievances were met by the Fund. Drawings up to 100 per cent of the quota have been authorized, with the reservation that they will not be authorized above 50 per cent unless the member country "co-operates in finding appropriate solutions to its balance of payments difficulties". The optional inclusion of remittances of emigrant workers was included into the calculation of the deficit on forecast income, if adequate data exists. Moreover, it is stipulated that the trend value of export income will be calculated as a geometric not an arithmetic average.(2) However, these measures continue to be insufficient in relation to the extent of the problem.

E. The creation of a new financial facility

When a country is facing severe balance of payment difficulties what really counts is avoiding the critical point of exhausting reserves and suspending payments

In this respect, the less the capacity to pay, and the greater the degree of indebtedness of a country, the smaller its chances of finding financial resources to face its liabilities. In these circumstances the only effective solution is international action, facilitating the restructuring of debt before a critical point is reached allowing escape from the vicious circle of "less capacity to pay, less ability to obtain resources".

(1) IMF Survey, 2 October 1978, pp. 306-307.
(2) Finances et Développement, September 1979, p. 6.

When a country reaches this critical point, it is no alternative to refinancing debt. This involves a negotiation usually including aspects separate from the debt itself, and tending to seriously limit the possibilities of action of the debtor country in various fields. It also requires the establishment of a heavy mechanism to adjust operations implied in the refinancing process, and finally it does not ensure that the problem will be entirely solved. The best proof of the latter is the resort of these same countries to the refinancing process, sometimes at very close intervals.

The creation of a special refinancing service would be one way of avoiding these drawbacks and ensuring a more durable solution to the problems of the structure of external debt. This facility, which could deal with a problem which is both short and long term, could be jointly administered by the International Monetary Fund and the World Bank, and its main objective would be to channel resources to countries with a high proportion of their debt consisting of short-term liabilities, with serious balance of payments problems, and who were in danger of not being able to face their obligations. This kind of financing should be on a medium-term basis and the user country would have to be able to count on the certainty of resorting to it in advance of the "critical" moment.(1)

The objective of this facility would be to iron out the bunching of the debt profile, thus allowing the debtor country to face the short-term problem. They would also have a margin of time and manoeuver to adopt measures to avoid the repetition of bottlenecks originating in an excessive concentration of debt over a very short period. Criteria for resort to this type of service could be an adequate combination of objective criteria, and case-by-case analysis. Thus a country would have access to this facility when faced with a concentration of maturities of its external debt over a two year period, above a certain percentage -which could be between 25 and 30 per cent- of the total value of the debt, and moreover when its reserves have fallen or are falling considerably in spite of efforts to balance its external payments. Additional criteria could also be retained, such as the fact that the service of the debt for the period considered as critical, exceed a given percentage of its exports forecast for the same period.

In view of the debt service volume of many developing countries, their drawing rights on this new facility would have to be well above their IMF quotas. However, just the Fund's resources need to be used to amortize all the debt service of those years in which critical situations are foreseen; especially if there is a possibility of resort to such service in advance and necessary adjustment measures are taken in due time.

(1) At present, the IMF has an extended facility on a medium-term basis (2 to 3 years), but subject to severe conditionality and exclusively aimed at the solution of balance of payments problems, avoiding any reference to the structure of indebtedness: "A request for an extended arrangement is met only if the Fund is satisfied that the solution to the member's balance of payments problem will require a longer period than is provided for use of resources of the Fund that are available under existing tranche policies. In addition, the member is expected to present a programme setting forth the objectives and policies for the whole period of the extended arrangement, as well as a detailed statement of the policies and measures that it will follow in each 12-month period to meet the objectives of the programme. Purchases are phased and made subject to performance clauses relating to implementation of key policy measures. Purchases outstanding under the extended facility may normally not exceed 140 per cent of the member's quota". (<u>IMF Survey</u>, September 1979).

This type of facility would have to be subject to some kind of conditionality, especially as regards future indebtedness and the profile of this indebtedness. But this can be done without applying the recessionary policies normally proposed by the Fund, but by fixing maximum limits to the future balance of payments deficit and indebtedness on the basis of a reasonable forecast of imports and exports.

Resort to compensatory finance would remain when factors outside the control of the debtor country brought the balance of payments deficits to levels much higher than those forecast. In this way, whether or not the conditions of access to the facility were fulfilled or not would be the responsibility of the beneficiary country, which aside from the development of its balance of payments and its indebtedness, would not be obliged to account to the IMF for the policies adopted to attain agreed objectives.

As regards resources, there are the general resources of the IMF, which could be used to create the new facility, through a simple decision of the Executive Directors, as was the case with the Compensatory Financing Facility. Also, other resources should be sought. Faced with the option of restrictive policies and the failure to serve debt by so many developing countries, the worsening of the international financial situation may lead industrialized countries to accept modifying conditionality conditions and increasing available resources. This is in fact what happened with the establishment of the Oil Facility.

F. Access to long-term financial markets

Access of the LDCs to the financial markets (Eurobond and internal bond markets) should be understood as comprising the following: the problems posed by restrictions and other obstacles to access to markets, direct measures which could be taken to strengthen the capacity of the LDCs to borrow on the financial markets,in particular the possibility of recourse to multilateral guarantees or the active use of the guarantee of the international lending institutions, and also the problem of the secondary markets.

At each of its meetings the Group of 24 has dealt with this problem. At the meeting in Paris, in June 1975, it called for "the creation of a multilateral guarantee fund" to facilitate the access of the LDCs to the financial markets (Article 20 of the communique). At the meeting in Kingston in 1976, the Twenty-four also emphasized the "need for the international financial institutions to help with the creation of a secondary market for securities issued by the LDCs by investing part of their liquid assets in such securities, or in other ways" (Article 21 of the communique). At the Manila meeting in October 1976, the Twenty-four made it clear that "the countries having financial markets should make known their intention to carry out a progressive liberalization of capital exports, and that the authorities of countries having capital markets should grant favourable treatment to the developing countries and show flexibility by authorizing those countries to sell bonds written in currencies for which demand is strong on both local markets and the Eurobond market" (Article 16 of the communique).

The adoption of this type of measure will contribute to increasing funds available to developing countries which are free from conditionality. However, problems can arise from an indiscriminate and permanent resort to this type of funds, especially when they are aimed at financing a balance of payments deficit or investments with a doubtful capacity for generating income necessary to cover their amortization, without mentioning the high long-term financial cost these type of funds tend to have, nor the political cost implied in increasing dependence on private international banking.

G. The improvement of the institutional framework for debt renegotiation

In the view of the Group of 77 the present international system of debt reorganization is characterized by the following shortcomings:

"(a) Debt relief was often delayed until the last stage of financial difficulties, when it was already too late for the country to recover its rate of growth. (...) practice was generally to respond to debt relief only in cases of acute debt crisis.

(b) The conditions under which debt relief was provided were too severe.

(c) Debt reorganizations had taken place in the past on an ad hoc basis and in the light of short-term considerations without providing long-term solutions to the debt problems of debtor countries.

(d) The clear distinction drawn between debt relief provided to facilitate the correction of balance-of-payments difficulties, on the one hand, and provision of development assistance, on the other, had brought about a disregard of the development prospects and needs of the debtor countries in such renegotiations. Debt relief had in most cases been provided on commercial or quasi-commercial terms.

(e) Multilateral debt renegotiation exercises had to be followed up by bilateral negotiations between each creditor government and the debtor country with a view to reaching agreement on terms of the debt relief. This created problems of interpretation of original multilateral agreements and resulted in delays which complicated the debt situation of the debtor countries.

(f) Short-term analysis of the economic situation of the debtor country as practised in the past tended to highlight the immediate domestic factors and policies at the expense of the underlying external factors at work prior to the emergence of a crises situation. To correct this shortcoming, the analysis should give adequate consideration of the debtor country's long-term capital requirements and growth prospects.

(g) There was a lack of institutional arrangements for dealing with private loans not guaranteed by governments. It should be underlined that such loans had, in the recent past, been the most dynamic component of total financial flows".(1)

This opinion led developing countries taking part in the Conference on International Economic Co-operation in Paris between 1976 and 1977 to present a detailed proposal on the establishment of a new mechanism to renegotiate debts which would include both the functions of clubs and consortia. This proposal was based mainly on the need to ensure to LDCs a constant and regular flow of resources to ensure the financing of their development. The criterion is perhaps too mechanical but it is a good basis on which to discuss the subject with industrialized countries. The latter submitted two proposals: one aimed at institutionalizing the functioning of consortia and the other to establish rules for renegotiations inside "clubs". Both proposals were discussed in various UNCTAD and Development Committee meetings without any substantial agreement emerging. At UNCTAD V in Manila, the Group of 77

(1) See UNCTAD document TD/B/685.

presented a new proposal, but if any progress is to be made, it should be around the contents of the proposals originally presented in Paris. A detailed analysis of both could lead to the conclusion that, despite the different philosophies inspiring them, on the institutional level, there is some basis for bringing the two sides together. The risk is that in the near future there will be a multiplication of renegotiation processes, which may be an element contributing to the elimination of differences permitting the establishment of a more appropriate institutional framework.

Finally, another factor which could contribute to improving the position of LDCs inside present renegotiation frameworks could be to have the technical assistance of United Nations experts.

UNDP could be authorized to give this kind of assistance either through the UNCTAD secretariat or by hiring independent experts. Anyone associated with such a complex process as renegotiation, would have been able to observe the urgent need of many developing countries for advice, in order to be able to escape from the network of conditions and obligations usually forced upon them by creditors.

II. Style of Development and Indebtedness

The problems presented by the excessive indebtedness of the Third World could be dealt with on the first level, mentioned above, i.e. by measures within the specific framework of existing international financial structures. But the limits of such action are comparable to treating symptoms and manifestations of any illness, avoiding any treatment of its causes. Here we encounter the complex process inducing massive external indebtedness, in which the ultimate causal relation derives from the style of development.

Thus it is pertinent to refer to the second level of the problem: only a new concept of development, and the questioning of the myth of industrialization by the passive import of technology will allow introduction of methods of economic planning and regulation which can open the way to growth not accompanied by massive external indebtedness.

The notion of economic development is based on an extrapolation into the socio-economic field of the biological notion of development. Biological organisms do indeed develop from an ovum during a period with a parallel growth of their constituent parts and potential. But this is the cyclic occurrence of a genetically registered past, and not the untried construction of the future.(1) The status of industrial growth is thus justified as essential to development under the appearance of self-evident truth. The myth is born of Third World growth by the diffusion of science and technology generated by industrial centres and its transnational enterprises, the messengers of prosperity. This legitimates historical evolution of world capitalism and its expansion towards the periphery which has moved from the initial cycle of internationalization of capital-merchandise to the contemporary cycles of internationalization of capital-money and productive capital.(2)

---

(1) See Edgar Morin "Le développement de la crise du développement", in <u>Le Mythe du développement</u>, Seuil 1977. ed. Candido Mendes.

(2) See Christian Palloix <u>L'internationalisation du capital</u>, Maspero, Paris, 1977.

As J. M. Domenach points out:

"Development in the correct sense of the term, implies taking the 'base' into consideration i.e. that which is latent in a group and needs to be developed: its language, temperament, culture, autonomy, everything giving rhythm and meaning to the collective effort. But the overriding concept of development only integrates this dynamism as a means at the service of a process whose orientation and speed are subject to calculations determined by the imitation of the industrial model and the general mechanism of competition. Far from arriving at a dynamic balance between town and country, between 'base' and administrative superstructure, almost everywhere huge metropolises are emerging, popular communities are declining, sub-cultures are disappearing to the benefit of hypertrophied tools, bureaucratised administration and prefabricated cultures. The development discourse becomes tautological and finally contradictory. Instead of dynamic equilibrium being created, there emerges a suffocating disequilibrium; and far from being stimulated originalities are paralyzed. It is envelopment, rather than development".(1)

Where there were obvious replies we must see interrogations: science, techniques, rationality, development in their present form, tend to be the cause of some of the problems which they are supposed to solve.

Hence the need to reformulate the notion of development, under the general criterion of not subordinating development to growth, but growth to development with all its multidimensionality (especially social, cultural, human, i.e. qualitative) overcoming the analogy with biological processes.

As pointed out by E. Morin in the work cited:

"Development problems should be approached in the same way as all human and social theoretical problems, at the reflexive level of second order concepts, i.e. which always imply recurrence of the object (development) to the subject (society, man); which needs the introduction of the prefix 'auto'. The key concept thus should be auto-development... We are persuaded of the development possibilities of man and society. But we are also persuaded that this development is inseparable from a social metamorphosis".

This should be the point of departure for the reflexion on the styles of development which can break the vicious circle of economic and financial dependence.

But the development crisis has broken out openly. The prolonged recession of industrialized countries has put an end to the myth of limitless growth, while the various "decades for development" launched by the United Nations for the Third World have failed, the gap between the situation of the industrialized world and the misery and decline of the Third World becoming ever wider. The development crisis has fed the crisis in development ideology.

This situation has given rise to proposals on "new styles of development" appearing as antithesis to the central features of the predominating development model. Thus, instead of dependent development, there is "self-reliant" development; instead of development for the minority, a development for the people as a whole; instead of rigid centralization of power, popular participation; instead of excessive consumption, austere development; instead of unilateral emphasis on production of material goods, the emphasis is placed on the development of the human being and of all humanity.

(1) J.M. Domenach, "Crise du Développement, Crise de la Rationalité", in Le Mythe du Développement, op.cit.

Concrete efforts to introduce new styles of development will require methods of economic regulation operating through new planning methods. In general terms, as pointed out by I. Sachs: "it appears reasonable to reject optimization as a central concept of planning, and to reconsider the dialectic of the means and ends in the context of heuristic methods, instead of formal ones, of a multi-dimensional planning".(1)

It is not pertinent to continue commenting here on this problem except to mention the specific problem of the links between the generation and spread of technology and external financing, in so far as the first broadly determines the second.

The deepening of scientific knowledge, the capacity for management and innovation constitute the pillars of autonomous technological development. Thus planning of these elements should be emphasized as an alternative to the trap of the indiscriminate import of sophisticated "ready to use" technology aimed at producing superfluous prestige consumer goods, and to the vicious circle of external indebtedness which is involved to ensure such imports.

It is not the mere acquisition of means of production which will permit a self-supported accumulation and the increase in levels of production, but the creation of better conditions of use of means of production and the progressive creation of capacity to generate and adapt technology. The inadequacies of research and development in Third World countries is one of the basic problems to be overcome. On an average, only 0.1 per cent of their GNP is used for this, as against 1 to 3 per cent in the industrialized countries.

This problem needs to be overcome under present productivity conditions and not as a function of the norms and specification of transnational enterprises and their experts and consultants. The accumulation of scientific knowledge, of management and innovation capacities, should have been previously consolidated or in parallel to the technology imports, so as to adapt and spread it without excess costs and breakages in the national economic tissue. A basic condition implied in this is an end of the reverse transfer of technological generating capacity, via the so-called "brain drain" which benefits industrialized countries. The latter costs a good deal more than foreign aid to Third World countries (60 billion dollars between 1961 and 1972, as against 46.3 billion dollars of aid).(2)

This approach could generate modalities which would permit a successful injection of modern technologies. There would not be an opposition between the acquisition of certain advanced technologies to the necessary use of intermediate technologies (with a low coefficient of capital use) but an internal generation of integral technological capacity, which can break the technological imitation and dependence with its inevitable corollary: major foreign exchange costs.

Only a technological policy of this type, inserted into a context of the progressive abandon of the consumption styles of industrialized countries, aimed at the minorities with purchasing power, and based on a high content of products, inputs and technology from abroad, can permit Third World countries to break out of the vicious circle of indebtedness. But this does not imply leaving aside the need to create an internal financial system which will encourage the growth of savings, channelled towards productive activities, nor going without external sources of savings when their costs and conditionality are not harmful to national interest.

---

(1) Sachs, Ignacy: Pour une économie politique du développement . Flammarion, 1977, p. 299.

(2) UNCTAD document TD/B/C.67.

This last option will only be open to those countries which have managed to escape from that vicious circle and are not financially strangled.

ABOUT THE EDITOR AND CONTRIBUTORS

JUAN CARLOS SÁNCHEZ ARNAU, of Argentina. Economist, specialist on international economic affairs. Is a former member of the Argentine foreign service and led his country's delegation to numerous international meetings, was also spokesman of the Group of 77 and of the Latin American Group at several international conferences. Member, in charge of financial issues, of the Supporting Team which advised the developing countries participating in the Conference on International Economic Co-operation (North-South dialogue). He is at present the Executive Director of the Centre International pour le Développement, in Paris, and a consultant of ECLA, SELA, UNESCO and UNDP. He is the author of several works published by these and other international organizations.

GEORGES CORM, from Lebanon, studied Law and Economics at the University of Paris. At present he is a professor at the St. Joseph University in Beirut. Was the representative of the National Bank of Algeria in Lebanon. Regular contributer to the newspaper "Le Monde diplomatique", he has been a consultant of the OCDE, United Nations and several Arab countries. He has published many works on the multinational corporations, transfer of technology, debt and the development theory.

ABDELKADER SID-AHMED, from Algeria, has a Ph.D. in Economics from the University of Paris. Has been the representative of his country in the Financial Committee of the Conference on International Economic Co-operation, in several committees and working groups in UNCTAD, the IMF and OPEC. He has also been a consultant in UNCTAD and a professor at the University of Paris-Dauphine. At present he is an advisor to the Algerian Ministry of Energy. He is the author of many books on economic development; one on the foreign debt of developing countries and another on the economy of the OPEC countries, the latter was recently published in France.

SAMUEL LICHTENSZTEJN, from Uruguay. Economist. Was the Director of Exchange of the Central Bank of Uruguay. Director of the Department of Economics and Dean of the National University of Montevideo. At present he is chief of research at the Centro de Investigaciones y Docencia Económica (CIDE) in Mexico. He directs the quarterly review "Economía de América Latina" and is also a member of "Cuadernos de Marcha". Has published several works on financial subjects, among them "El FMI y la crisis económica nacional" /"The IMF and the national economy crisis"/ and "Enfoque y papel de las políticas de estabilización" /"The role of estabilising policies"/.

JOSÉ MANUEL QUIJANO, from Uruguay. Economist. Worked at the National Chilean Bureau of Planification (ODEPLAN). Has carried out research on the economic and financial problems of Uruguay. Has published a major study on "Concentración, desnacionalización y crédito. El caso de Mexico 1970-1975". /"Concentration, denationalization and credit. The mexican case 1970-1975"/, which received the prize "Juan Noyola", the highest distinction of Economics in Mexico.

GONZALO DANIEL MARTNER, from Chili. Studied Economics at the University of Paris-La Sorbonne. Has done several studies on the financial aspects of development, the Chilean economy and the financial relations between Europe and Latin America. At present he is working as a researcher at the International Development Center in Paris